INUYASHA

VOL. 16
Action Edition

Story and Art by
RUMIKO TAKAHASHI

English Adaptation by Gerard Jones

Translation/Mari Morimoto
Touch-Up Art & Lettering/Bill Schuch
Cover Design/Yuki Ameda
Graphics & Design/Yuki Ameda
Editor/Julie Davis

Managing Editor/Annette Roman
Editor in Chief/William Flanagan
Production Manager/Noboru Watanabe
Sr. Dir. of Licensing and Acquisitions/Rika Inouye
VP of Sales & Marketing/Liza Coppola
Sr. VP of Editorial/Hyoe Narita
Publisher/Seiji Horibuchi

INUYASHA is rated "T+" for Older Teens. It may contain violence, language, alcohol or tobacco use, or suggestive situations.

Printed in Canada.

Published by VIZ, LLC
P.O. Box 77010
San Francisco, CA 94107

Action Edition
10 9 8 7 6 5 4 3 2 1
First printing, December 2003

www.viz.com

store.viz.com

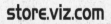

InuYasha

VOL. 16   Action Edition

STORY AND ART BY
RUMIKO TAKAHASHI

CONTENTS

THE STORY THUS FAR

Long ago, in the "Warring States" era of Japan's Muromachi period (Sengoku-jidai, approximately 1467-1568 CE) a legendary doglike half-demon called "Inu-Yasha" attempted to steal the Shikon Jewel, or "Jewel of Four Souls," from a village, but was stopped by the enchanted arrow of the village priestess, Kikyo. Inu-Yasha fell into a deep sleep, pinned to a tree by Kikyo's arrow, while the mortally wounded Kikyo took the Shikon Jewel with her into the fires of her funeral pyre. Years passed.

Fast forward to the present day. Kagome, a Japanese high school girl, is pulled into a well one day by a mysterious centipede monster, and finds herself transported into the past, only to come face to face with the trapped Inu-Yasha. She frees him, and Inu-Yasha easily defeats the centipede monster.

The residents of the village, now fifty years older, readily accept Kagome as the reincarnation of their deceased priestess Kikyo, a claim supported by the fact that the Shikon Jewel emerges from a cut on Kagome's body. Unfortunately, the jewel's rediscovery means that the village is soon under attack by a variety of demons in search of this treasure. Then, the jewel is accidentally shattered into many shards, each of which may have the fearsome power of the entire jewel.

Although Inu-Yasha says he hates Kagome because of her resemblance to Kikyo, the woman who "killed" him, he is forced to team up with her when Kaede, the village leader, binds him to Kagome with a powerful spell. Now the two grudging companions must fight to reclaim and reassemble the shattered shards of the Shikon Jewel before they fall into the wrong hands.

THIS VOLUME Naraku's demon offspring increase in number, and Inu-Yasha must face the demon within himself.

CHARACTERS

INU-YASHA
A half-demon hybrid, son of a human mother and a demon father. His necklace is enchanted, allowing Kagome to control him with a word.

KAGOME
A modern Japanese schoolgirl who can travel back and forth between the past and present through an enchanted well.

SANGO
A "Demon Exterminator" from the village where the Shikon Jewel was first born.

MIROKU
A lecherous Buddhist priest cursed with a mystical "hellhole" in his hand that is slowly killing him.

NARAKU
The enigmatic demon mastermind who has caused the miseries of nearly everyone in the story.

KAGURA
Created by Naraku to be his puppet, Kagura can manipulate the dead.

SHIPPO
An orphaned young fox-demon who likes to play shape-changing tricks.

SESSHO-MARU
Inu-Yasha's half-brother, Sessho-Maru is the full demon son of the same father.

KANNA
Another of Naraku's "offspring," Kanna uses a magic mirror to trap souls.

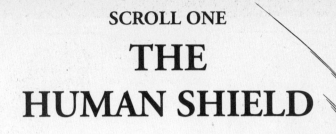

SCROLL ONE
THE HUMAN SHIELD

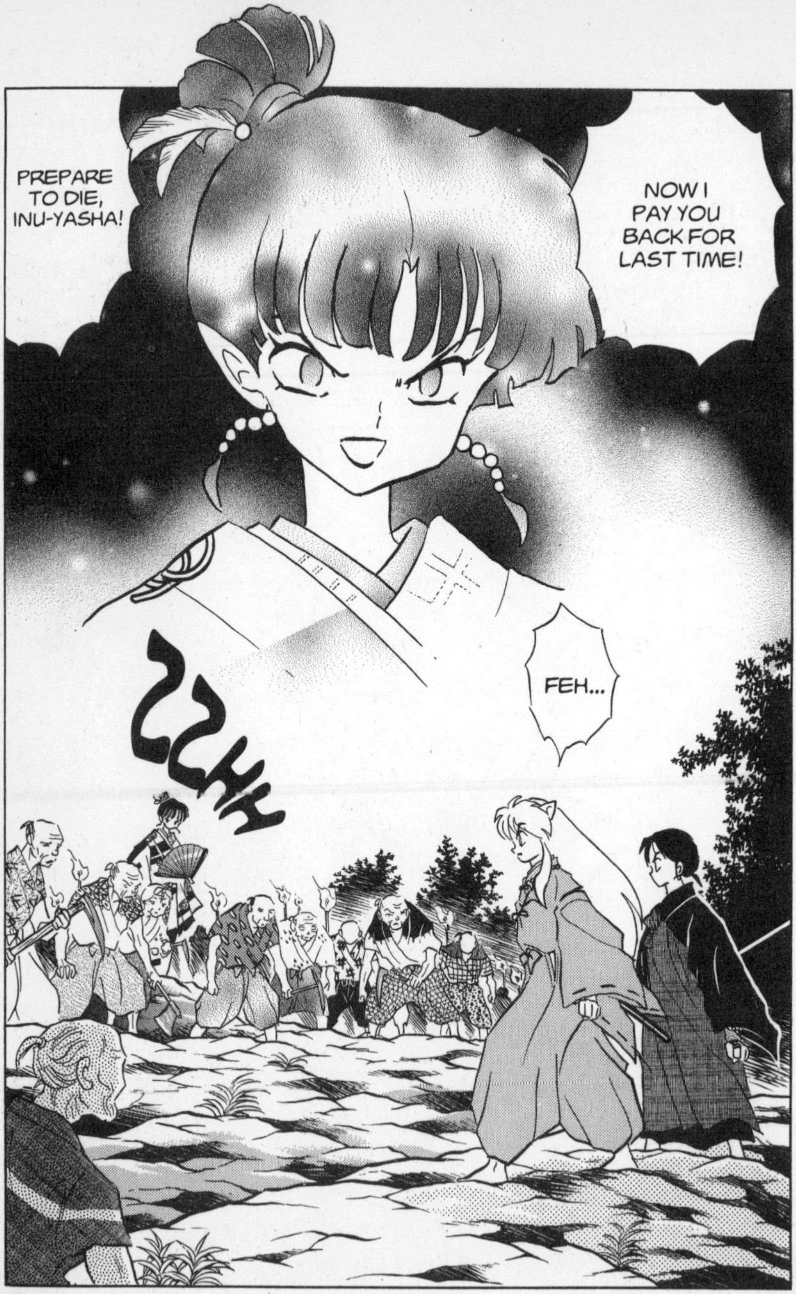
PREPARE TO DIE, INU-YASHA!
NOW I PAY YOU BACK FOR LAST TIME!
ZZHH
FEH...

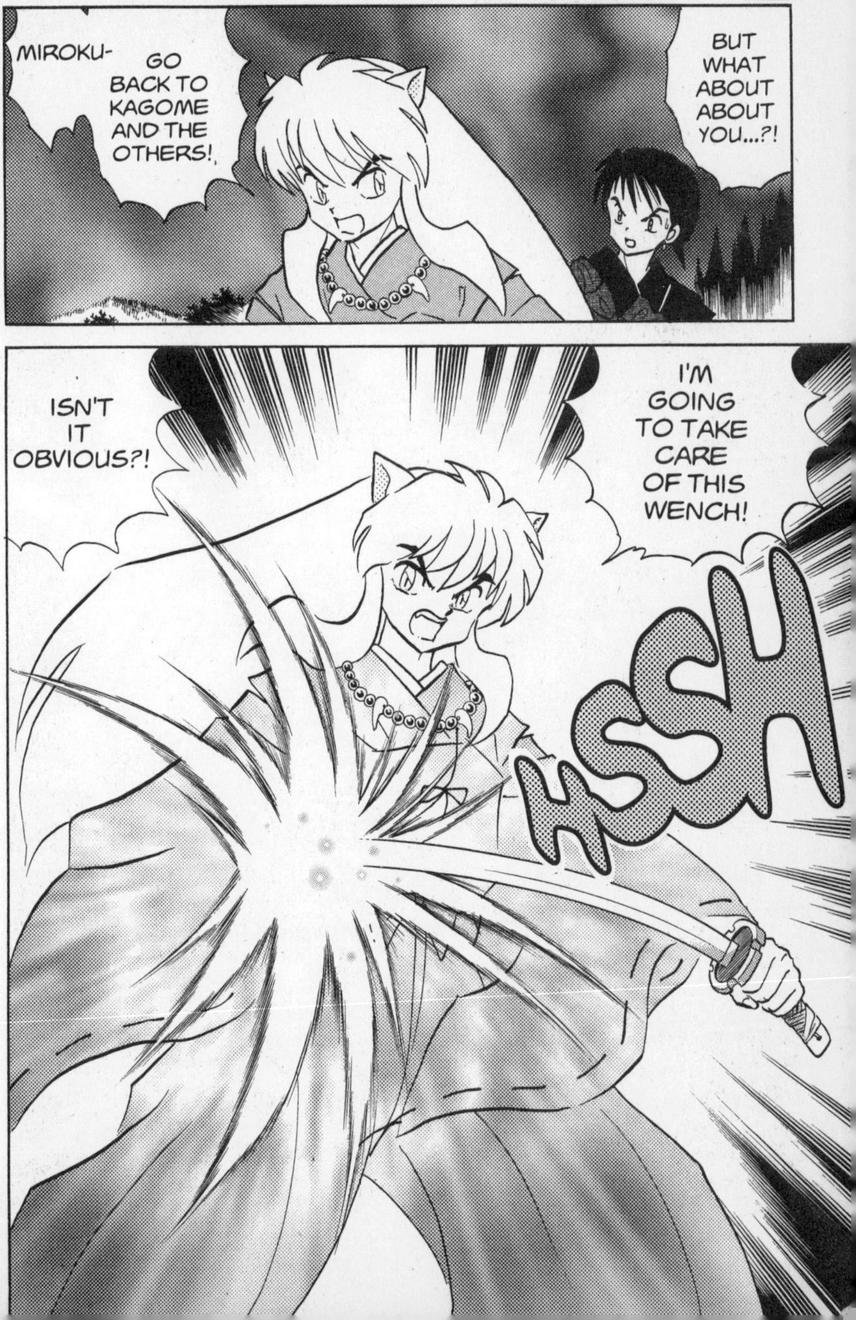
MIROKU-
GO BACK TO KAGOME AND THE OTHERS!
BUT WHAT ABOUT ABOUT YOU...?!
ISN'T IT OBVIOUS?!
I'M GOING TO TAKE CARE OF THIS WENCH!
HSSH

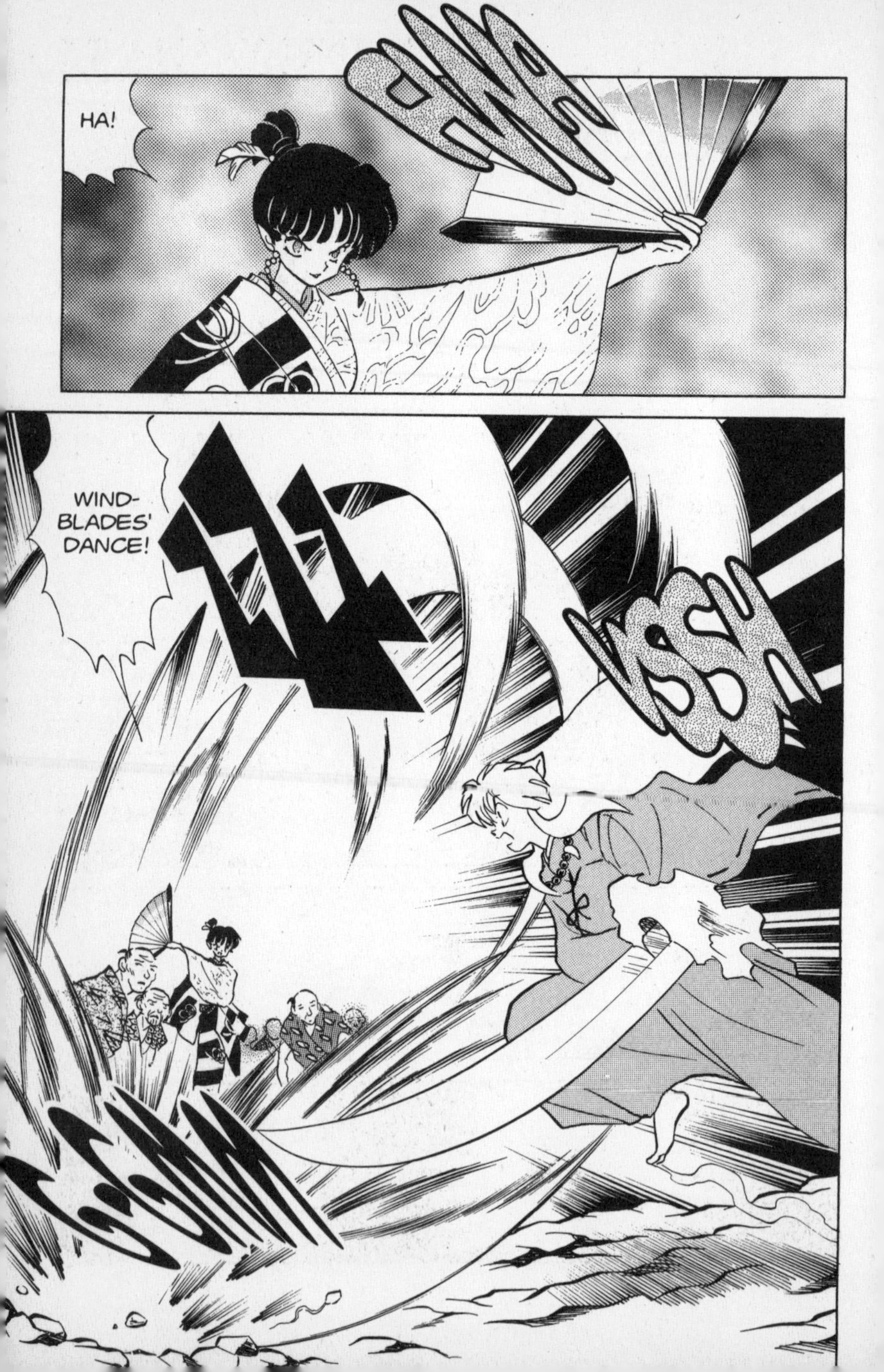
HA!
WIND-BLADES' DANCE!

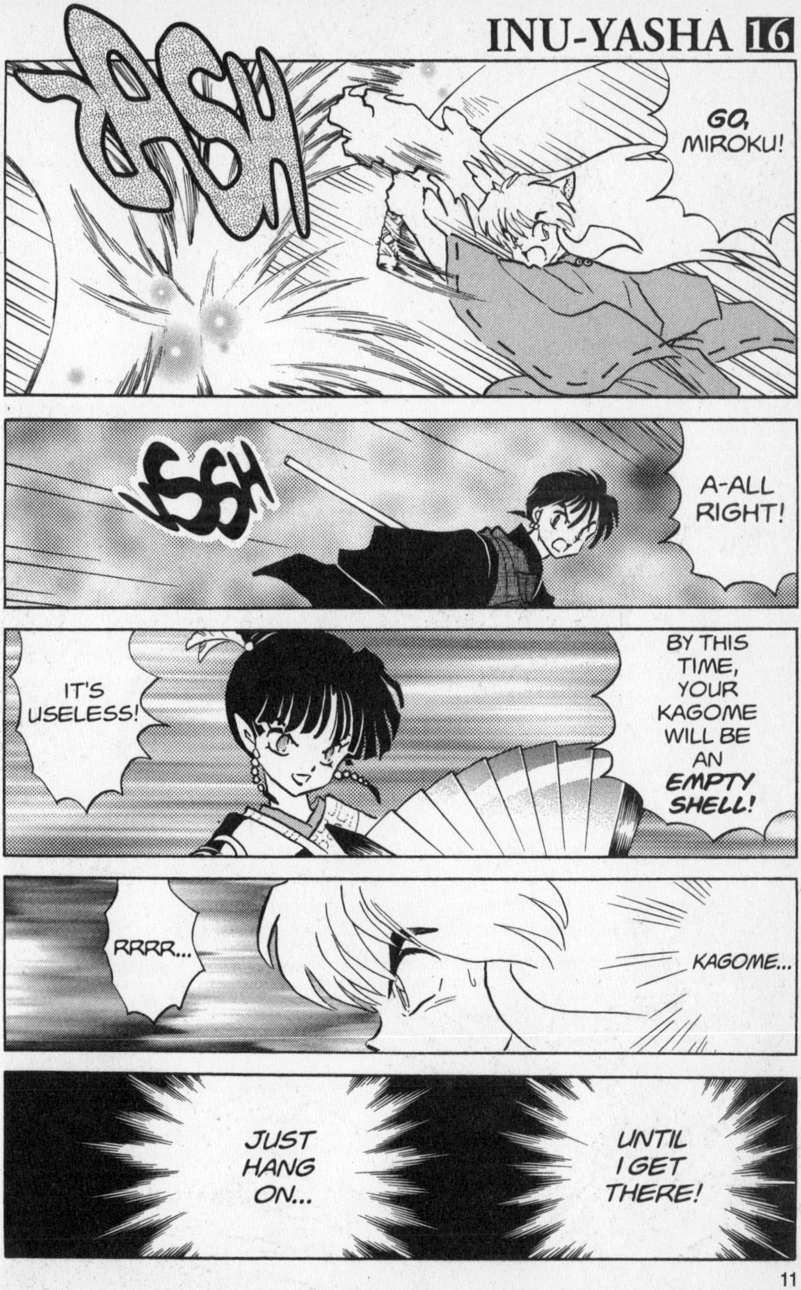
FSSH
GO, MIROKU!
VSSH
A-ALL RIGHT!
IT'S USELESS!
BY THIS TIME, YOUR KAGOME WILL BE AN EMPTY SHELL!
RRRR...
KAGOME...
JUST HANG ON...
UNTIL I GET THERE!

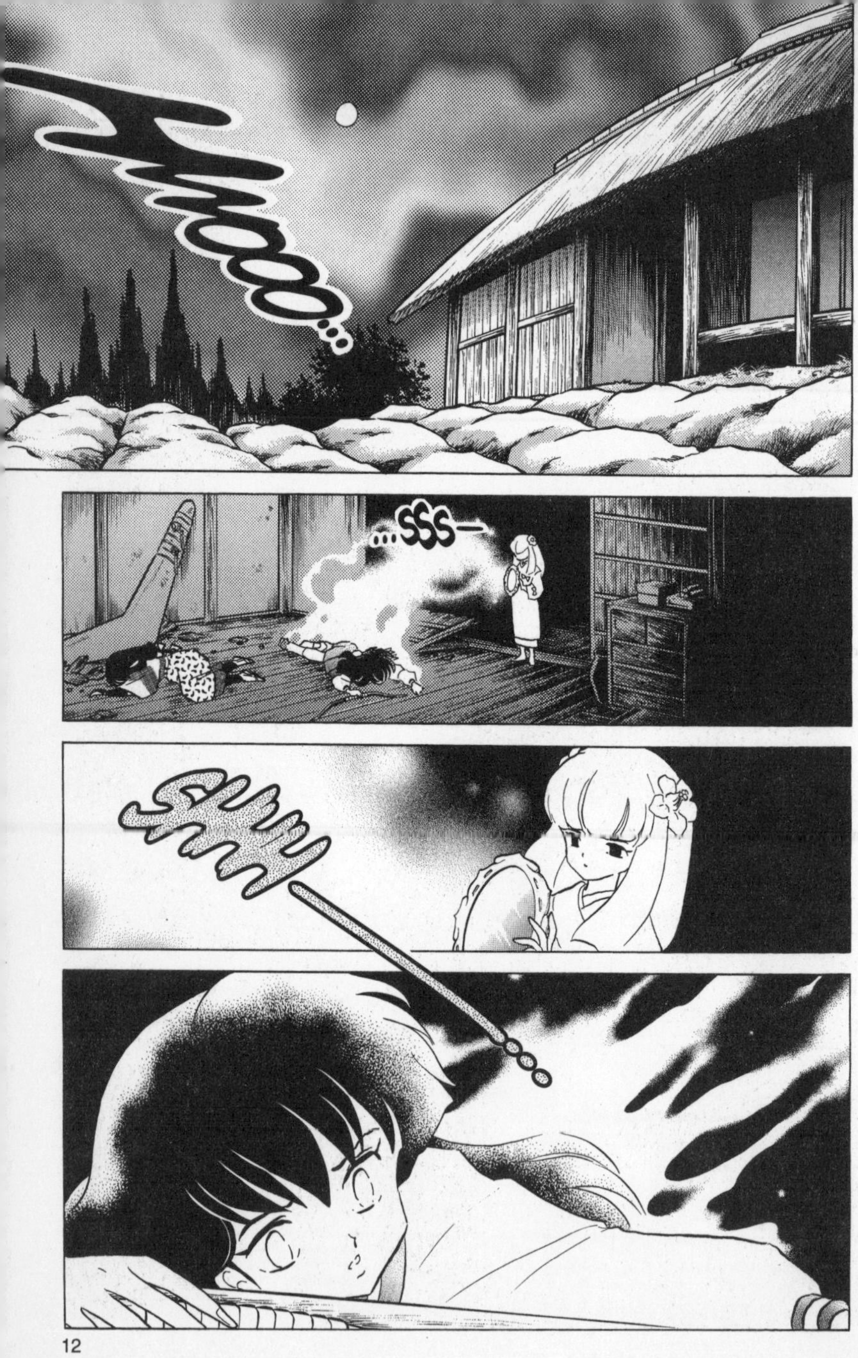
WHOOO…
…SSS—

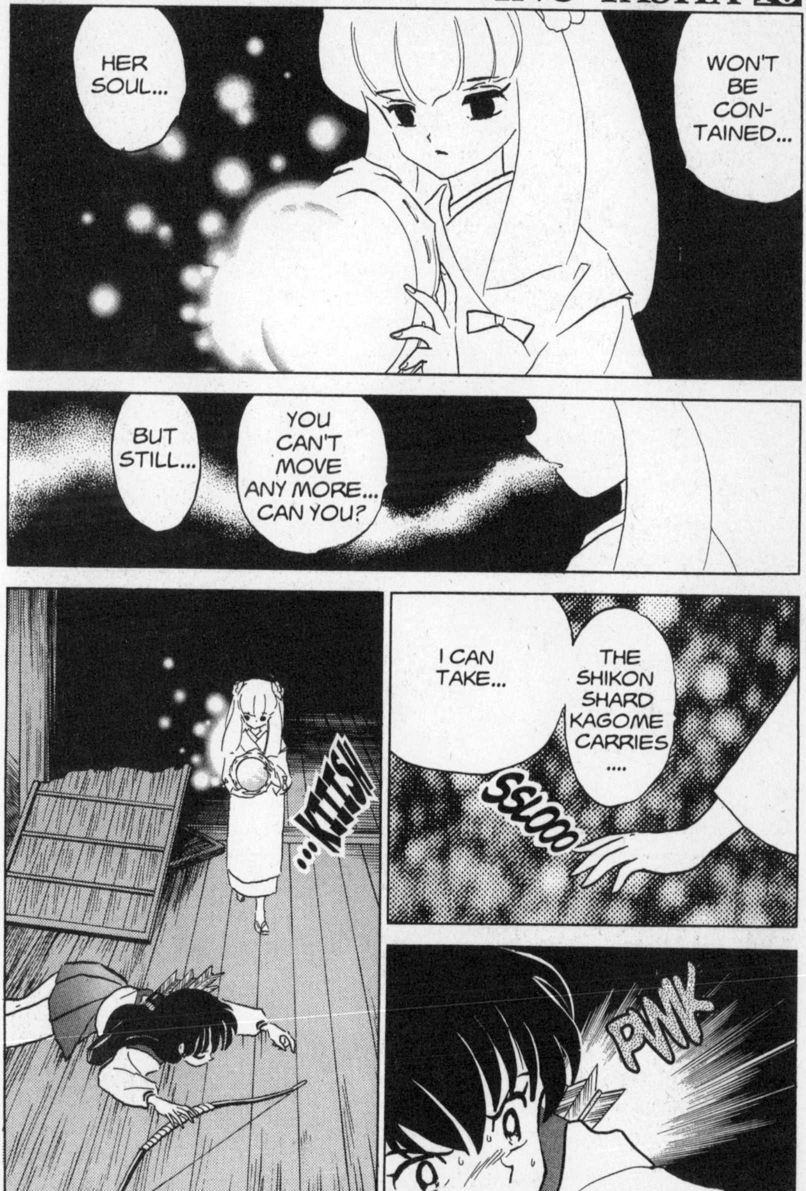
HER SOUL...
WON'T BE CON-TAINED...
BUT STILL...
YOU CAN'T MOVE ANY MORE... CAN YOU?
...KTTSH
I CAN TAKE...
THE SHIKON SHARD KAGOME CARRIES ....
SSLOOO
PWK

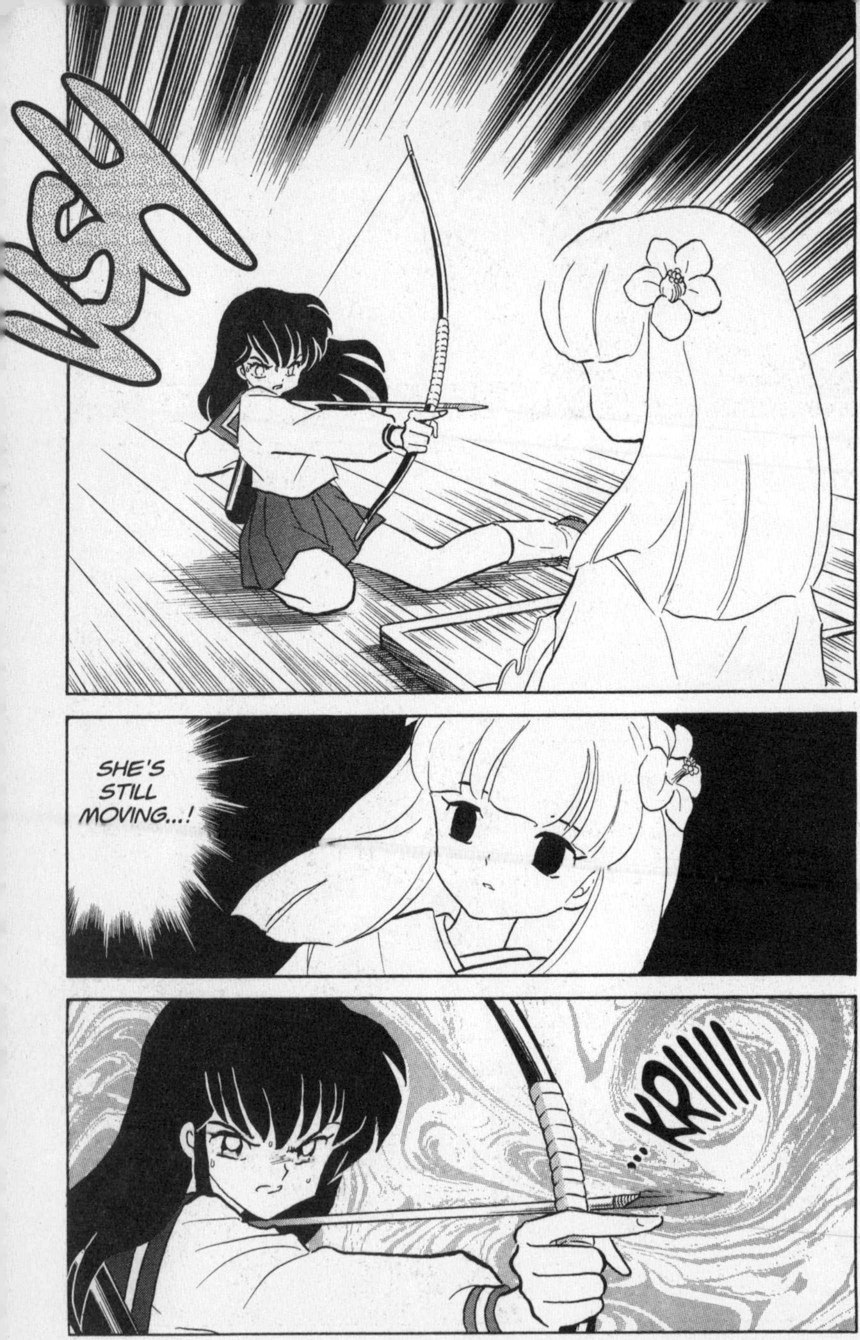
VSSH
SHE'S STILL MOVING...!
KRIII

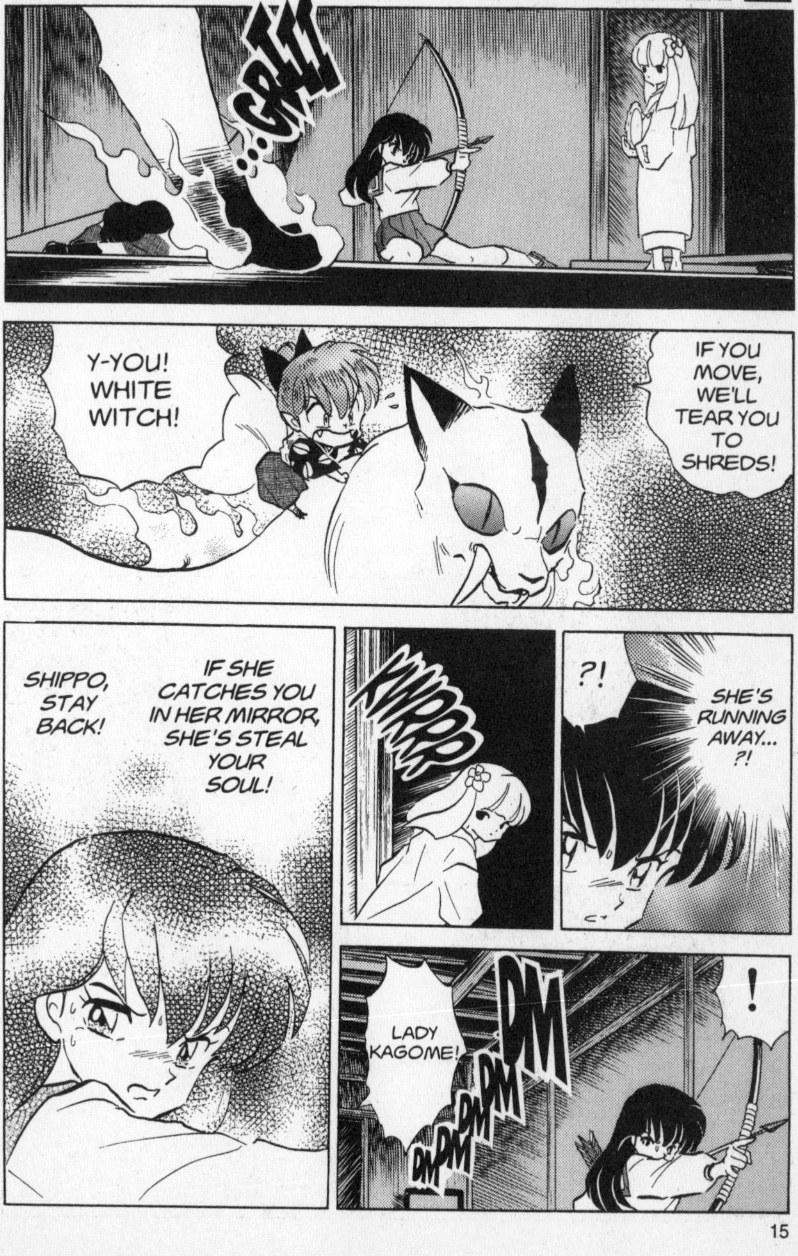
...GRIIT
Y-YOU! WHITE WITCH!
IF YOU MOVE, WE'LL TEAR YOU TO SHREDS!
SHIPPO, STAY BACK!
IF SHE CATCHES YOU IN HER MIRROR, SHE'S STEAL YOUR SOUL!
KWRRR
?!
SHE'S RUNNING AWAY...?!
LADY KAGOME!
DM DM DM DM DM DM
!

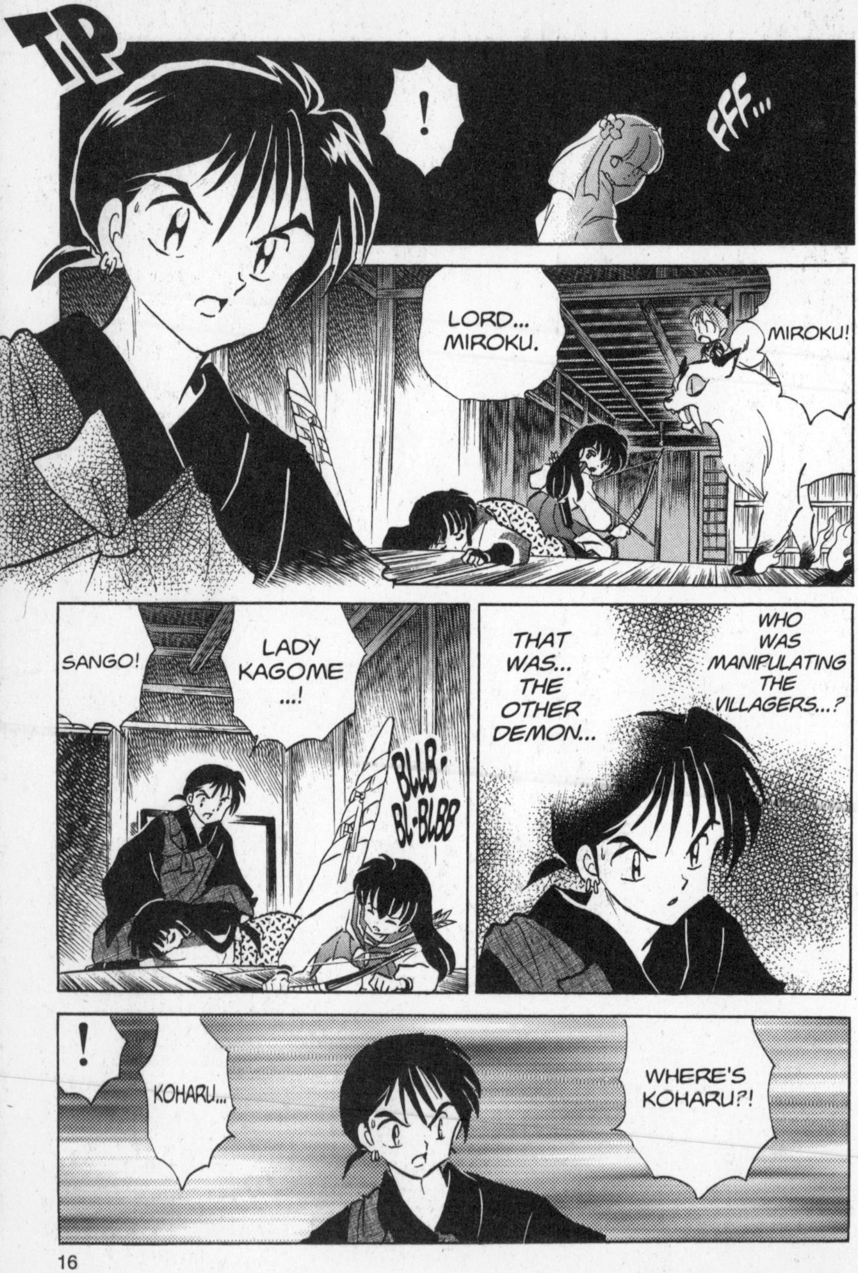
TP
!
FFF...
LORD... MIROKU.
MIROKU!
SANGO!
LADY KAGOME ...!
BLLB-BL-BLBB
THAT WAS... THE OTHER DEMON...
WHO WAS MANIPULATING THE VILLAGERS...?
!
KOHARU...
WHERE'S KOHARU?!

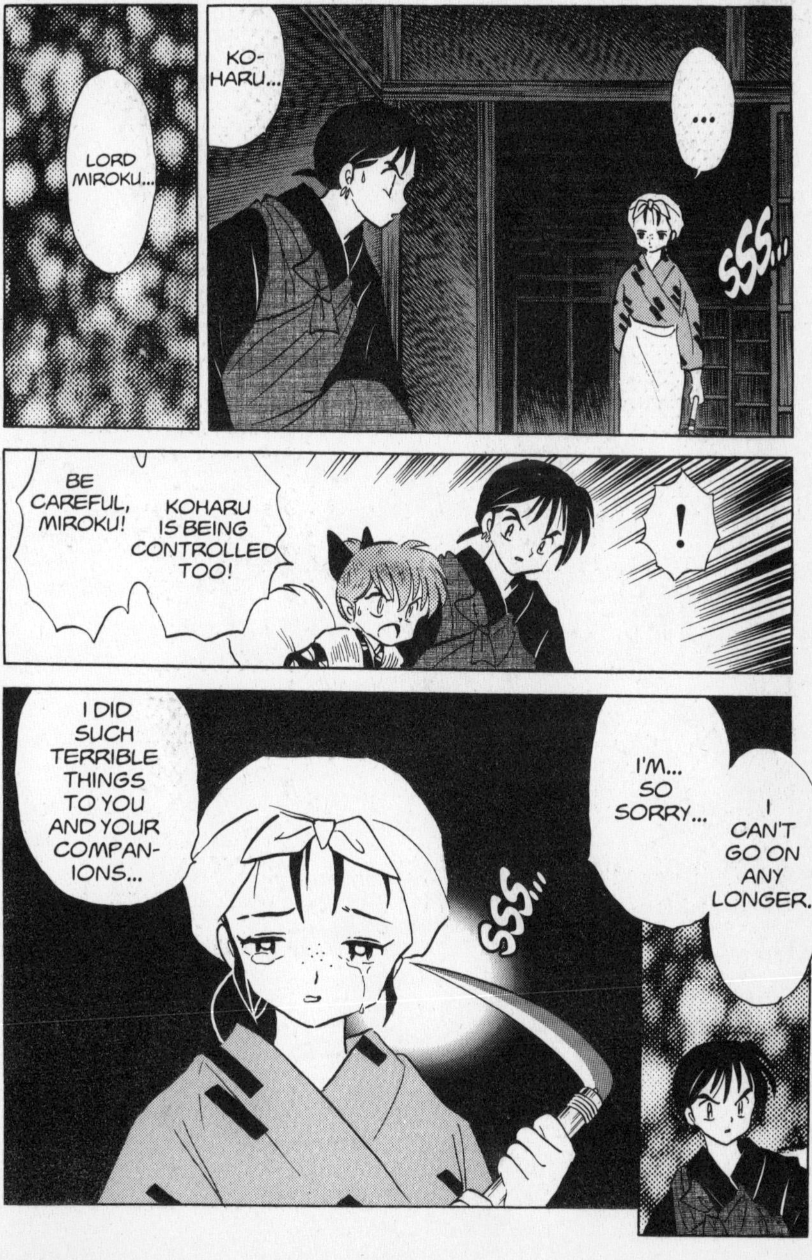
LORD MIROKU...
KO-HARU...
...
SSS...
BE CAREFUL, MIROKU!
KOHARU IS BEING CONTROLLED TOO!
!
I DID SUCH TERRIBLE THINGS TO YOU AND YOUR COMPAN-IONS...
SSS...
I'M... SO SORRY...
I CAN'T GO ON ANY LONGER...

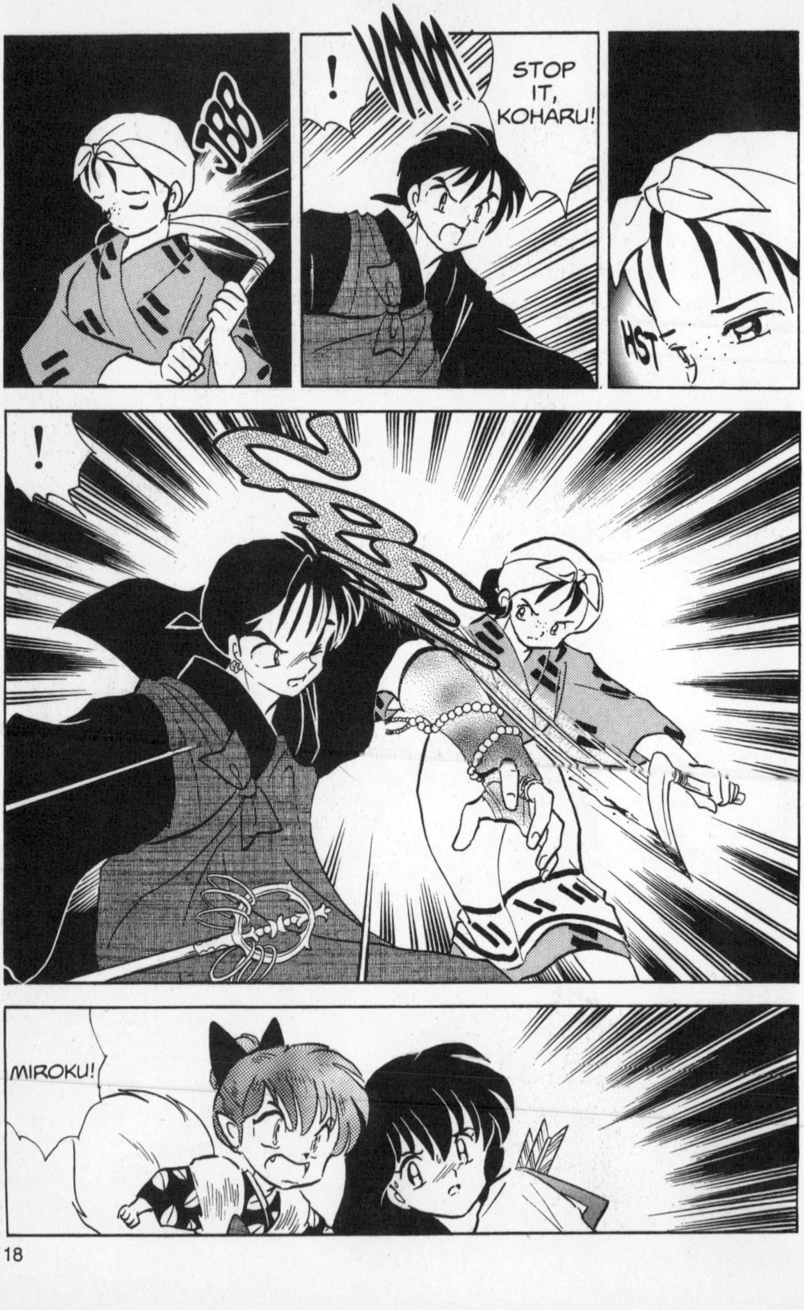
JBB
!
VMM
STOP IT, KOHARU!
HST
!
MIROKU!

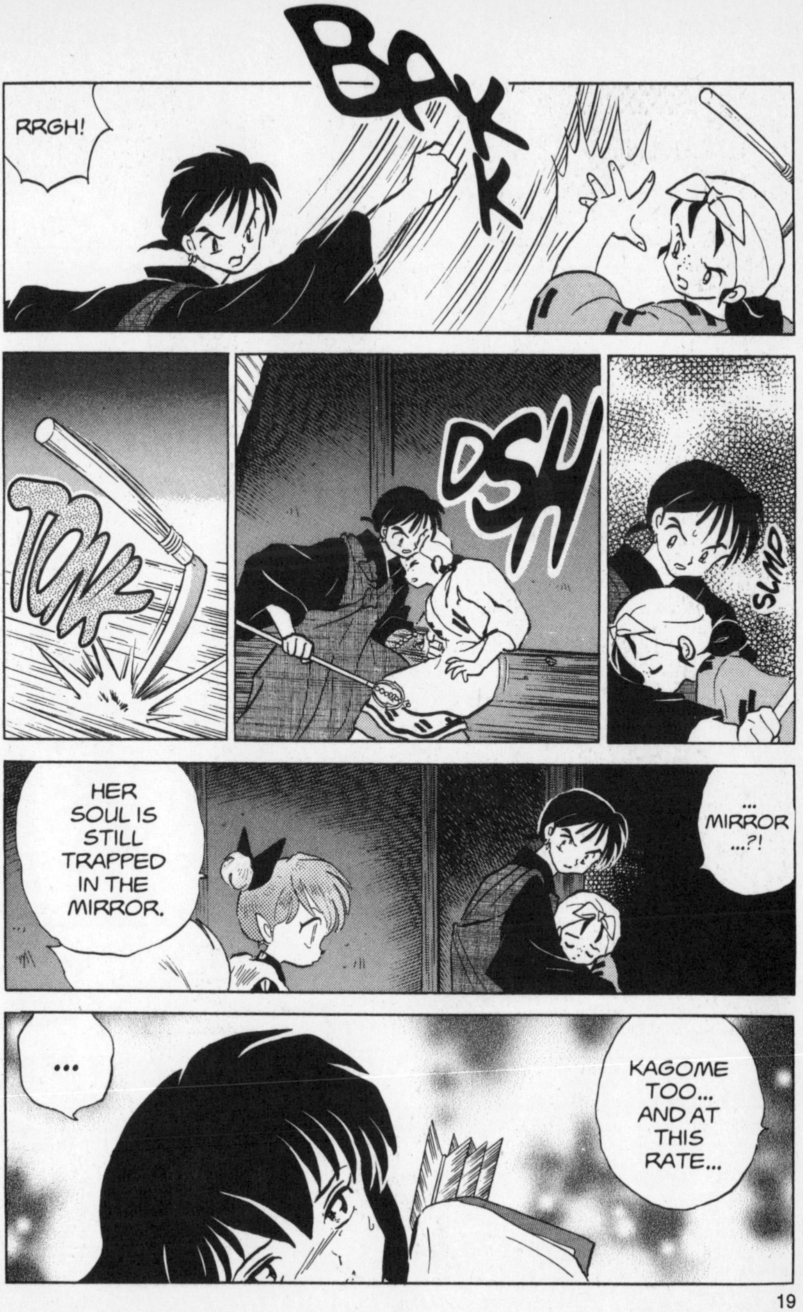
BAKK
RRGH!
TOK
DSH
SLMP
HER SOUL IS STILL TRAPPED IN THE MIRROR.
... MIRROR ...?!
...
KAGOME TOO... AND AT THIS RATE...

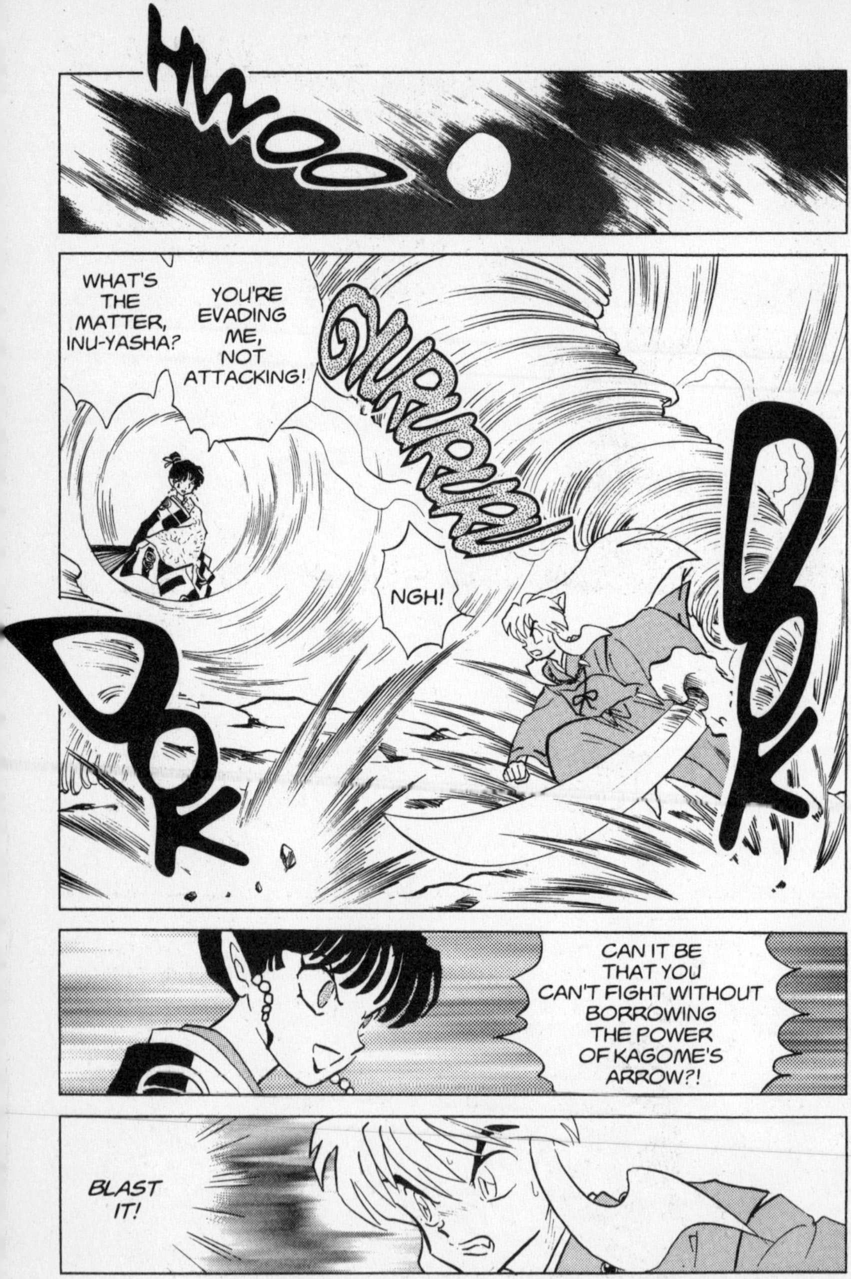
HWOO
WHAT'S THE MATTER, INU-YASHA?
YOU'RE EVADING ME, NOT ATTACKING!
GWURURU
NGH!
DOK
DOK
CAN IT BE THAT YOU CAN'T FIGHT WITHOUT BORROWING THE POWER OF KAGOME'S ARROW?!
BLAST IT!

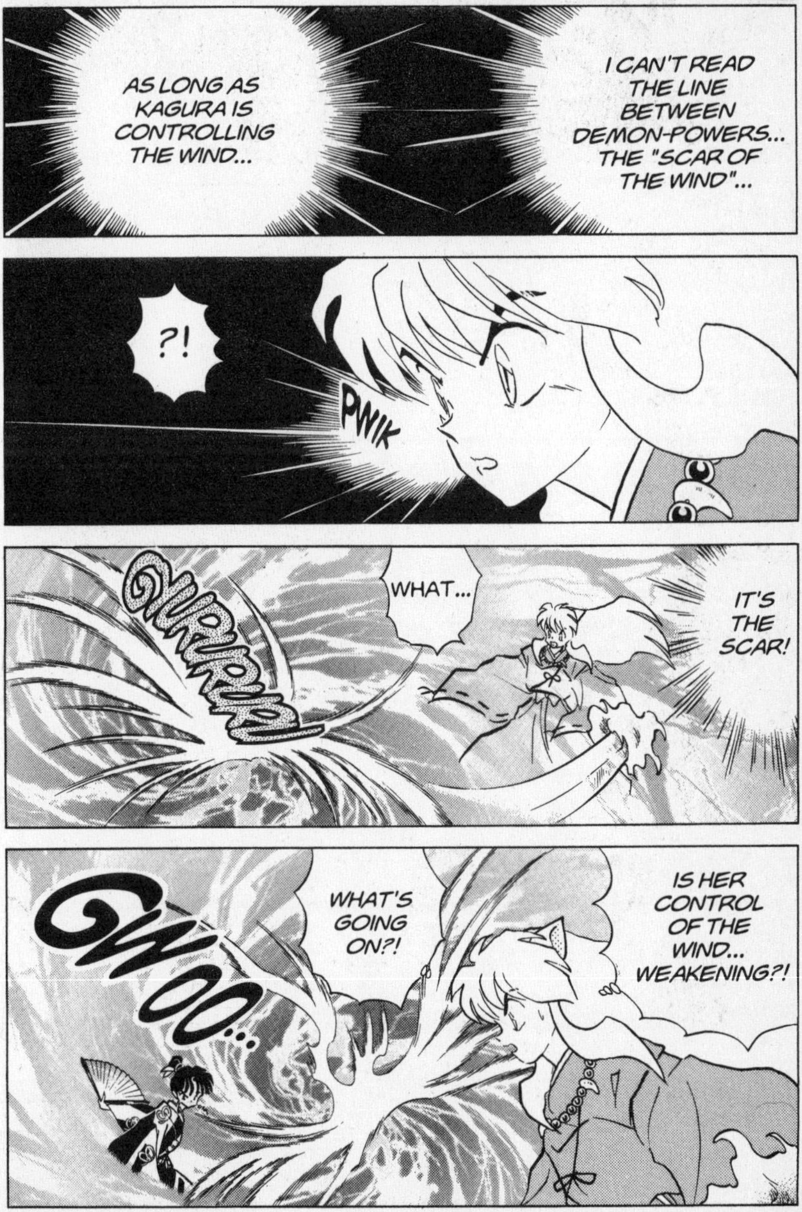
AS LONG AS KAGURA IS CONTROLLING THE WIND...
I CAN'T READ THE LINE BETWEEN DEMON-POWERS... THE "SCAR OF THE WIND"...
?!
PWIK
WHAT...
IT'S THE SCAR!
GWOO...
WHAT'S GOING ON?!
IS HER CONTROL OF THE WIND... WEAKENING?!

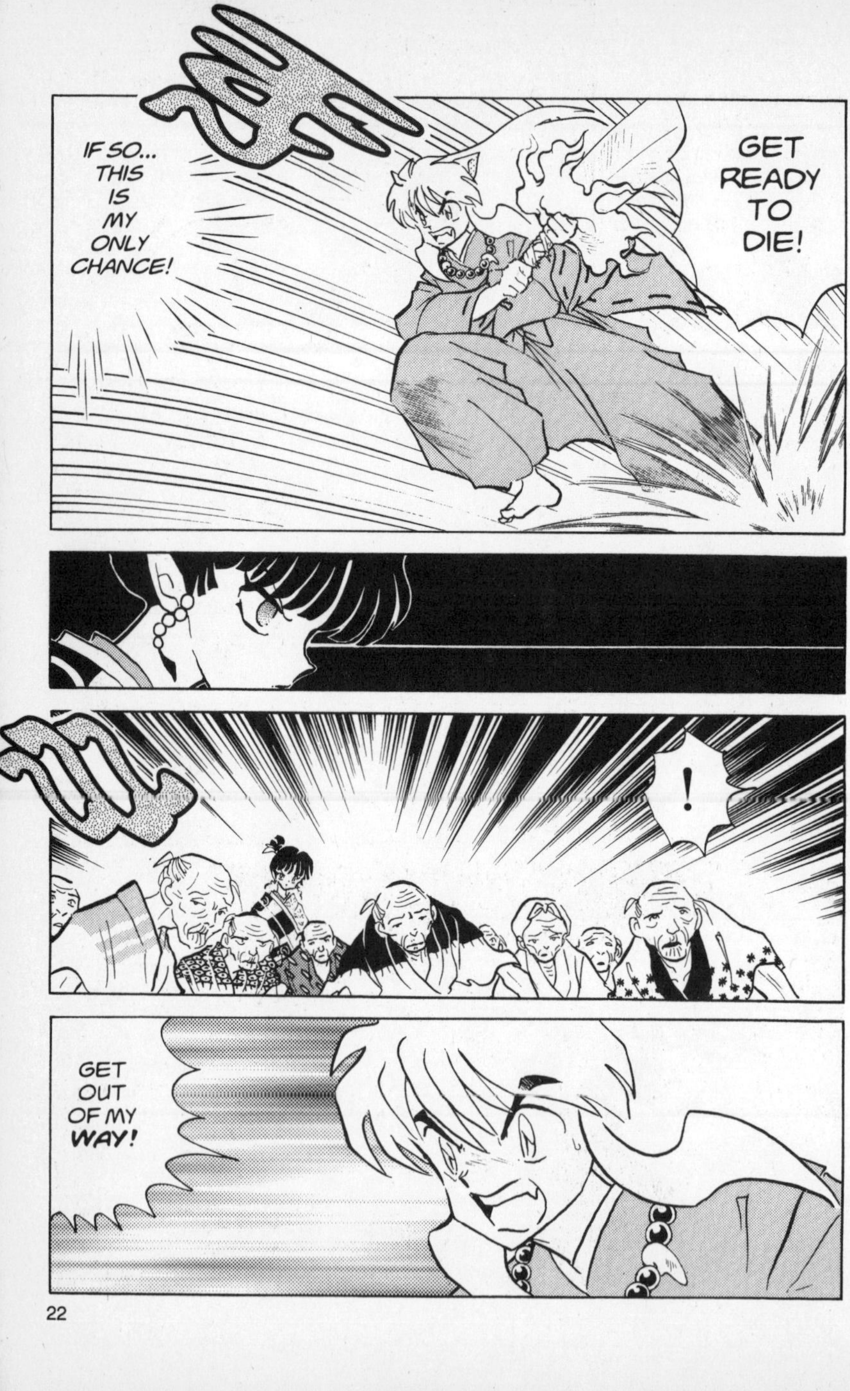

IF SO... THIS IS MY ONLY CHANCE!
GET READY TO DIE!
!
GET OUT OF MY WAY!

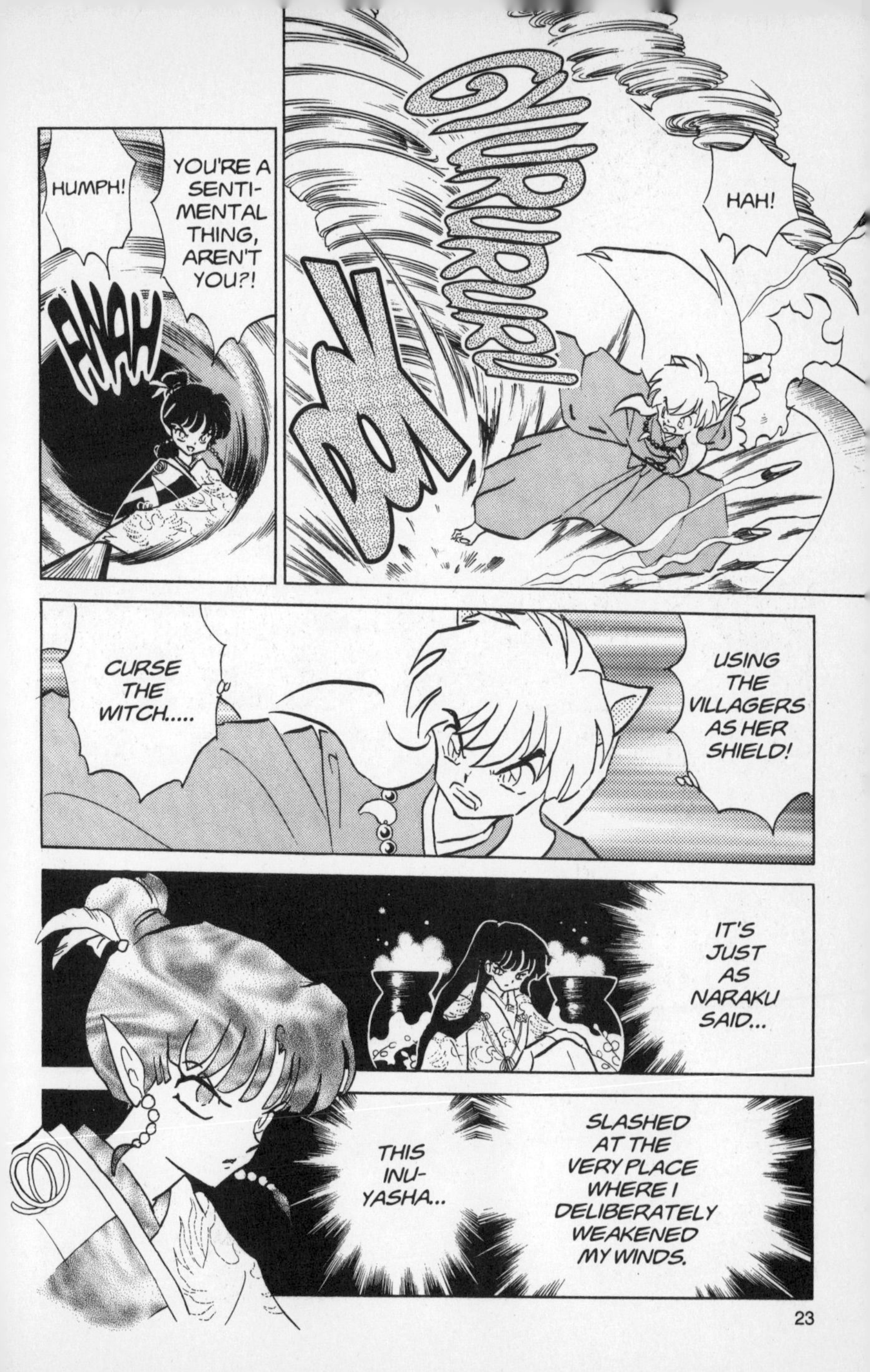
HUMPH!
YOU'RE A SENTI-MENTAL THING, AREN'T YOU?!
FWAH
GYURURURURU
DOH
HAH!
CURSE THE WITCH.....
USING THE VILLAGERS AS HER SHIELD!
IT'S JUST AS NARAKU SAID...
THIS INU-YASHA...
SLASHED AT THE VERY PLACE WHERE I DELIBERATELY WEAKENED MY WINDS.

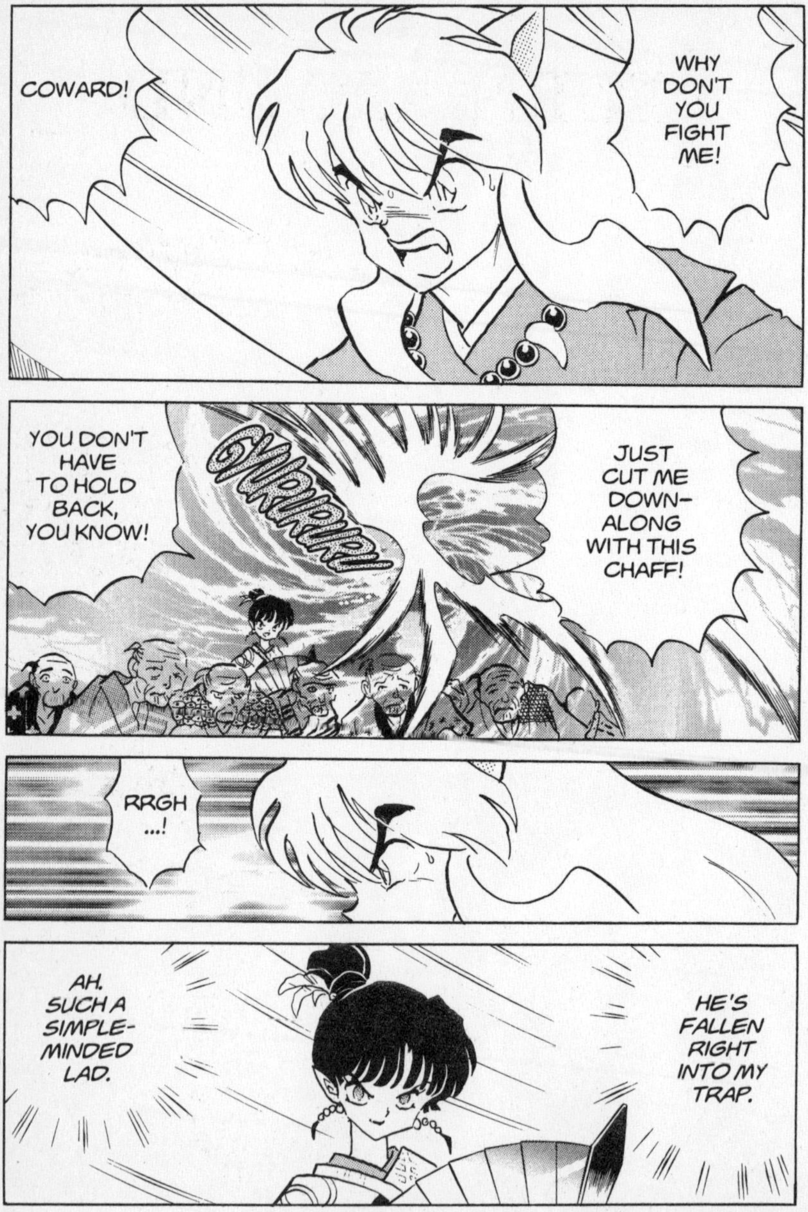
COWARD!
WHY DON'T YOU FIGHT ME!
YOU DON'T HAVE TO HOLD BACK, YOU KNOW!
JUST CUT ME DOWN—ALONG WITH THIS CHAFF!
RRGH ...!
AH. SUCH A SIMPLE-MINDED LAD.
HE'S FALLEN RIGHT INTO MY TRAP.

SCROLL TWO

TURN-AROUND

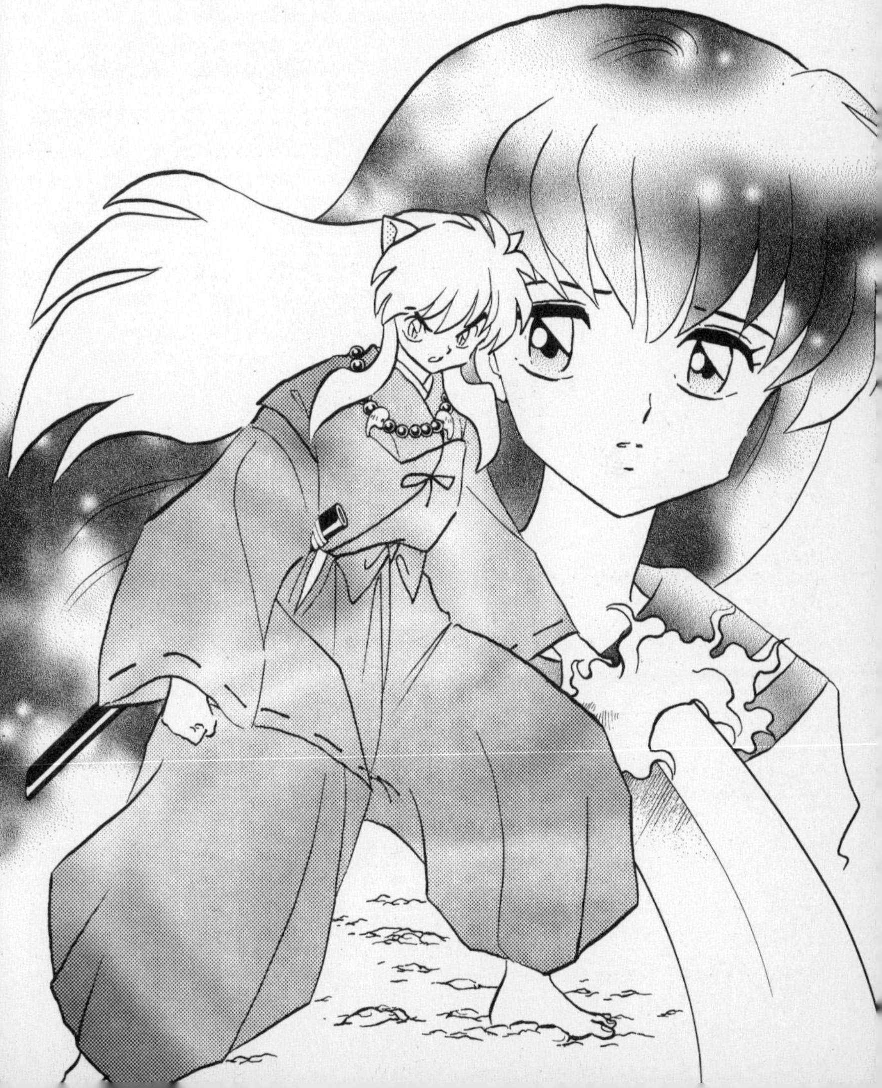

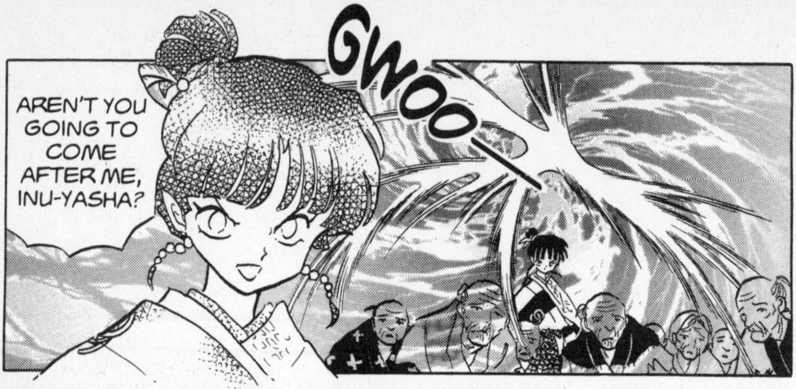
ARE N'T YOU GOING TO COME AFTER ME, INU-YASHA?
GWOO—
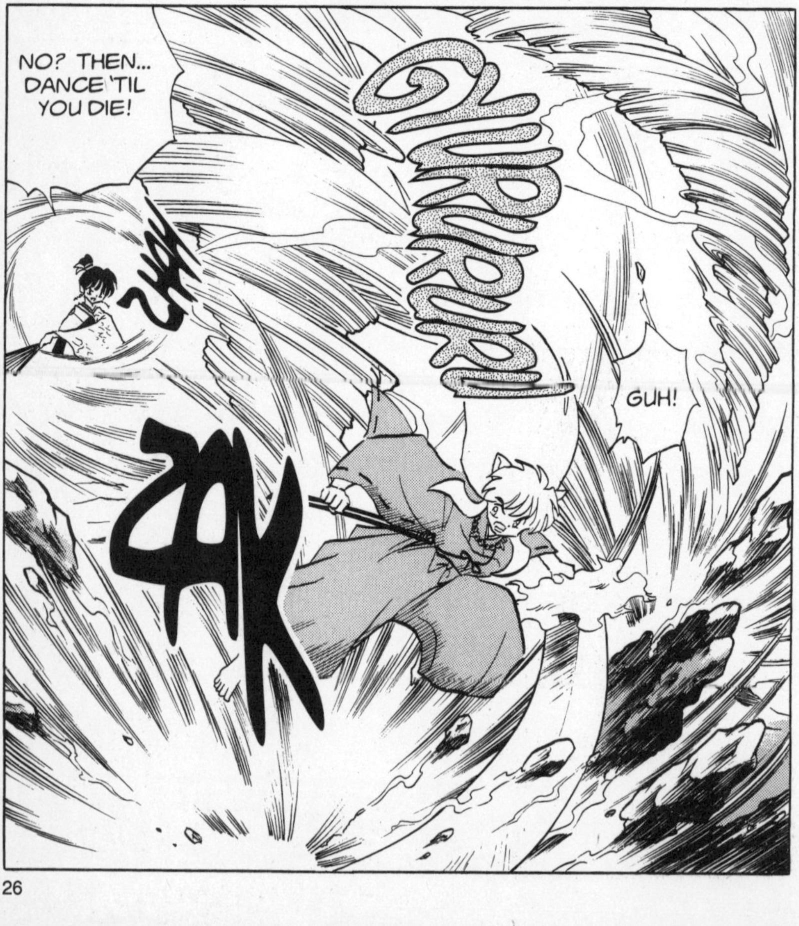
NO? THEN... DANCE 'TIL YOU DIE!
GYURURURU!
GUH!
ZAK

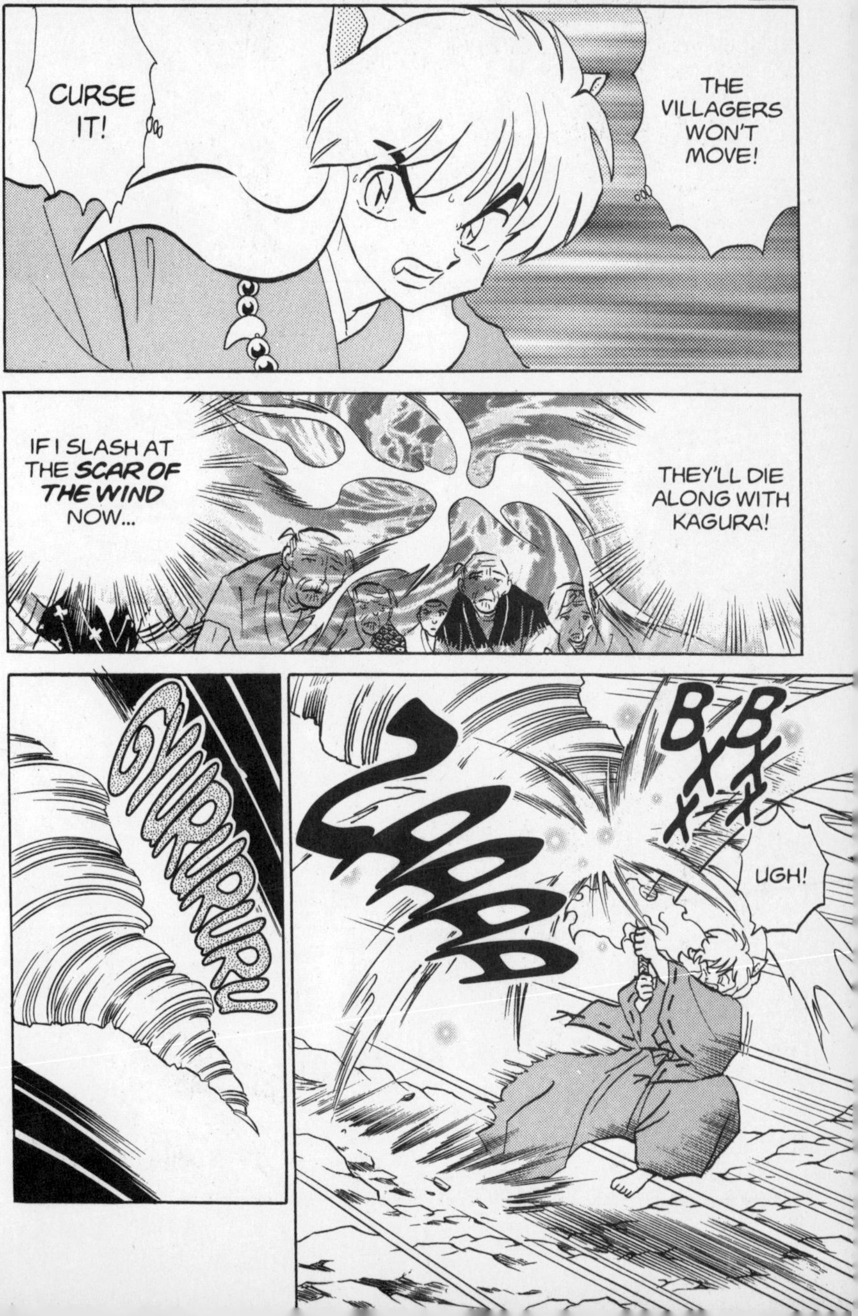
CURSE IT!
THE VILLAGERS WON'T MOVE!
IF I SLASH AT THE ***SCAR OF THE WIND*** NOW...
THEY'LL DIE ALONG WITH KAGURA!
GYURURURURU
ZAAAA
UGH!

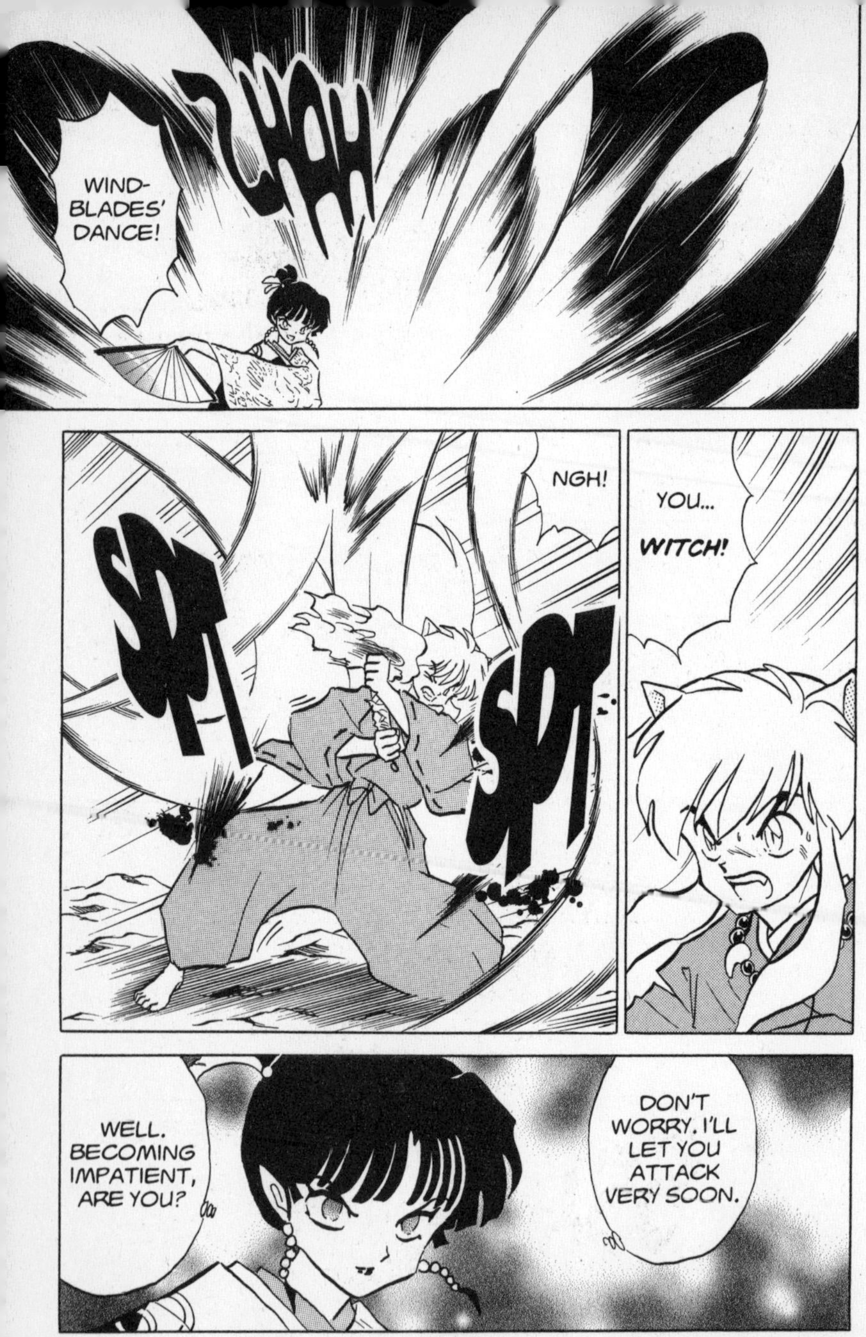
WIND-BLADES' DANCE!
SPT
NGH!
SPT
YOU...
WITCH!
WELL. BECOMING IMPATIENT, ARE YOU?
DON'T WORRY. I'LL LET YOU ATTACK VERY SOON.

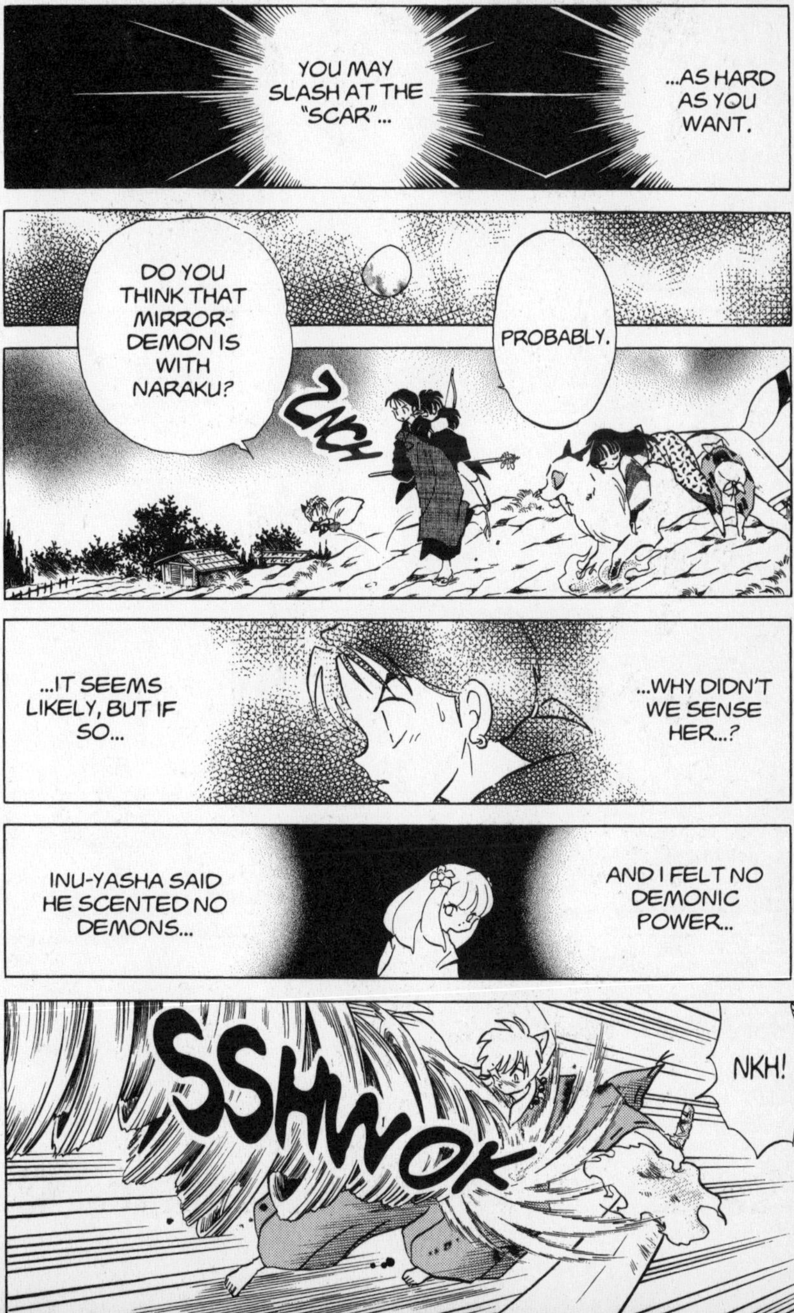
YOU MAY SLASH AT THE "SCAR"...
...AS HARD AS YOU WANT.
DO YOU THINK THAT MIRROR-DEMON IS WITH NARAKU?
PROBABLY.
ZNCH
...IT SEEMS LIKELY, BUT IF SO...
...WHY DIDN'T WE SENSE HER...?
INU-YASHA SAID HE SCENTED NO DEMONS...
AND I FELT NO DEMONIC POWER...
SSHWOK
NKH!

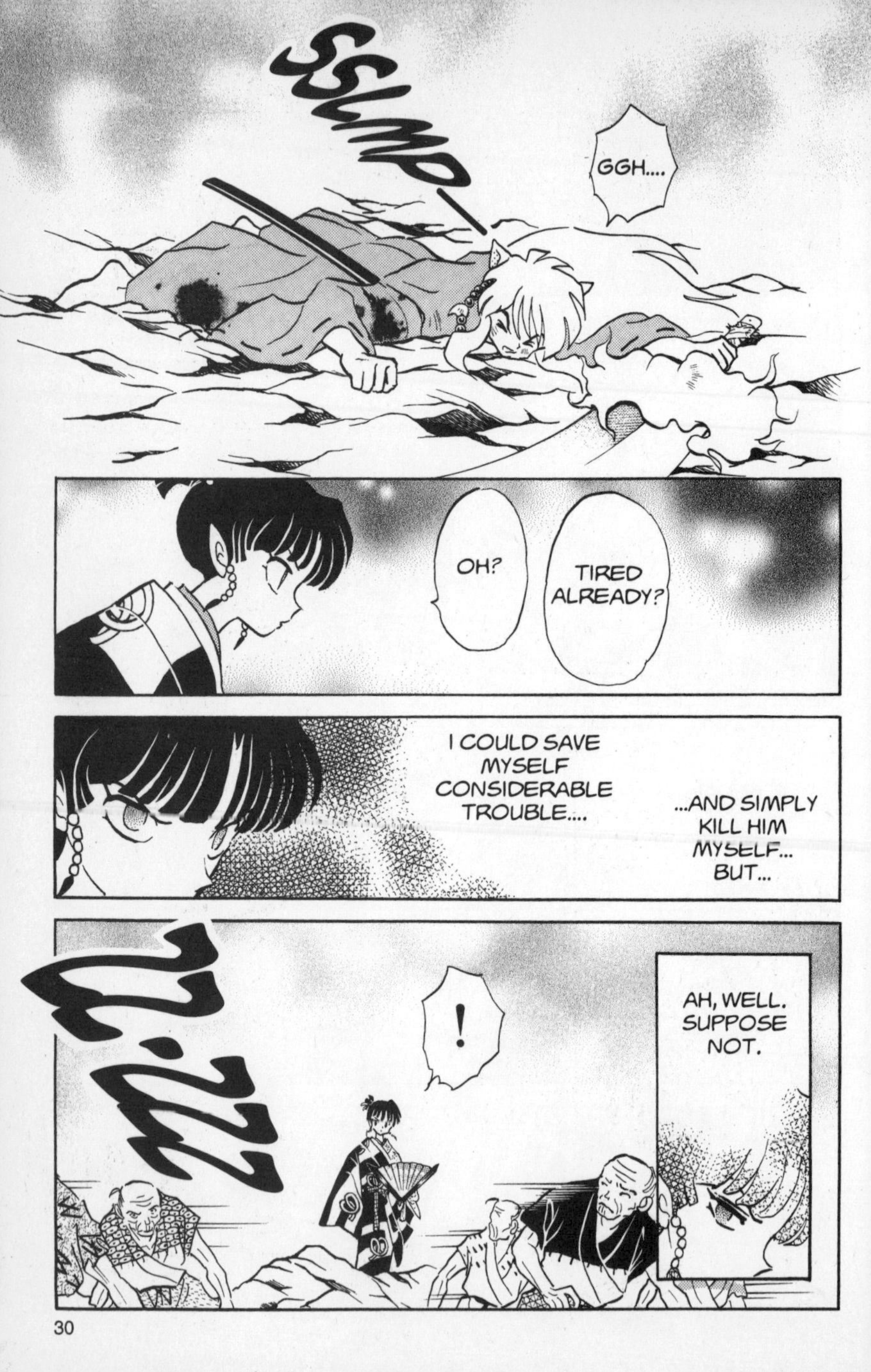
SSLMP
GGH....
OH?
TIRED ALREADY?
I COULD SAVE MYSELF CONSIDERABLE TROUBLE....
...AND SIMPLY KILL HIM MYSELF... BUT...
!
AH, WELL. SUPPOSE NOT.

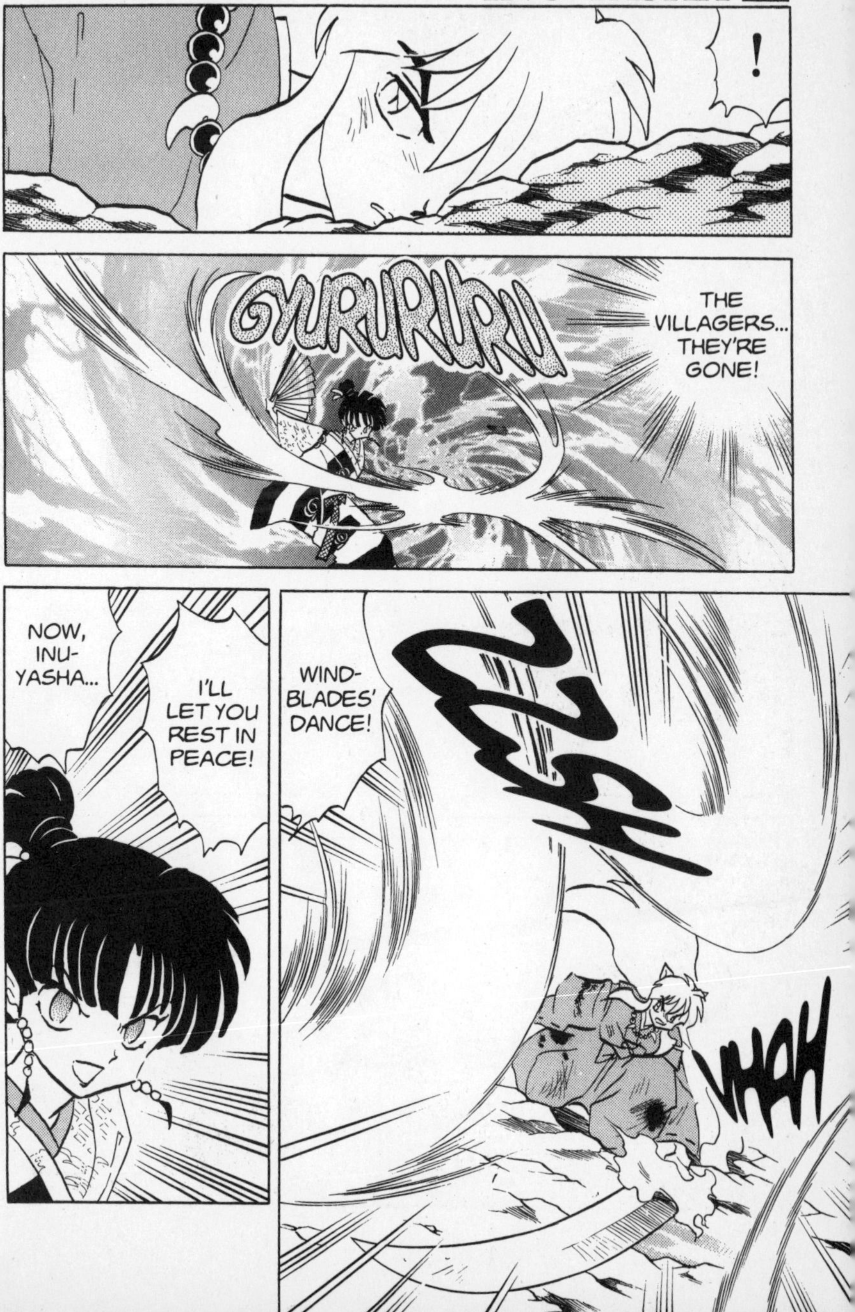
!
GYURURURU
THE VILLAGERS... THEY'RE GONE!
NOW, INU-YASHA...
I'LL LET YOU REST IN PEACE!
WIND-BLADES' DANCE!
ZZSH
VHOH

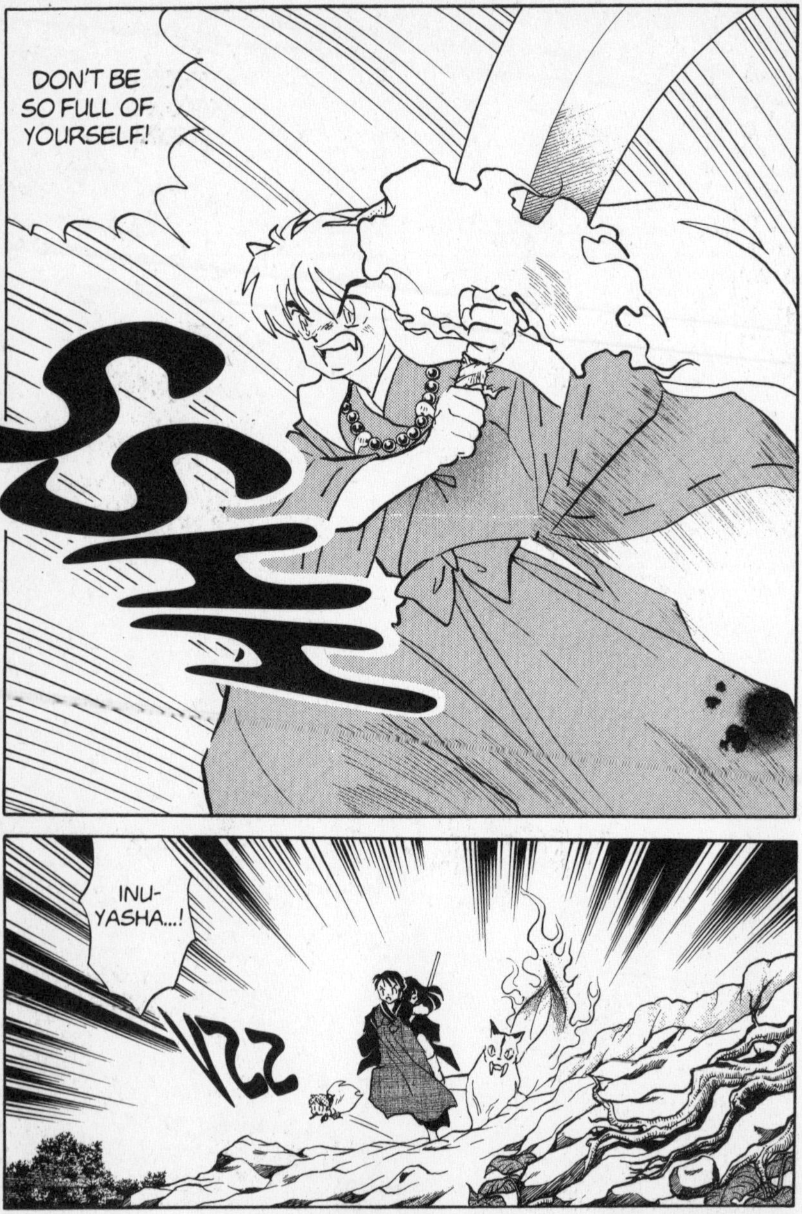
DON'T BE SO FULL OF YOURSELF!
SSH
INU-YASHA...!
VZZ

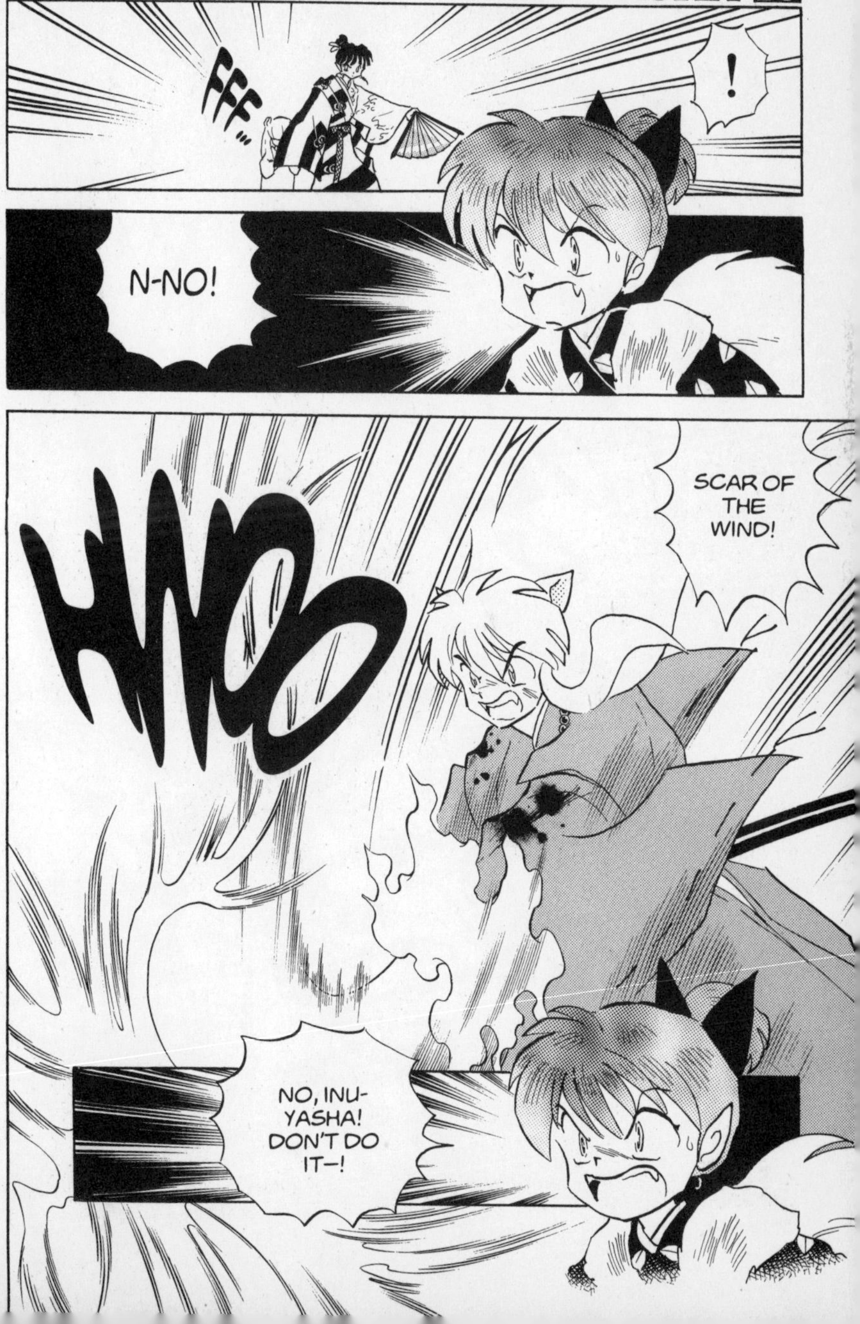
FFF...
!
N-NO!
SCAR OF THE WIND!
NO, INU-YASHA! DON'T DO IT—!

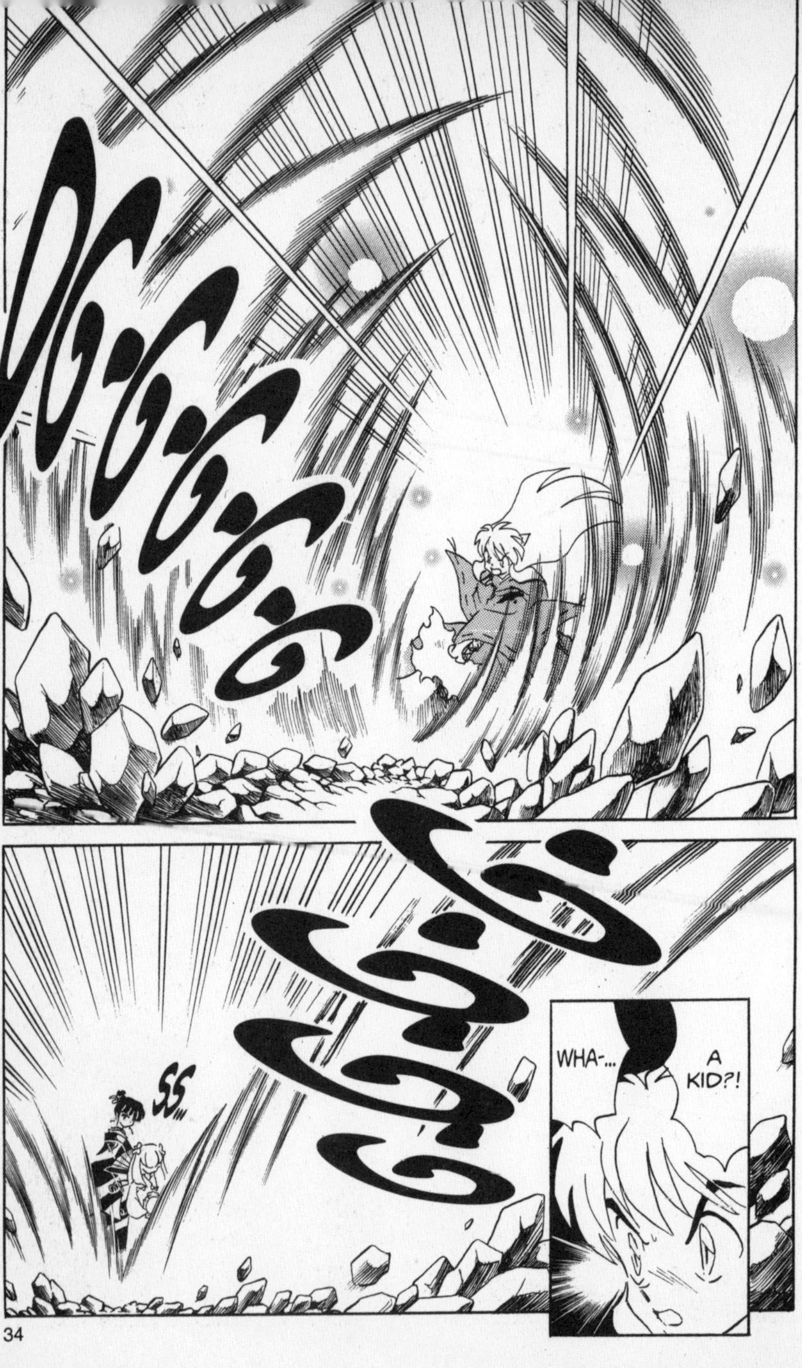
SS
WHA-...
A KID?!

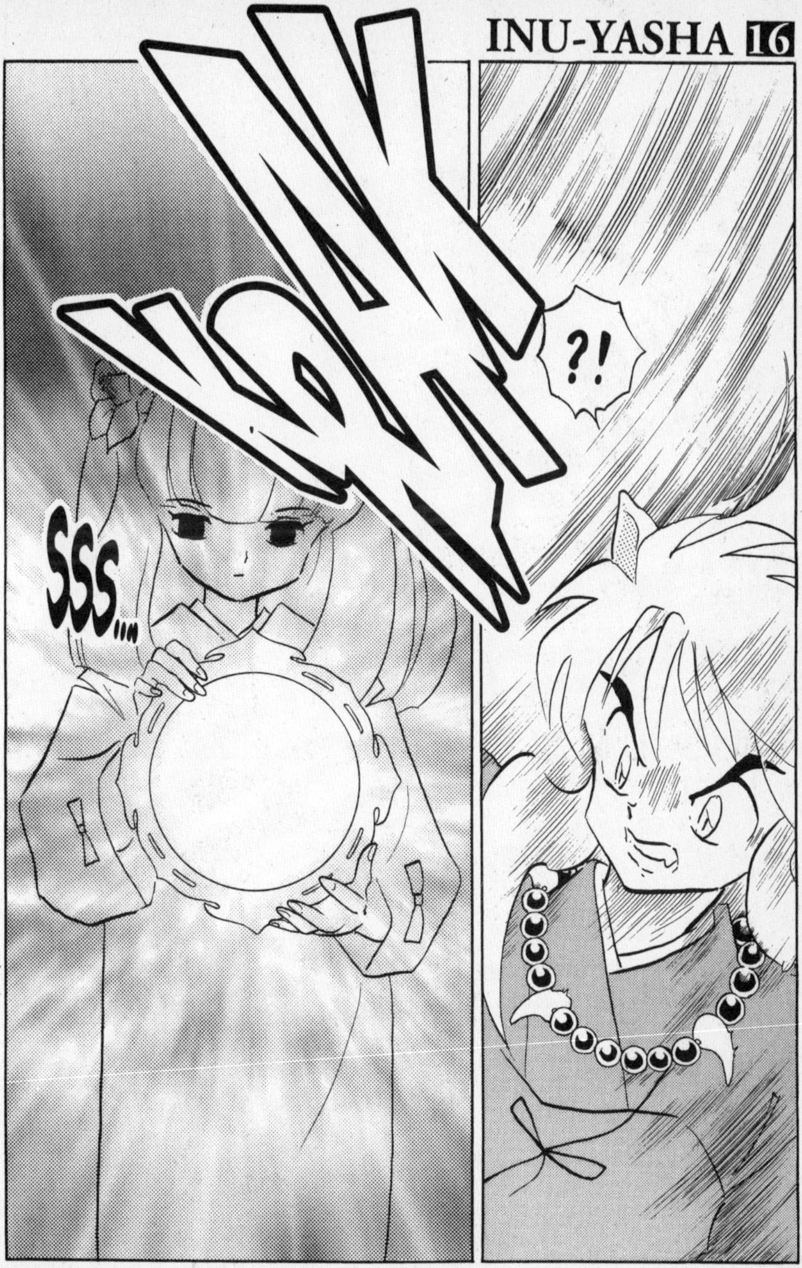
VWSH
SSS...
?!

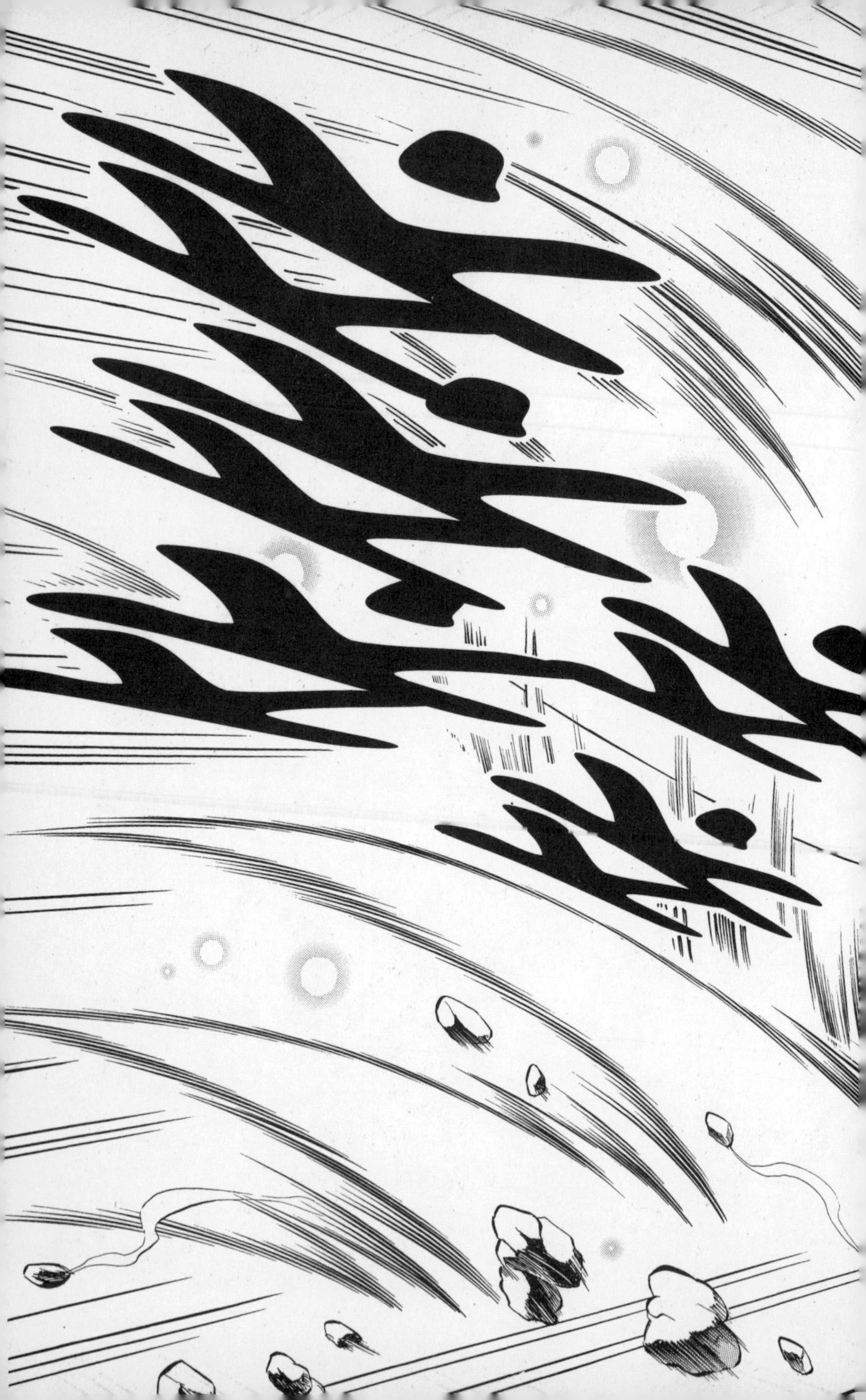

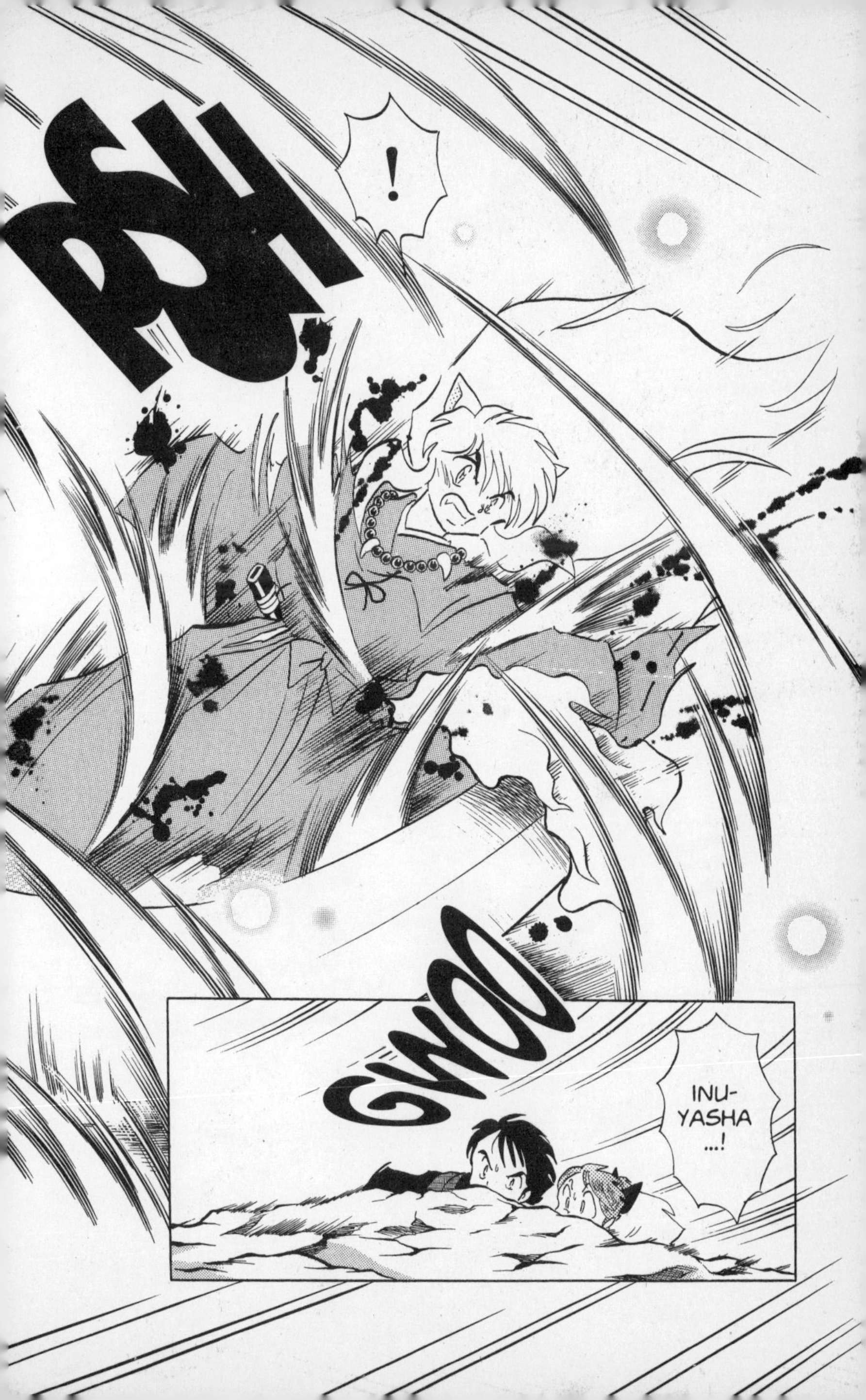

BSHH
!
GWOO
INU-YASHA ...!

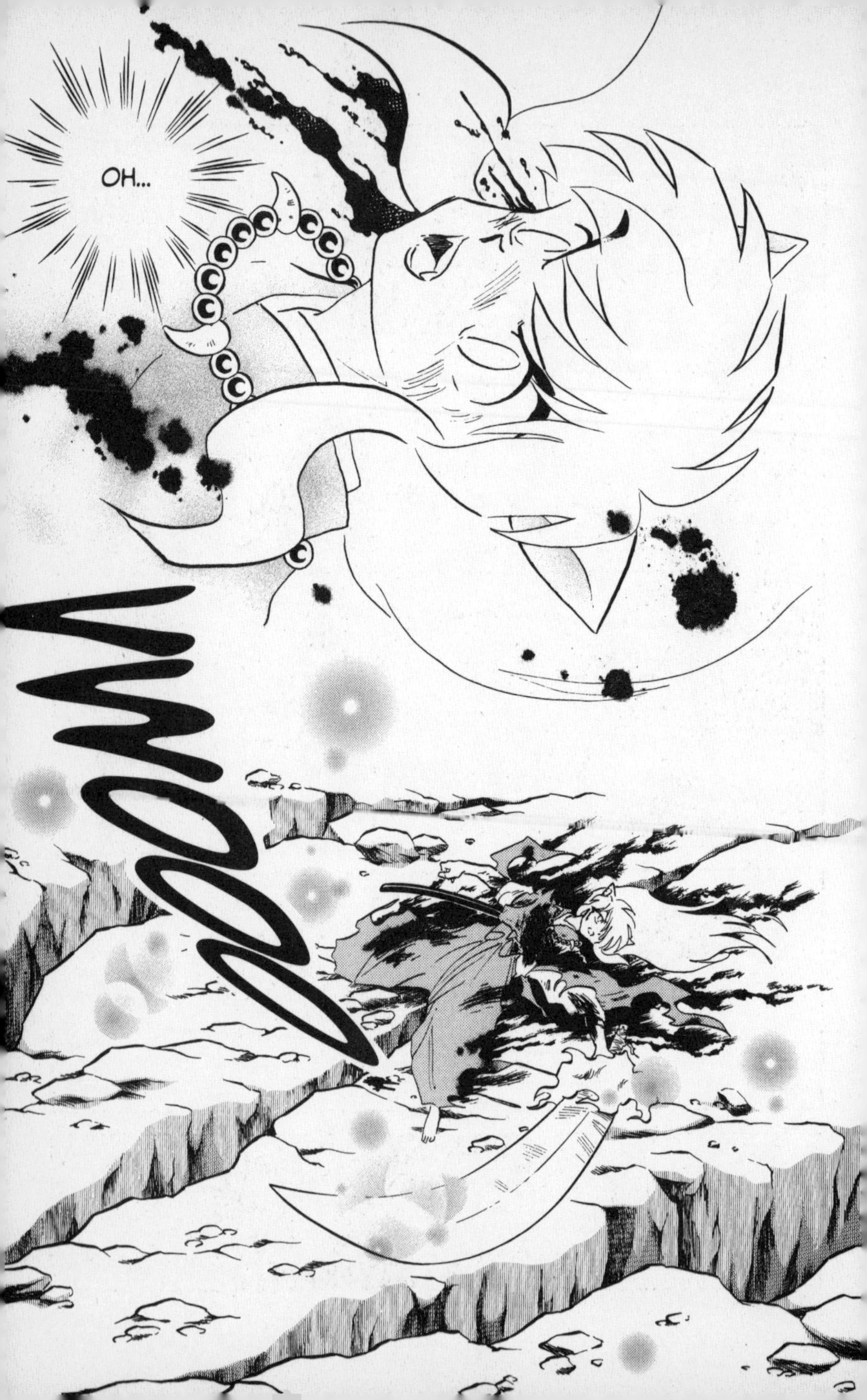
OH...

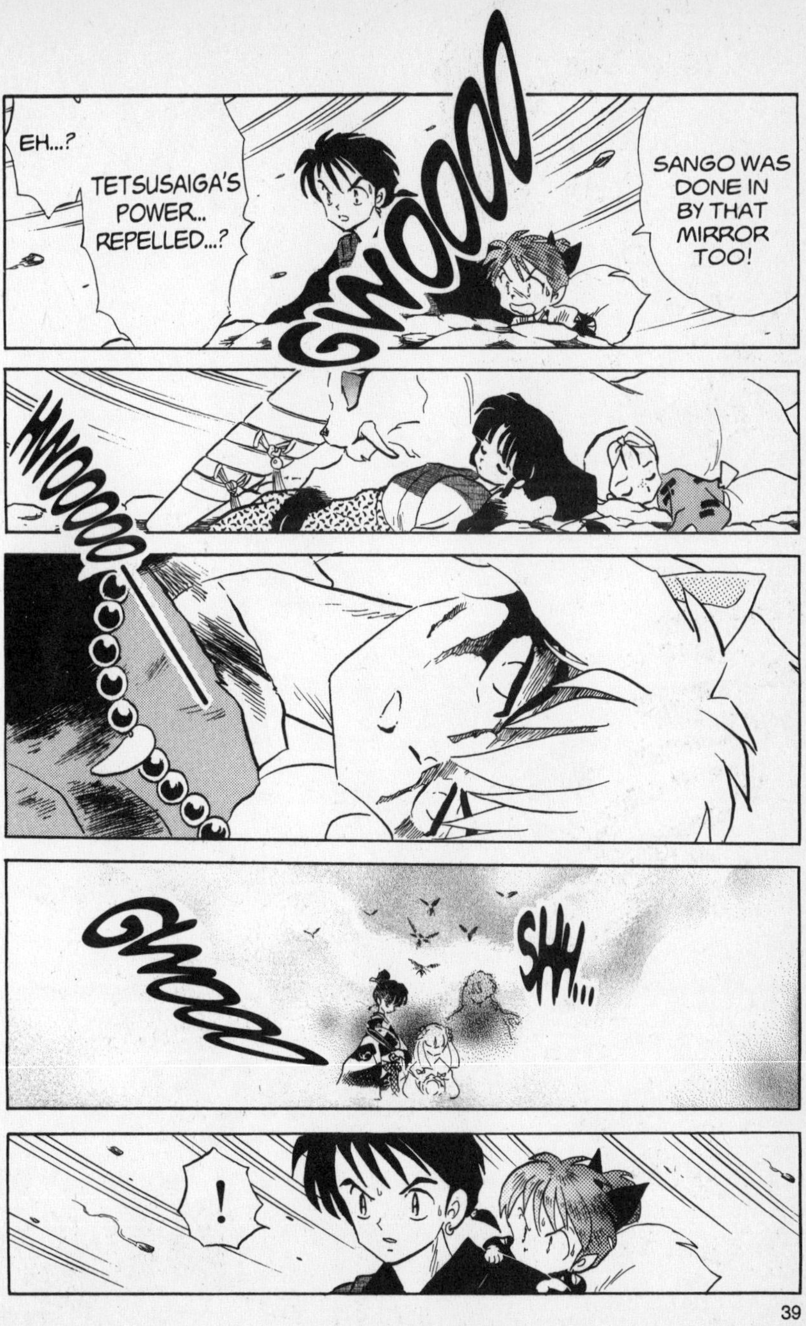
EH...?
TETSUSAIGA'S POWER... REPELLED...?
GWOOOO
SANGO WAS DONE IN BY THAT MIRROR TOO!
HWOOOOO
GWOOO
SHH...
!

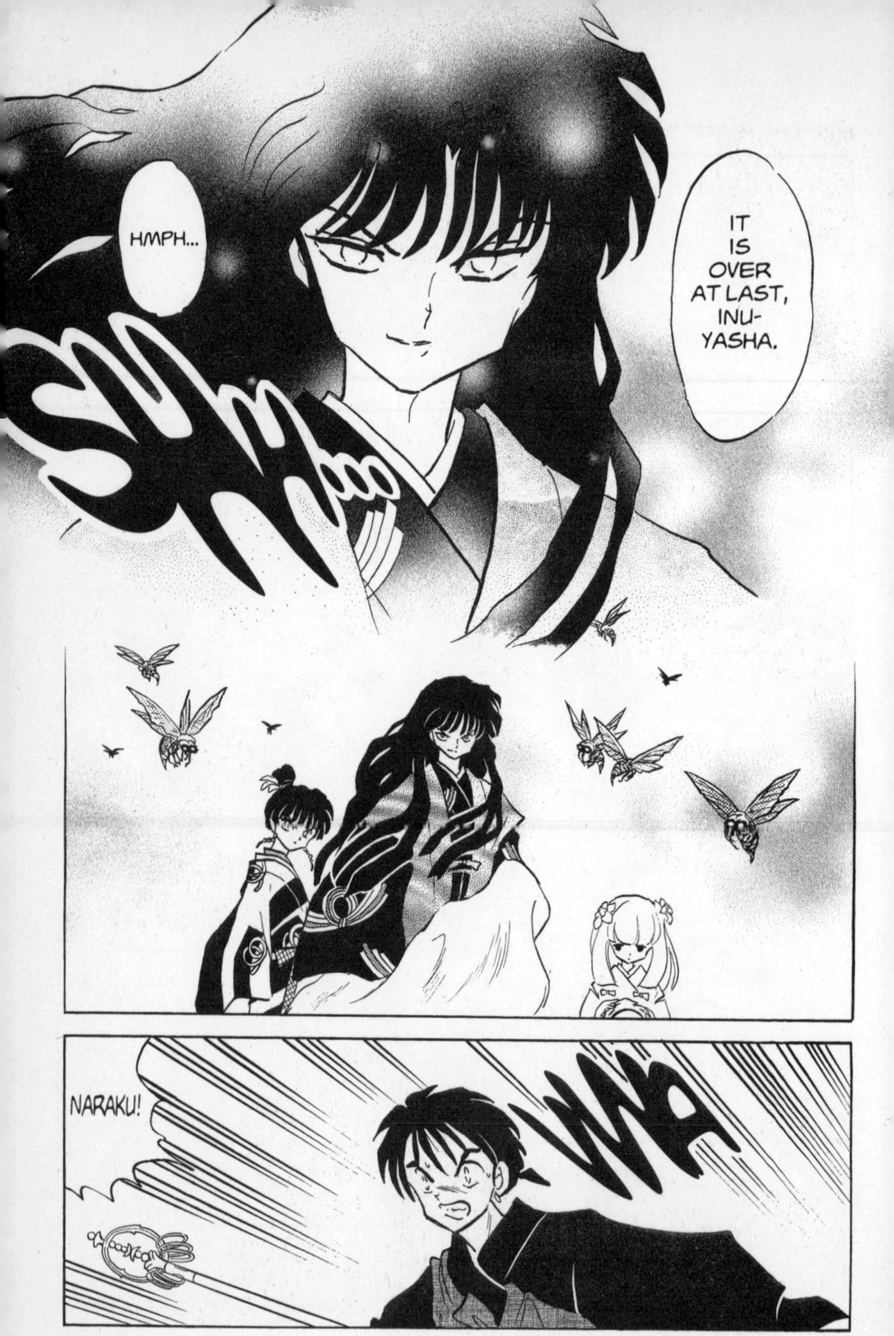
HMPH...
IT IS OVER AT LAST, INU-YASHA.
NARAKU!

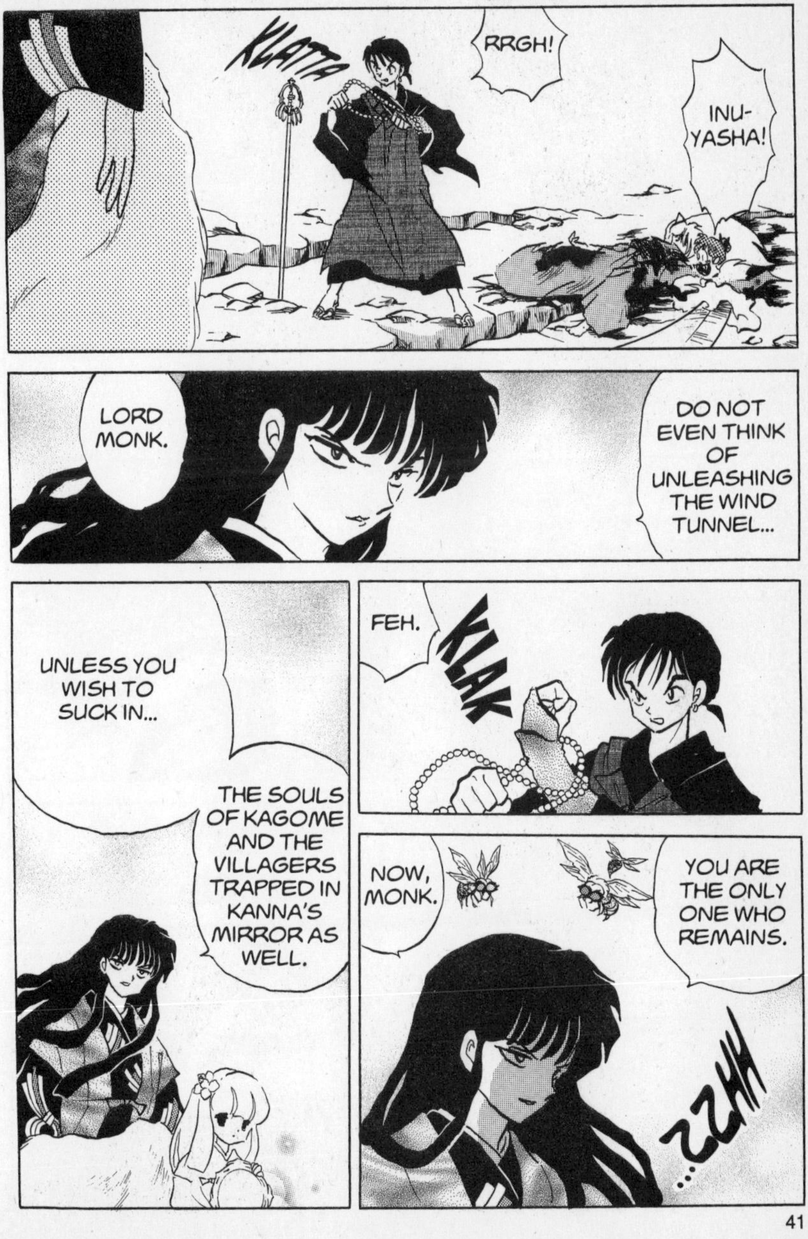
KLATTA
RRGH!
INU-YASHA!
LORD MONK.
DO NOT EVEN THINK OF UNLEASHING THE WIND TUNNEL...
UNLESS YOU WISH TO SUCK IN...
THE SOULS OF KAGOME AND THE VILLAGERS TRAPPED IN KANNA'S MIRROR AS WELL.
FEH.
KLAK
NOW, MONK.
YOU ARE THE ONLY ONE WHO REMAINS.
ZZZHH...

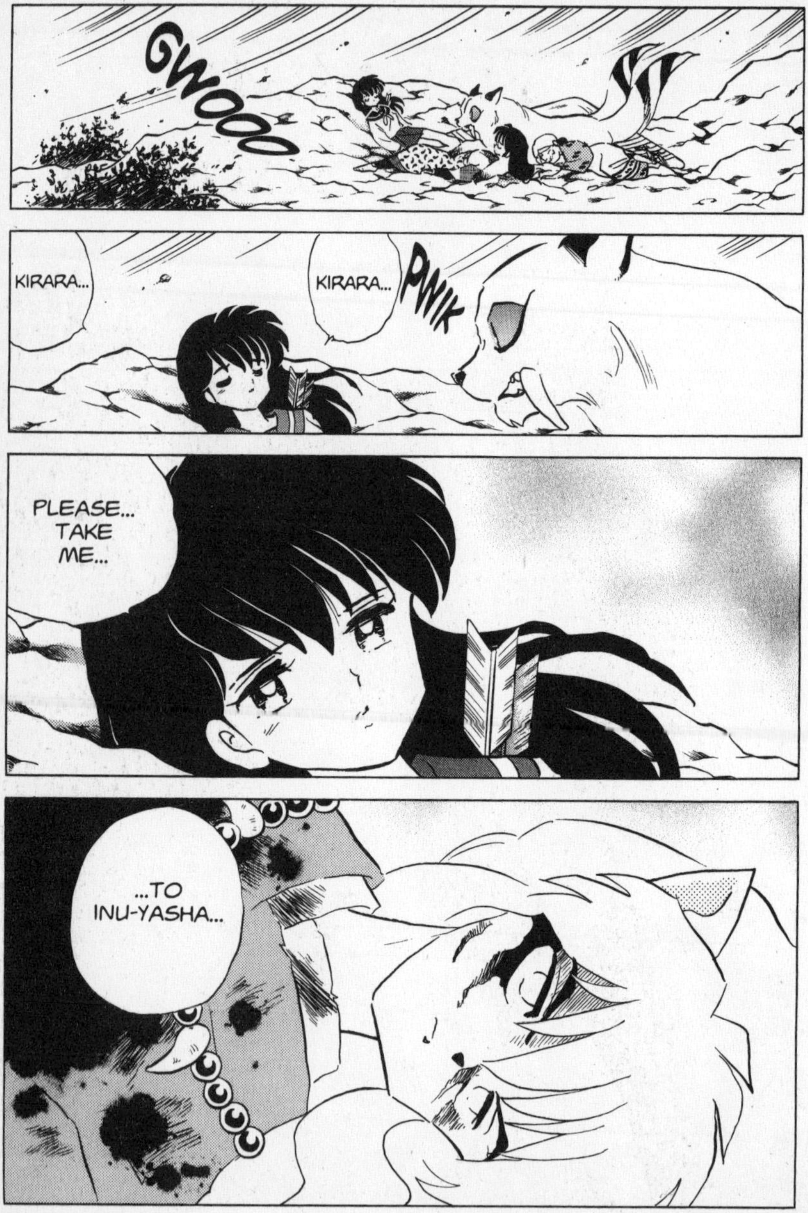
GWOOO
KIRARA...
KIRARA...
PWIK
PLEASE... TAKE ME...
...TO INU-YASHA...

SCROLL THREE

THE LIGHT OF THE SHIKON

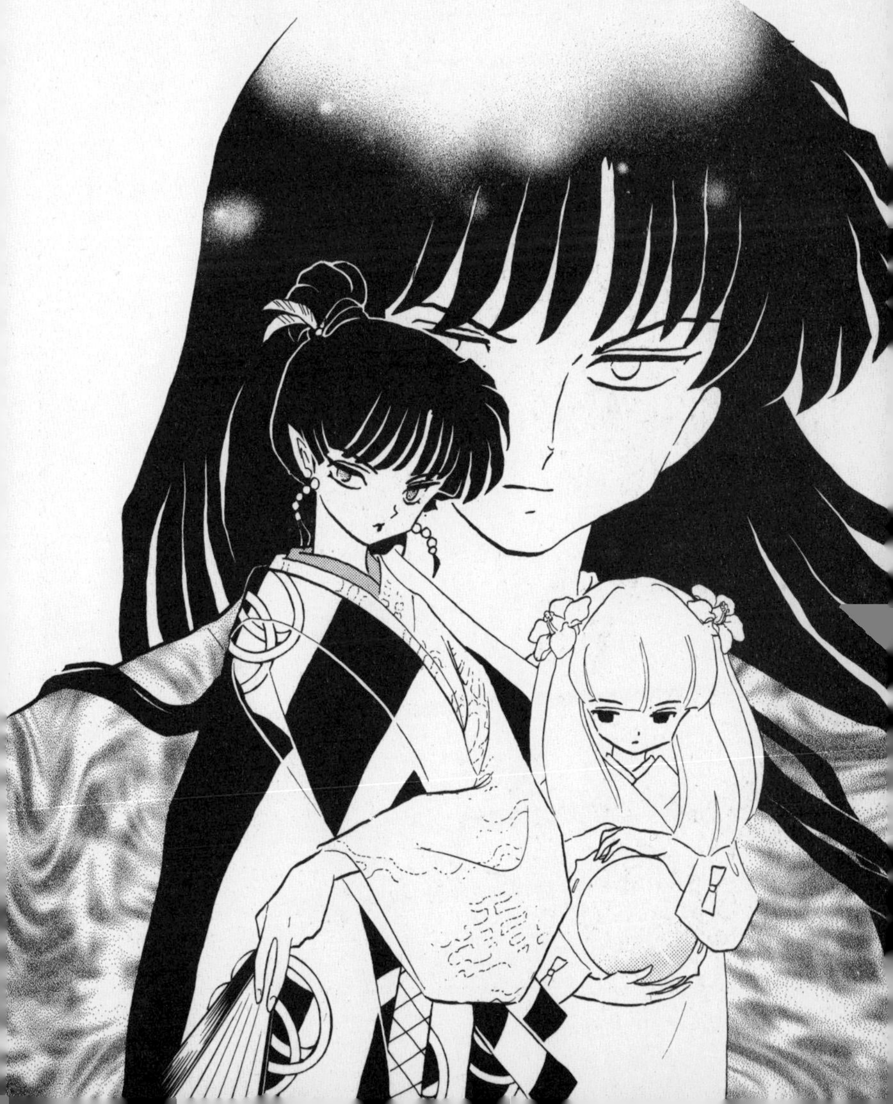

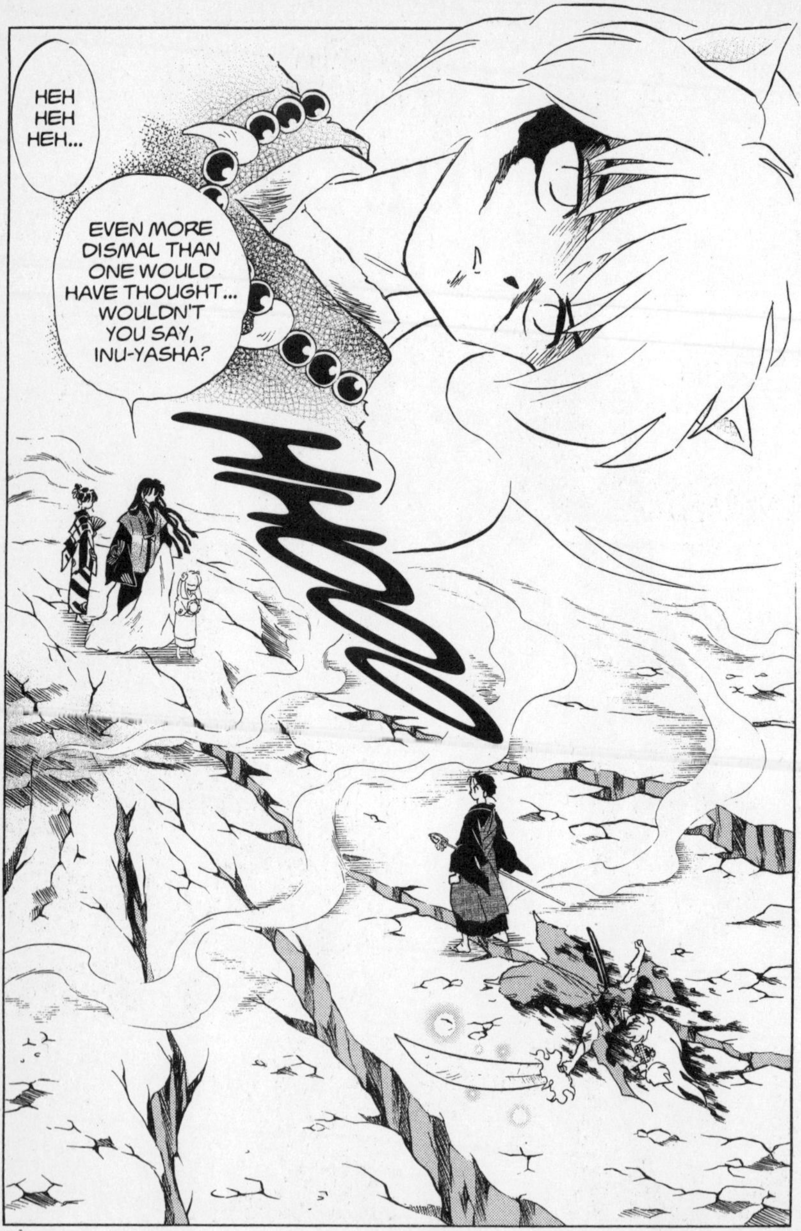
HEH HEH HEH...
EVEN MORE DISMAL THAN ONE WOULD HAVE THOUGHT... WOULDN'T YOU SAY, INU-YASHA?
HWOO

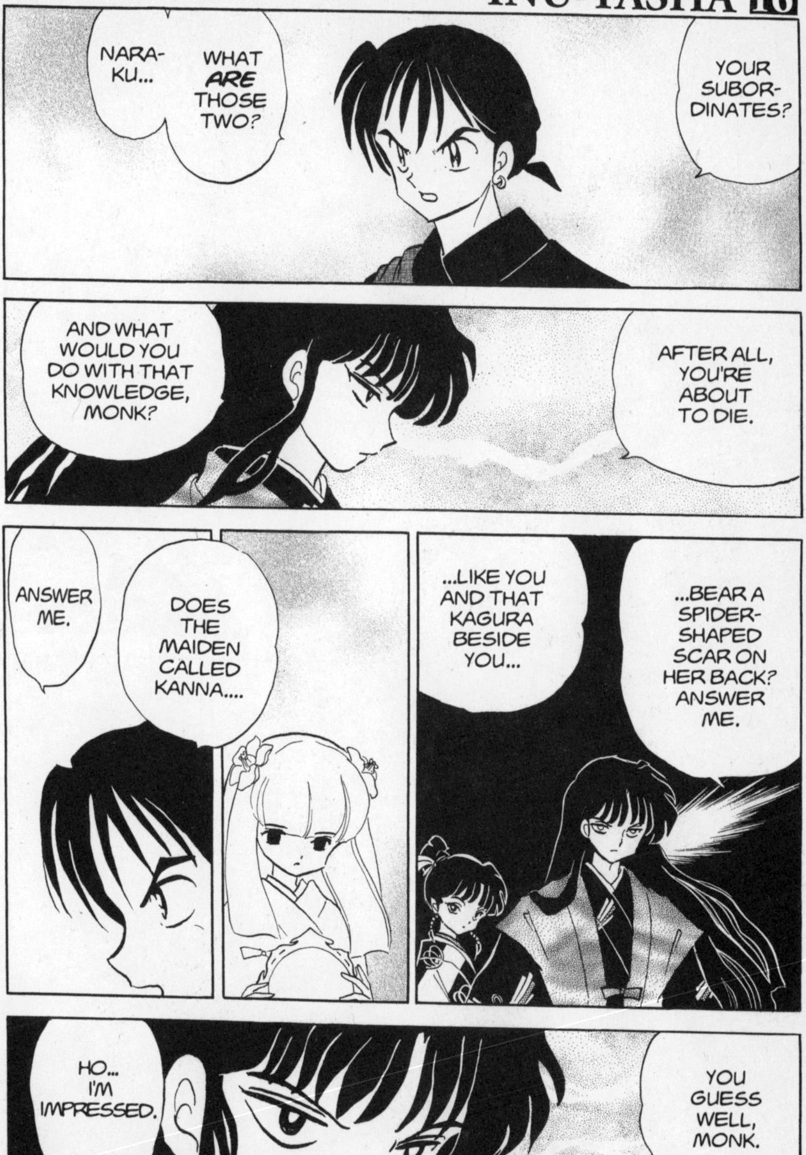
NARA-KU...
WHAT ARE THOSE TWO?
YOUR SUBOR-DINATES?
AND WHAT WOULD YOU DO WITH THAT KNOWLEDGE, MONK?
AFTER ALL, YOU'RE ABOUT TO DIE.
ANSWER ME.
DOES THE MAIDEN CALLED KANNA....
...LIKE YOU AND THAT KAGURA BESIDE YOU...
...BEAR A SPIDER-SHAPED SCAR ON HER BACK? ANSWER ME.
HO... I'M IMPRESSED.
YOU GUESS WELL, MONK.

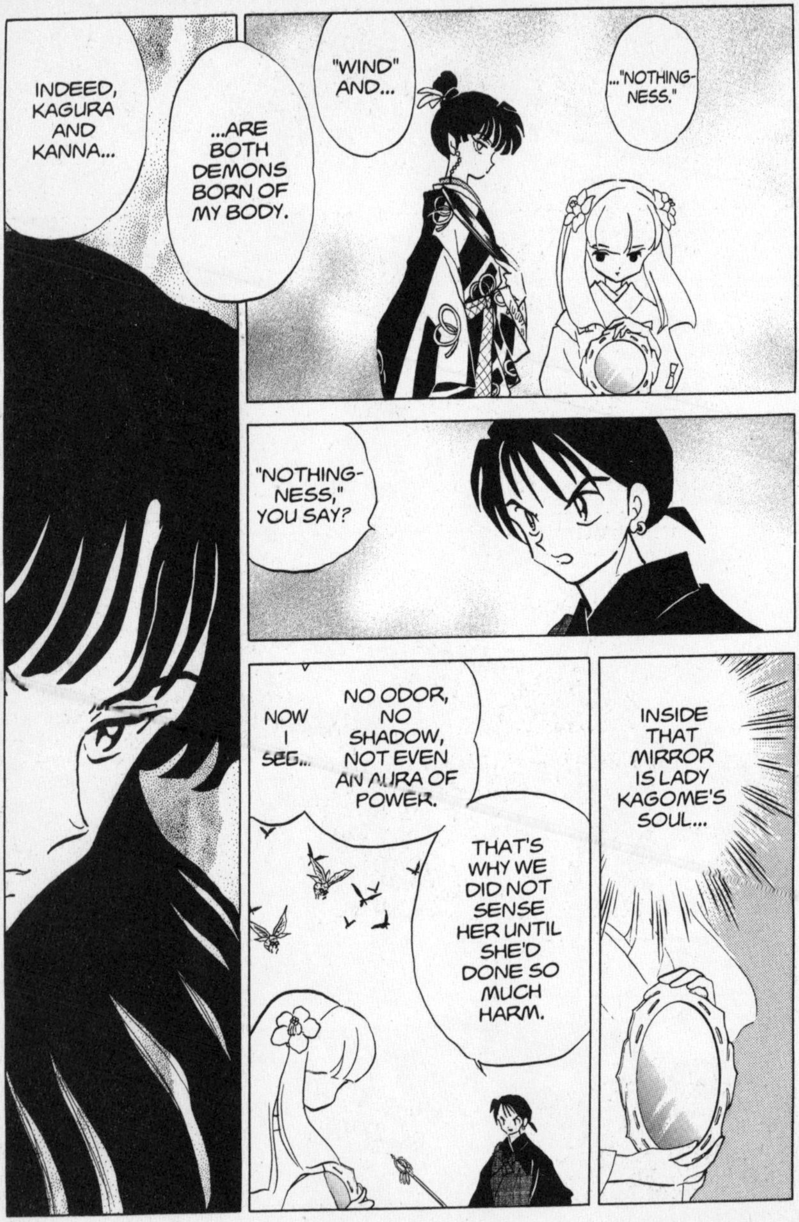
INDEED, KAGURA AND KANNA...
...ARE BOTH DEMONS BORN OF MY BODY.
"WIND" AND...
..."NOTHING-NESS."
"NOTHING-NESS," YOU SAY?
NOW I SEE...
NO ODOR, NO SHADOW, NOT EVEN AN AURA OF POWER.
THAT'S WHY WE DID NOT SENSE HER UNTIL SHE'D DONE SO MUCH HARM.
INSIDE THAT MIRROR IS LADY KAGOME'S SOUL...

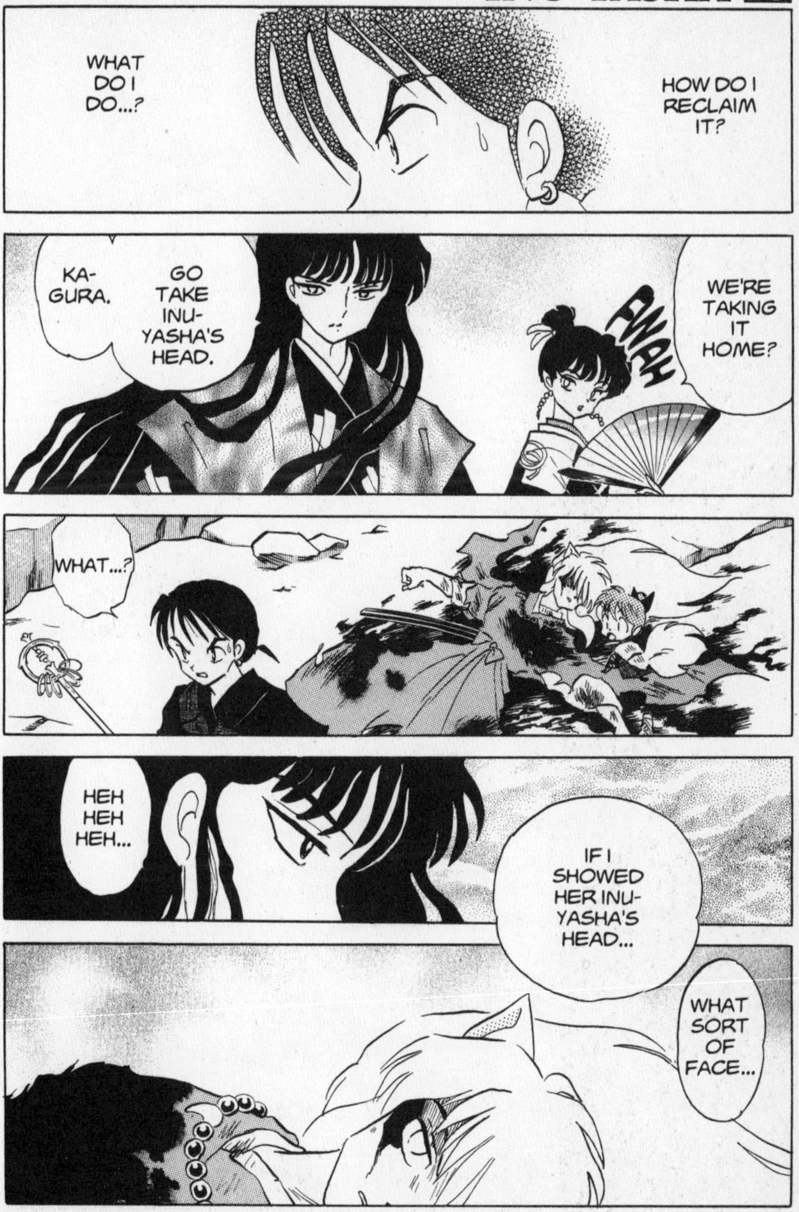
WHAT DO I DO...?
HOW DO I RECLAIM IT?
KA-GURA.
GO TAKE INU-YASHA'S HEAD.
AWAH
WE'RE TAKING IT HOME?
WHAT...?
HEH HEH HEH...
IF I SHOWED HER INU-YASHA'S HEAD...
WHAT SORT OF FACE...

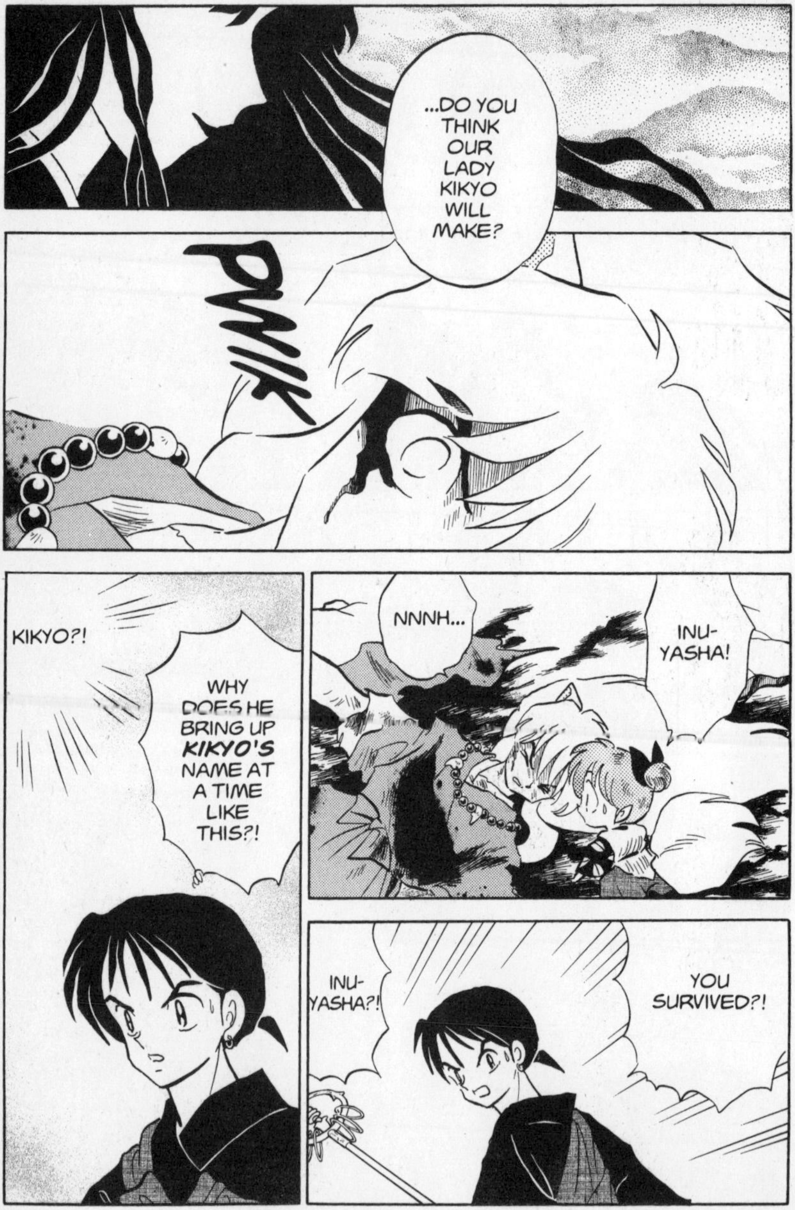
...DO YOU THINK OUR LADY KIKYO WILL MAKE?
PWNK
KIKYO?!
WHY DOES HE BRING UP KIKYO'S NAME AT A TIME LIKE THIS?!
NNNH...
INU-YASHA!
INU-YASHA?!
YOU SURVIVED?!

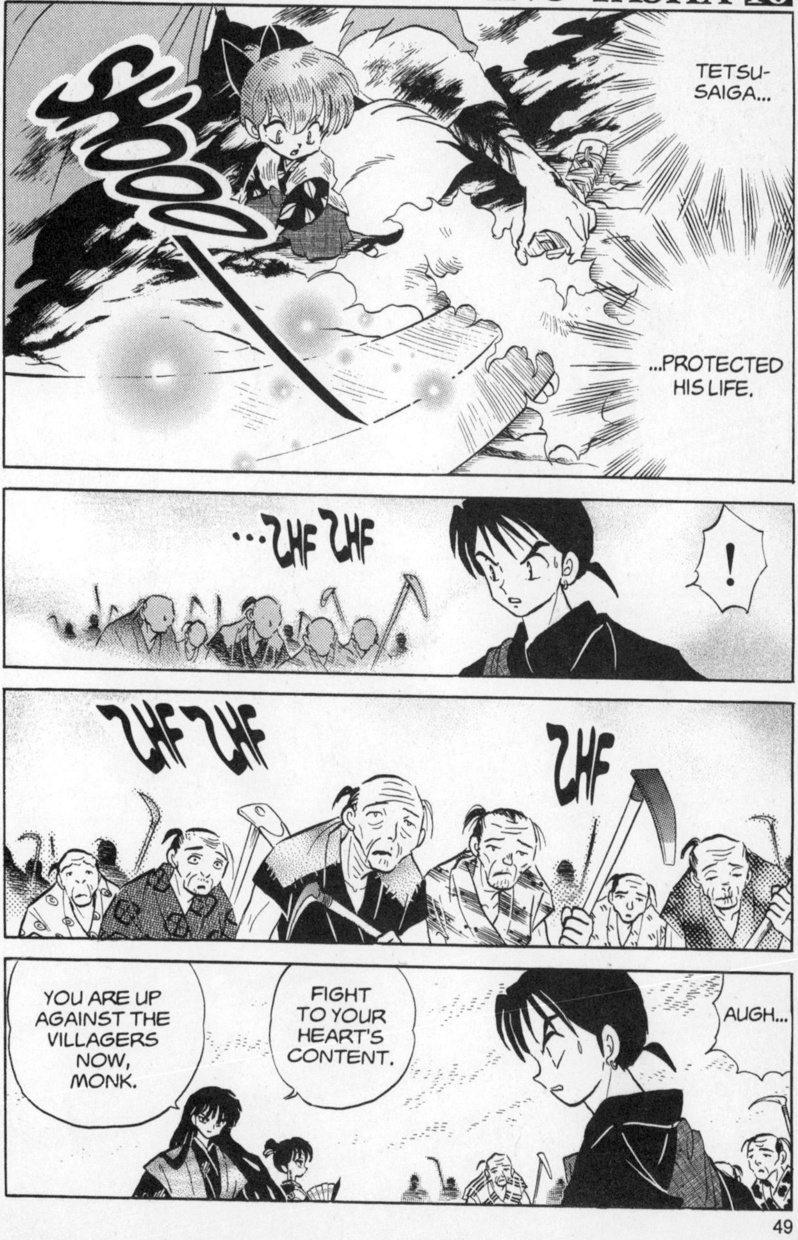
SHOOO
TETSU-SAIGA...
...PROTECTED HIS LIFE.
...ZHF ZHF
!
ZHF ZHF
ZHF
YOU ARE UP AGAINST THE VILLAGERS NOW, MONK.
FIGHT TO YOUR HEART'S CONTENT.
AUGH...

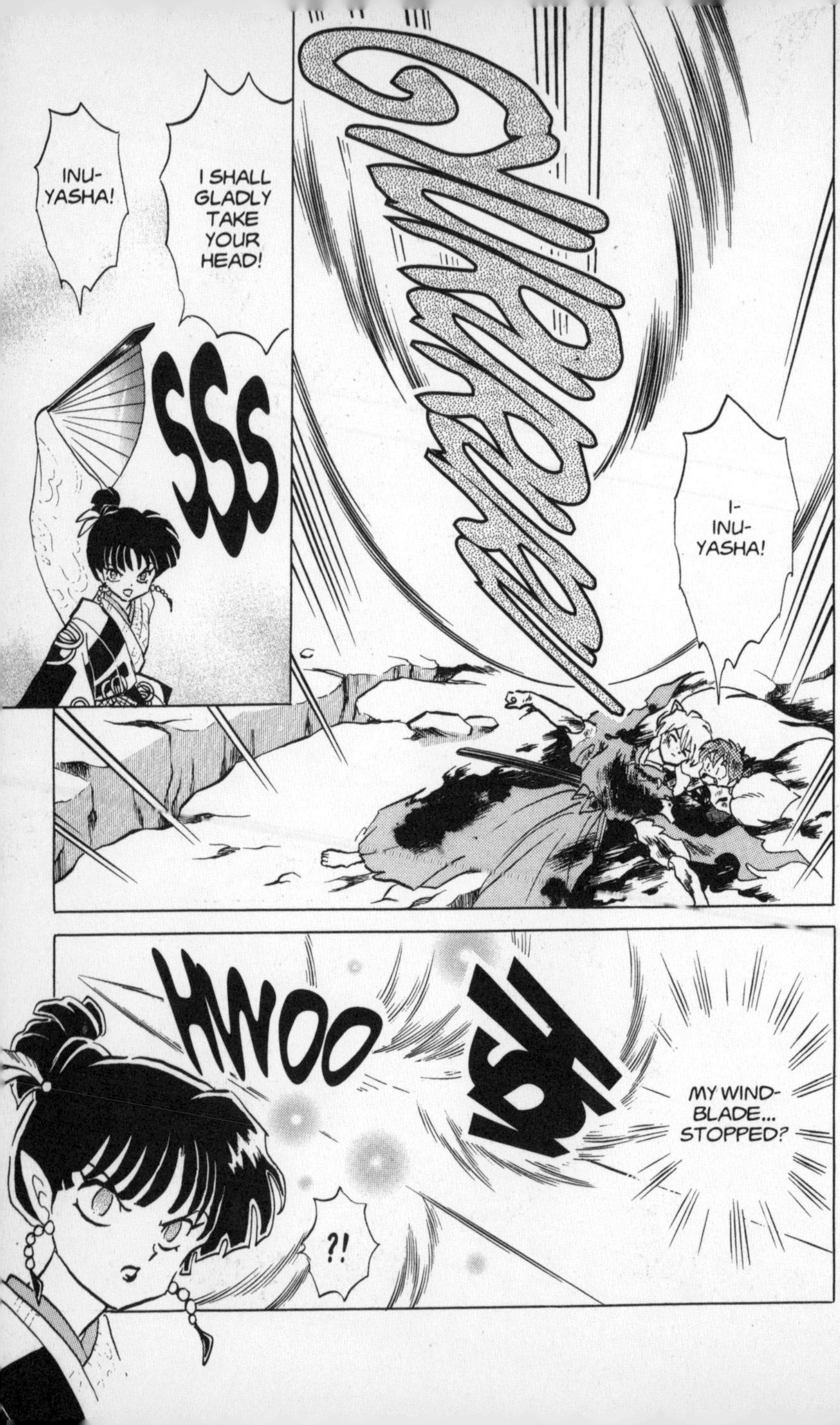

INU-YASHA!
I SHALL GLADLY TAKE YOUR HEAD!
SSS
I- INU-YASHA!
HWOO
MY WIND-BLADE... STOPPED?
?!

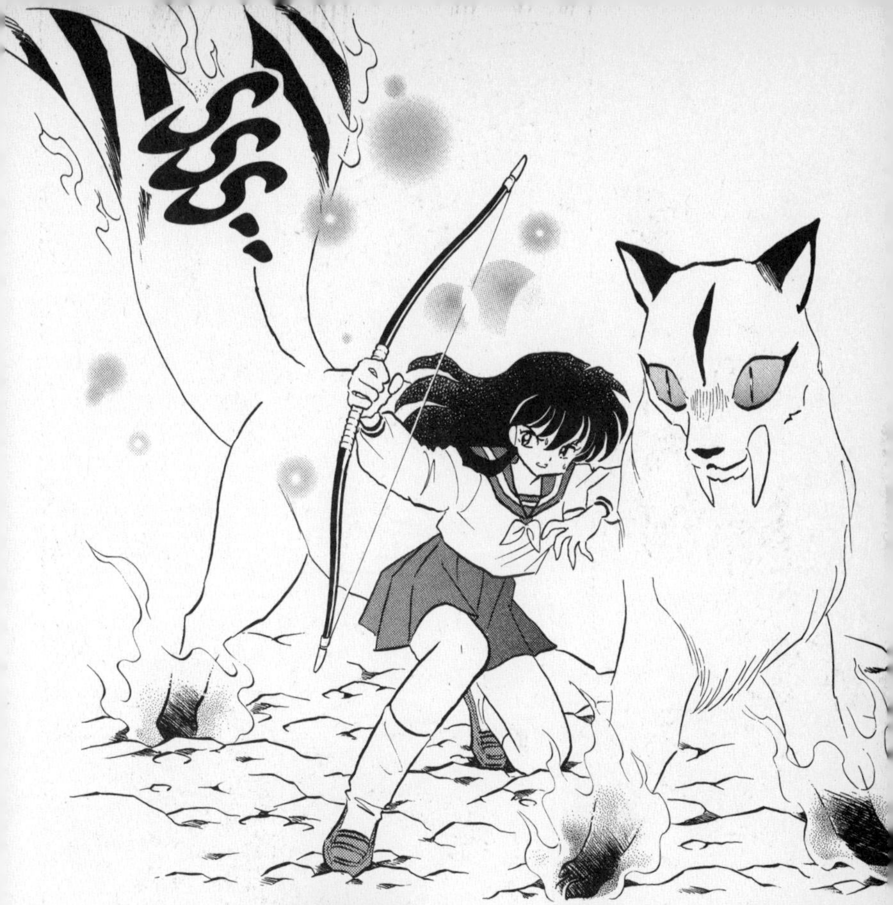
SSS...

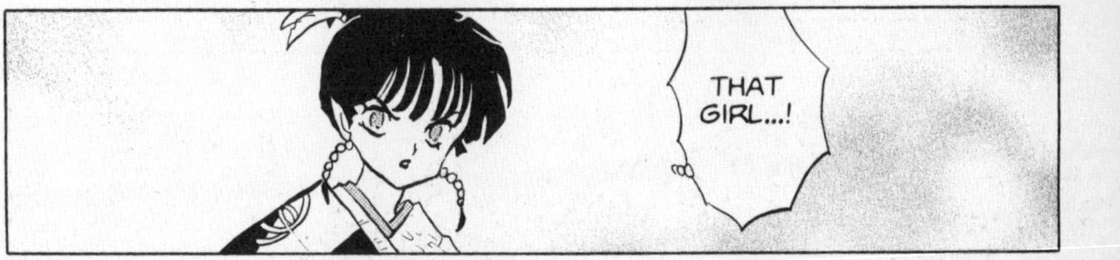
THAT GIRL...!

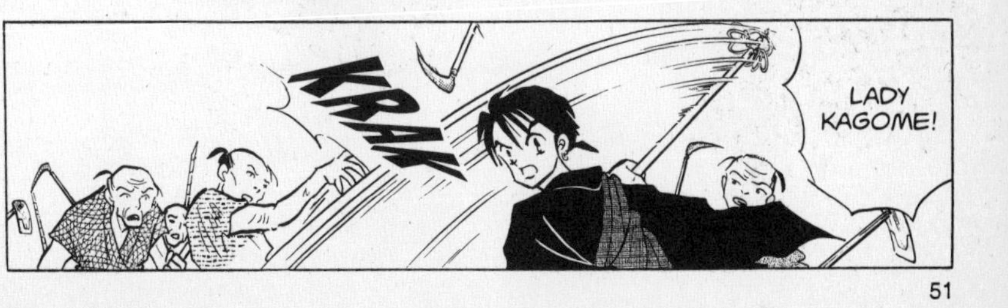
KRAK
LADY KAGOME!

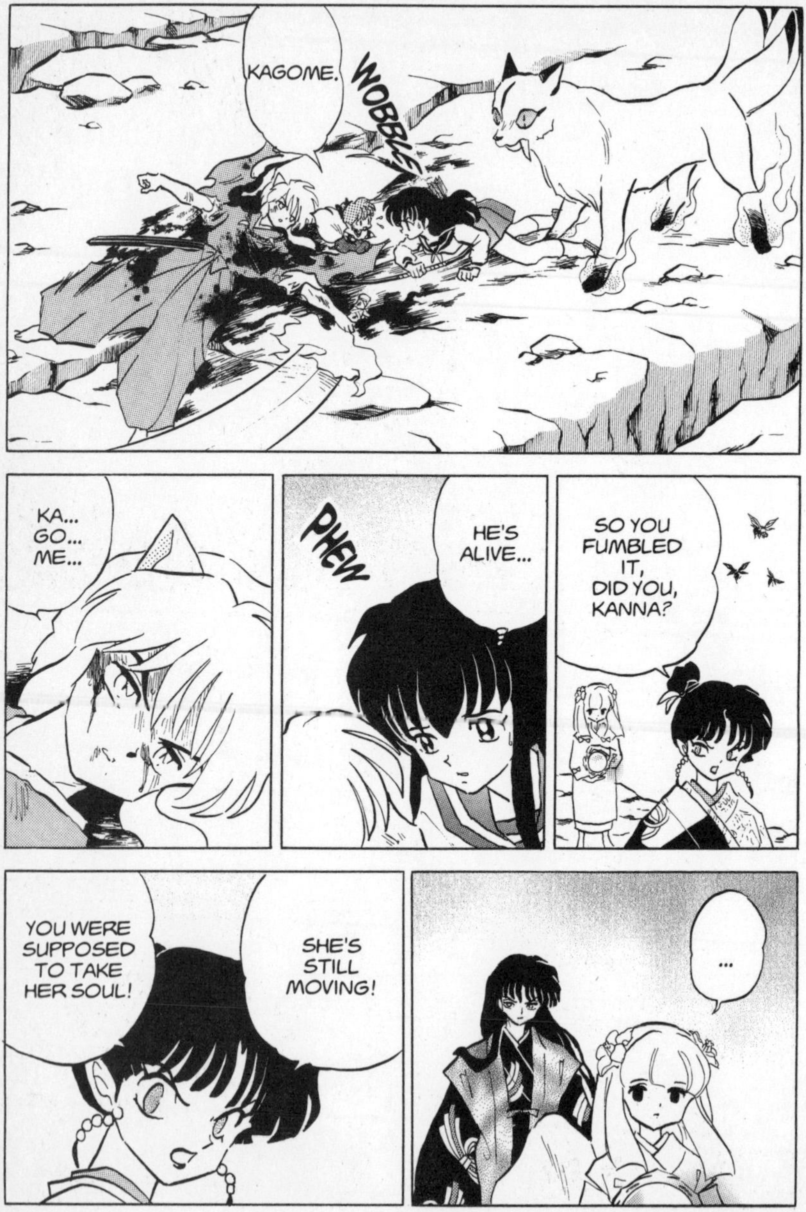
KAGOME.
WOBBLE
KA... GO... ME...
PHEW
HE'S ALIVE...
SO YOU FUMBLED IT, DID YOU, KANNA?
YOU WERE SUPPOSED TO TAKE HER SOUL!
SHE'S STILL MOVING!
...

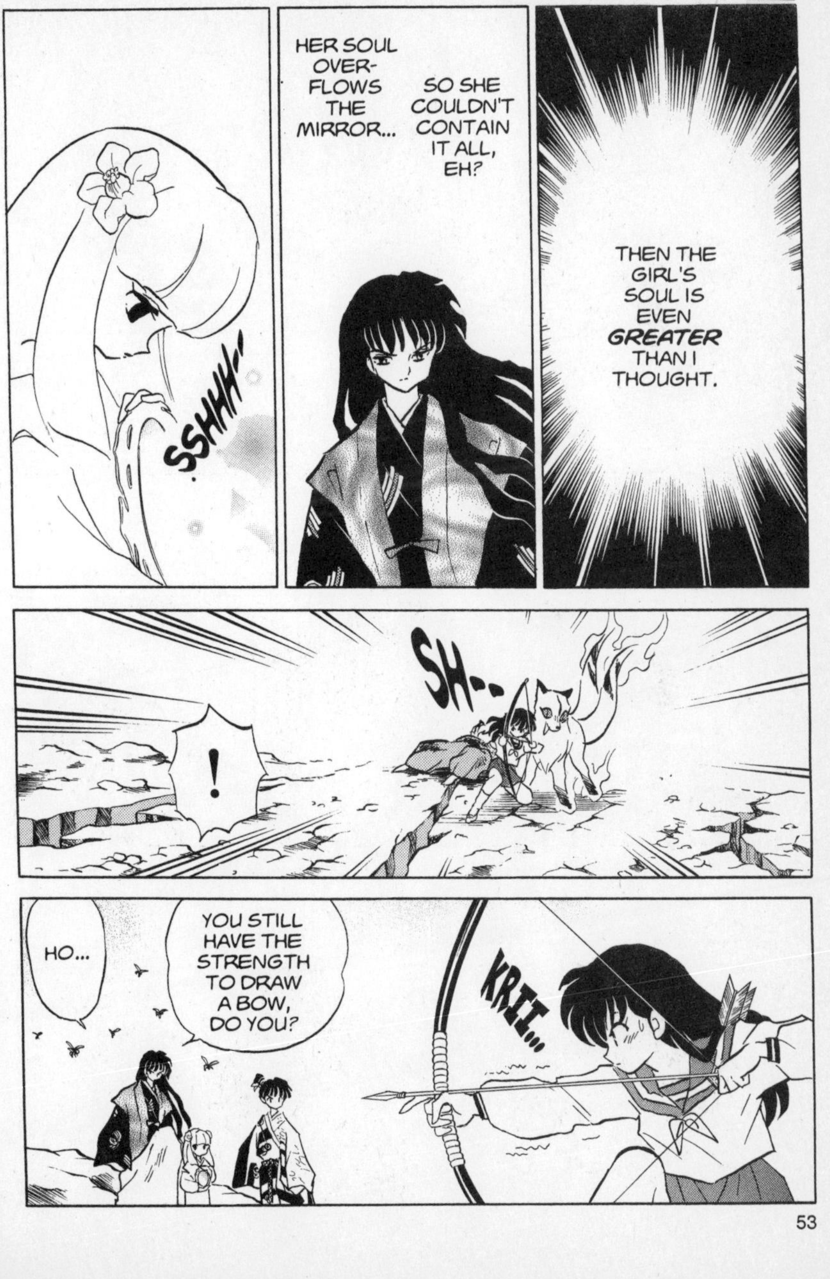
SSHHH..
HER SOUL OVER-FLOWS THE MIRROR...
SO SHE COULDN'T CONTAIN IT ALL, EH?
THEN THE GIRL'S SOUL IS EVEN **GREATER** THAN I THOUGHT.
SH..
!
HO...
YOU STILL HAVE THE STRENGTH TO DRAW A BOW, DO YOU?
KRII...

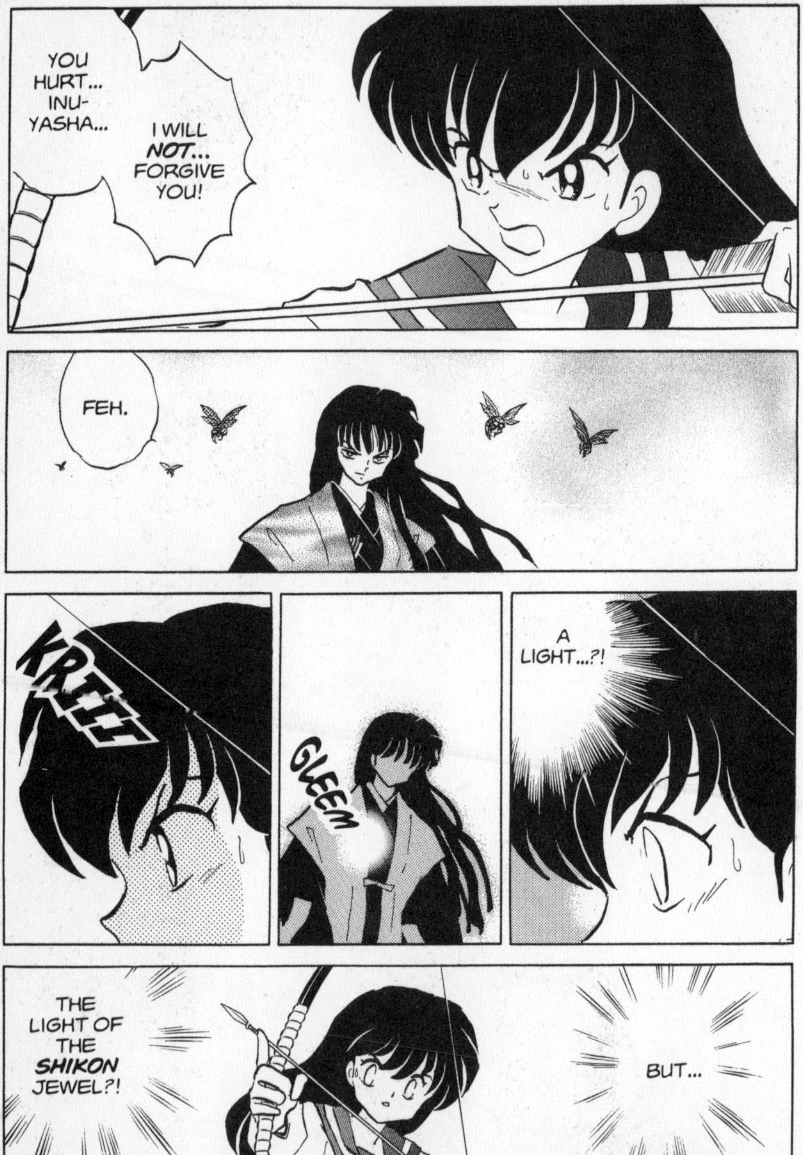
YOU HURT... INU-YASHA...
I WILL ***NOT***... FORGIVE YOU!
FEH.
KRIII
GLEEM
A LIGHT...?!
THE LIGHT OF THE ***SHIKON*** JEWEL?!
BUT...

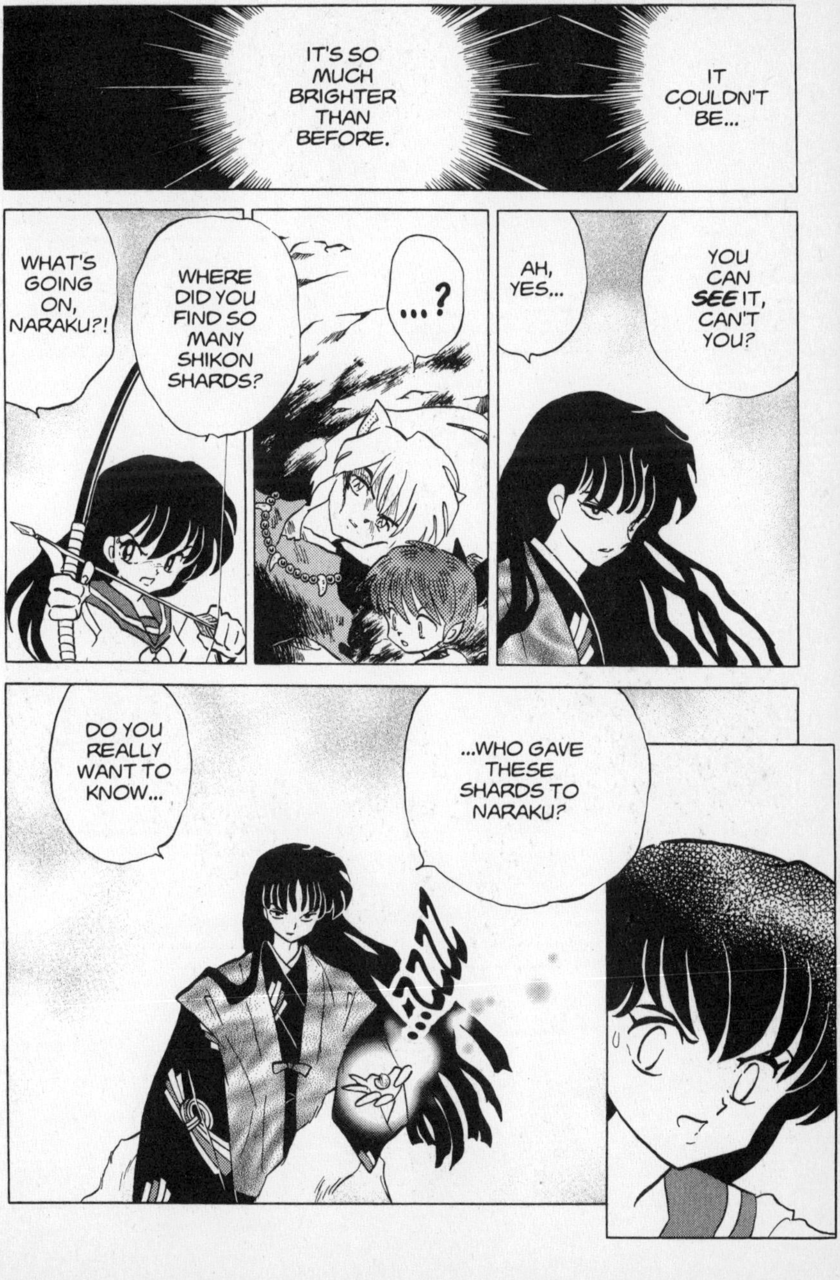
IT'S SO MUCH BRIGHTER THAN BEFORE.
IT COULDN'T BE...
WHAT'S GOING ON, NARAKU?!
WHERE DID YOU FIND SO MANY SHIKON SHARDS?
...?
AH, YES...
YOU CAN **SEE** IT, CAN'T YOU?
DO YOU REALLY WANT TO KNOW...
...WHO GAVE THESE SHARDS TO NARAKU?

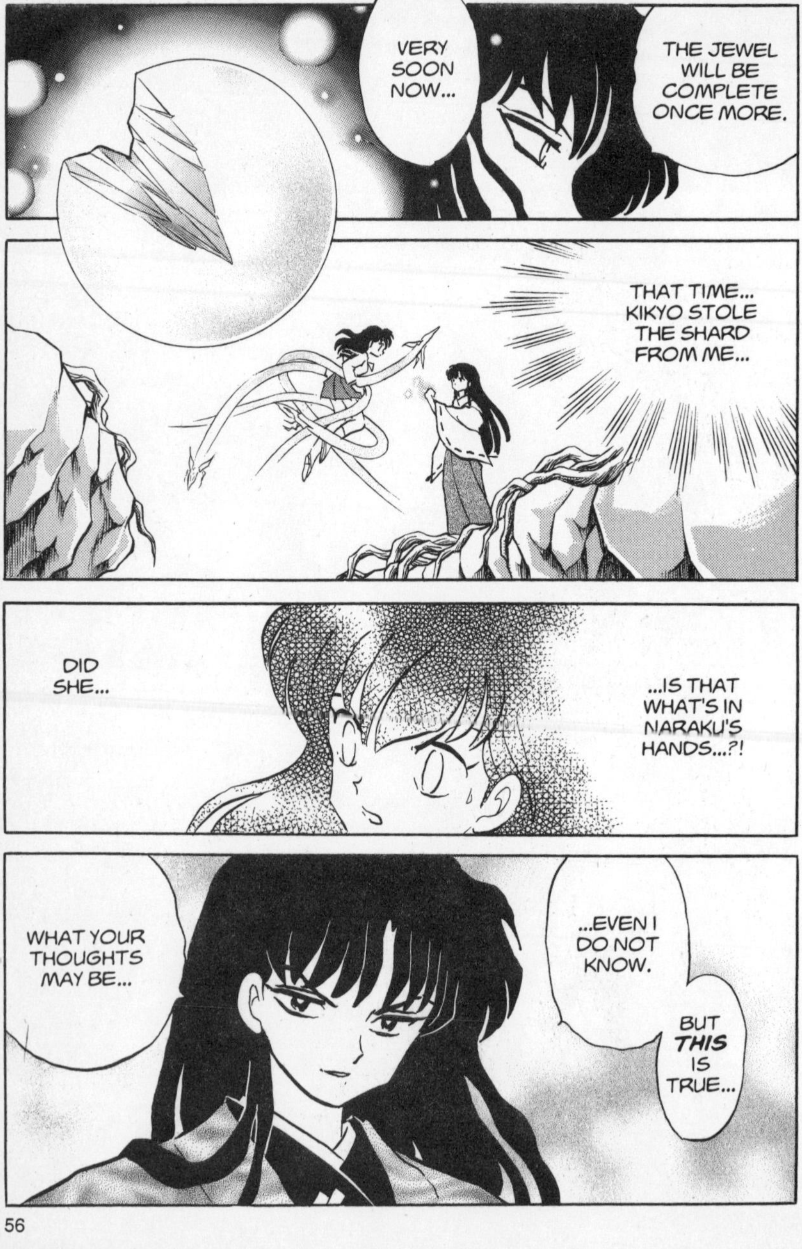
VERY SOON NOW...
THE JEWEL WILL BE COMPLETE ONCE MORE.
THAT TIME... KIKYO STOLE THE SHARD FROM ME...
DID SHE...
...IS THAT WHAT'S IN NARAKU'S HANDS...?!
WHAT YOUR THOUGHTS MAY BE...
...EVEN I DO NOT KNOW.
BUT THIS IS TRUE...

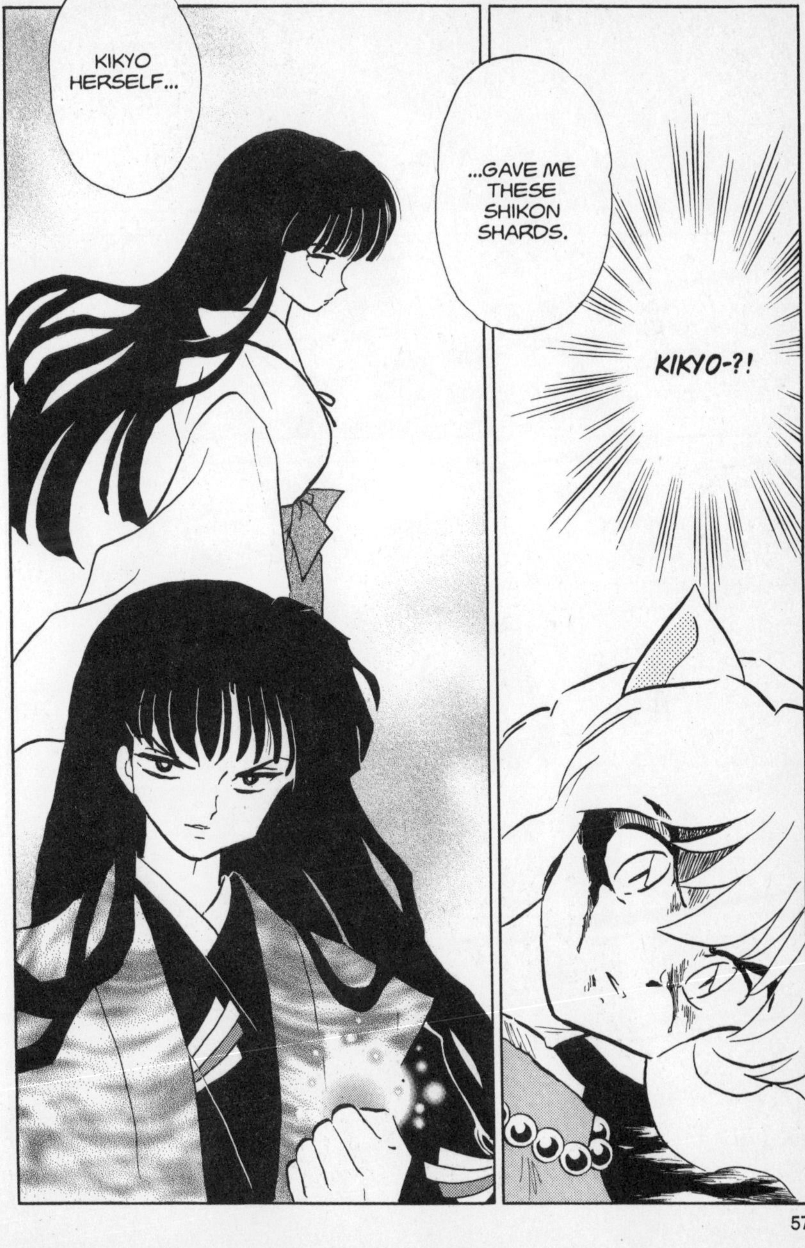
KIKYO HERSELF...
...GAVE ME THESE SHIKON SHARDS.
KIKYO-?!

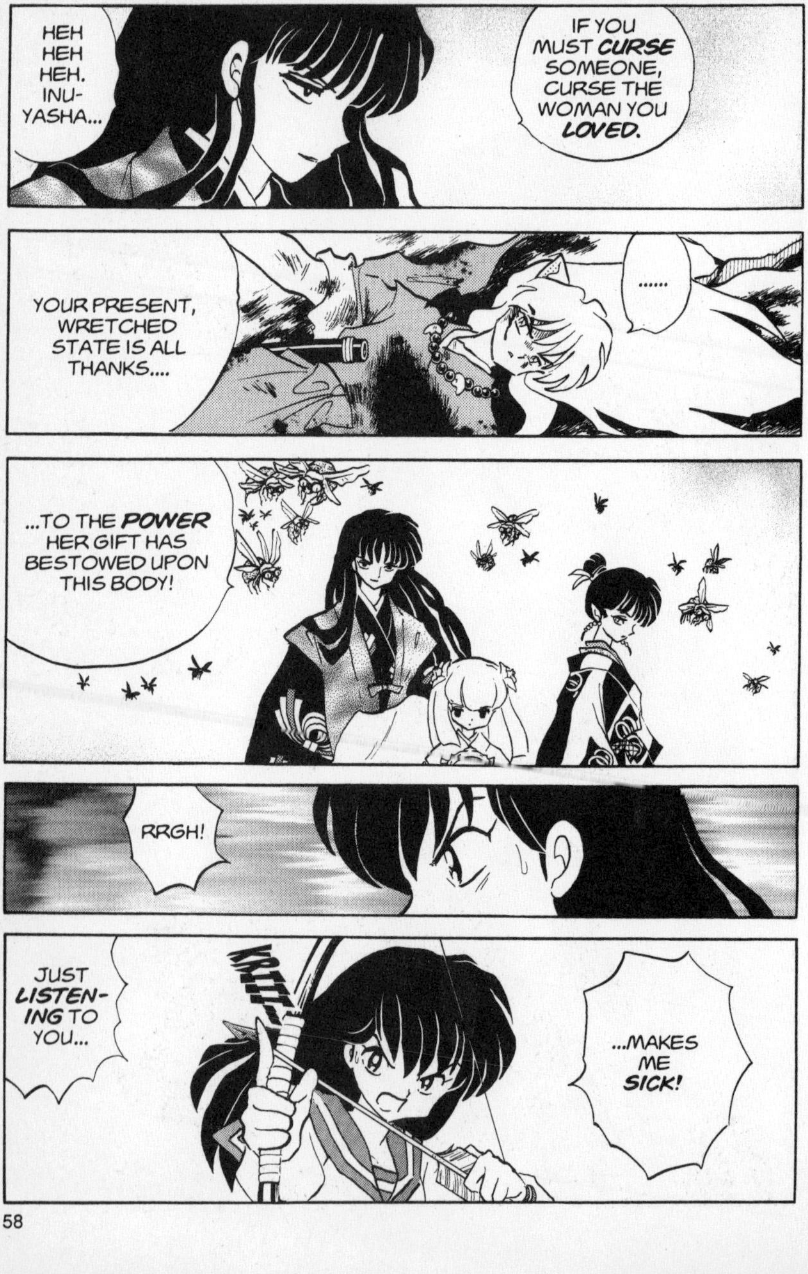
HEH HEH HEH. INU-YASHA...
IF YOU MUST **CURSE** SOMEONE, CURSE THE WOMAN YOU **LOVED.**
YOUR PRESENT, WRETCHED STATE IS ALL THANKS....
......
...TO THE **POWER** HER GIFT HAS BESTOWED UPON THIS BODY!
RRGH!
JUST **LISTEN-ING** TO YOU...
...MAKES ME **SICK!**

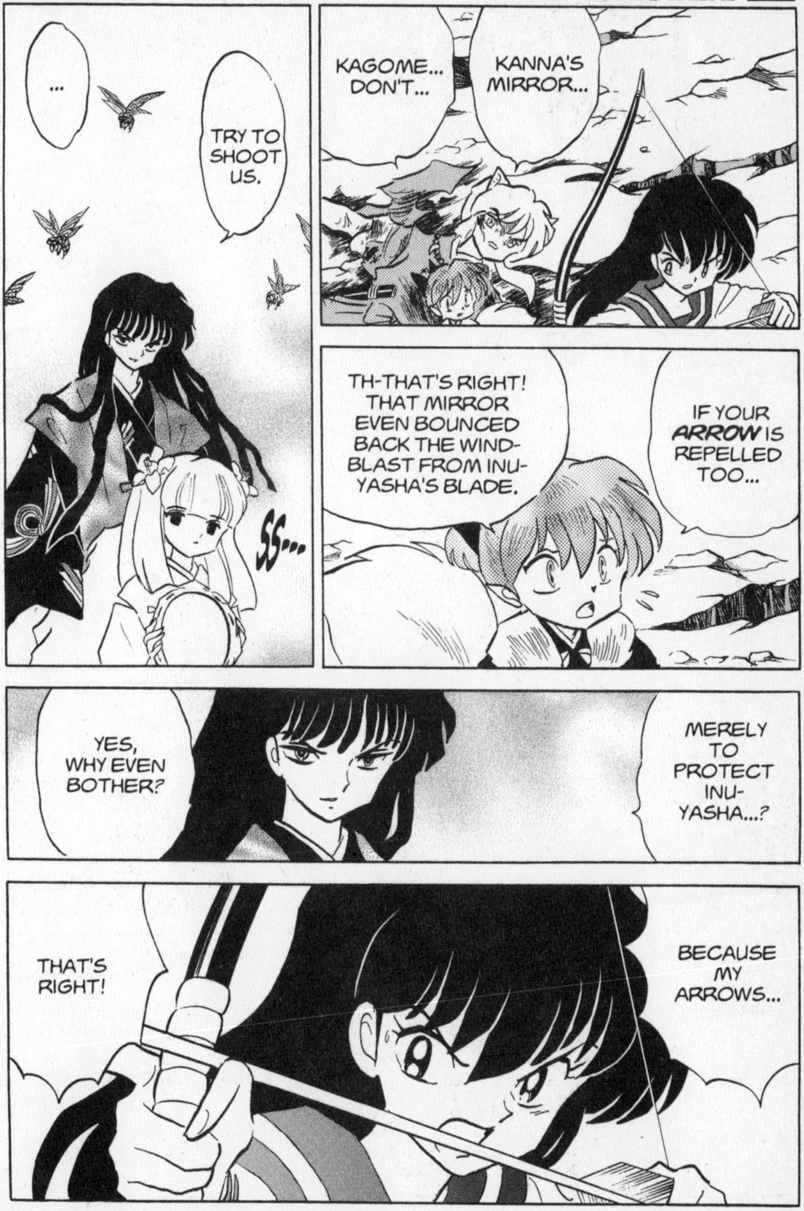
...
TRY TO SHOOT US.
SS...
KAGOME... DON'T...
KANNA'S MIRROR...
TH-THAT'S RIGHT! THAT MIRROR EVEN BOUNCED BACK THE WIND-BLAST FROM INU-YASHA'S BLADE.
IF YOUR ARROW IS REPELLED TOO...
YES, WHY EVEN BOTHER?
MERELY TO PROTECT INU-YASHA...?
THAT'S RIGHT!
BECAUSE MY ARROWS...

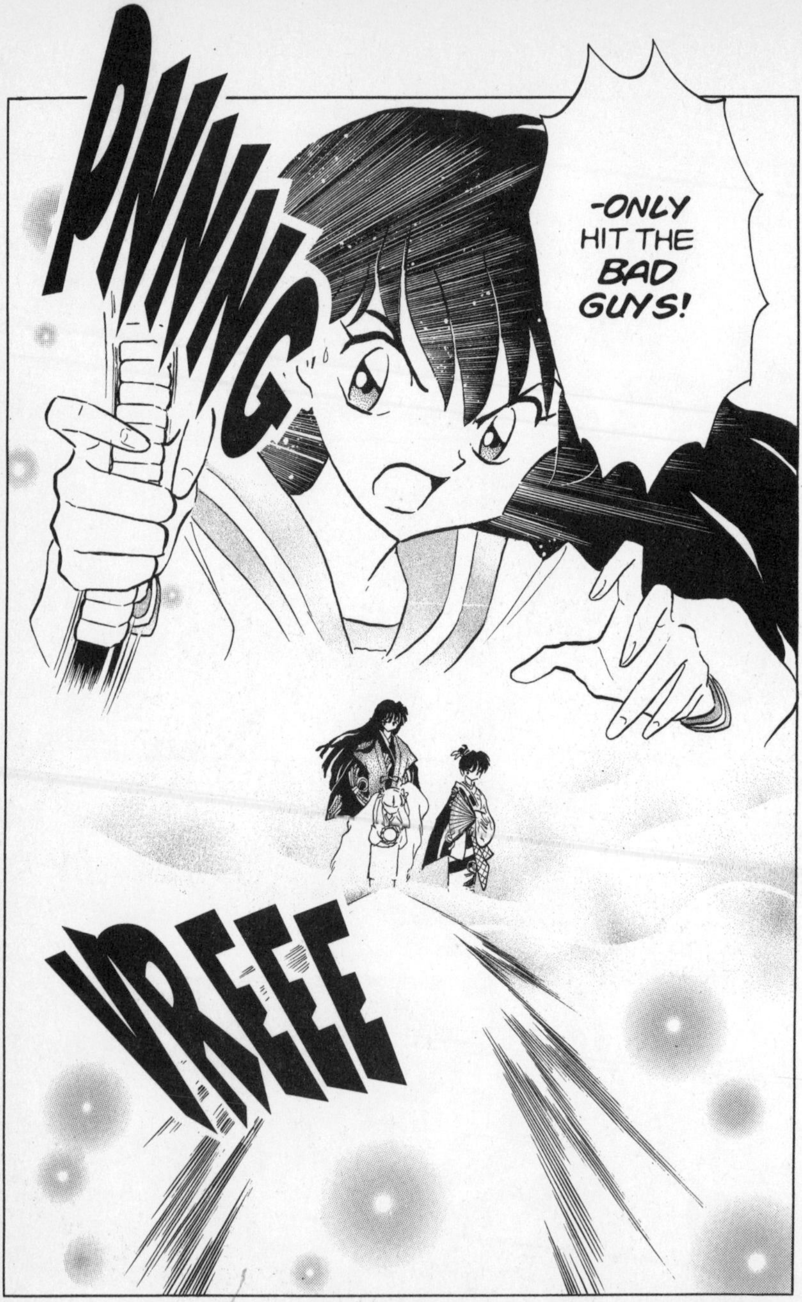
PNNG
-ONLY HIT THE BAD GUYS!
VREEE

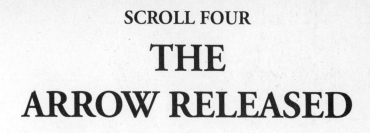

SCROLL FOUR

THE ARROW RELEASED

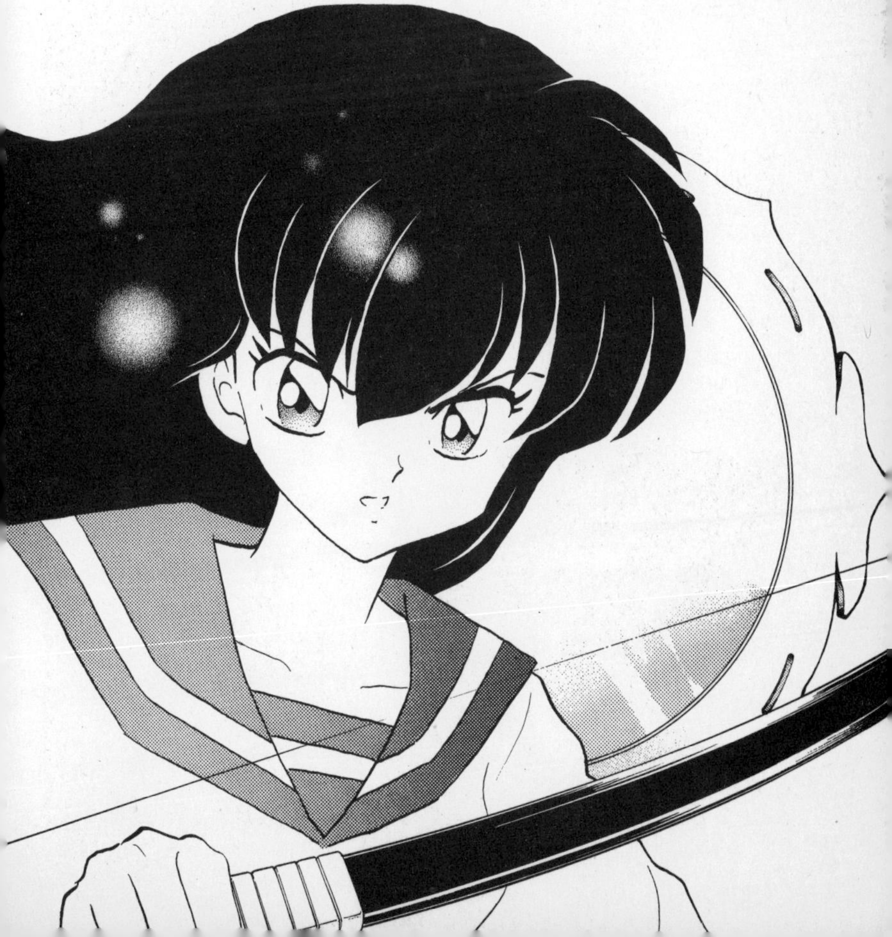

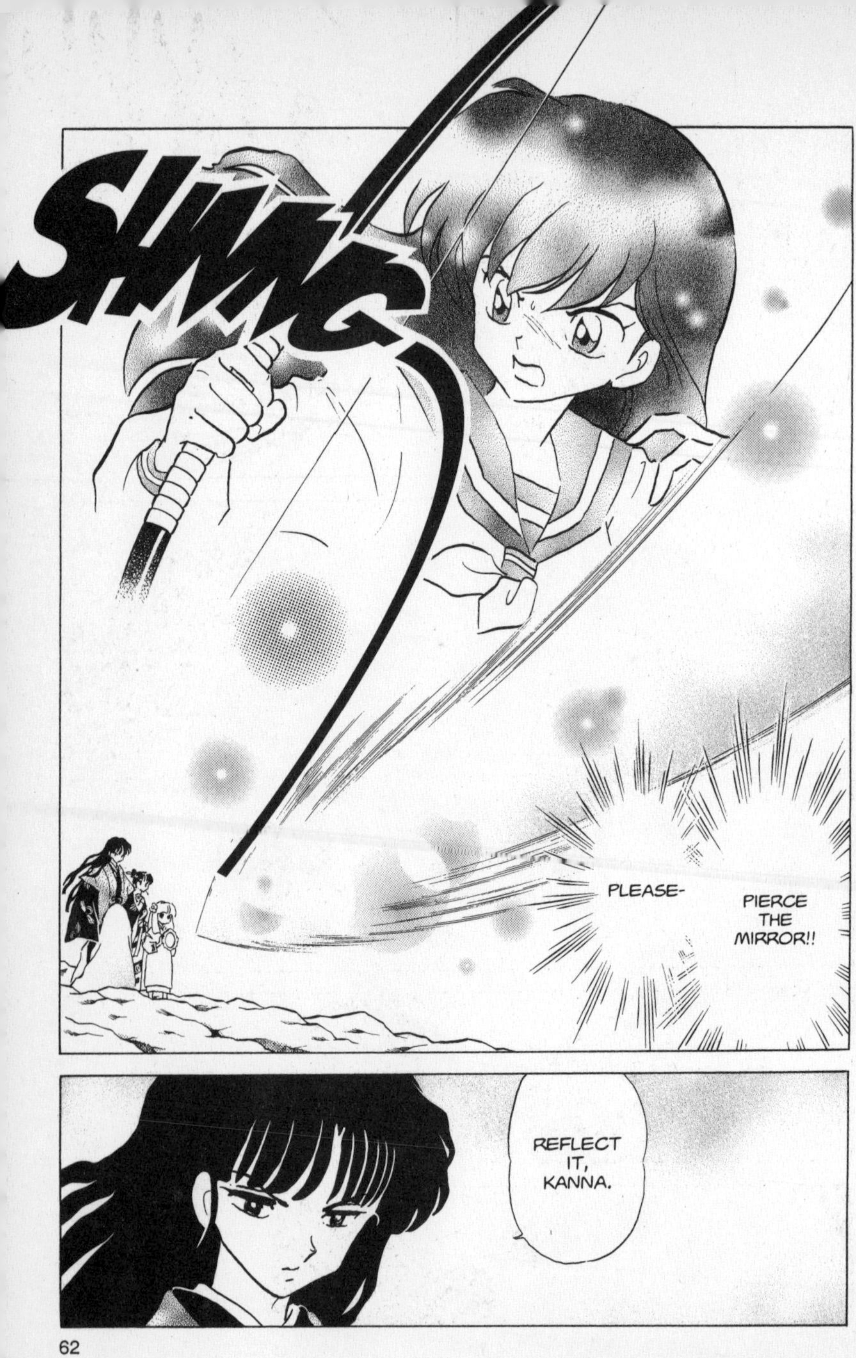
SHING
PLEASE-
PIERCE THE MIRROR!!
REFLECT IT, KANNA.

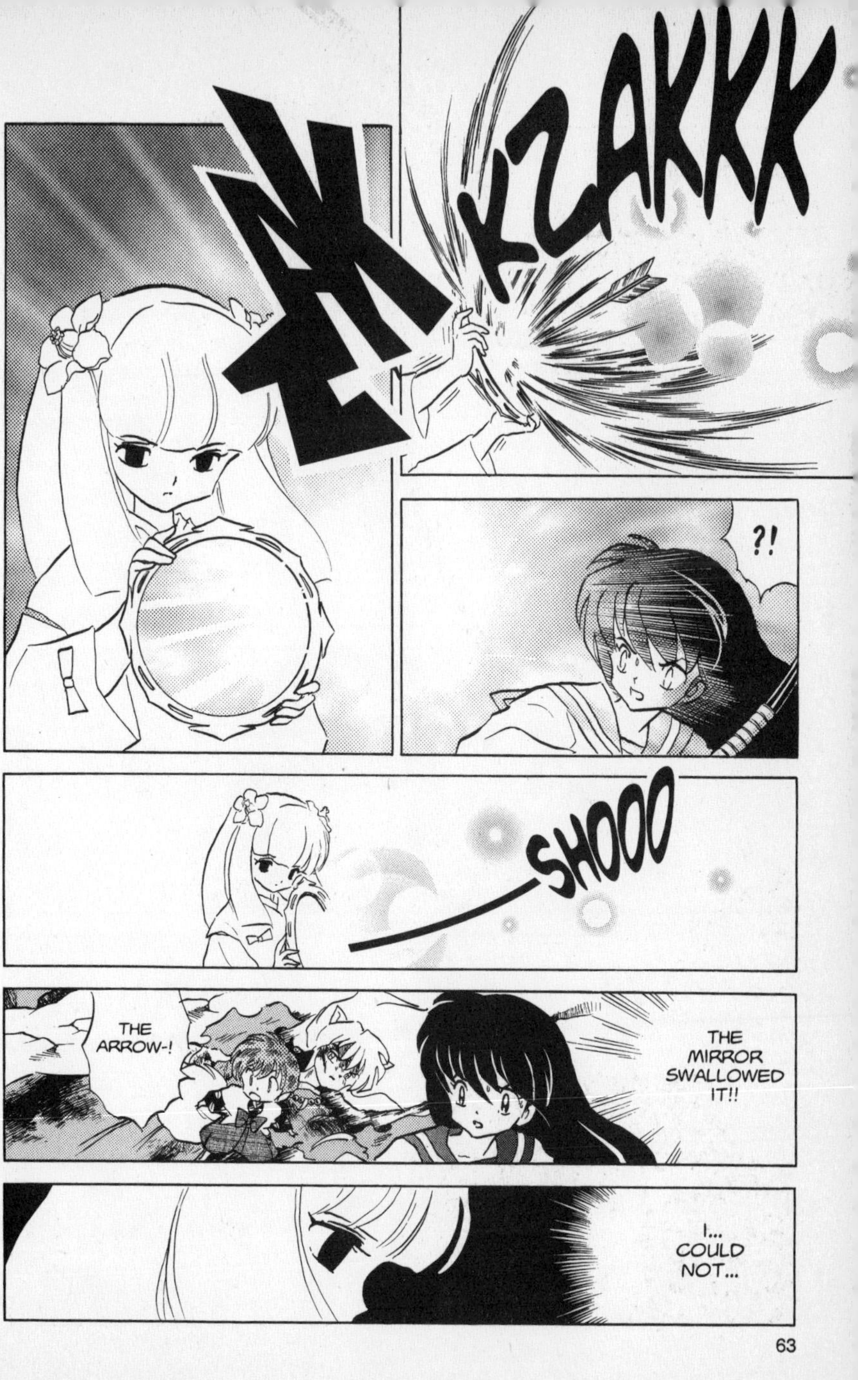
ZAKKK
KZAKKK
?!
SHOOO
THE ARROW-!
THE MIRROR SWALLOWED IT!!
I... COULD NOT...

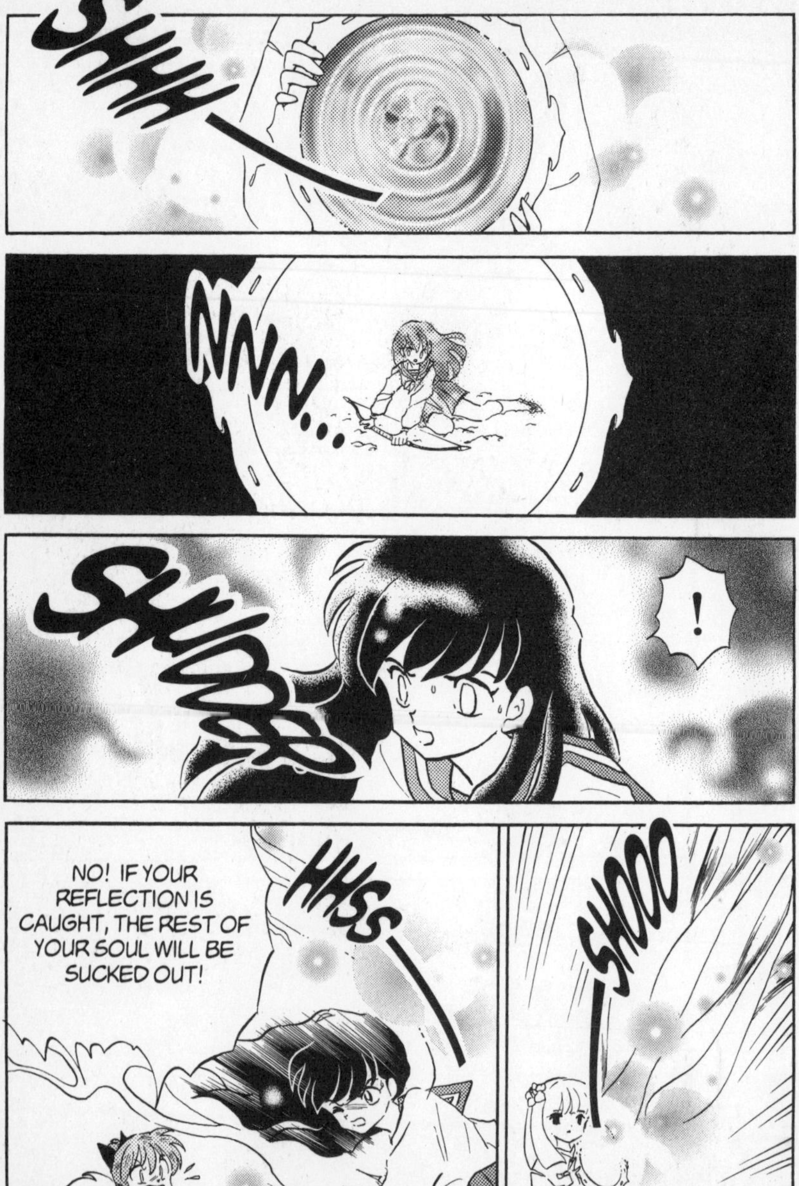
SHHH—
ZNNN...
SHOOP
!
NO! IF YOUR REFLECTION IS CAUGHT, THE REST OF YOUR SOUL WILL BE SUCKED OUT!
HHSS—
—SHOOO

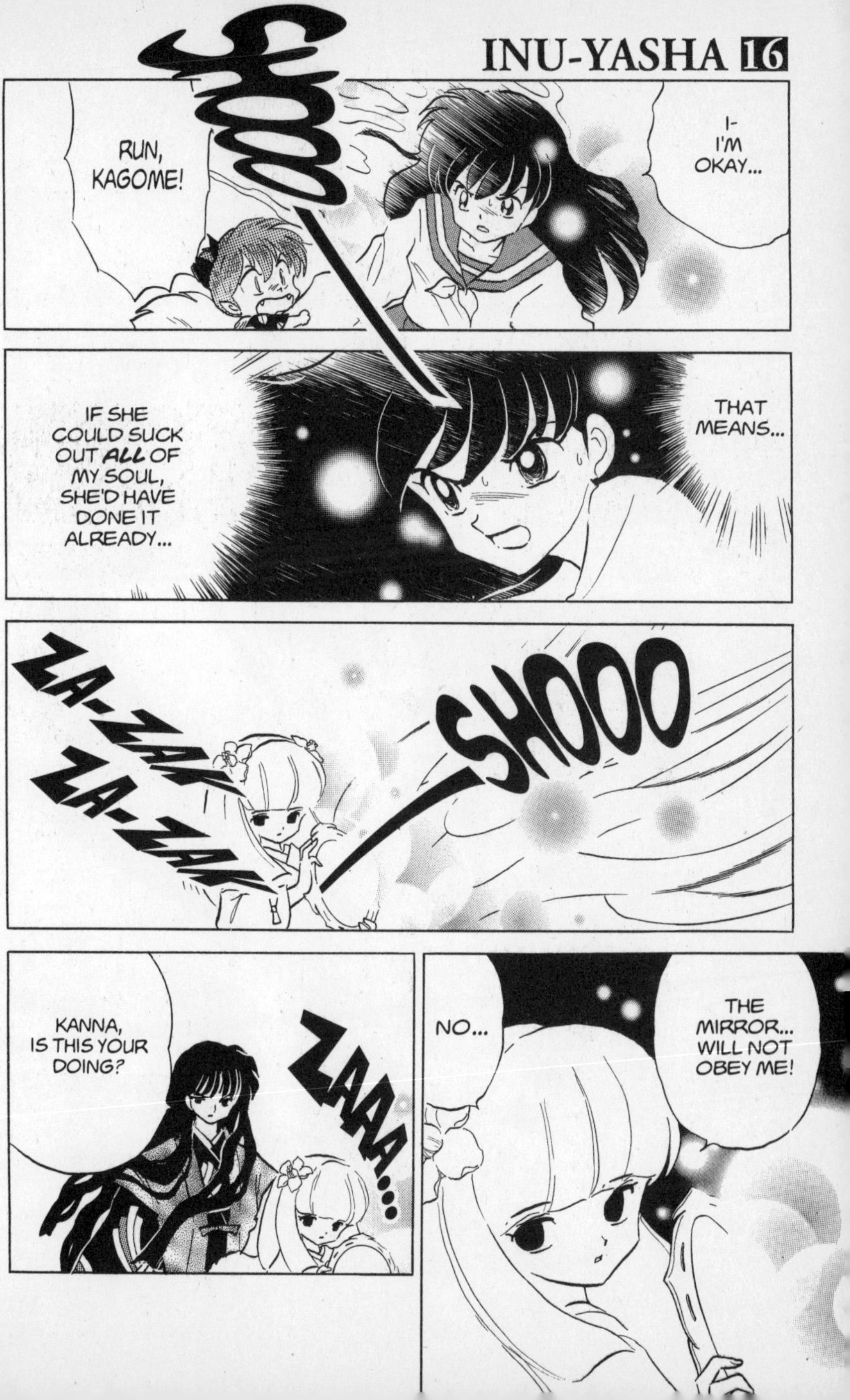
SHOOO
RUN, KAGOME!
I- I'M OKAY...
IF SHE COULD SUCK OUT **ALL** OF MY SOUL, SHE'D HAVE DONE IT ALREADY...
THAT MEANS...
ZA-ZAK ZA-ZAK
SHOOO
KANNA, IS THIS YOUR DOING?
ZAAA...
NO...
THE MIRROR... WILL NOT OBEY ME!

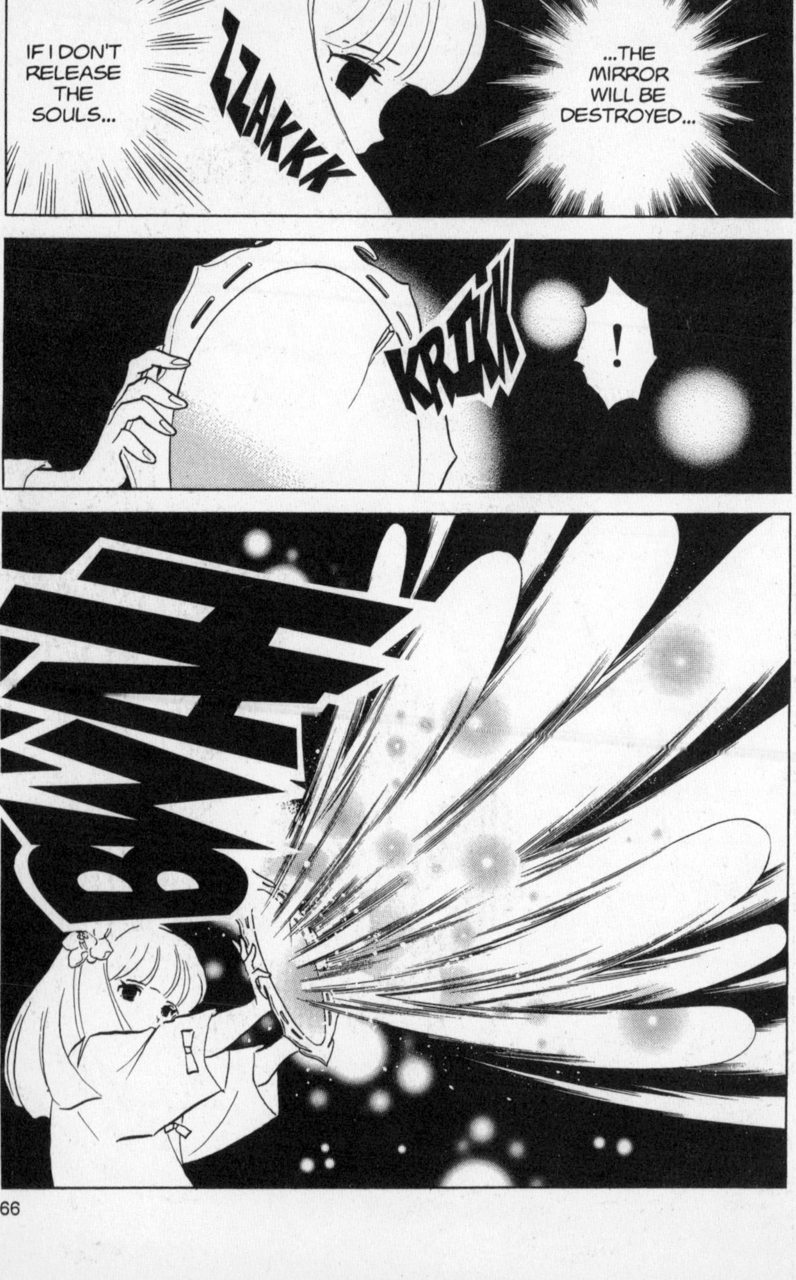
IF I DON'T RELEASE THE SOULS...
ZZAKKK
...THE MIRROR WILL BE DESTROYED...
KRIKK
!
BWHH

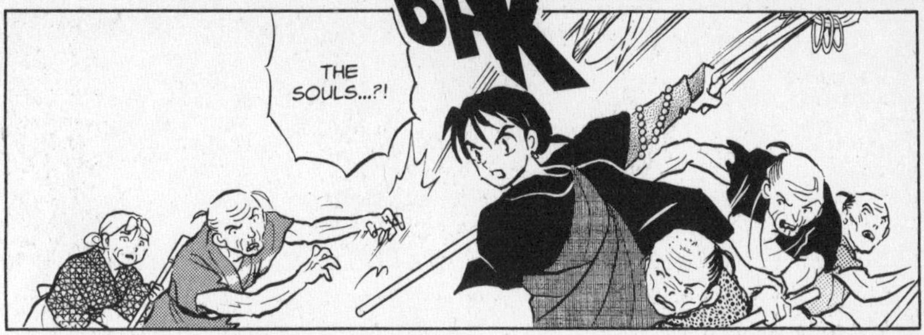
BAK
THE SOULS...?!

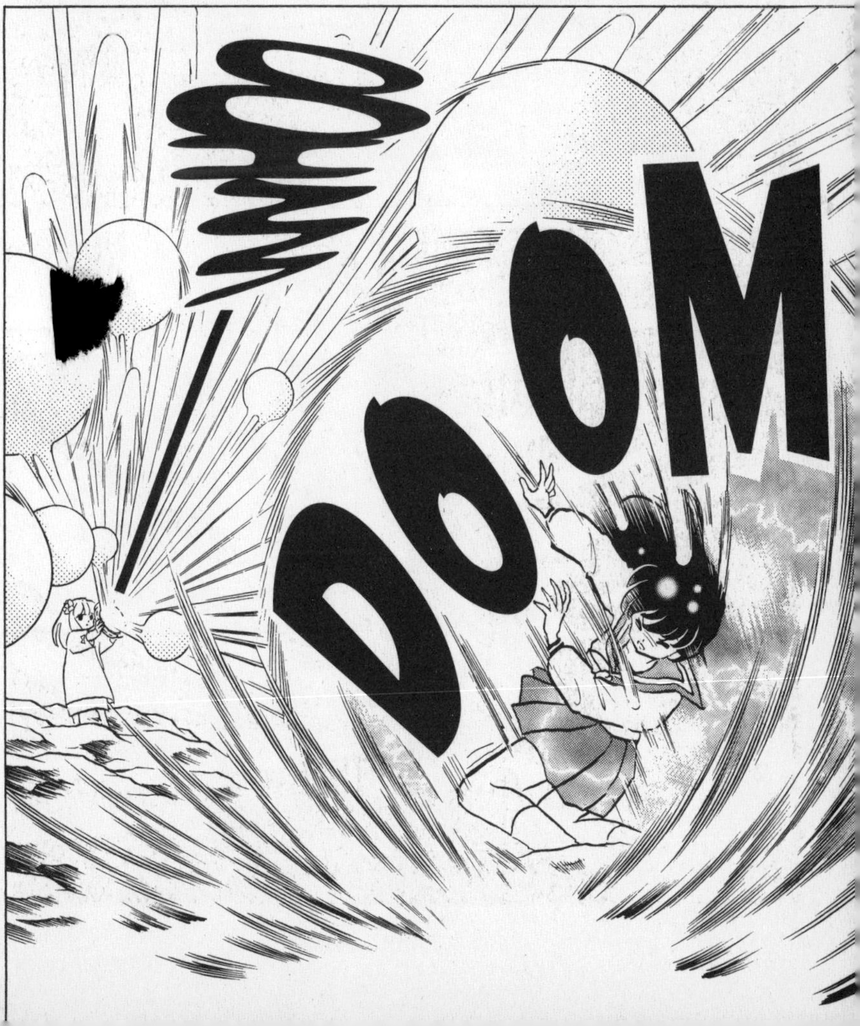
WHOOO
DOOOM

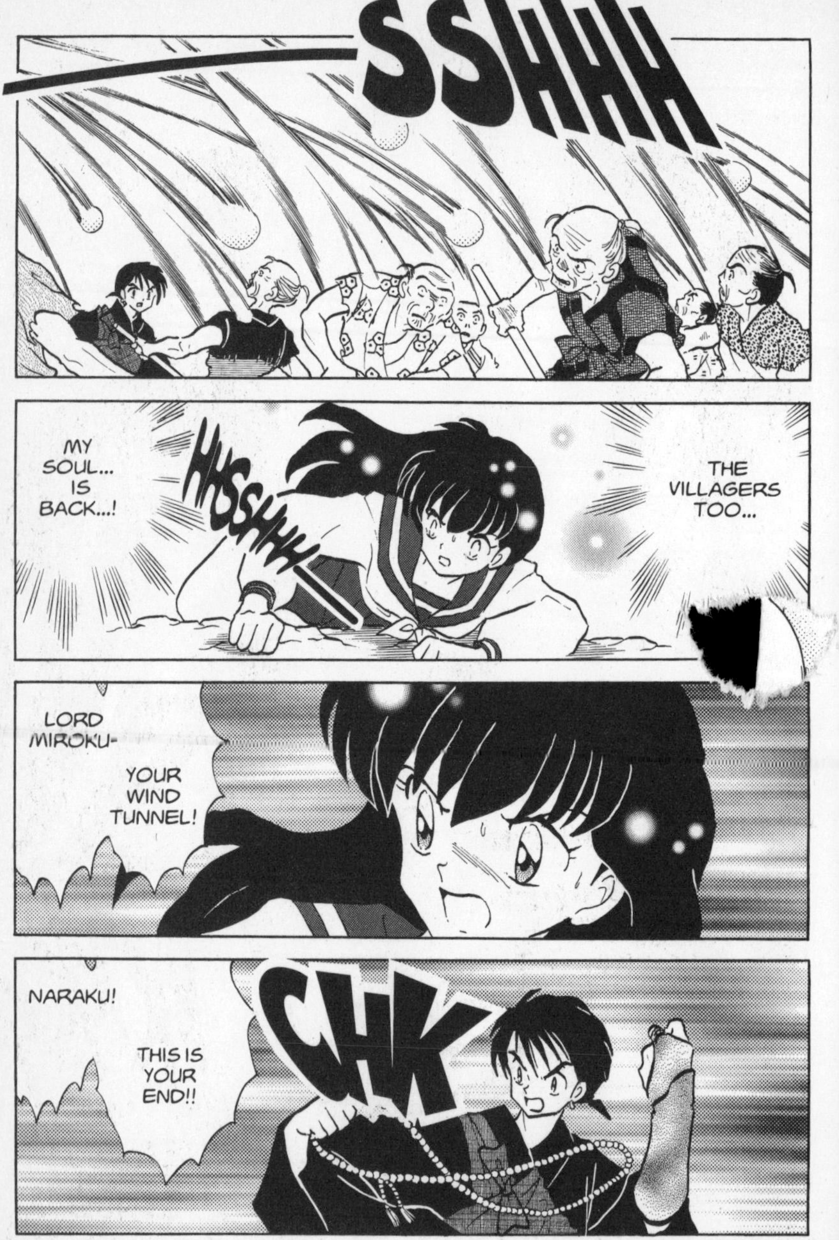
SSHHHH
MY SOUL... IS BACK...!
HHSSHHH
THE VILLAGERS TOO...
LORD MIROKU-
YOUR WIND TUNNEL!
NARAKU!
CHK
THIS IS YOUR END!!

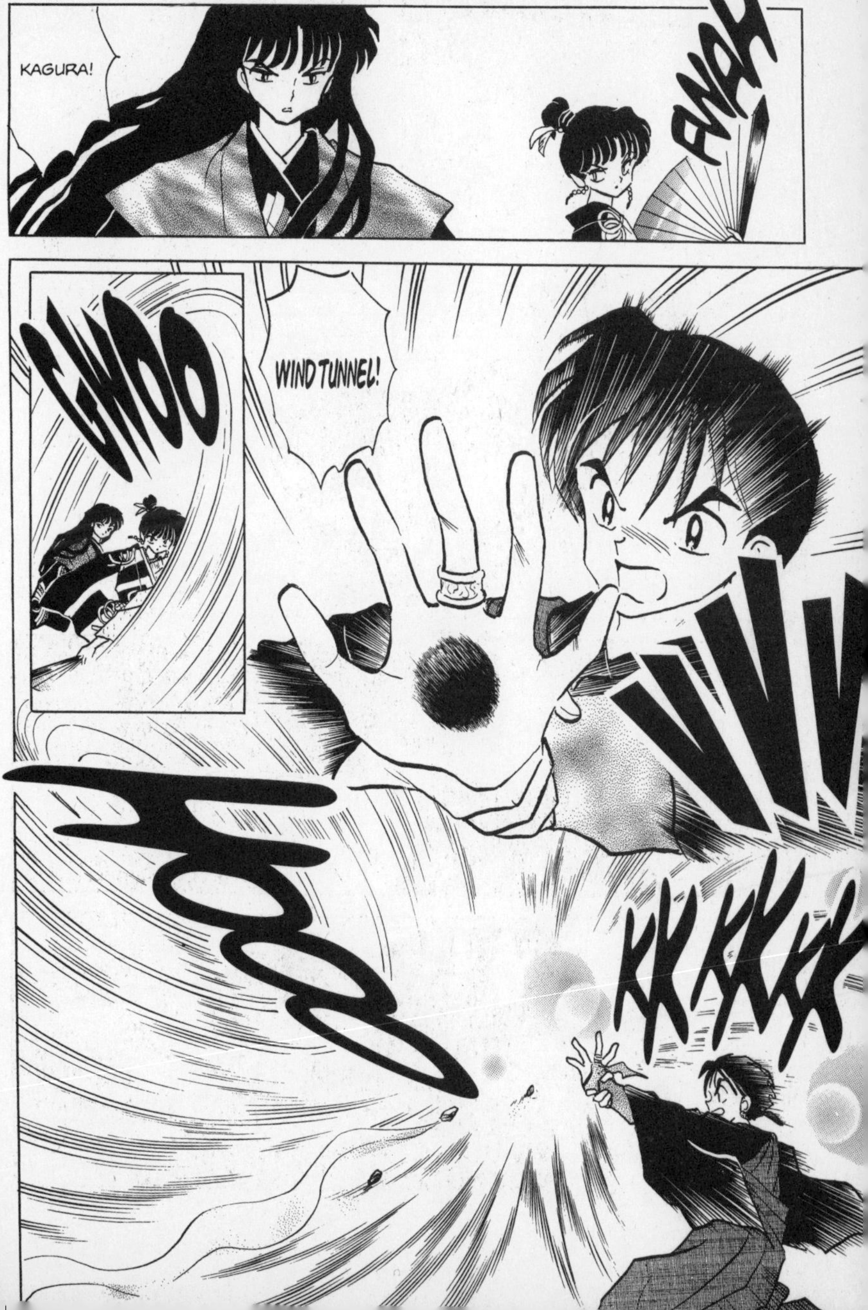
KAGURA!
AWAH
GWOO
WIND TUNNEL!
HOOO

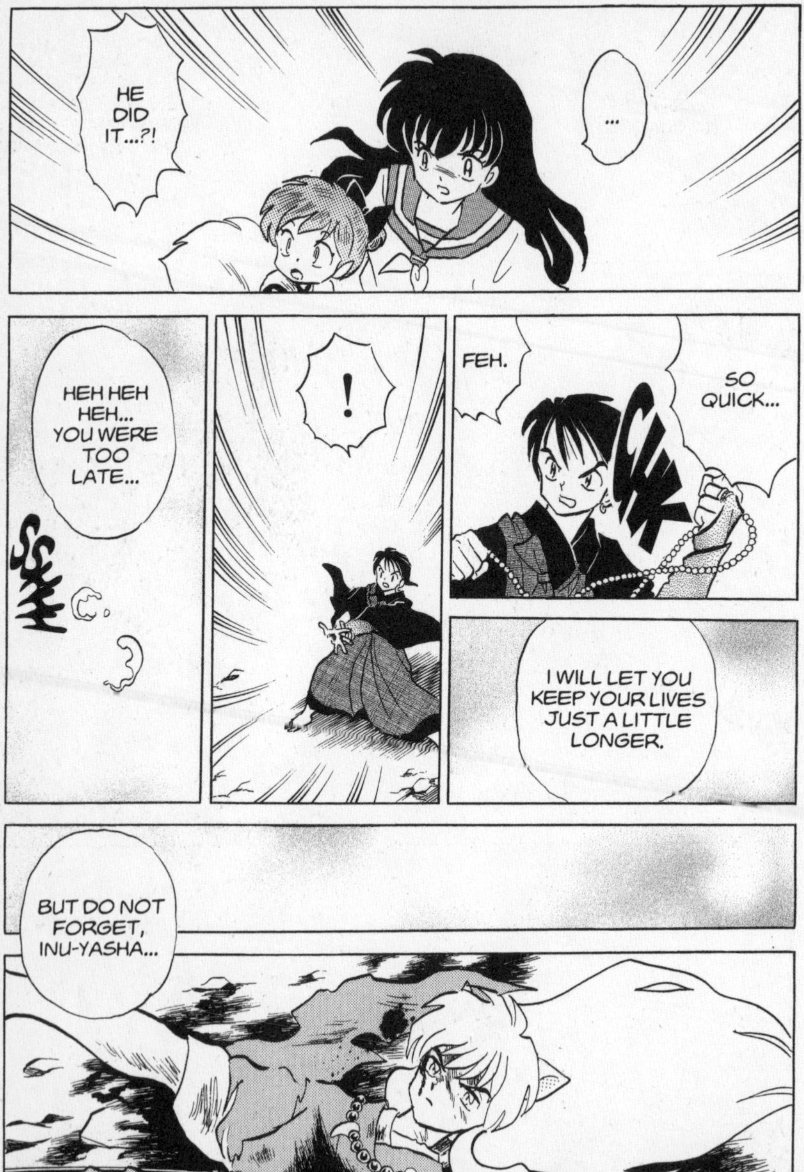
HE DID IT...?!
...
HEH HEH HEH... YOU WERE TOO LATE...
!
FEH.
SO QUICK...
I WILL LET YOU KEEP YOUR LIVES JUST A LITTLE LONGER.
BUT DO NOT FORGET, INU-YASHA...

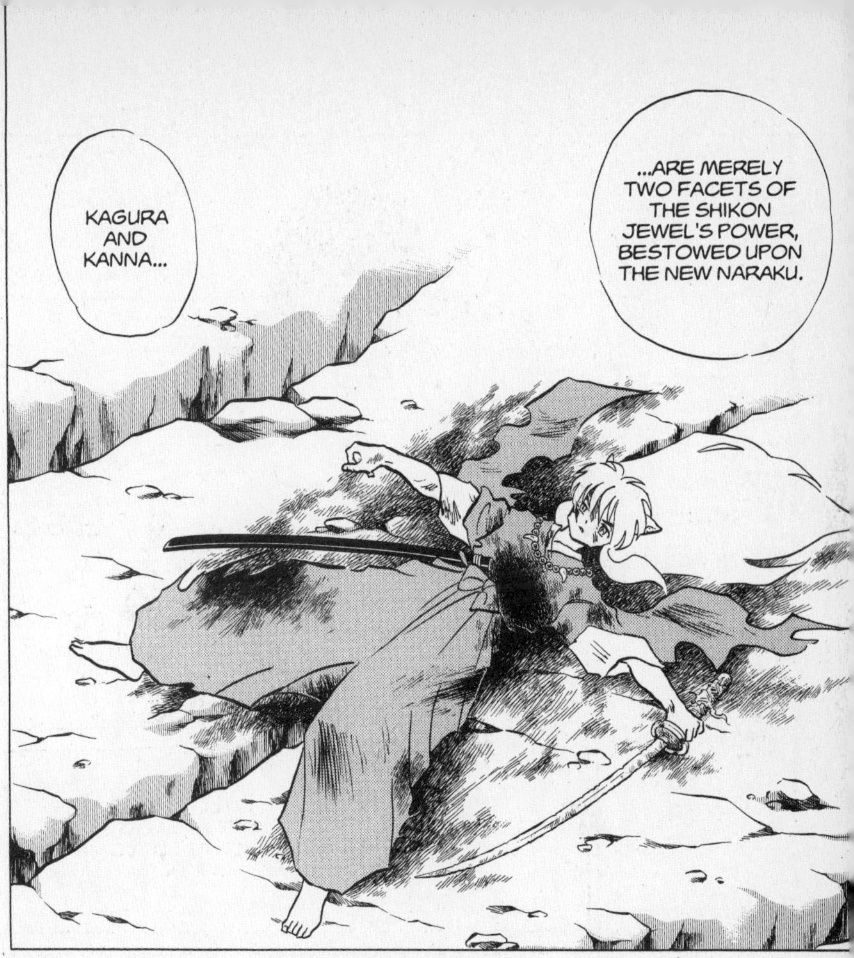
KAGURA AND KANNA...
...ARE MERELY TWO FACETS OF THE SHIKON JEWEL'S POWER, BESTOWED UPON THE NEW NARAKU.

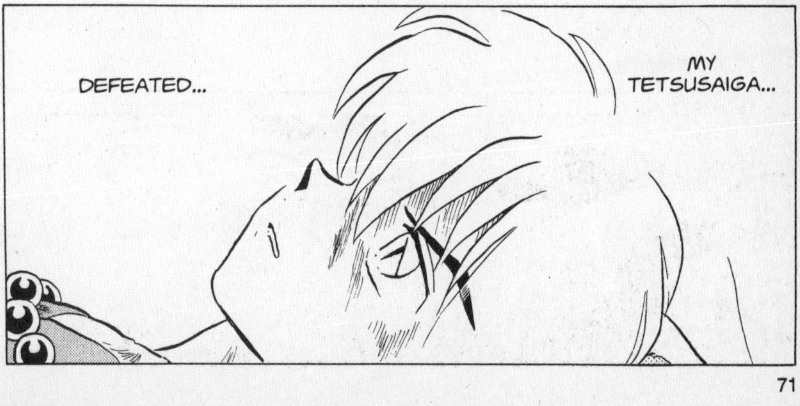
DEFEATED...
MY TETSUSAIGA...

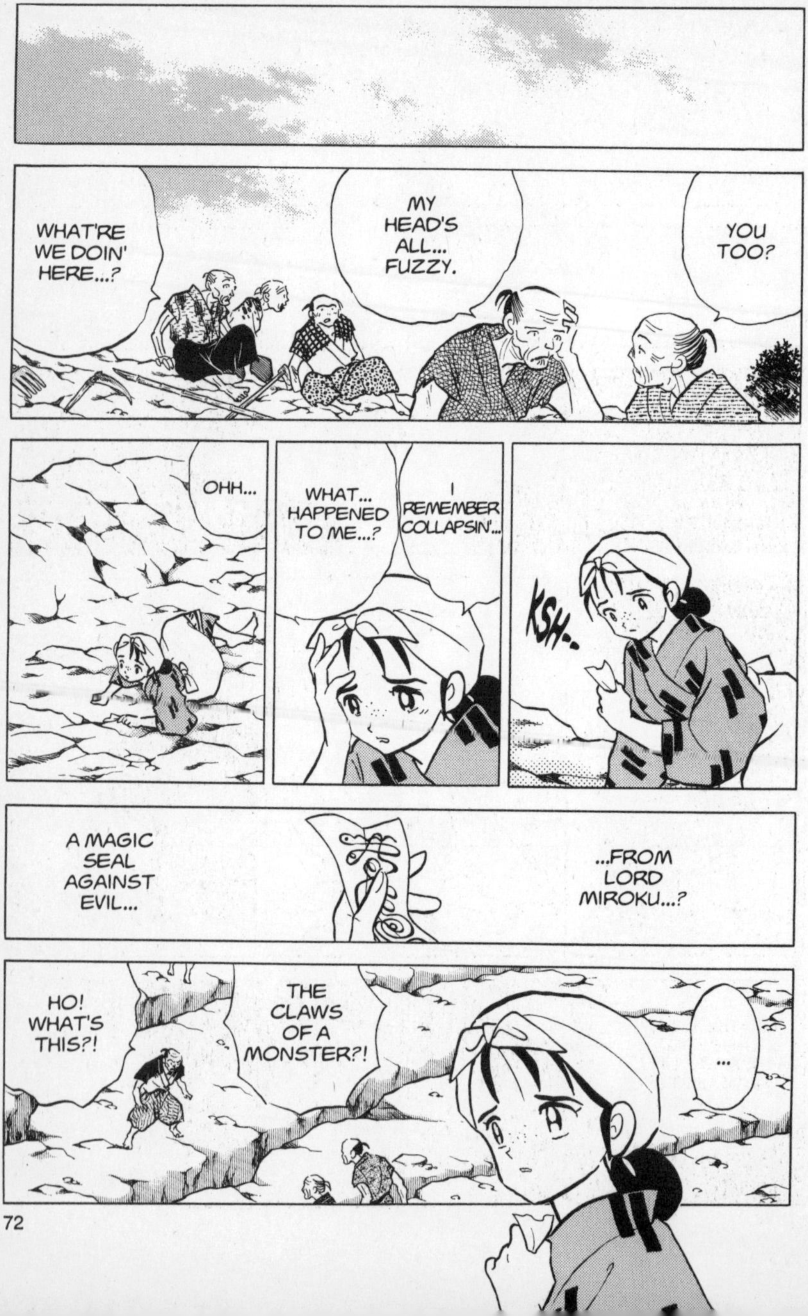
WHAT'RE WE DOIN' HERE...?
MY HEAD'S ALL... FUZZY.
YOU TOO?
OHH...
WHAT... HAPPENED TO ME...?
I REMEMBER COLLAPSIN'...
KSH-
A MAGIC SEAL AGAINST EVIL...
...FROM LORD MIROKU...?
HO! WHAT'S THIS?!
THE CLAWS OF A MONSTER?!
...

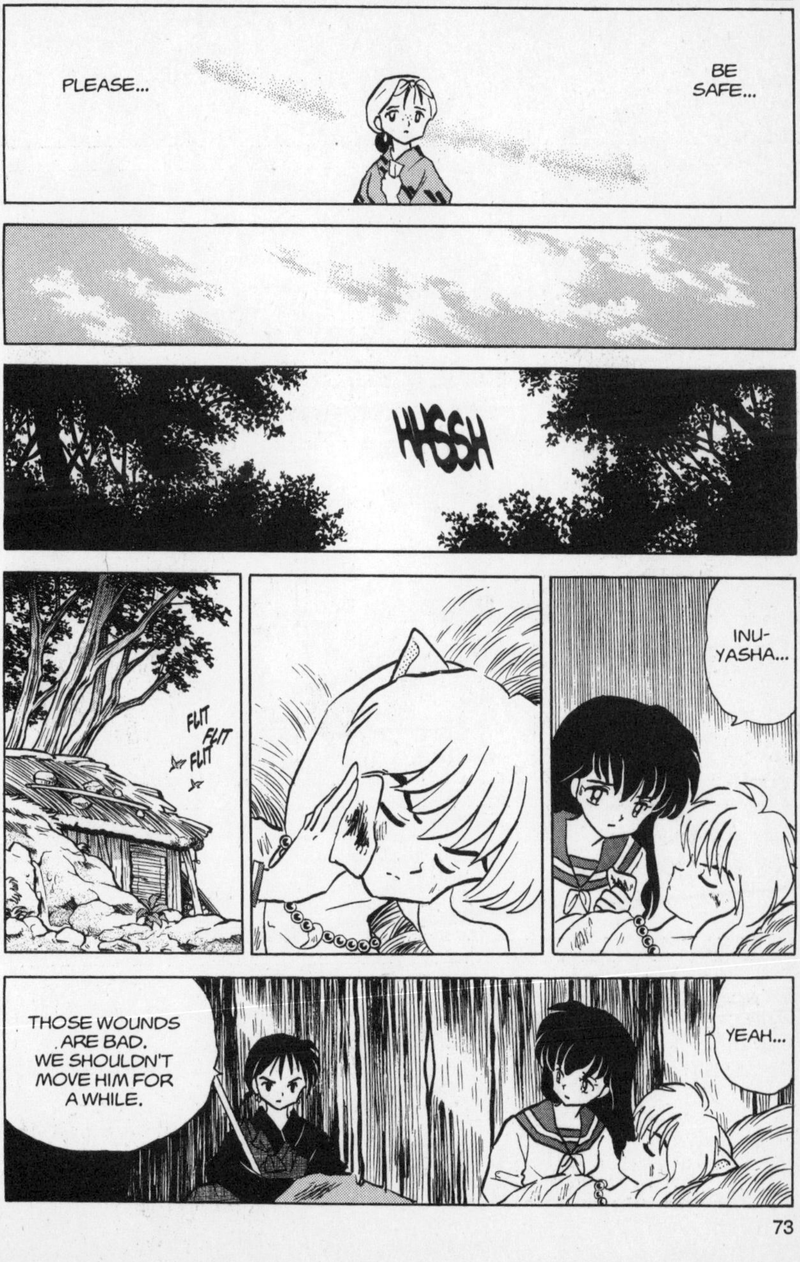
PLEASE...
BE SAFE...
HUSSH
FLIT FLIT FLIT
INU-YASHA...
THOSE WOUNDS ARE BAD. WE SHOULDN'T MOVE HIM FOR A WHILE.
YEAH...

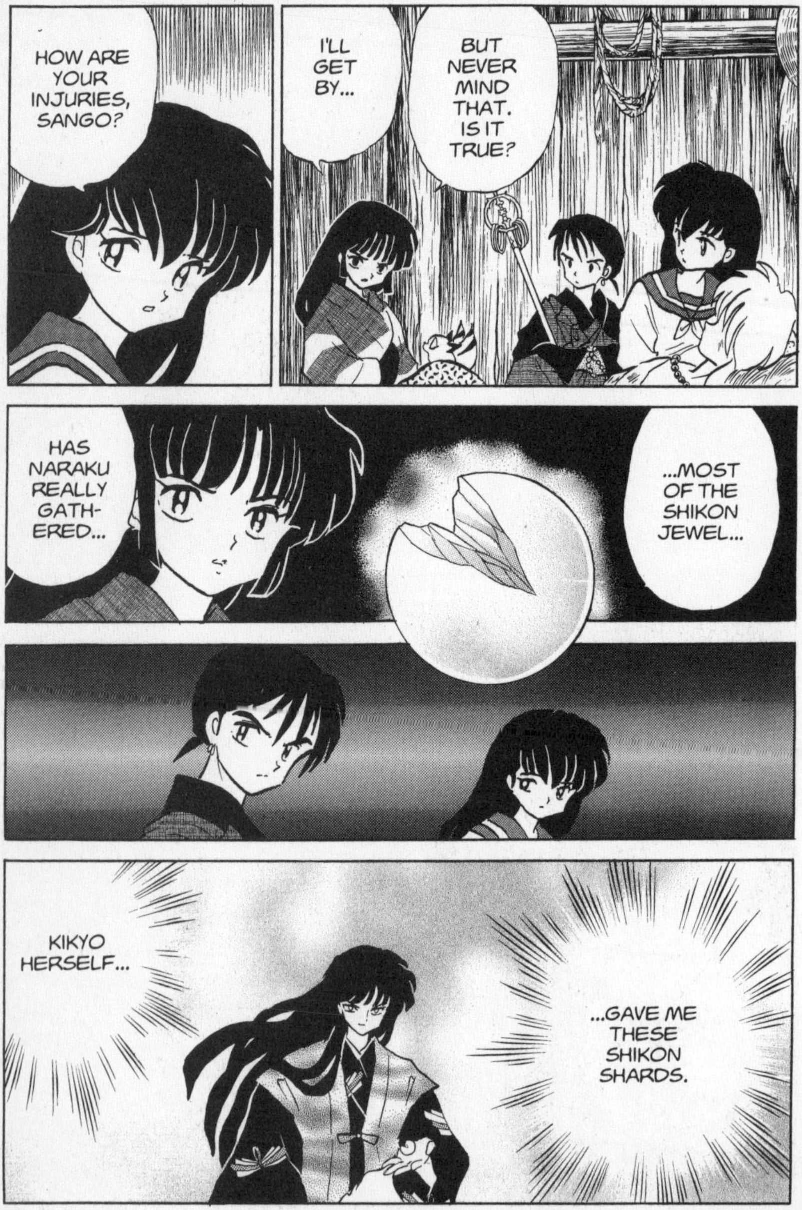
HOW ARE YOUR INJURIES, SANGO?
I'LL GET BY...
BUT NEVER MIND THAT. IS IT TRUE?
HAS NARAKU REALLY GATHERED...
...MOST OF THE SHIKON JEWEL...
KIKYO HERSELF...
...GAVE ME THESE SHIKON SHARDS.

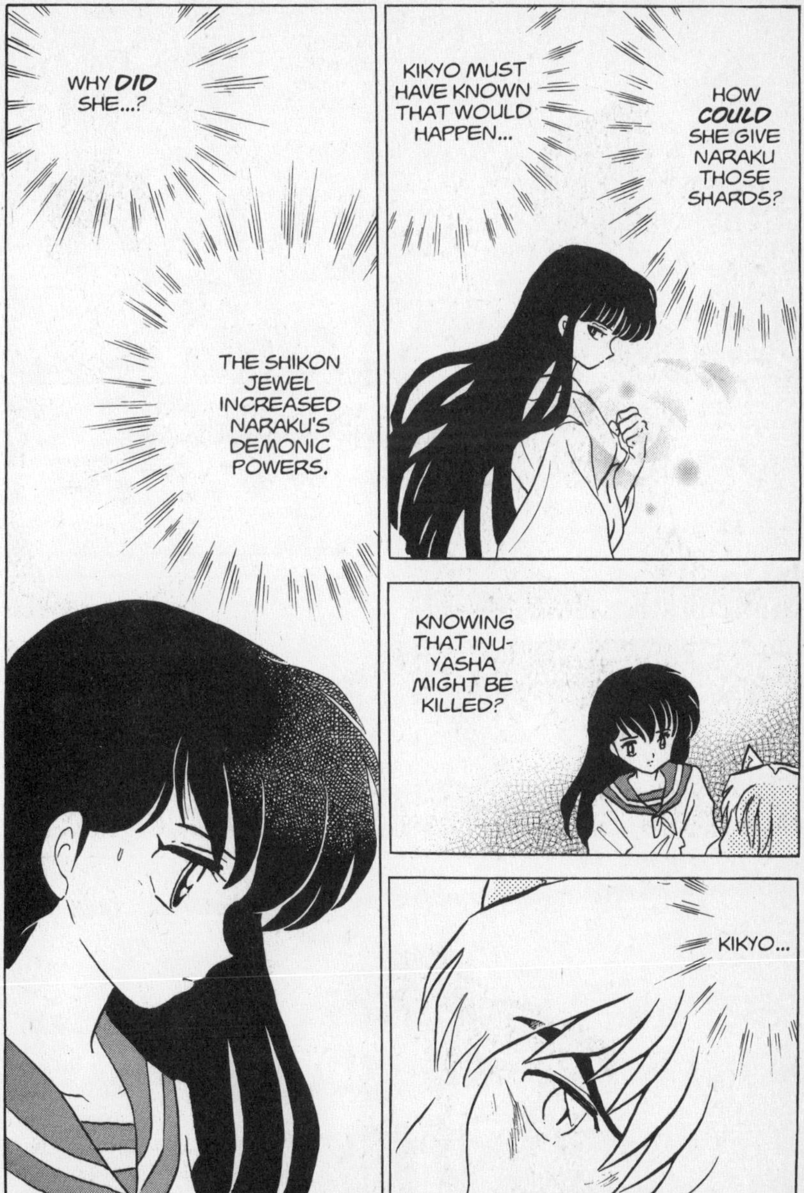
WHY DID SHE...?
THE SHIKON JEWEL INCREASED NARAKU'S DEMONIC POWERS.
KIKYO MUST HAVE KNOWN THAT WOULD HAPPEN...
HOW COULD SHE GIVE NARAKU THOSE SHARDS?
KNOWING THAT INU-YASHA MIGHT BE KILLED?
KIKYO...

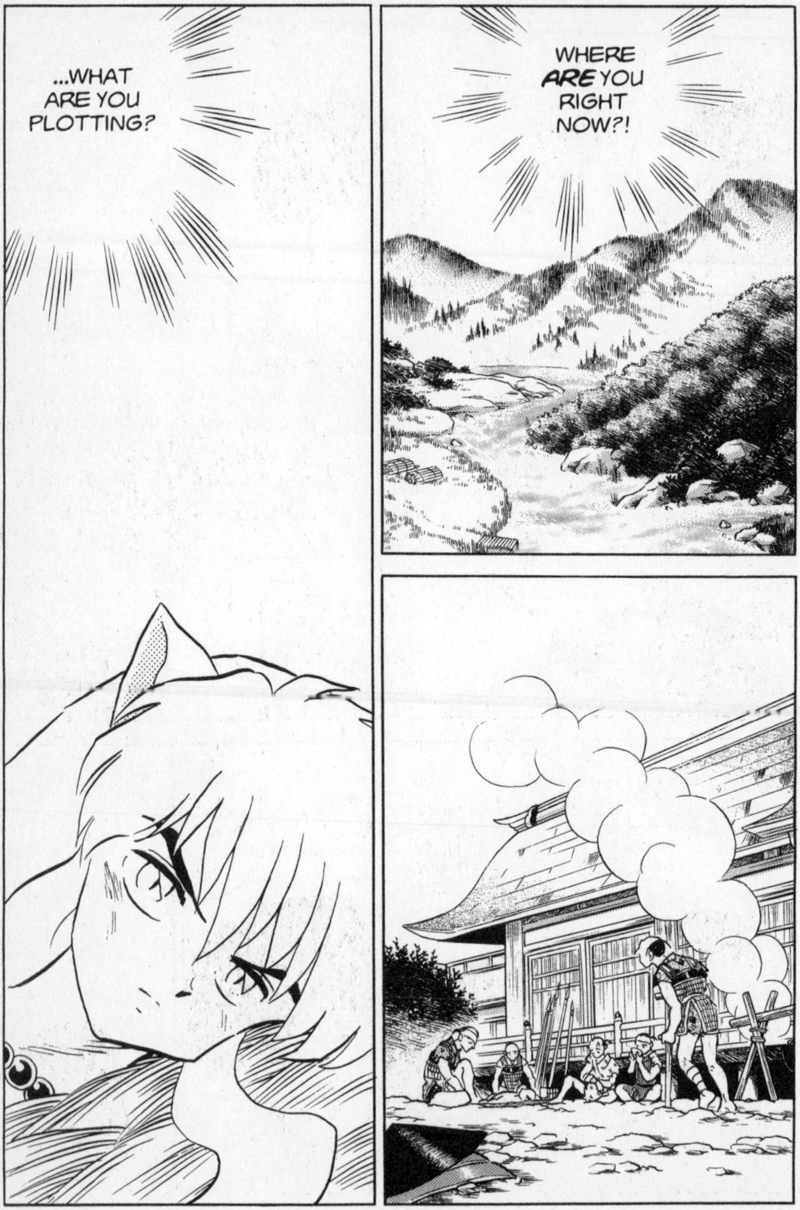
...WHAT ARE YOU PLOTTING?
WHERE ARE YOU RIGHT NOW?!

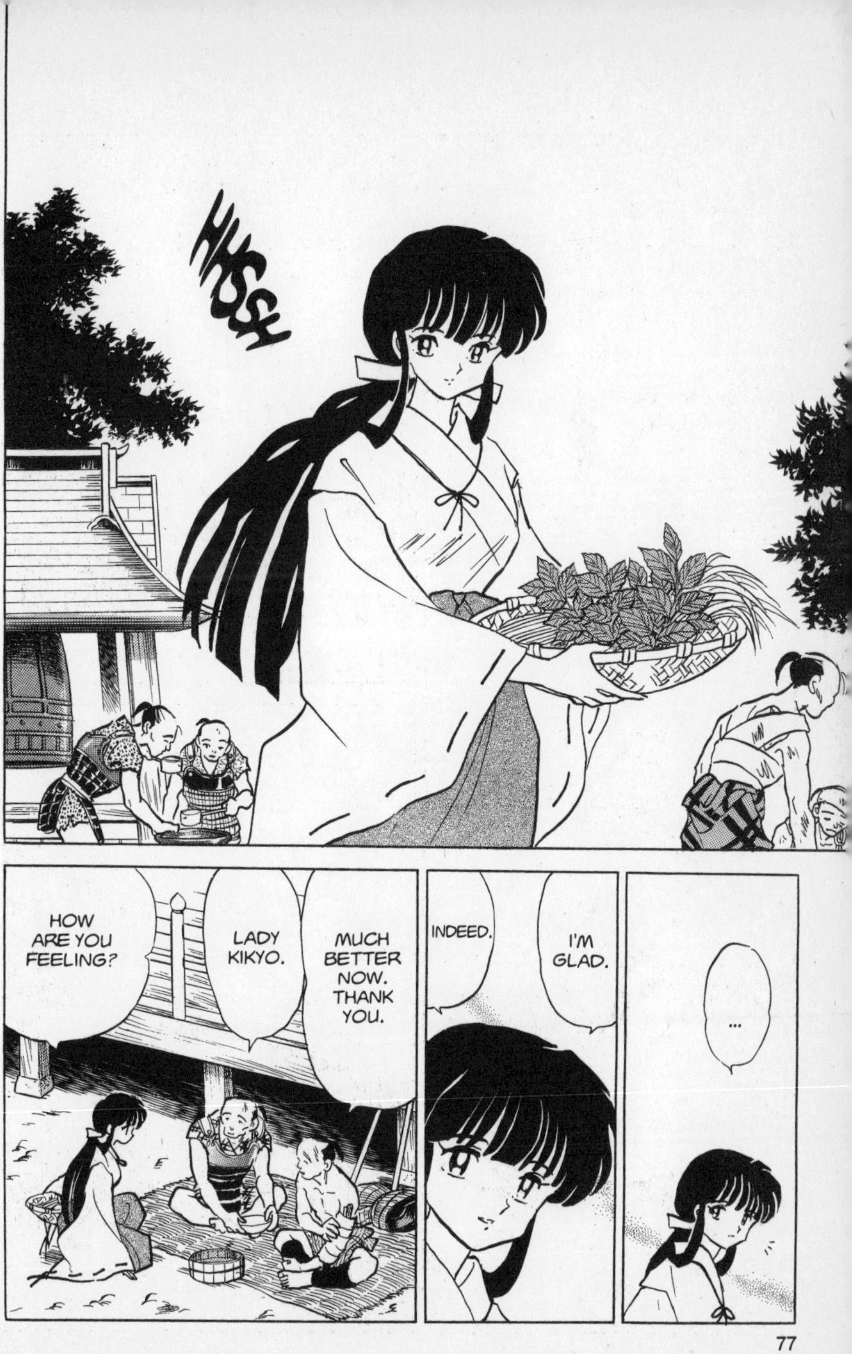
HISSH
HOW ARE YOU FEELING?
LADY KIKYO.
MUCH BETTER NOW. THANK YOU.
INDEED.
I'M GLAD.
...

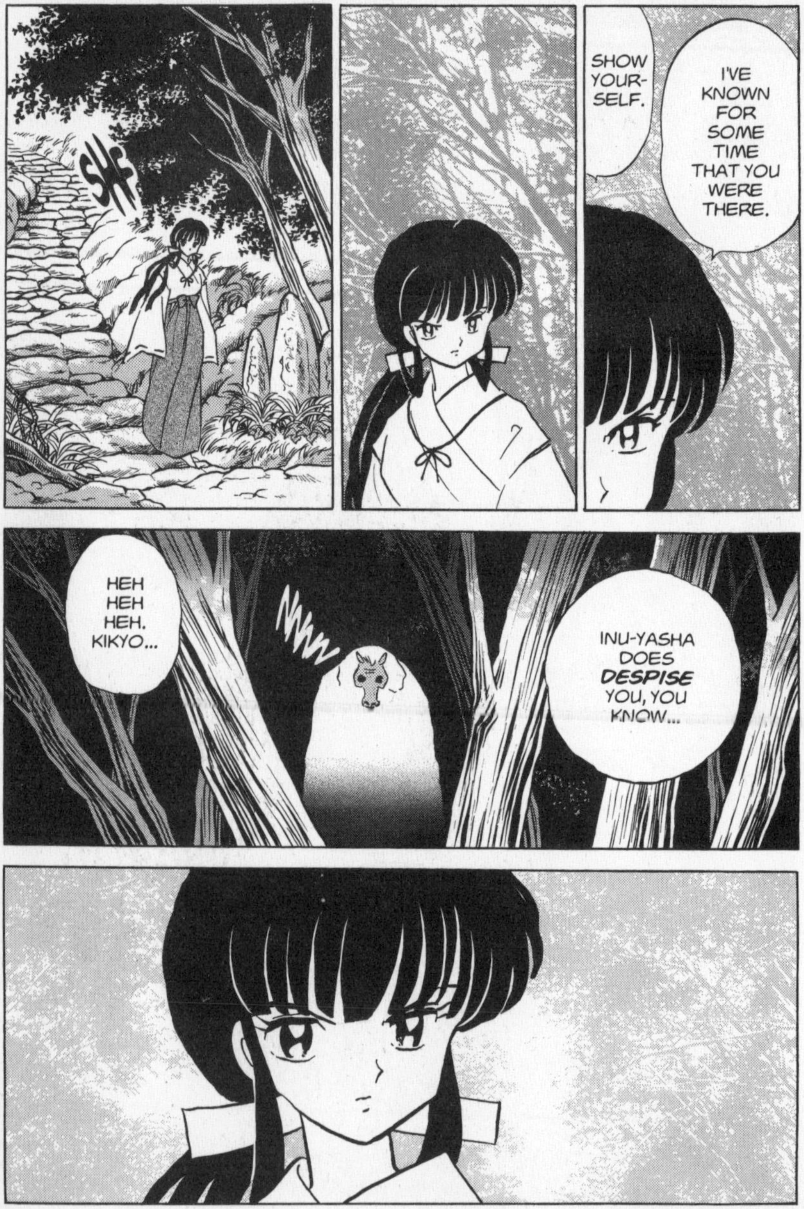
SHF
SHOW YOURSELF.
I'VE KNOWN FOR SOME TIME THAT YOU WERE THERE.
HEH HEH HEH. KIKYO...
INU-YASHA DOES **DESPISE** YOU, YOU KNOW...

SCROLL FIVE

KIKYO'S PLAN

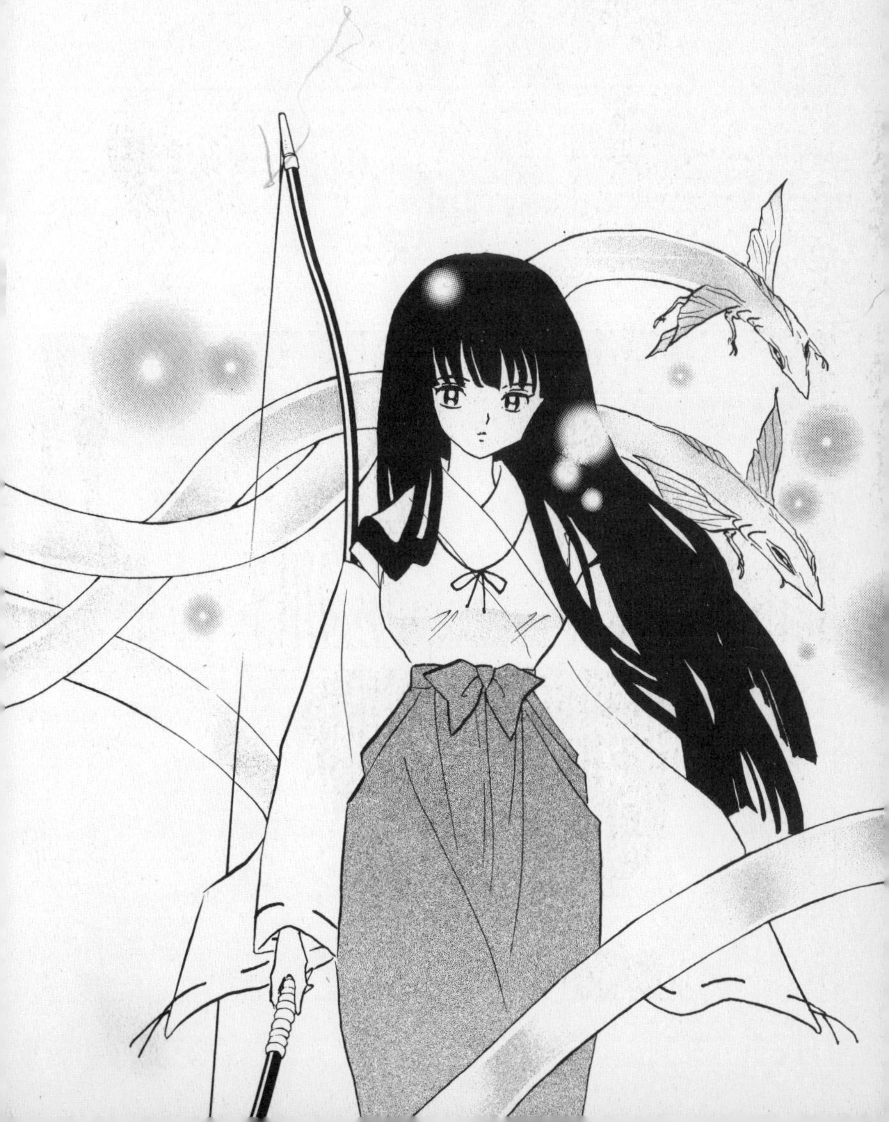

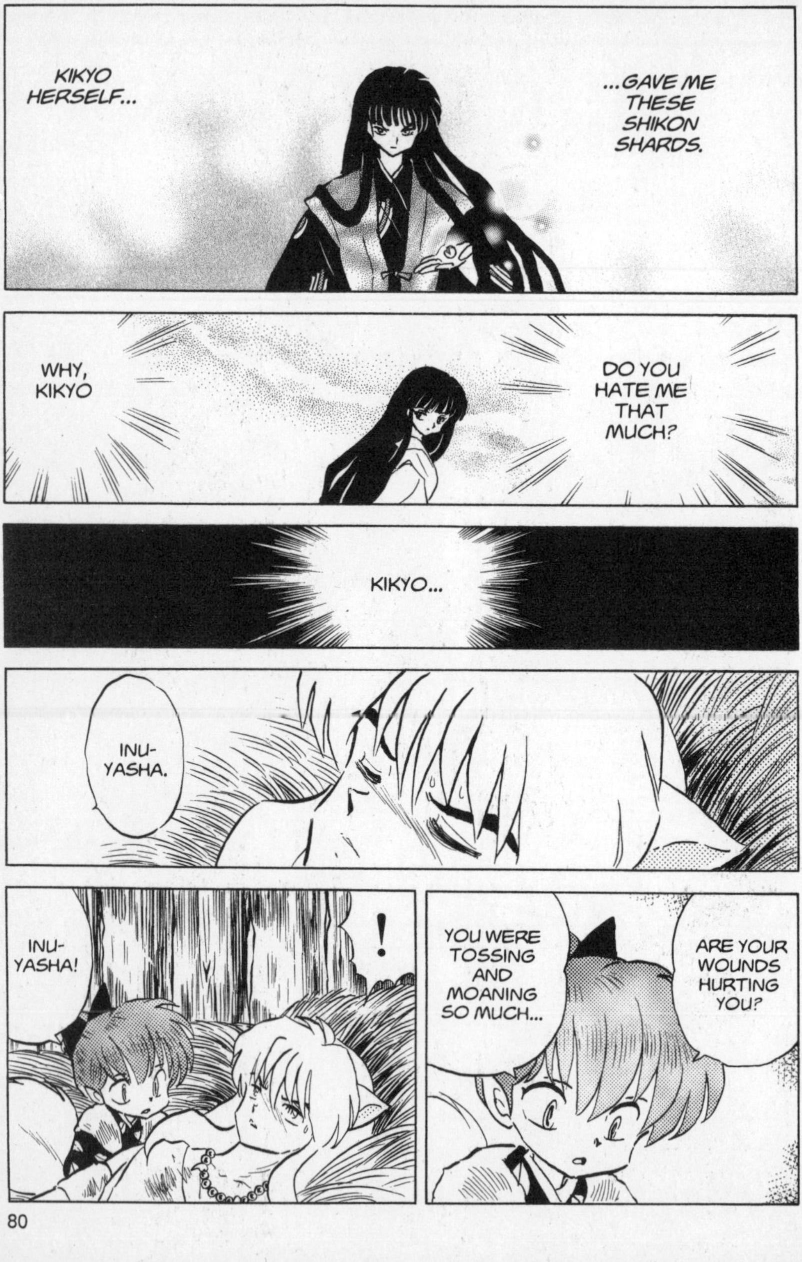
KIKYO HERSELF...
...GAVE ME THESE SHIKON SHARDS.
WHY, KIKYO
DO YOU HATE ME THAT MUCH?
KIKYO...
INU-YASHA.
INU-YASHA!
!
YOU WERE TOSSING AND MOANING SO MUCH...
ARE YOUR WOUNDS HURTING YOU?

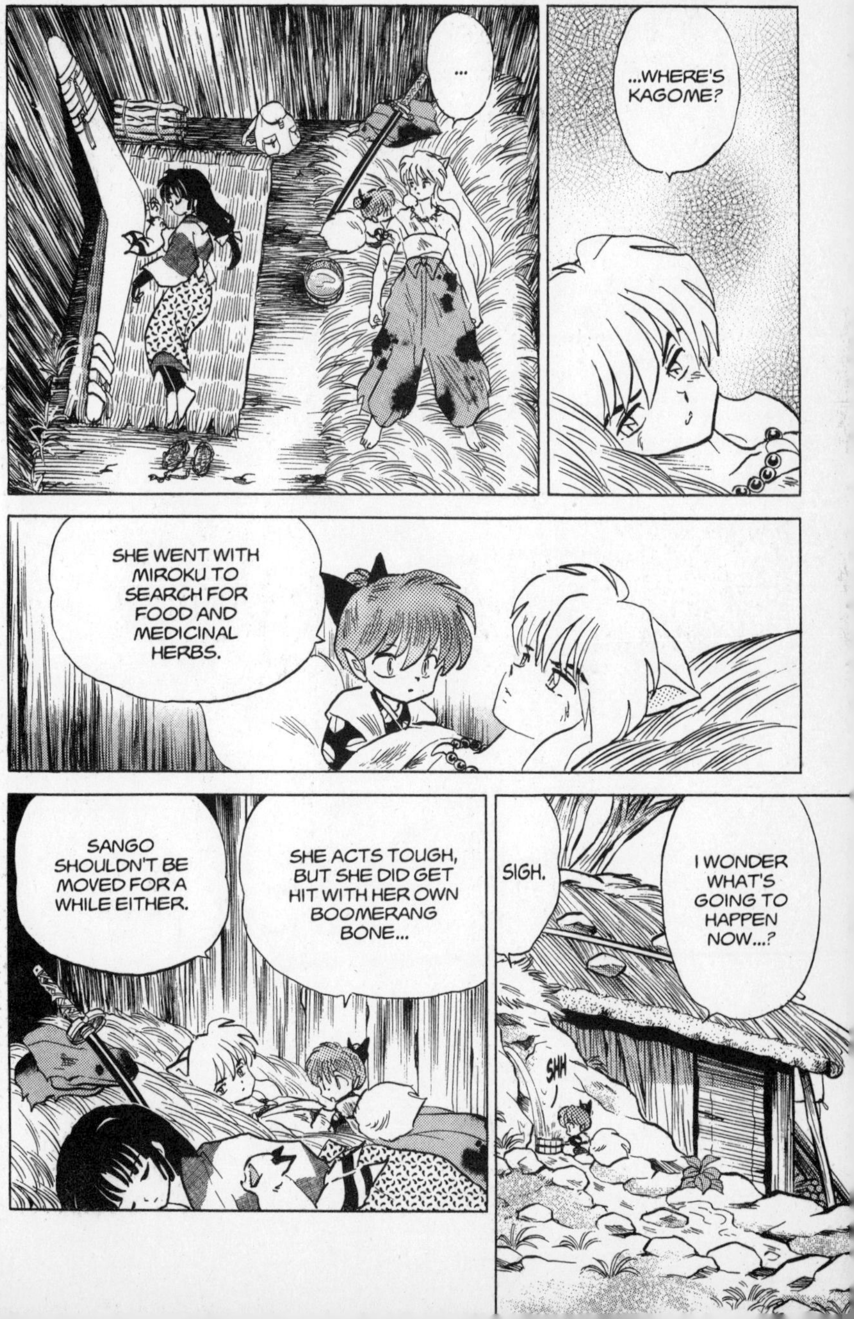
...
...WHERE'S KAGOME?
SHE WENT WITH MIROKU TO SEARCH FOR FOOD AND MEDICINAL HERBS.
SANGO SHOULDN'T BE MOVED FOR A WHILE EITHER.
SHE ACTS TOUGH, BUT SHE DID GET HIT WITH HER OWN BOOMERANG BONE...
SIGH.
I WONDER WHAT'S GOING TO HAPPEN NOW...?
SHH

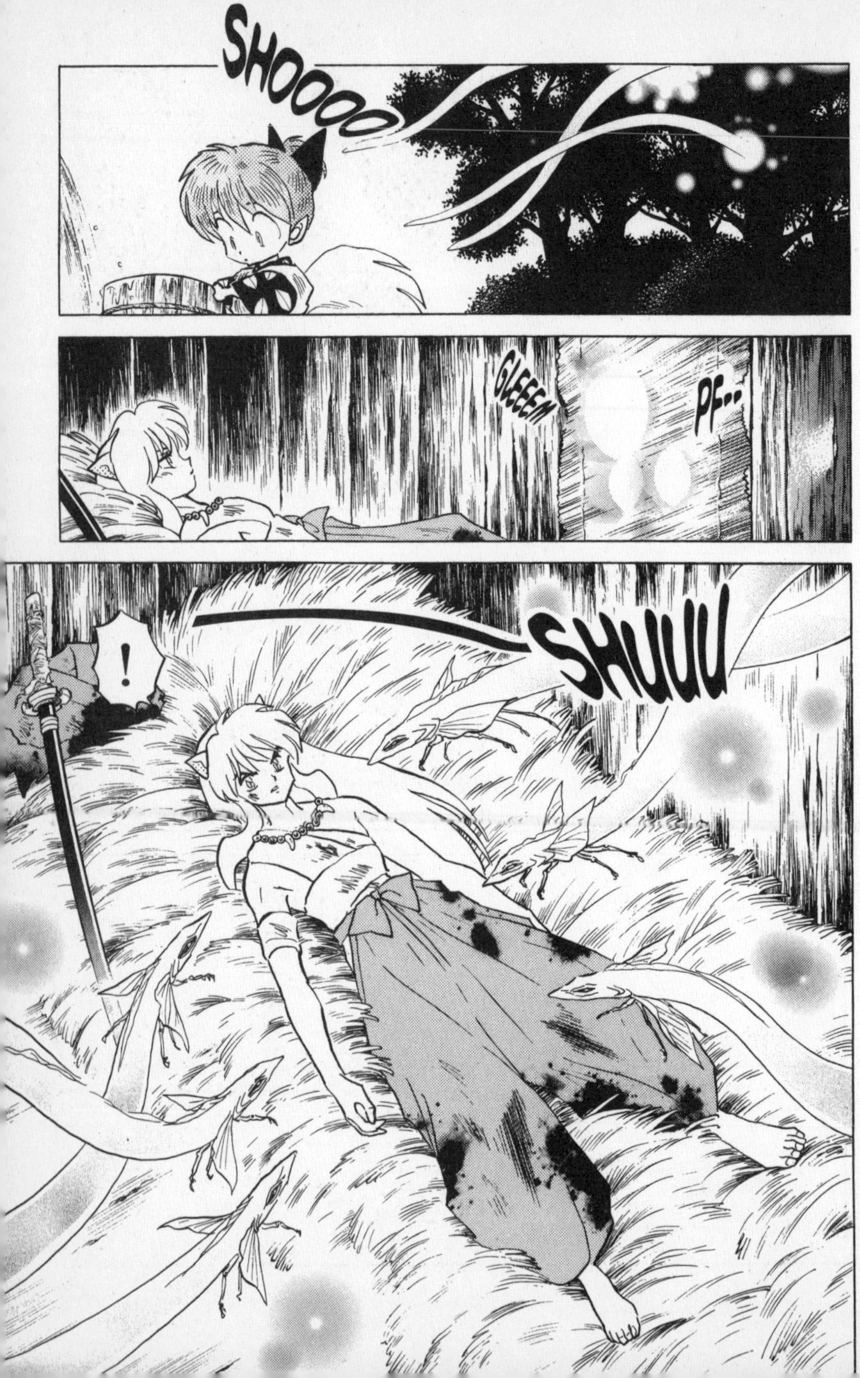
SHOOOO
GLEEEM
PF..
!
SHUUU

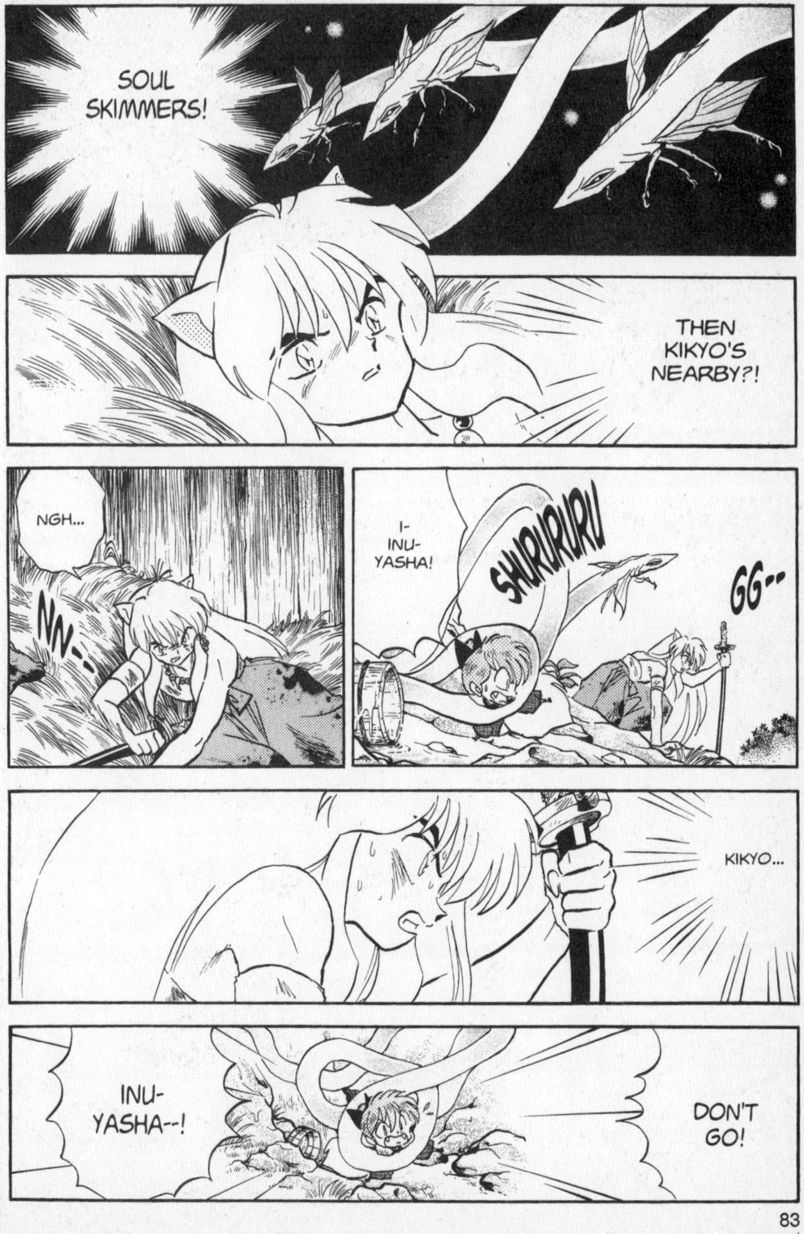
SOUL SKIMMERS!
THEN KIKYO'S NEARBY?!
I- INU-YASHA!
SHURURURU
GG--
NGH...
NN--
KIKYO...
DON'T GO!
INU-YASHA--!

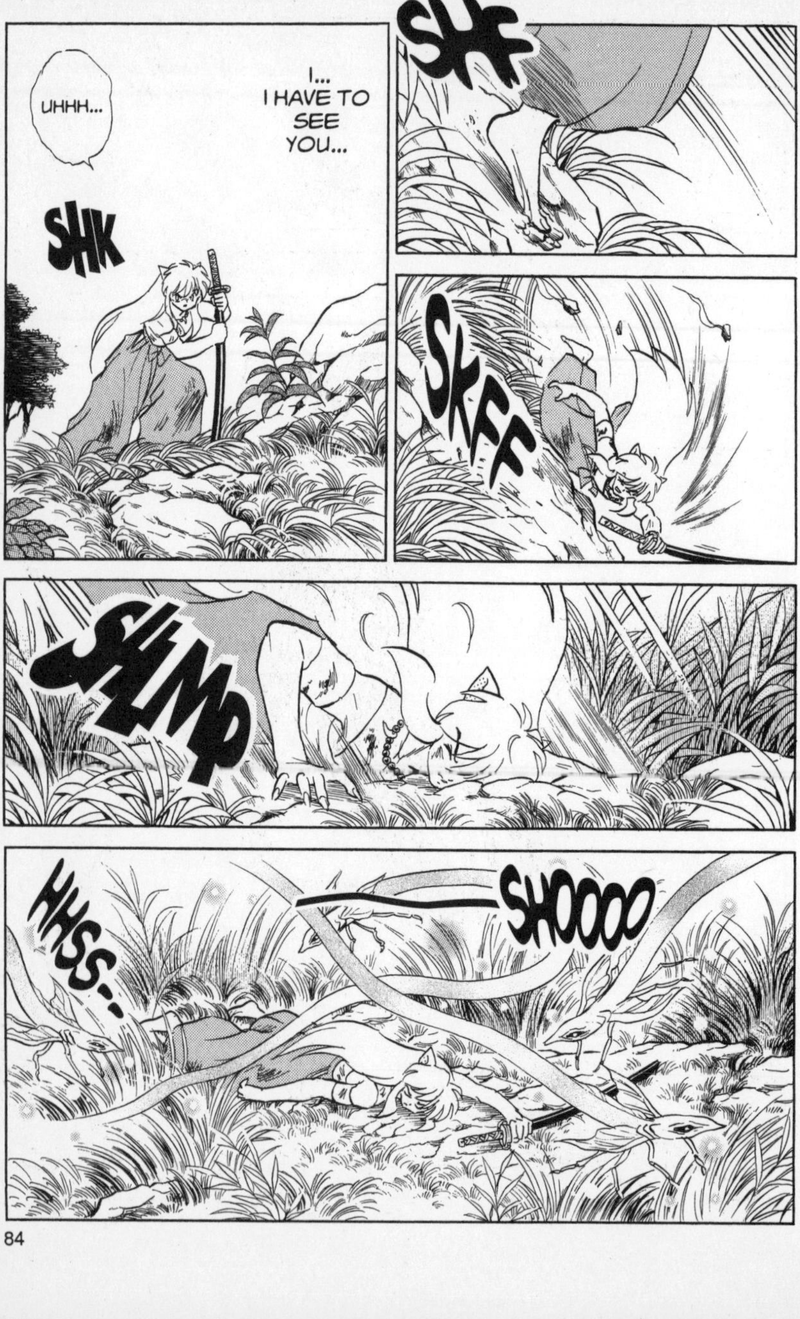
UHHH...
I... I HAVE TO SEE YOU...
SHK
SHF
SKFF
SHLMP
HHSS..
SHOOOO

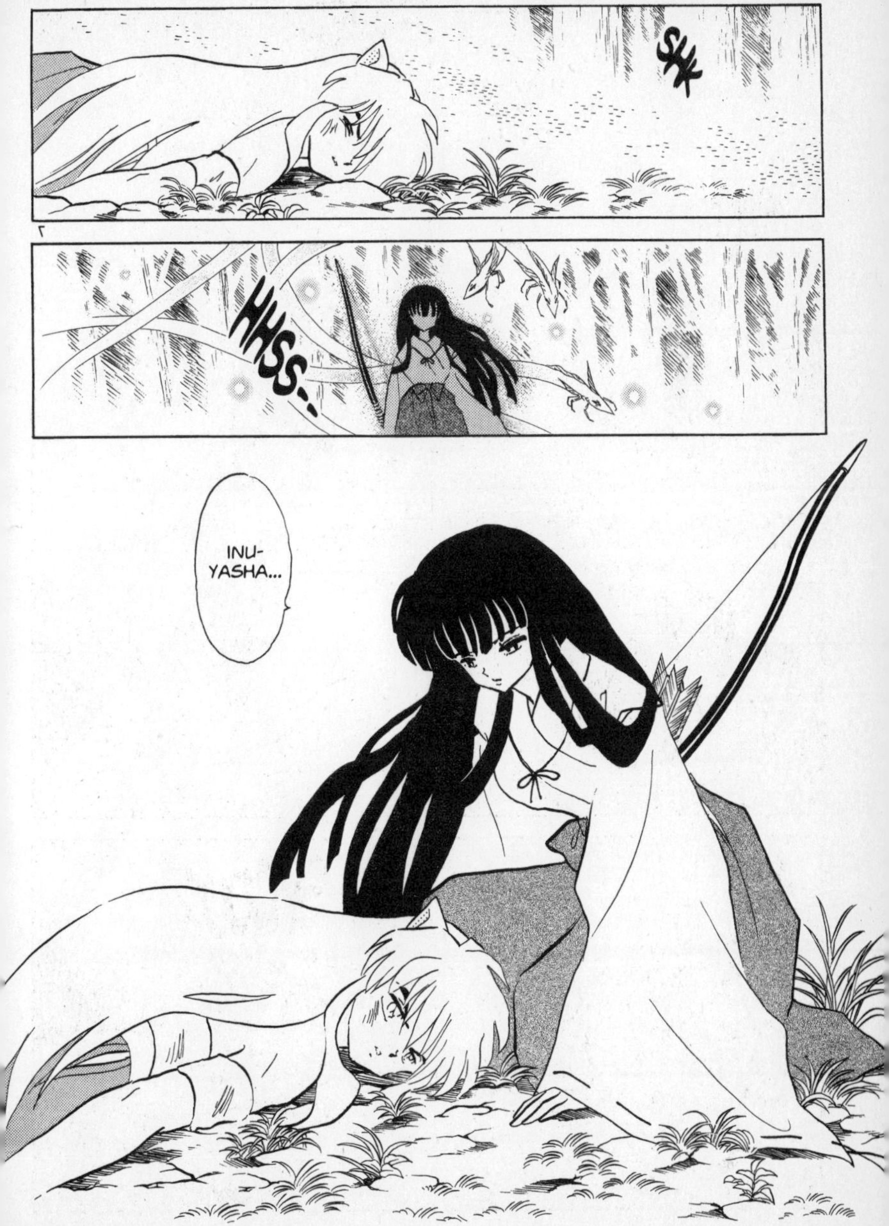
SHK
HHSS...
INU-YASHA...

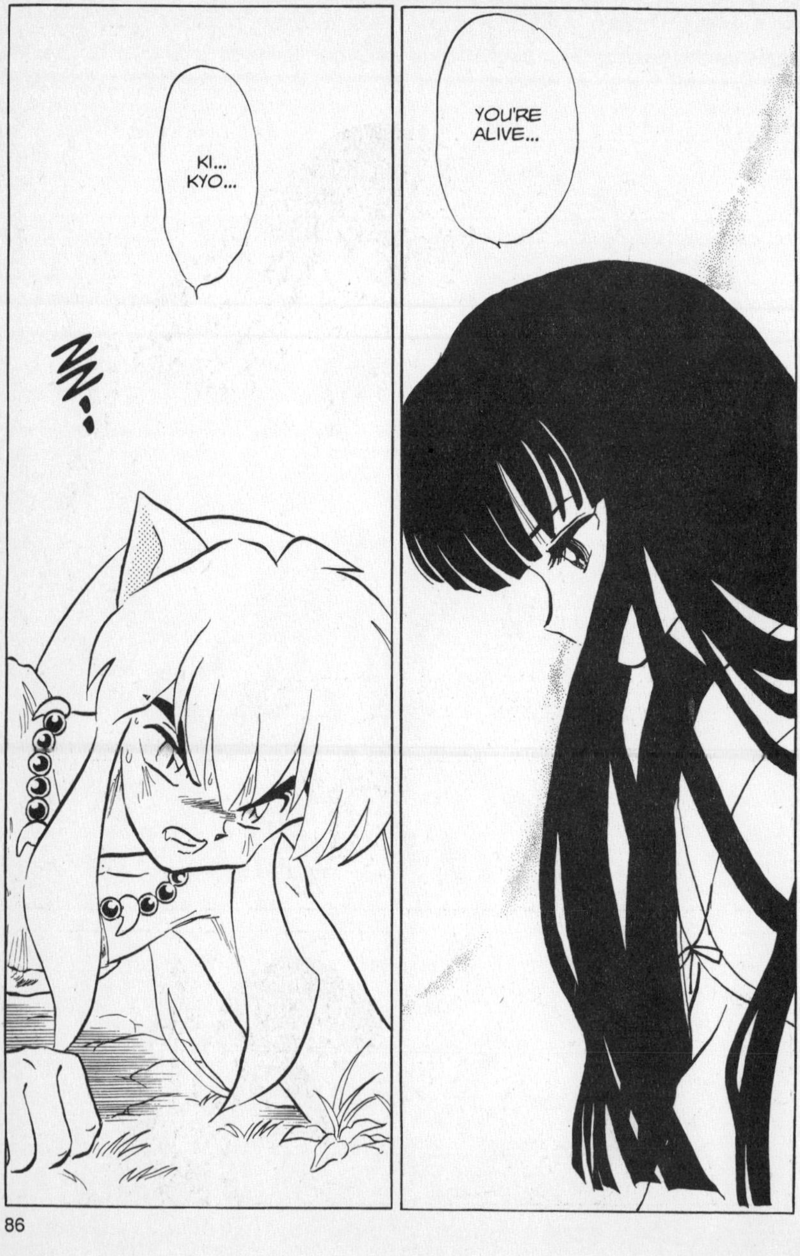
KI... KYO...
YOU'RE ALIVE...

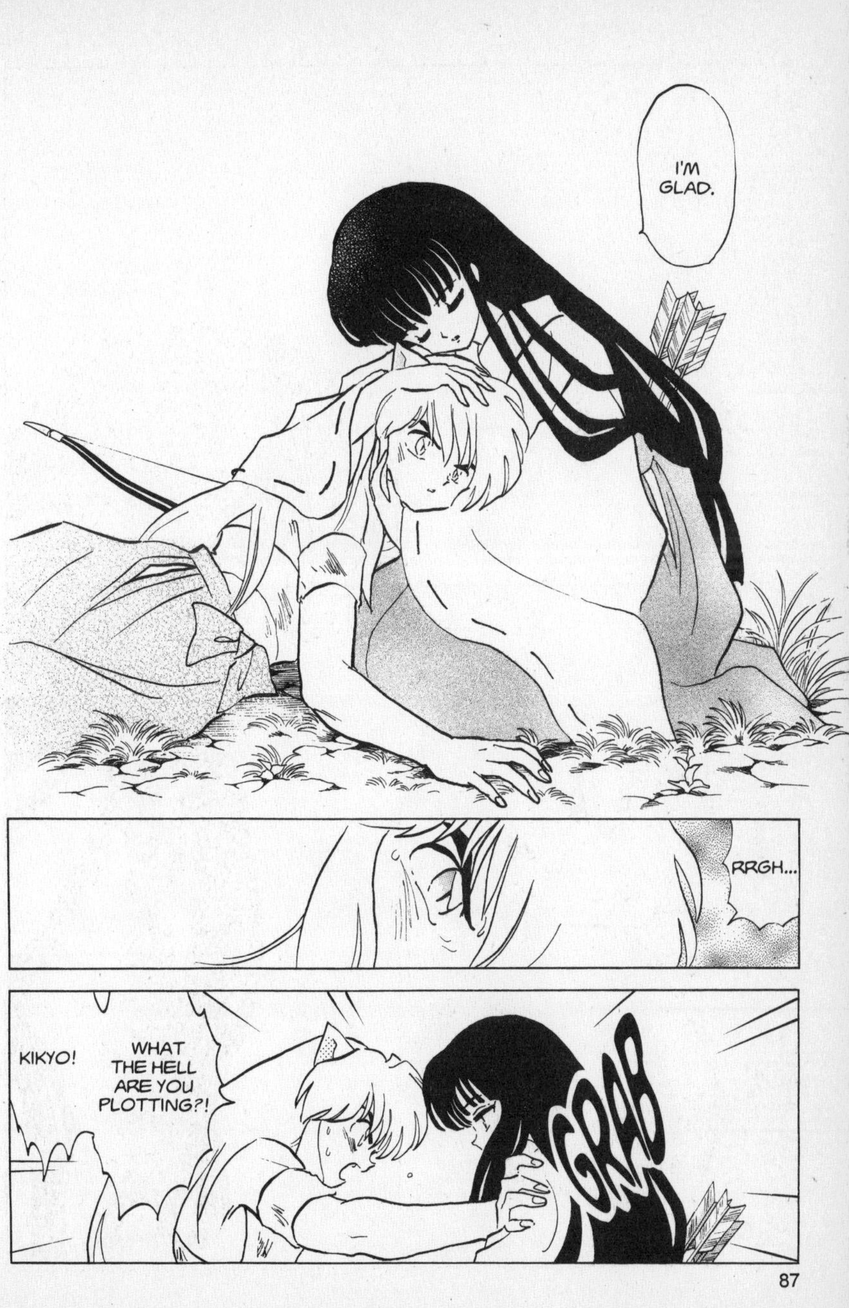
I'M GLAD.
RRGH...
KIKYO!
WHAT THE HELL ARE YOU PLOTTING?!
GRAB

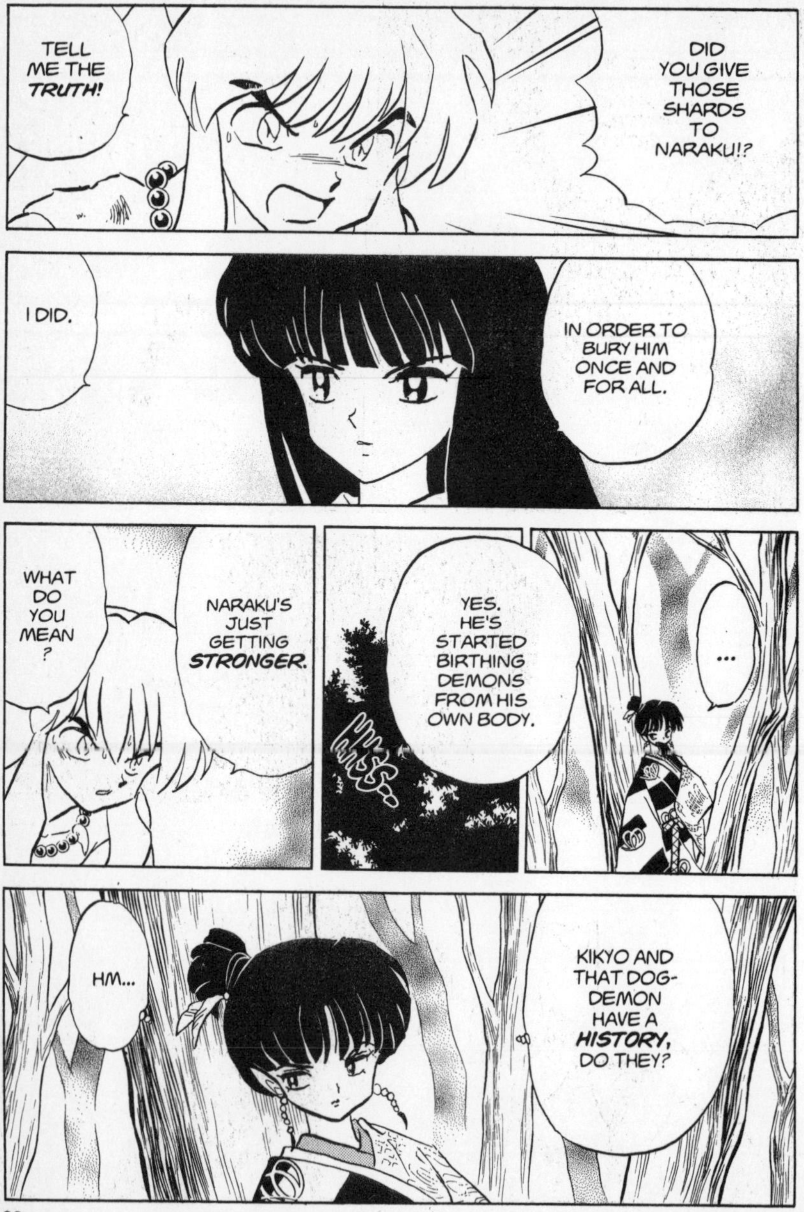
TELL ME THE *TRUTH!*
DID YOU GIVE THOSE SHARDS TO NARAKU!?
I DID.
IN ORDER TO BURY HIM ONCE AND FOR ALL.
WHAT DO YOU MEAN?
NARAKU'S JUST GETTING *STRONGER.*
YES. HE'S STARTED BIRTHING DEMONS FROM HIS OWN BODY.
...
HM...
KIKYO AND THAT DOG-DEMON HAVE A *HISTORY,* DO THEY?

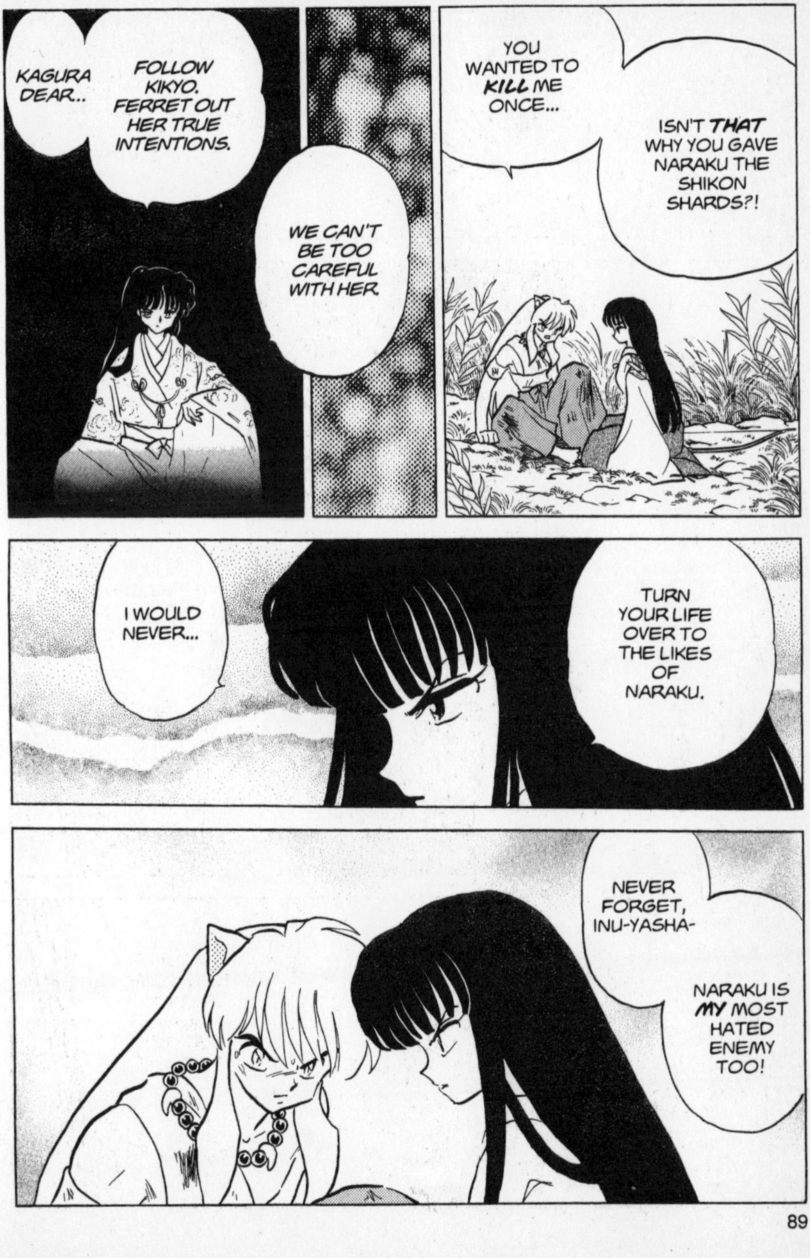
KAGURA DEAR...
FOLLOW KIKYO. FERRET OUT HER TRUE INTENTIONS.
WE CAN'T BE TOO CAREFUL WITH HER.
YOU WANTED TO KILL ME ONCE...
ISN'T THAT WHY YOU GAVE NARAKU THE SHIKON SHARDS?!
I WOULD NEVER...
TURN YOUR LIFE OVER TO THE LIKES OF NARAKU.
NEVER FORGET, INU-YASHA-
NARAKU IS MY MOST HATED ENEMY TOO!

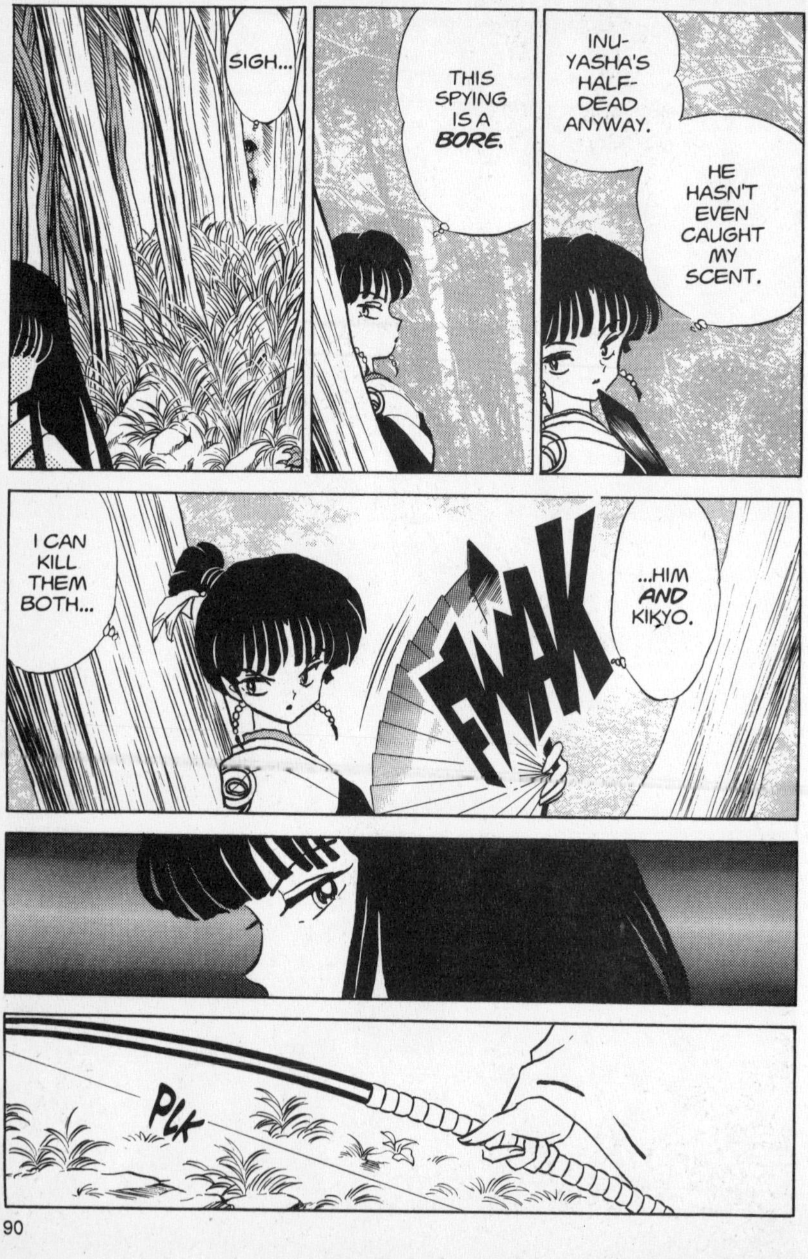

SIGH...
THIS SPYING IS A *BORE.*
INU-YASHA'S HALF-DEAD ANYWAY.
HE HASN'T EVEN CAUGHT MY SCENT.
I CAN KILL THEM BOTH...
FWAK
...HIM *AND* KIKYO.
PLK

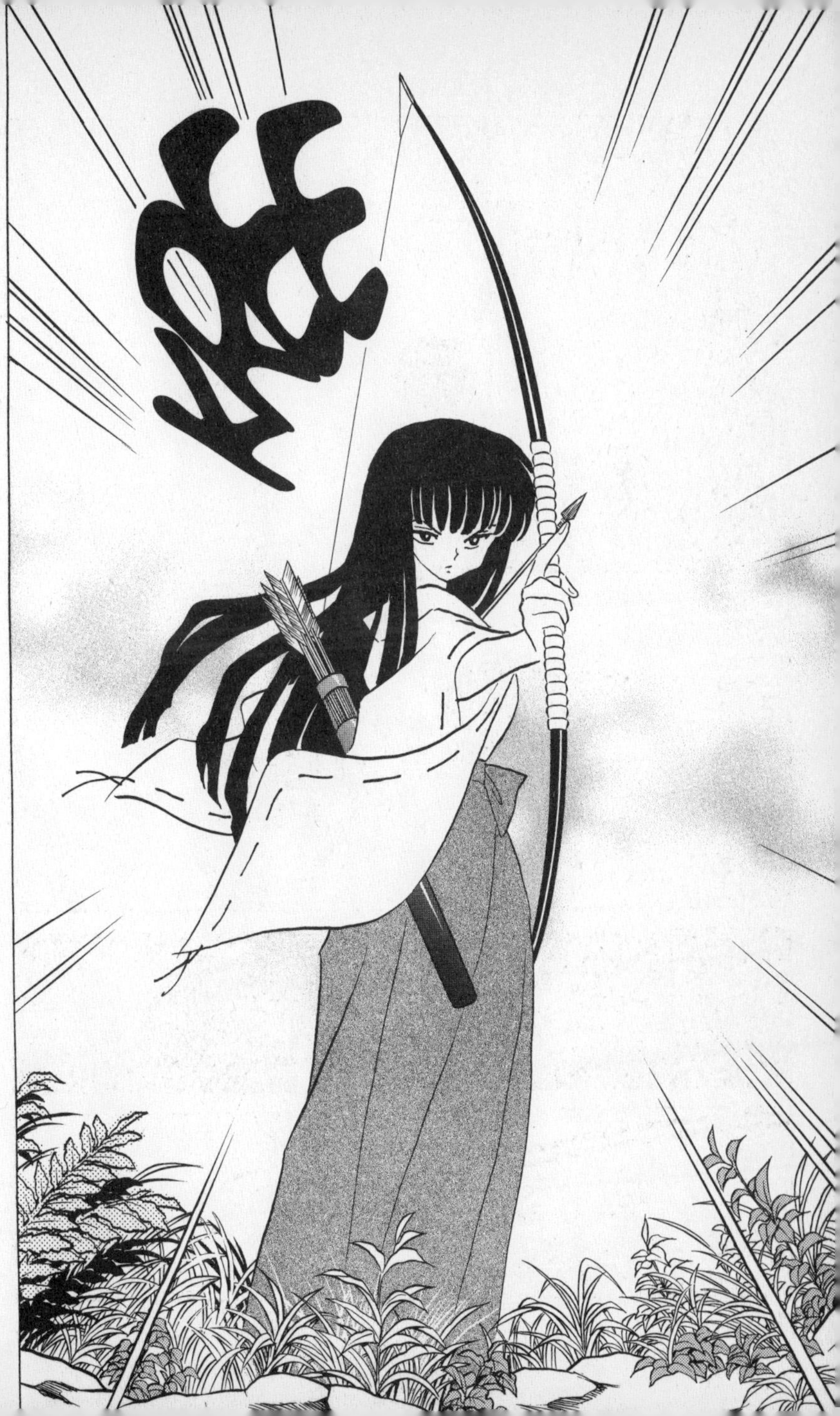

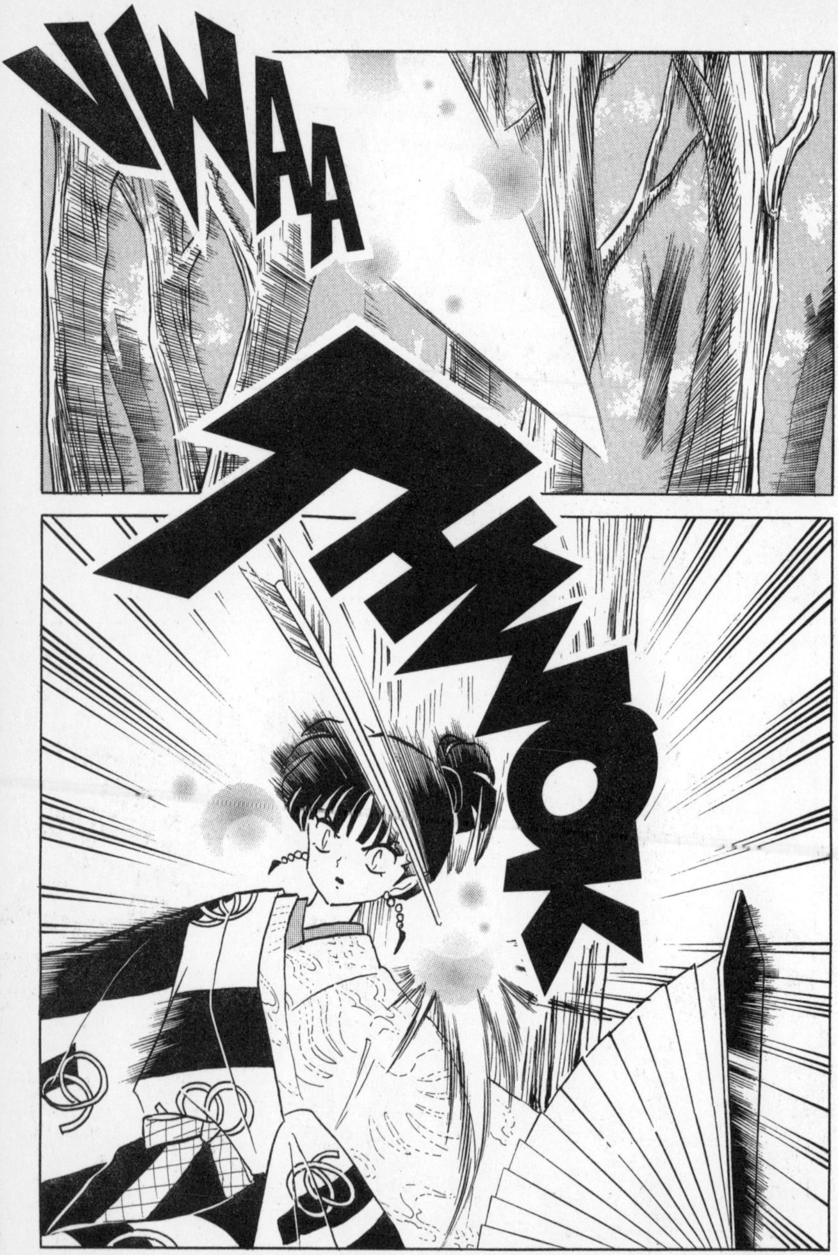
VWAA
THWOK

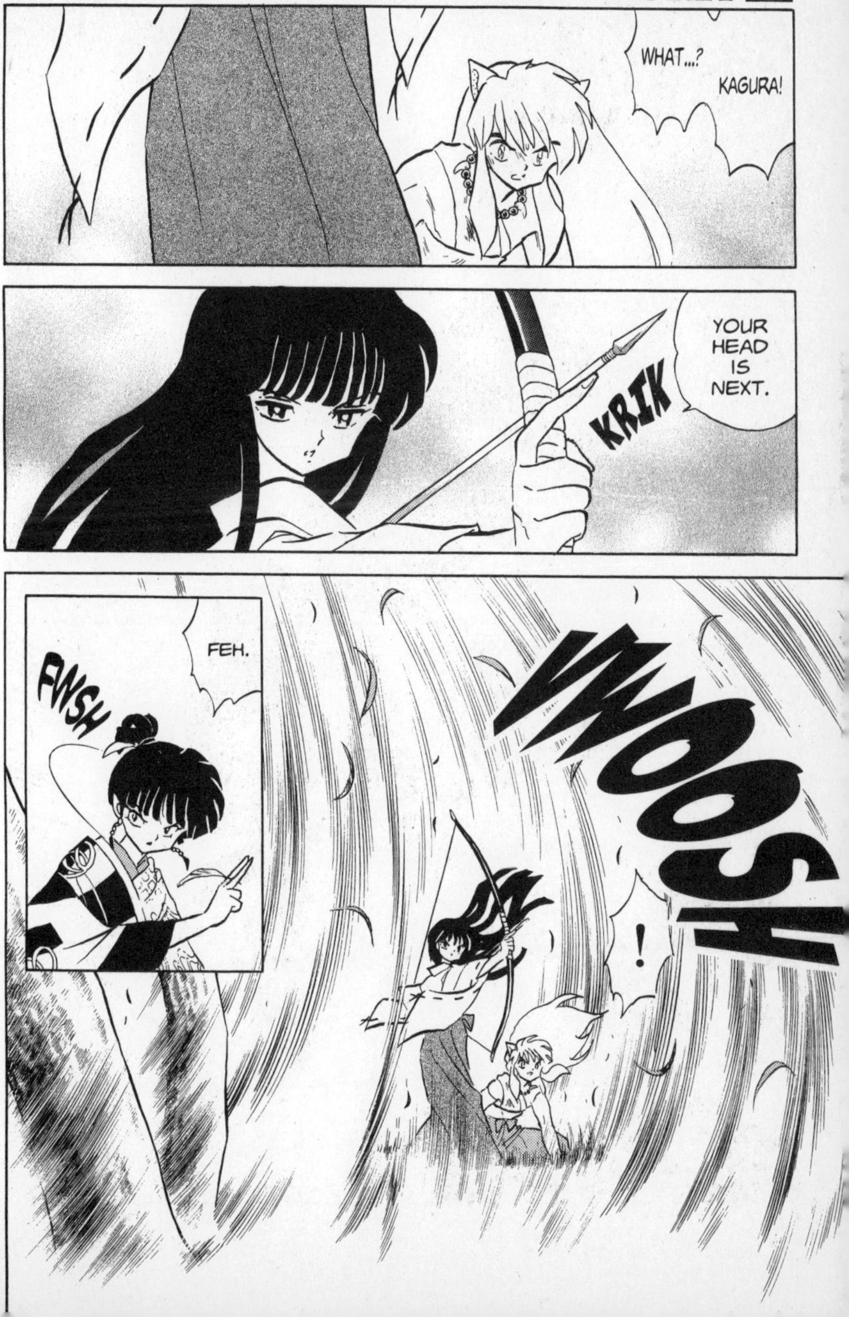
WHAT...?
KAGURA!
KRIK
YOUR HEAD IS NEXT.
FEH.
FWSH
WOOSH
!

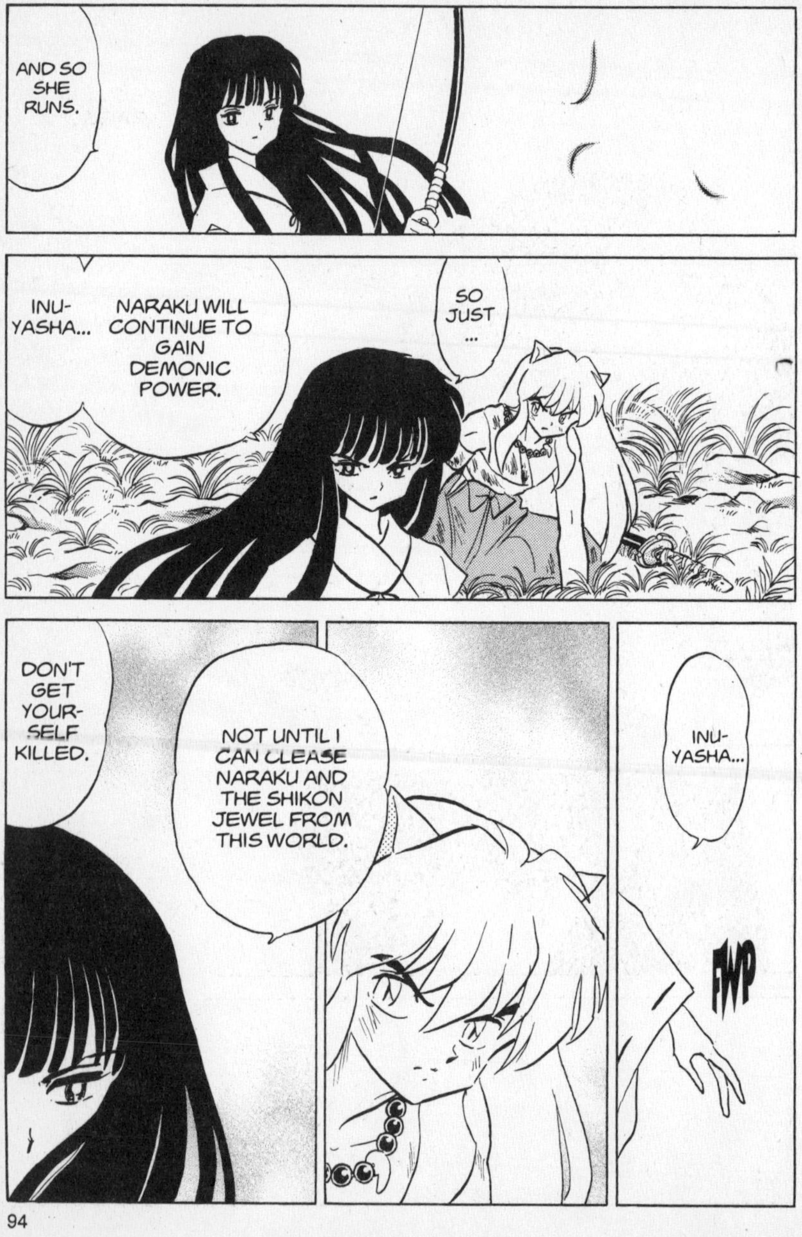

AND SO SHE RUNS.
INU-YASHA...
NARAKU WILL CONTINUE TO GAIN DEMONIC POWER.
SO JUST ...
DON'T GET YOUR-SELF KILLED.
NOT UNTIL I CAN CLEASE NARAKU AND THE SHIKON JEWEL FROM THIS WORLD.
INU-YASHA...
FWP

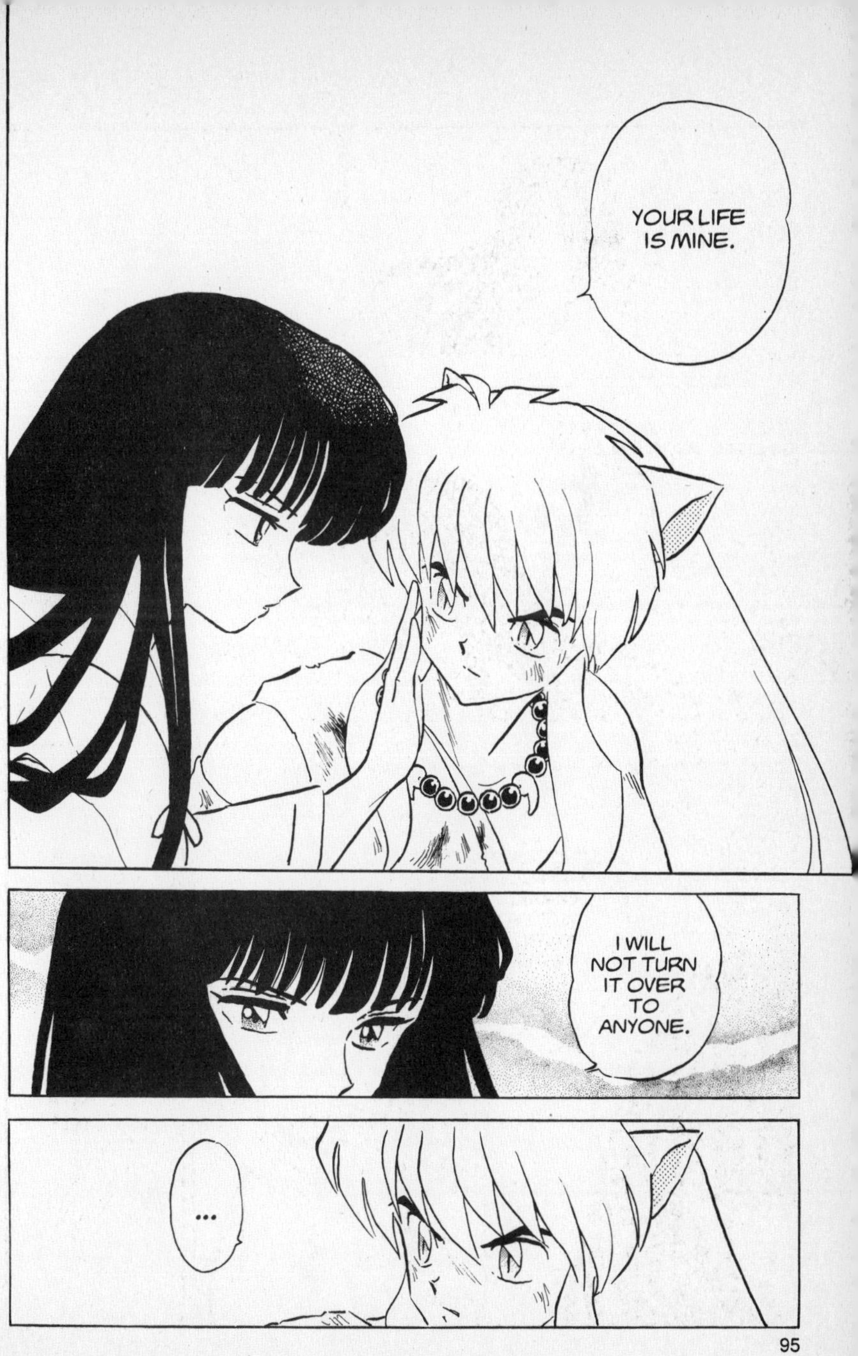
YOUR LIFE IS MINE.
I WILL NOT TURN IT OVER TO ANYONE.
...

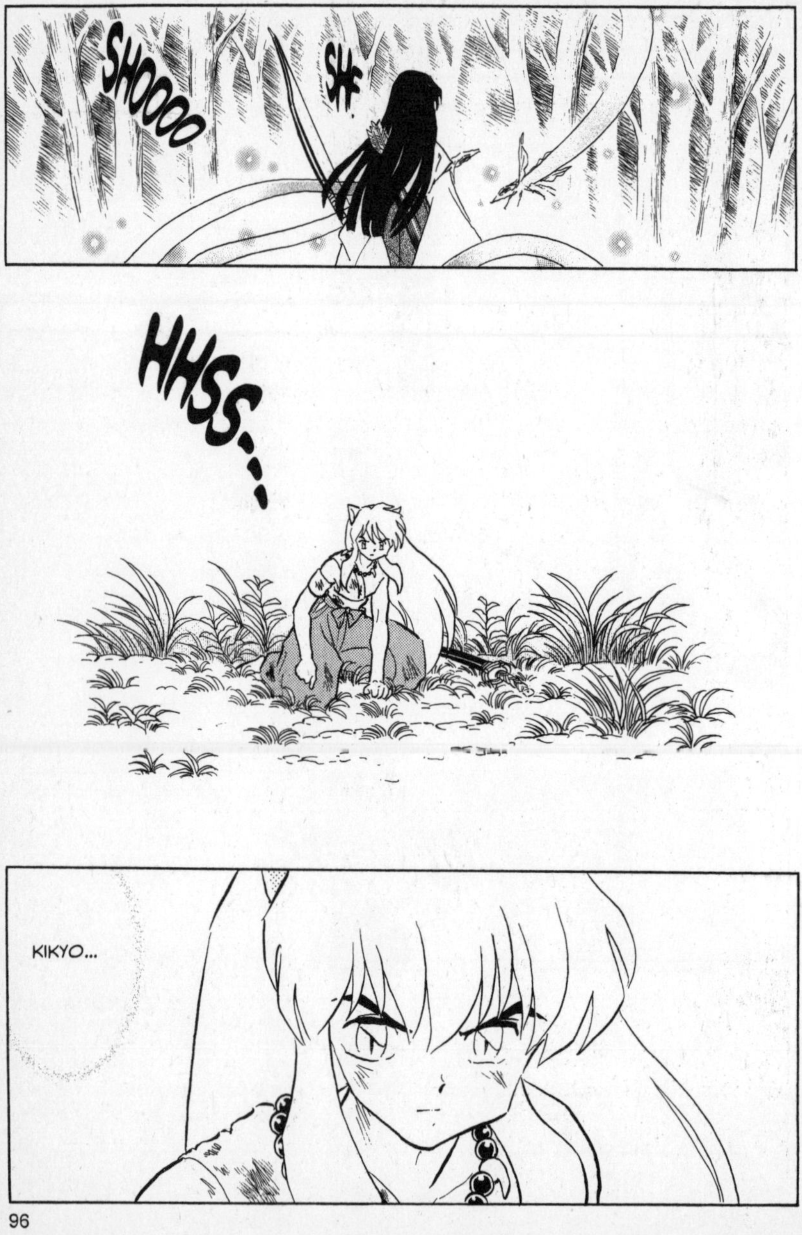
SHOOOO
SH
HHSS...
KIKYO...

SCROLL SIX

THE THIRD DEMON

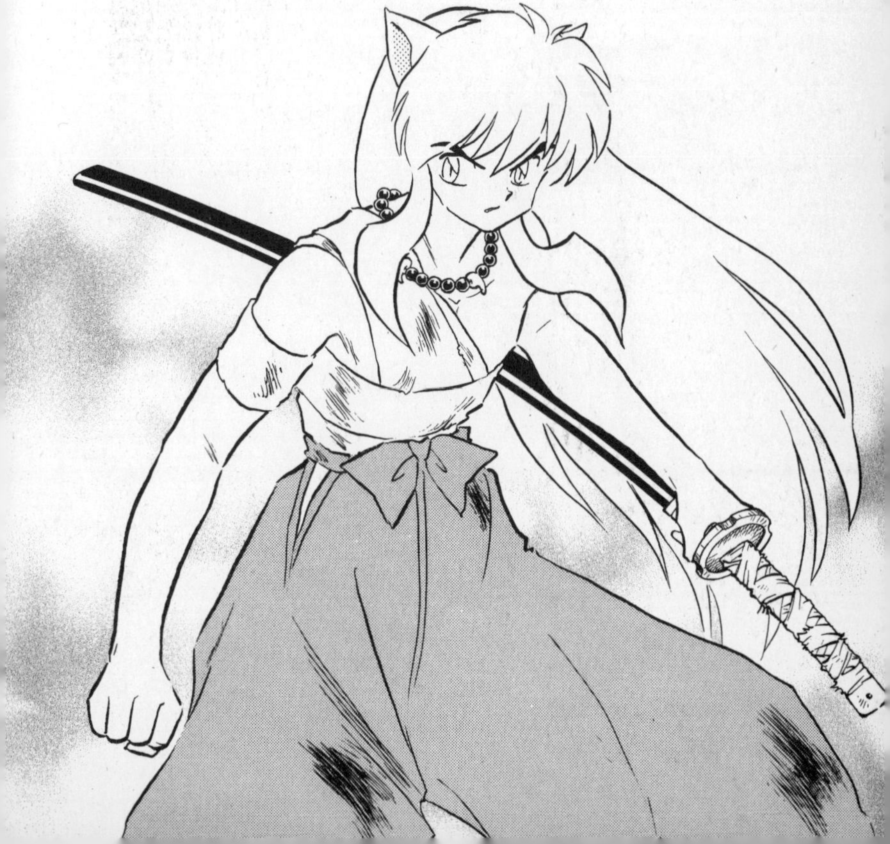

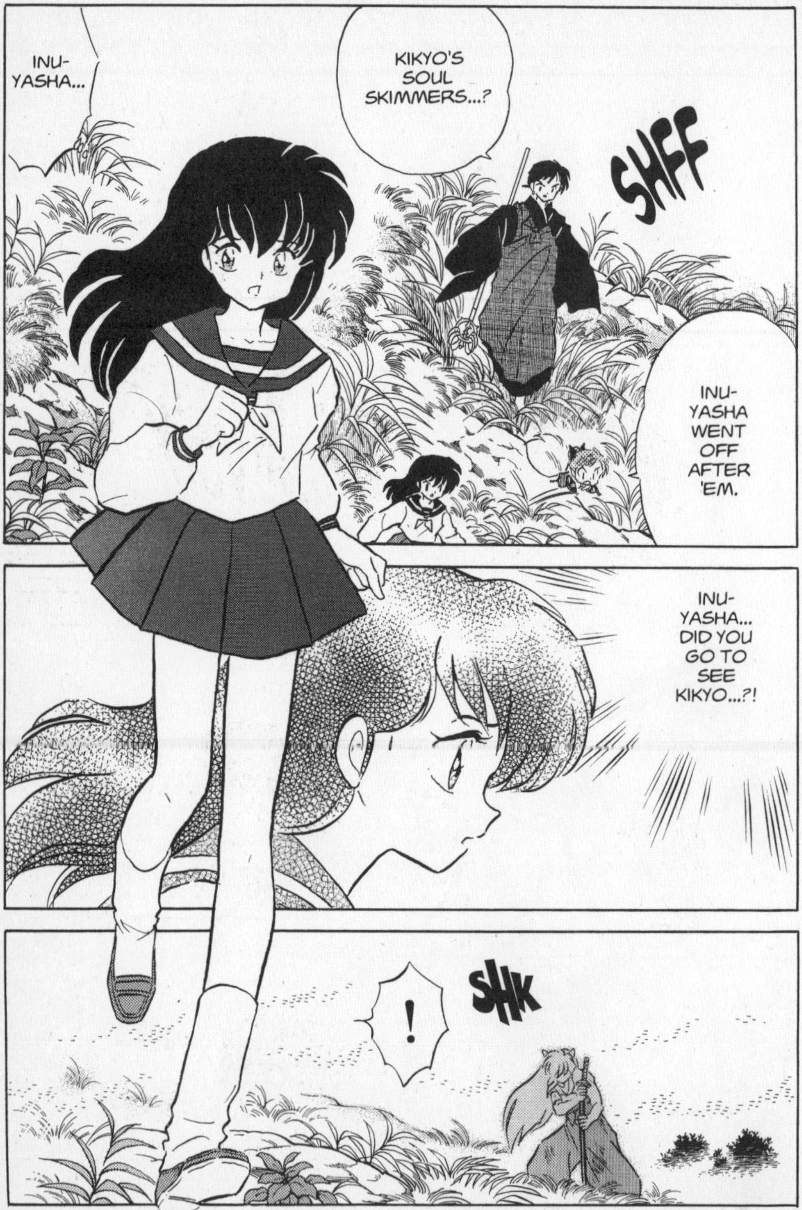
INU-YASHA...
KIKYO'S SOUL SKIMMERS...?
SHFF
INU-YASHA WENT OFF AFTER 'EM.
INU-YASHA... DID YOU GO TO SEE KIKYO...?!
!
SHK

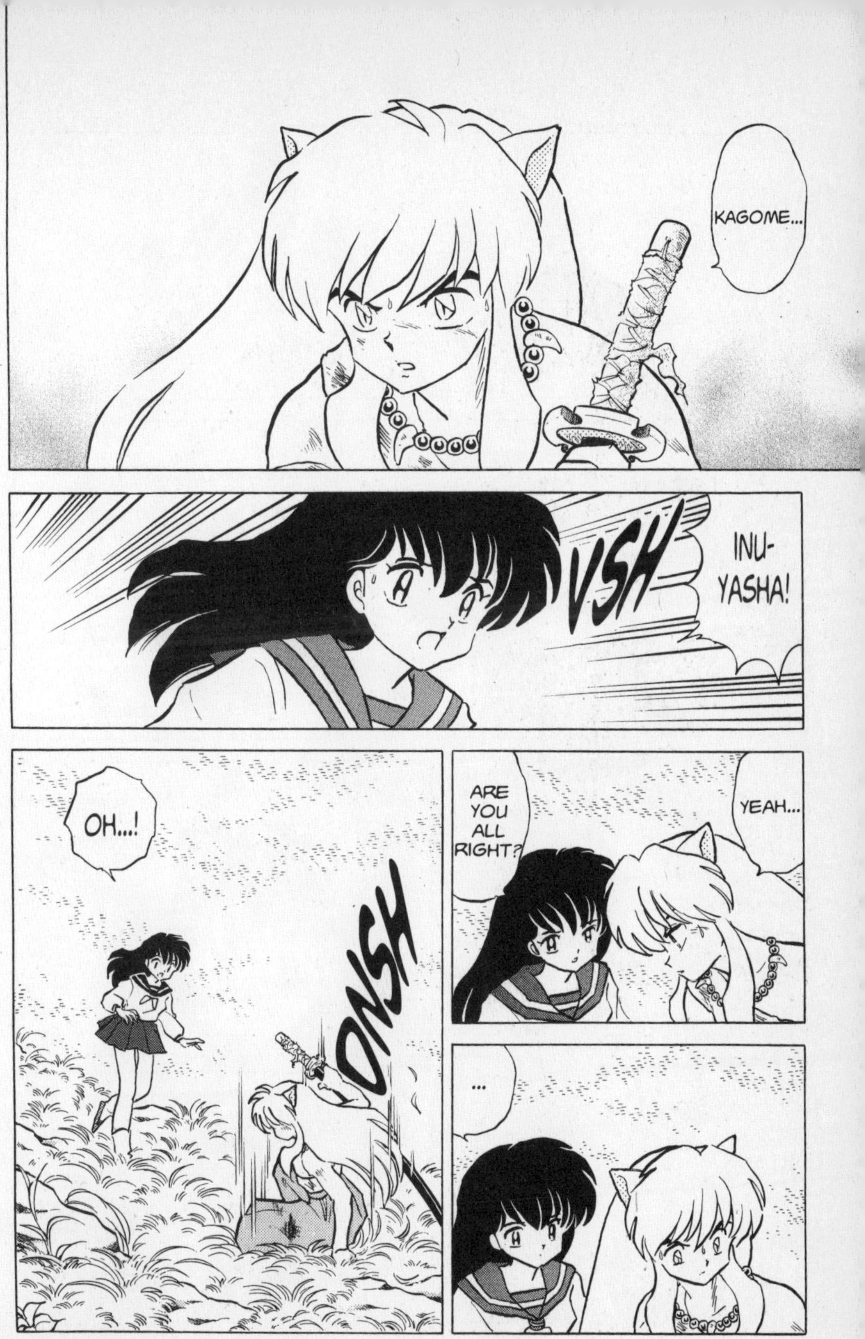
KAGOME...
VSH
INU-YASHA!
OH...!
ARE YOU ALL RIGHT?
YEAH...
...

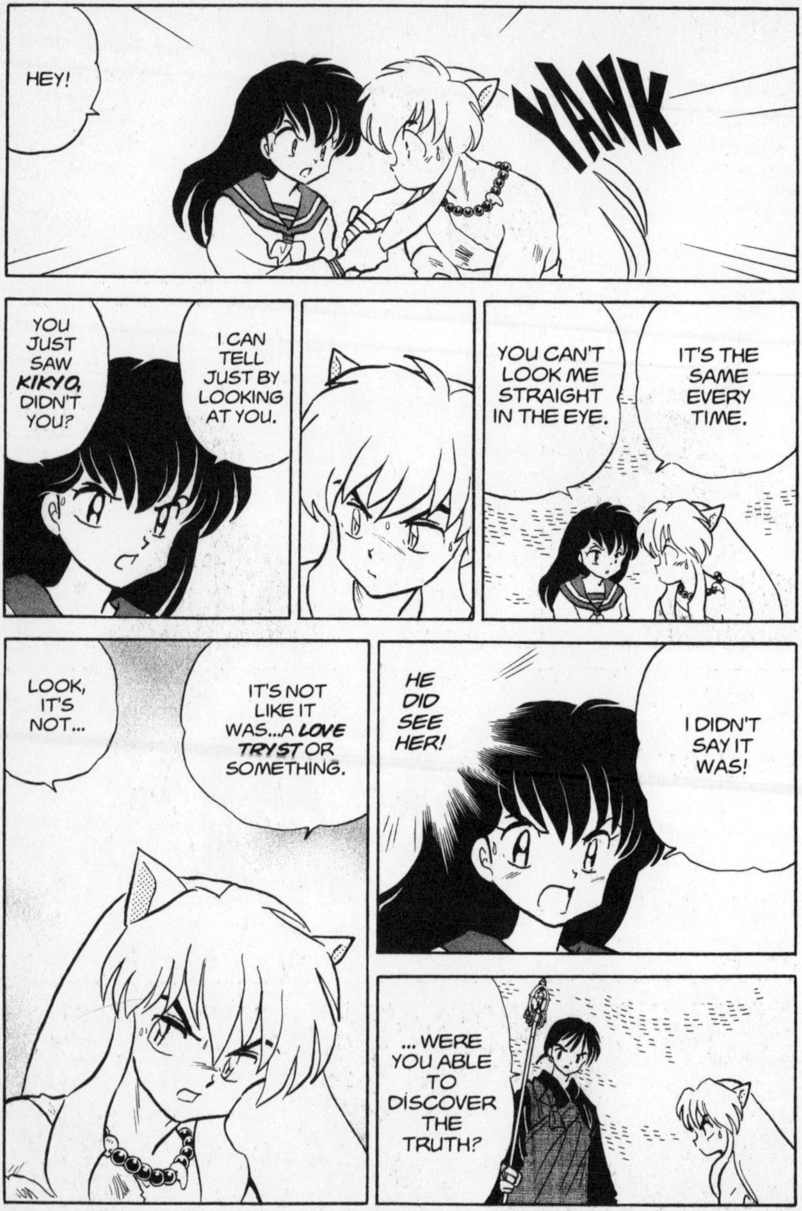
HEY!
YANK
YOU JUST SAW KIKYO, DIDN'T YOU?
I CAN TELL JUST BY LOOKING AT YOU.
YOU CAN'T LOOK ME STRAIGHT IN THE EYE.
IT'S THE SAME EVERY TIME.
LOOK, IT'S NOT...
IT'S NOT LIKE IT WAS...A LOVE TRYST OR SOMETHING.
HE DID SEE HER!
I DIDN'T SAY IT WAS!
...WERE YOU ABLE TO DISCOVER THE TRUTH?

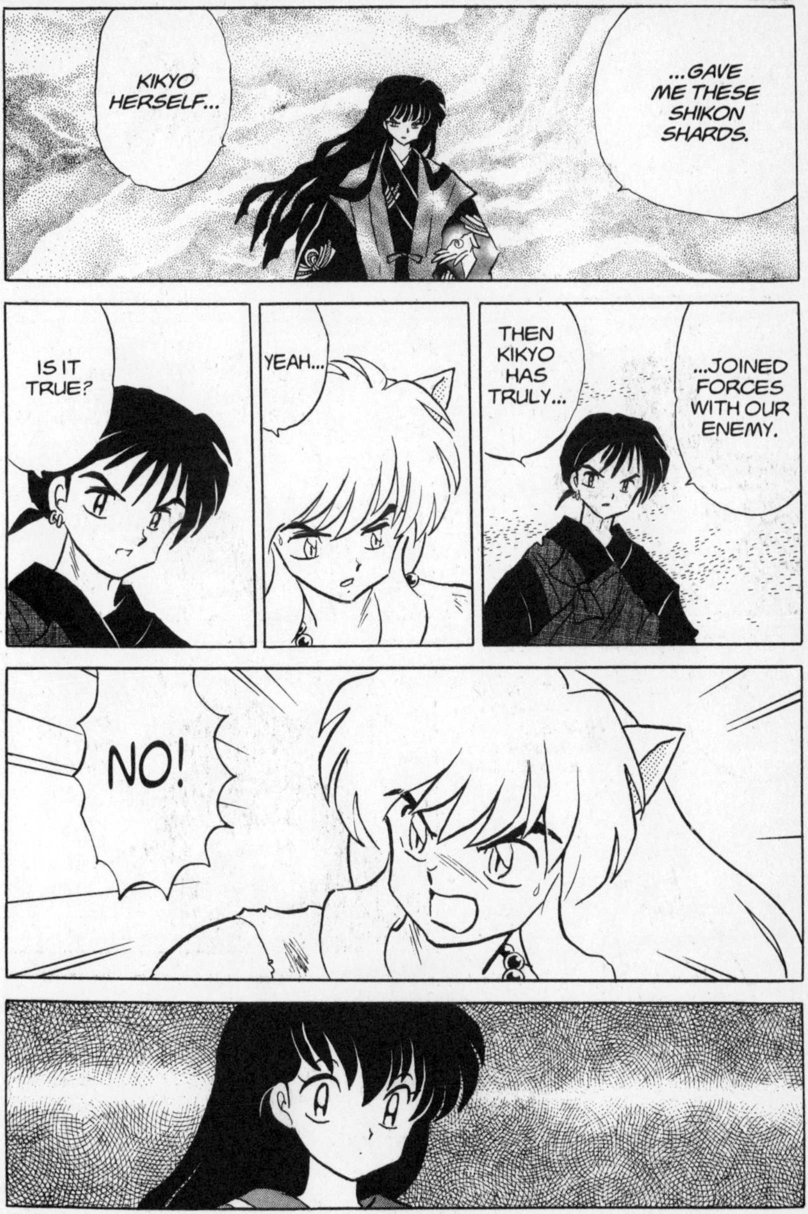
KIKYO HERSELF...
...GAVE ME THESE SHIKON SHARDS.
IS IT TRUE?
YEAH...
THEN KIKYO HAS TRULY...
...JOINED FORCES WITH OUR ENEMY.
NO!

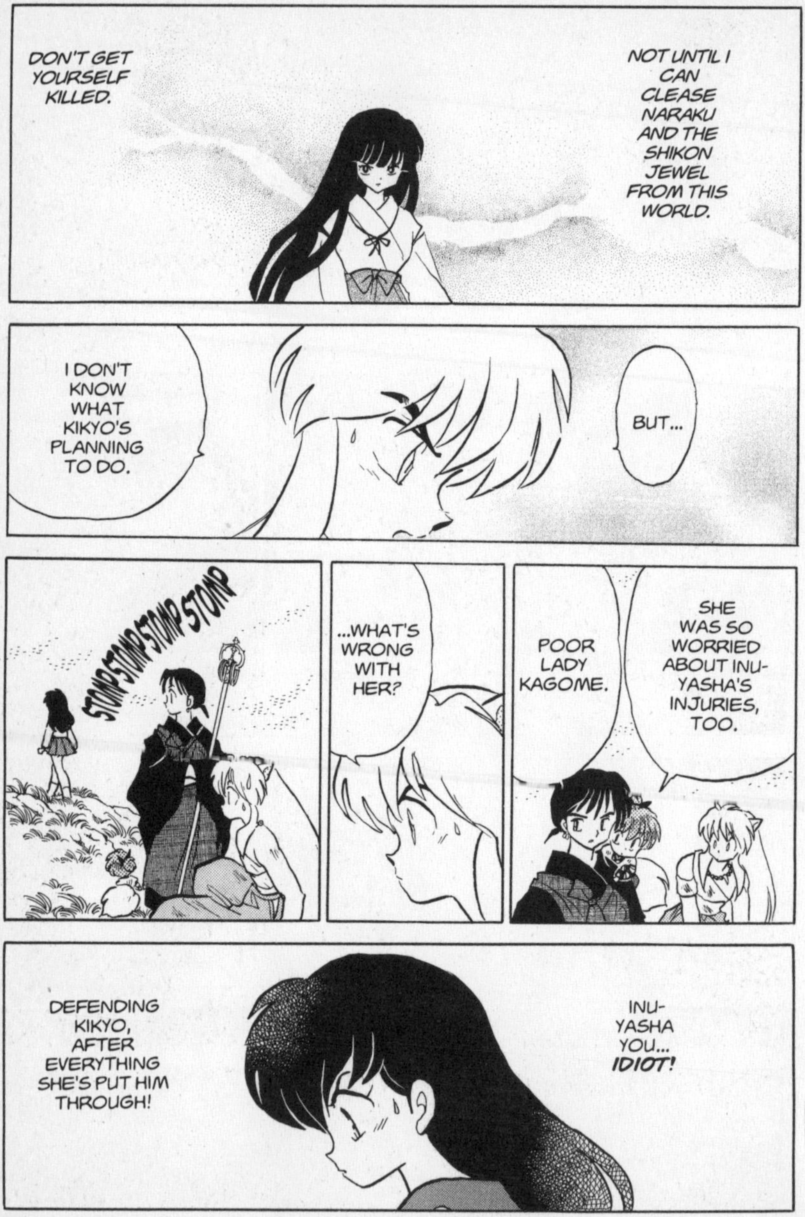
DON'T GET YOURSELF KILLED.
NOT UNTIL I CAN CLEASE NARAKU AND THE SHIKON JEWEL FROM THIS WORLD.
I DON'T KNOW WHAT KIKYO'S PLANNING TO DO.
BUT...
STOMP STOMP STOMP STOMP
...WHAT'S WRONG WITH HER?
POOR LADY KAGOME.
SHE WAS SO WORRIED ABOUT INU-YASHA'S INJURIES, TOO.
DEFENDING KIKYO, AFTER EVERYTHING SHE'S PUT HIM THROUGH!
INU-YASHA YOU... ***IDIOT!***

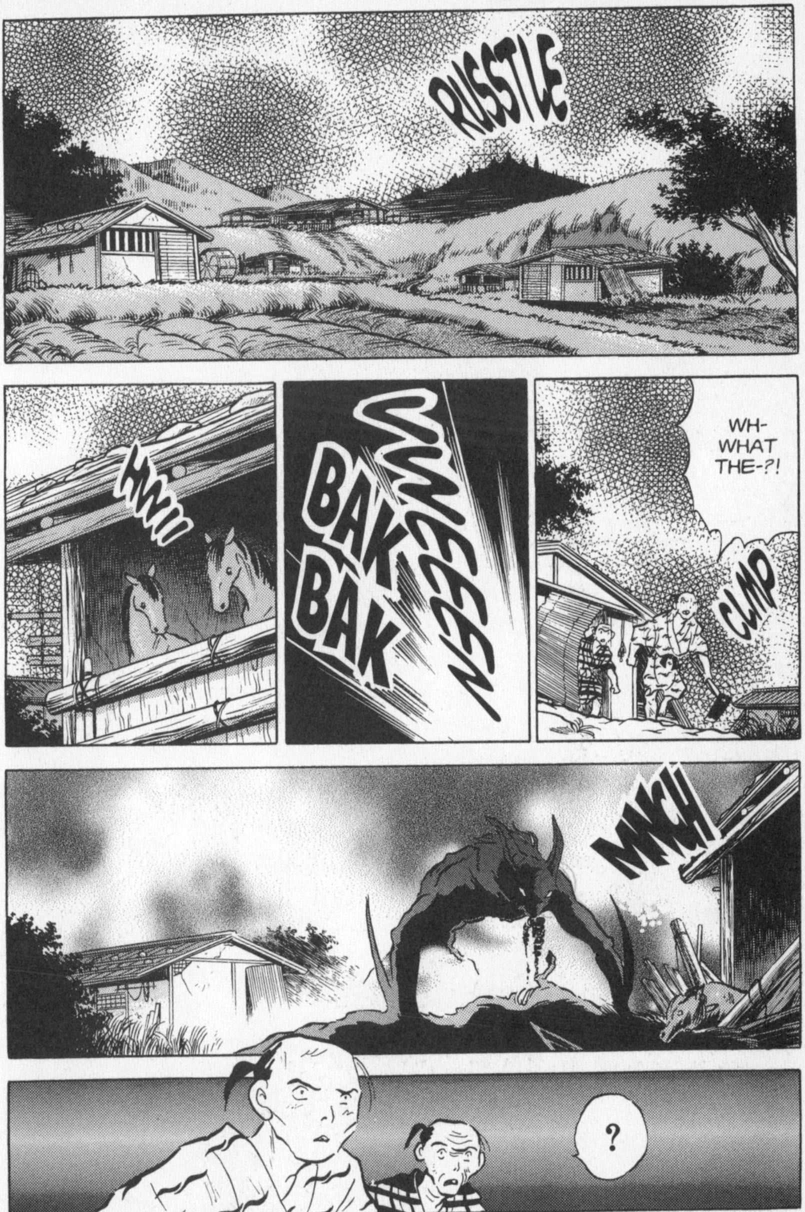
RUSSTLE
HNN!!
BAK BAK
WH- WHAT THE-?!
CLUMP
?

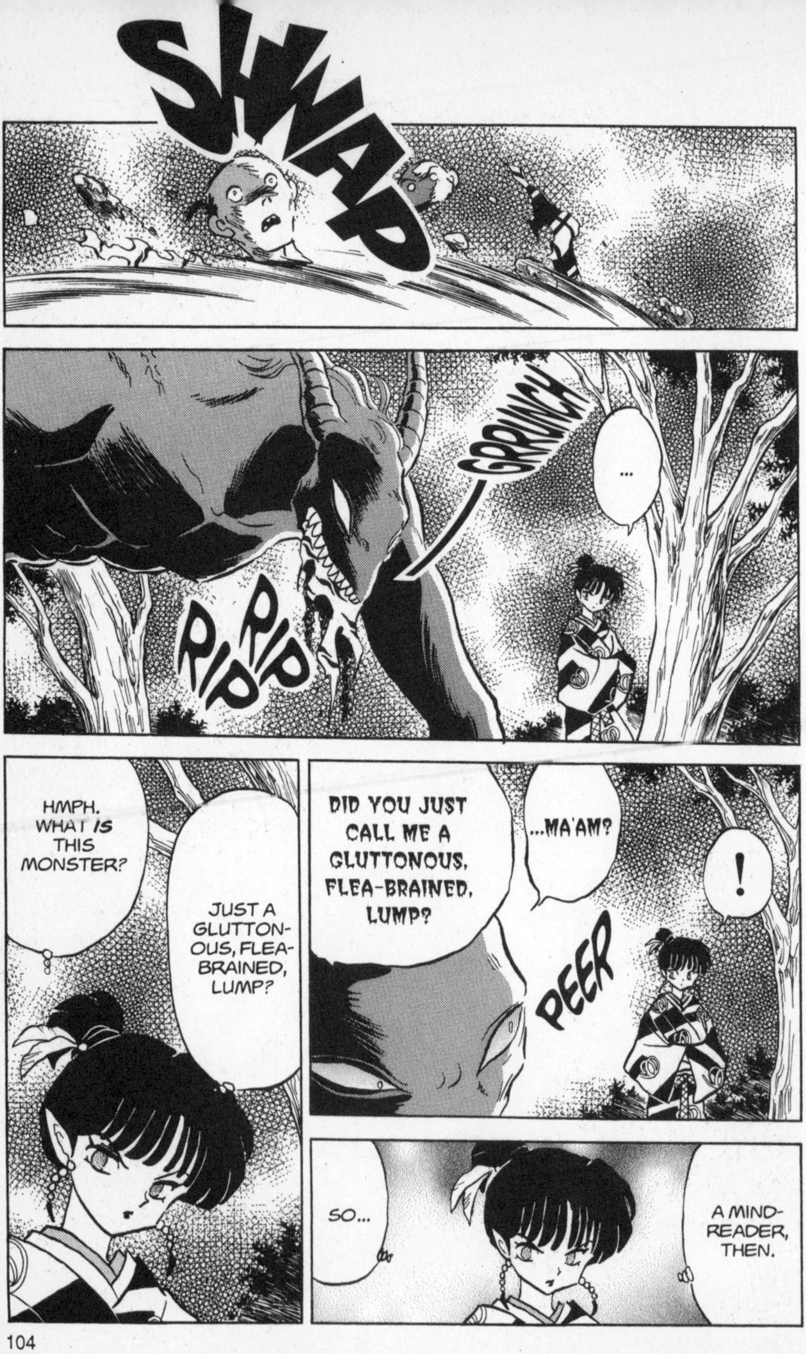
SHWAP
GRRUNCH
RIP RIP
...
HMPH. WHAT *IS* THIS MONSTER?
JUST A GLUTTONOUS, FLEA-BRAINED, LUMP?
DID YOU JUST CALL ME A GLUTTONOUS, FLEA-BRAINED, LUMP?
...MA'AM?
!
PEER
SO...
A MIND-READER, THEN.

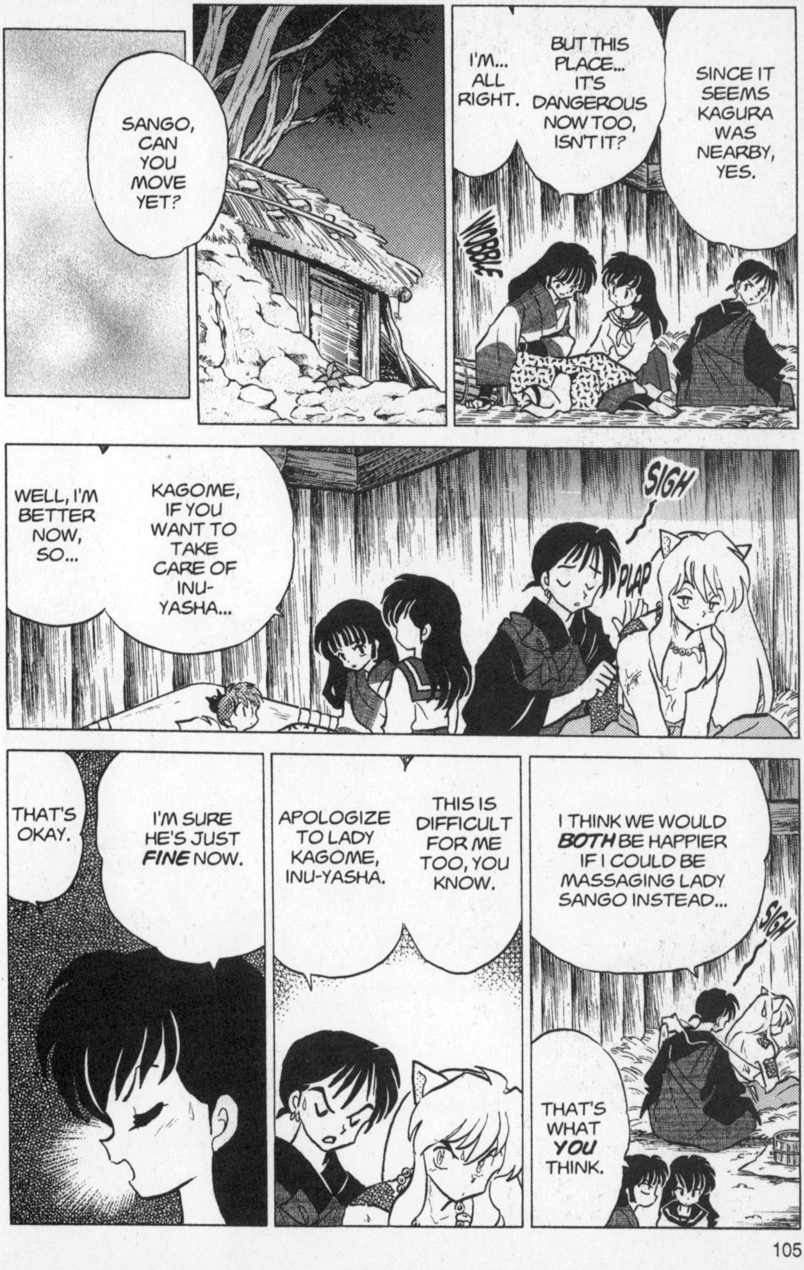
SANGO, CAN YOU MOVE YET?
I'M... ALL RIGHT.
BUT THIS PLACE... IT'S DANGEROUS NOW TOO, ISN'T IT?
SINCE IT SEEMS KAGURA WAS NEARBY, YES.
WOBBLE
WELL, I'M BETTER NOW, SO...
KAGOME, IF YOU WANT TO TAKE CARE OF INU-YASHA...
SIGH
PLAP
THAT'S OKAY.
I'M SURE HE'S JUST *FINE* NOW.
APOLOGIZE TO LADY KAGOME, INU-YASHA.
THIS IS DIFFICULT FOR ME TOO, YOU KNOW.
I THINK WE WOULD *BOTH* BE HAPPIER IF I COULD BE MASSAGING LADY SANGO INSTEAD...
SIGH
THAT'S WHAT *YOU* THINK.

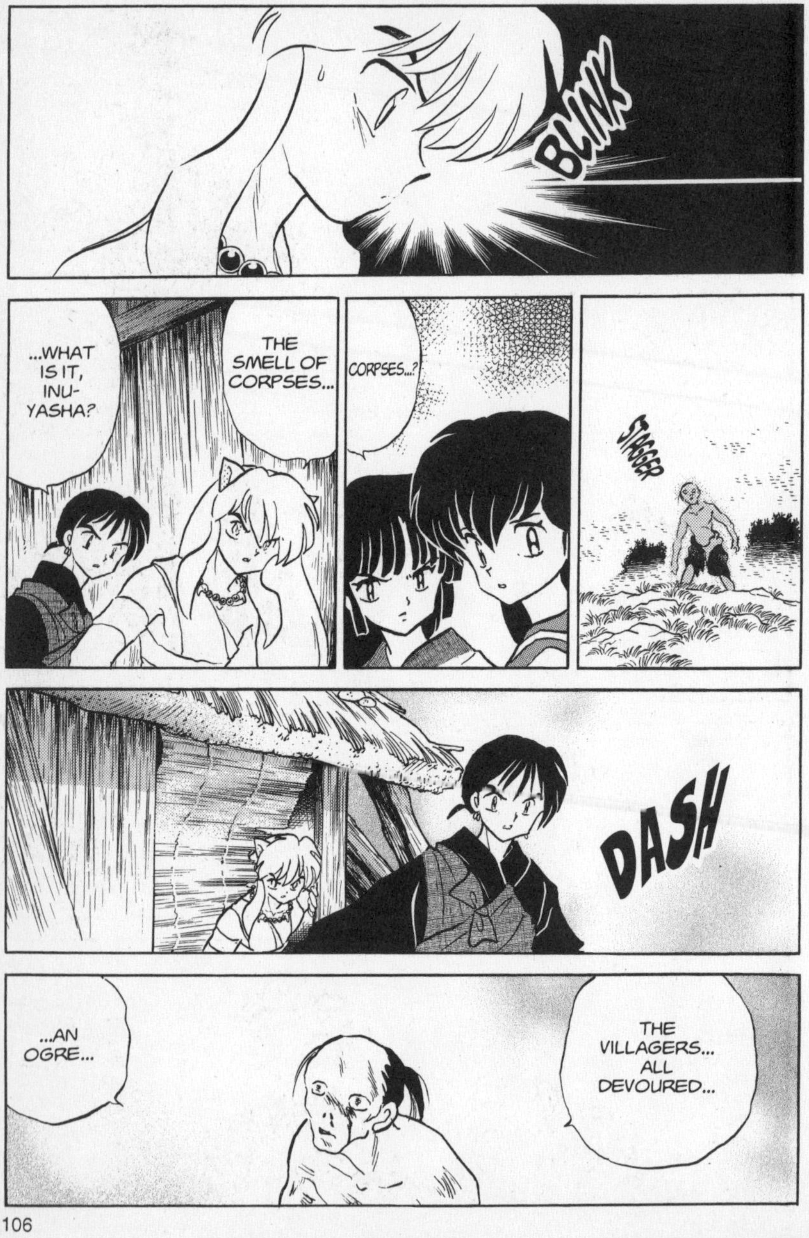
BLINK
...WHAT IS IT, INU-YASHA?
THE SMELL OF CORPSES...
CORPSES...?
STAGGER
DASH
...AN OGRE...
THE VILLAGERS... ALL DEVOURED...

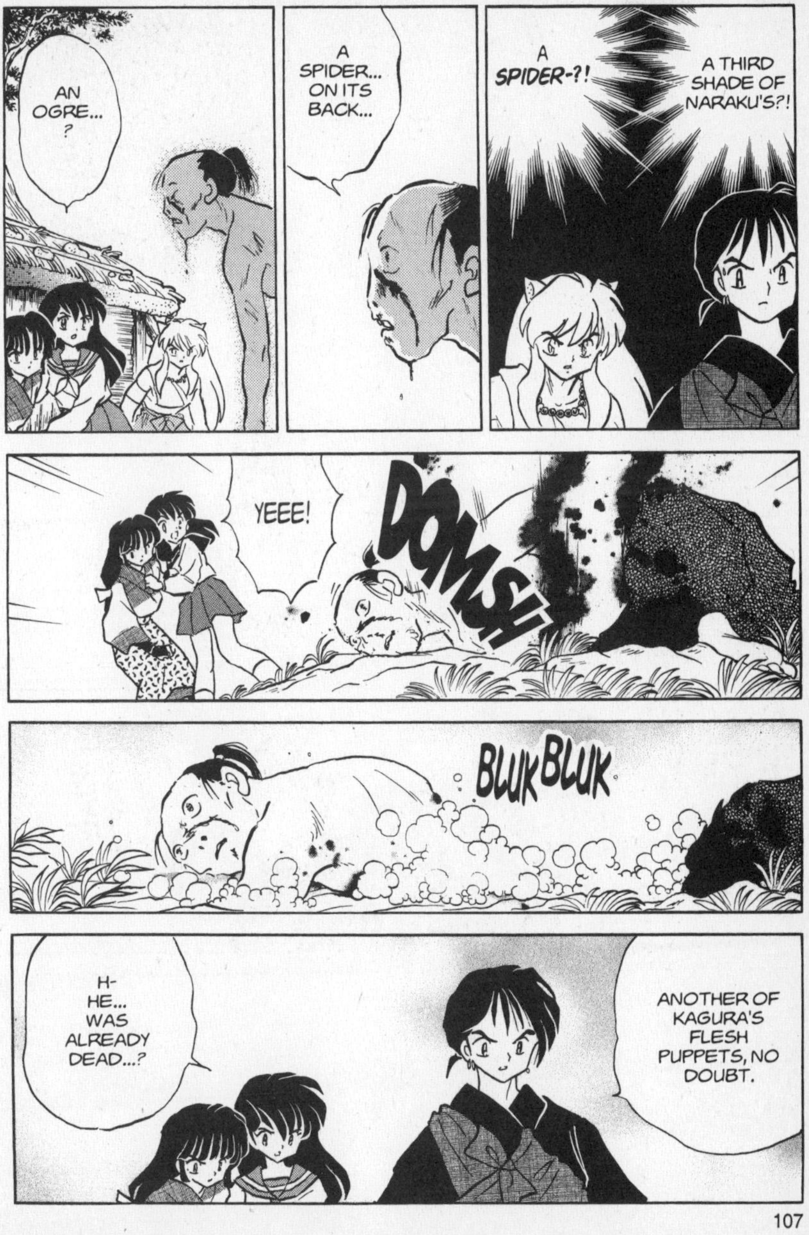
AN OGRE... ?
A SPIDER... ON ITS BACK...
A SPIDER-?!
A THIRD SHADE OF NARAKU'S?!
YEEE!
DOMSH
BLUK BLUK
H- HE... WAS ALREADY DEAD...?
ANOTHER OF KAGURA'S FLESH PUPPETS, NO DOUBT.

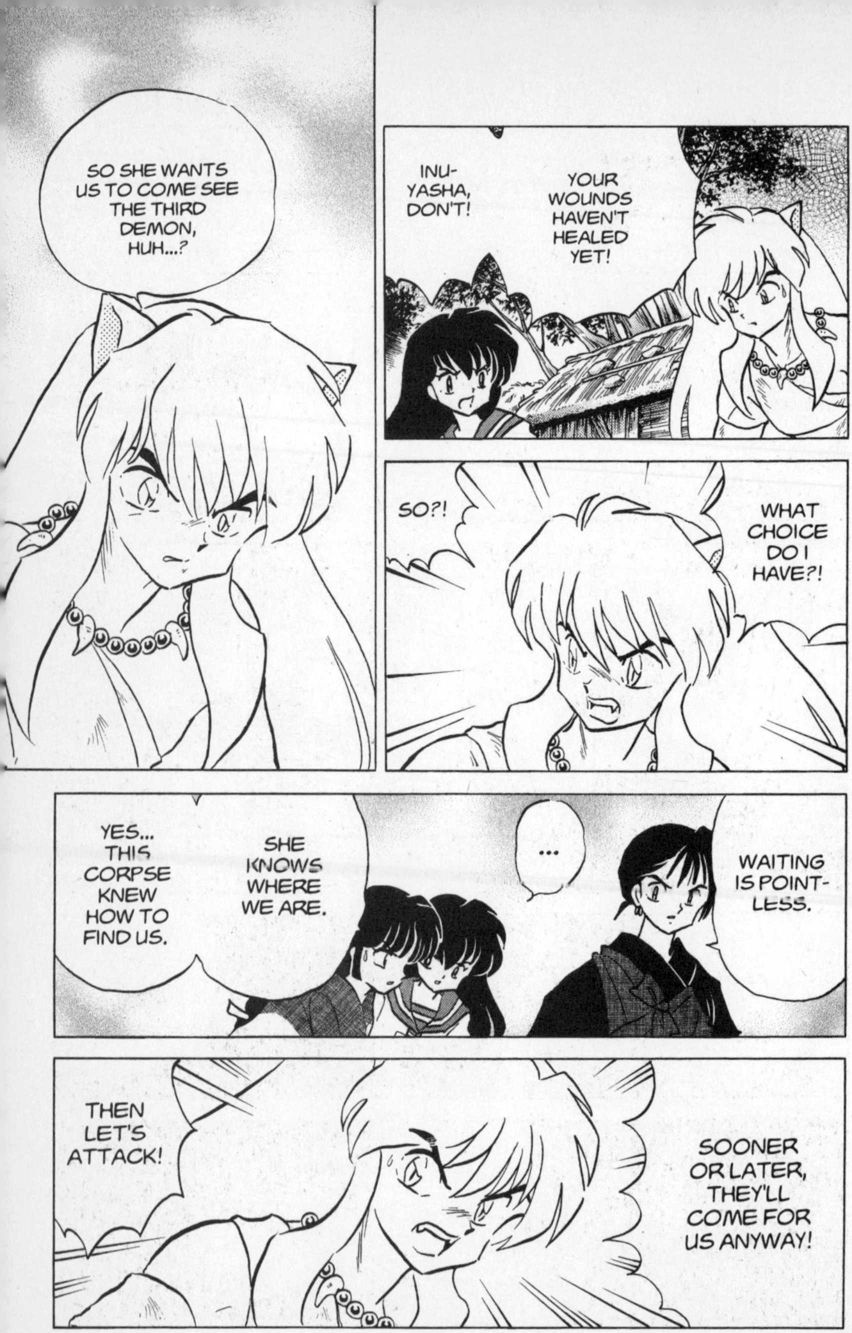
SO SHE WANTS US TO COME SEE THE THIRD DEMON, HUH...?
INU-YASHA, DON'T!
YOUR WOUNDS HAVEN'T HEALED YET!
SO?!
WHAT CHOICE DO I HAVE?!
YES... THIS CORPSE KNEW HOW TO FIND US.
SHE KNOWS WHERE WE ARE.
...
WAITING IS POINT-LESS.
THEN LET'S ATTACK!
SOONER OR LATER, THEY'LL COME FOR US ANYWAY!

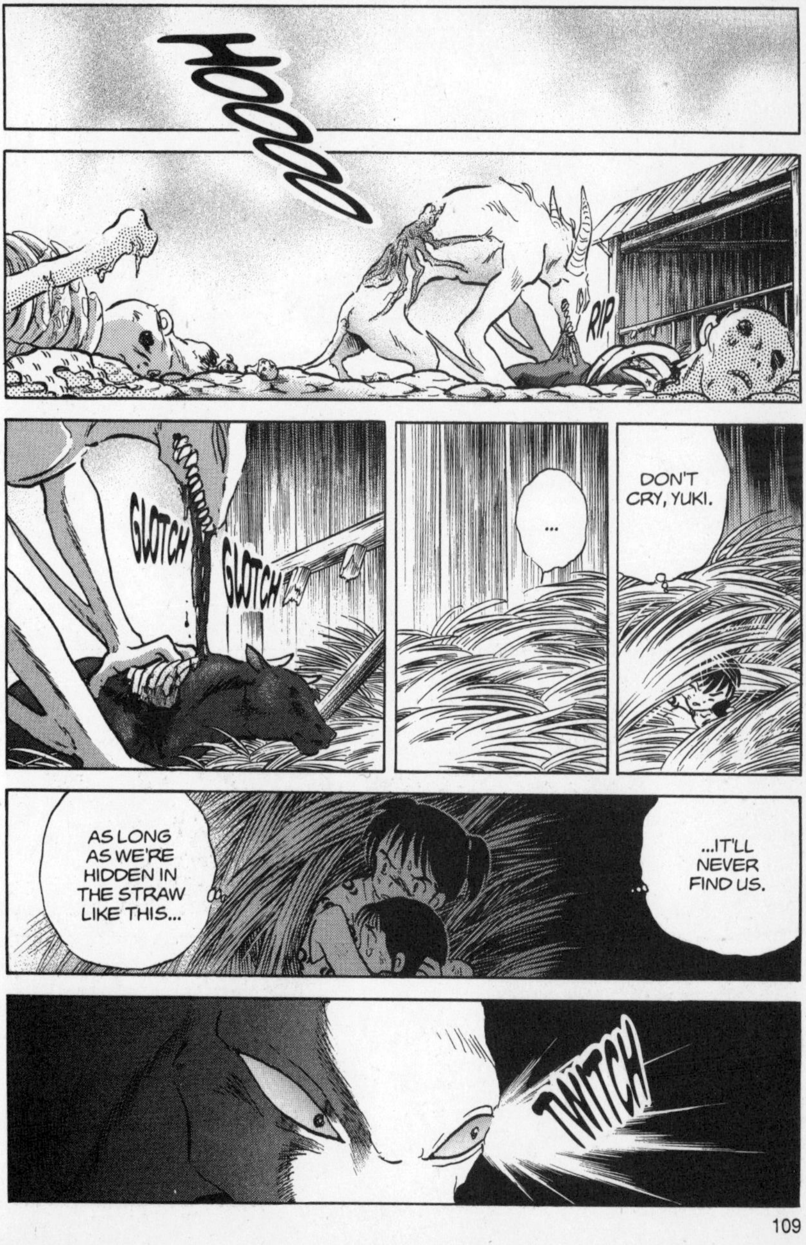
HOOOO
RIP
GLOTCH
GLOTCH
...
DON'T CRY, YUKI.
AS LONG AS WE'RE HIDDEN IN THE STRAW LIKE THIS...
...IT'LL NEVER FIND US.
TWITCH

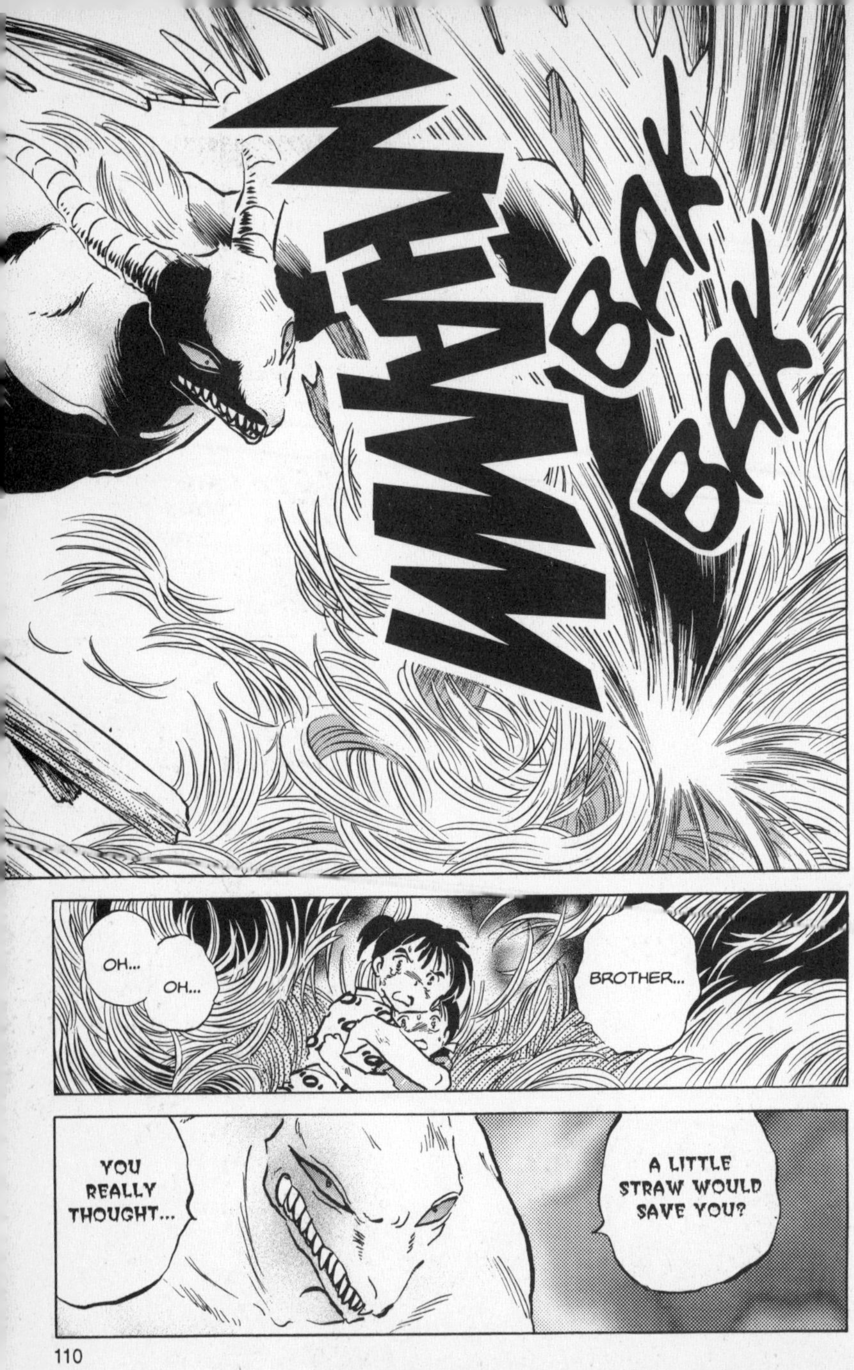
WHAMM
BAK BAK
OH...
OH...
BROTHER...
YOU REALLY THOUGHT...
A LITTLE STRAW WOULD SAVE YOU?

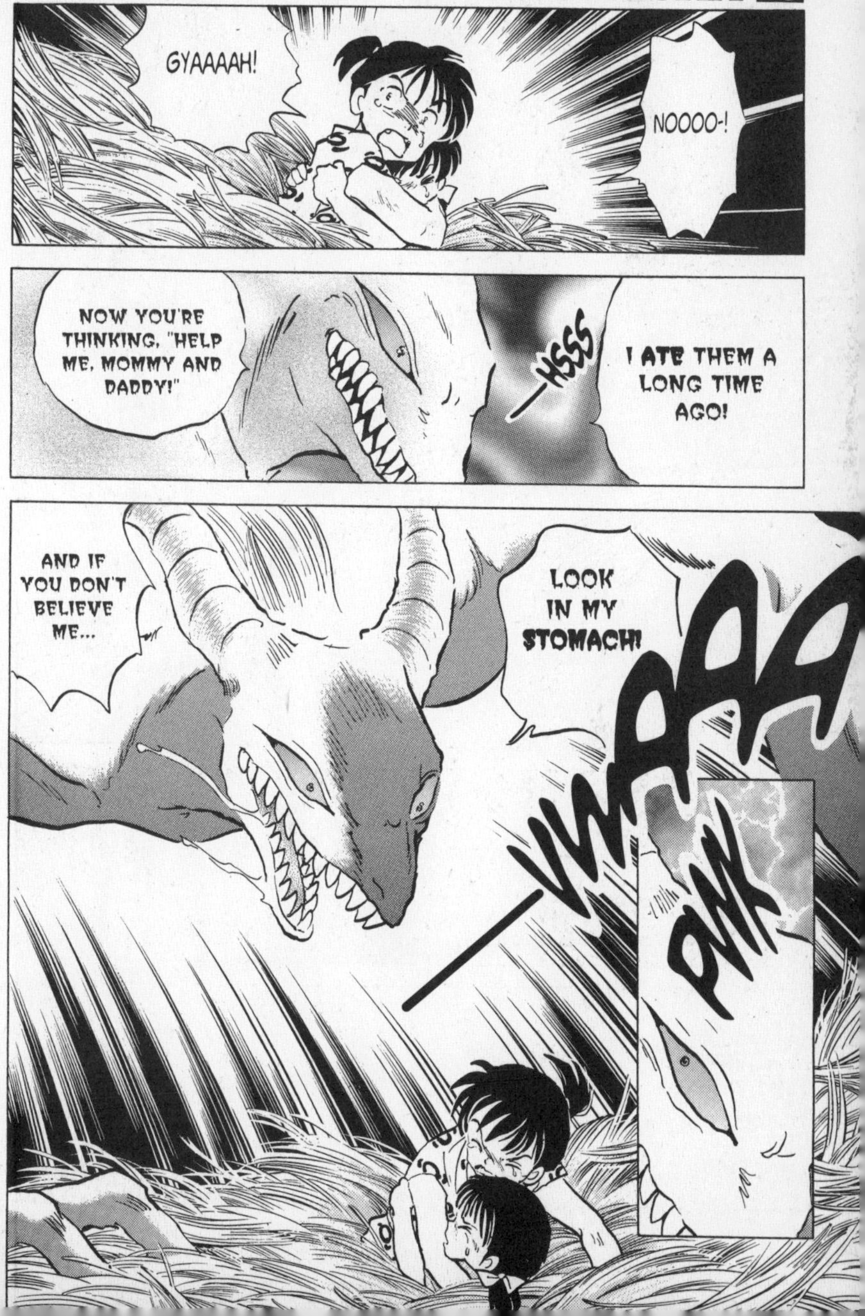
GYAAAAH!
NOOOO-!
NOW YOU'RE THINKING, "HELP ME, MOMMY AND DADDY!"
—HSSS
I ATE THEM A LONG TIME AGO!
AND IF YOU DON'T BELIEVE ME...
LOOK IN MY STOMACH!
—VVVRRR
RNNK

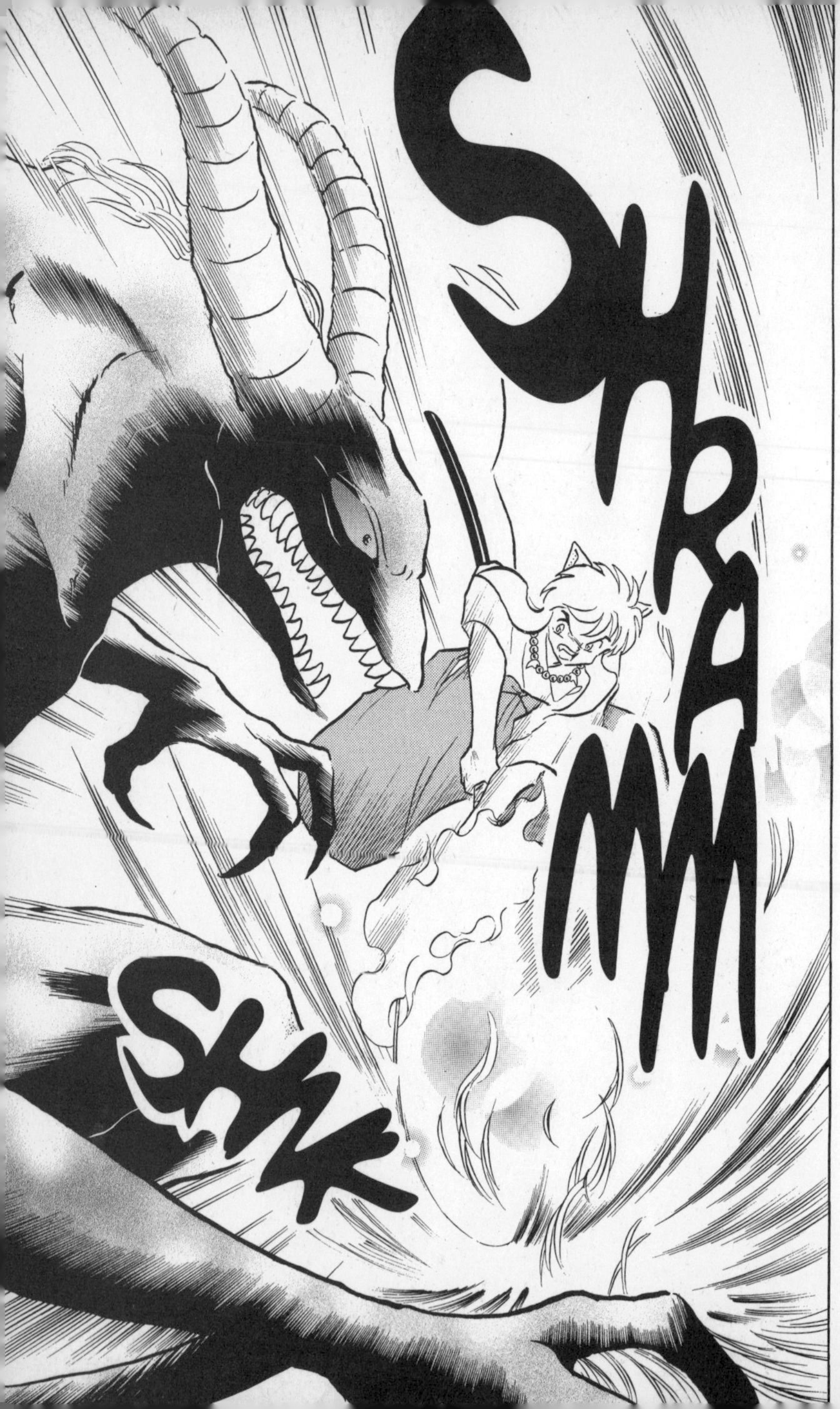
SHRAMM
SHK

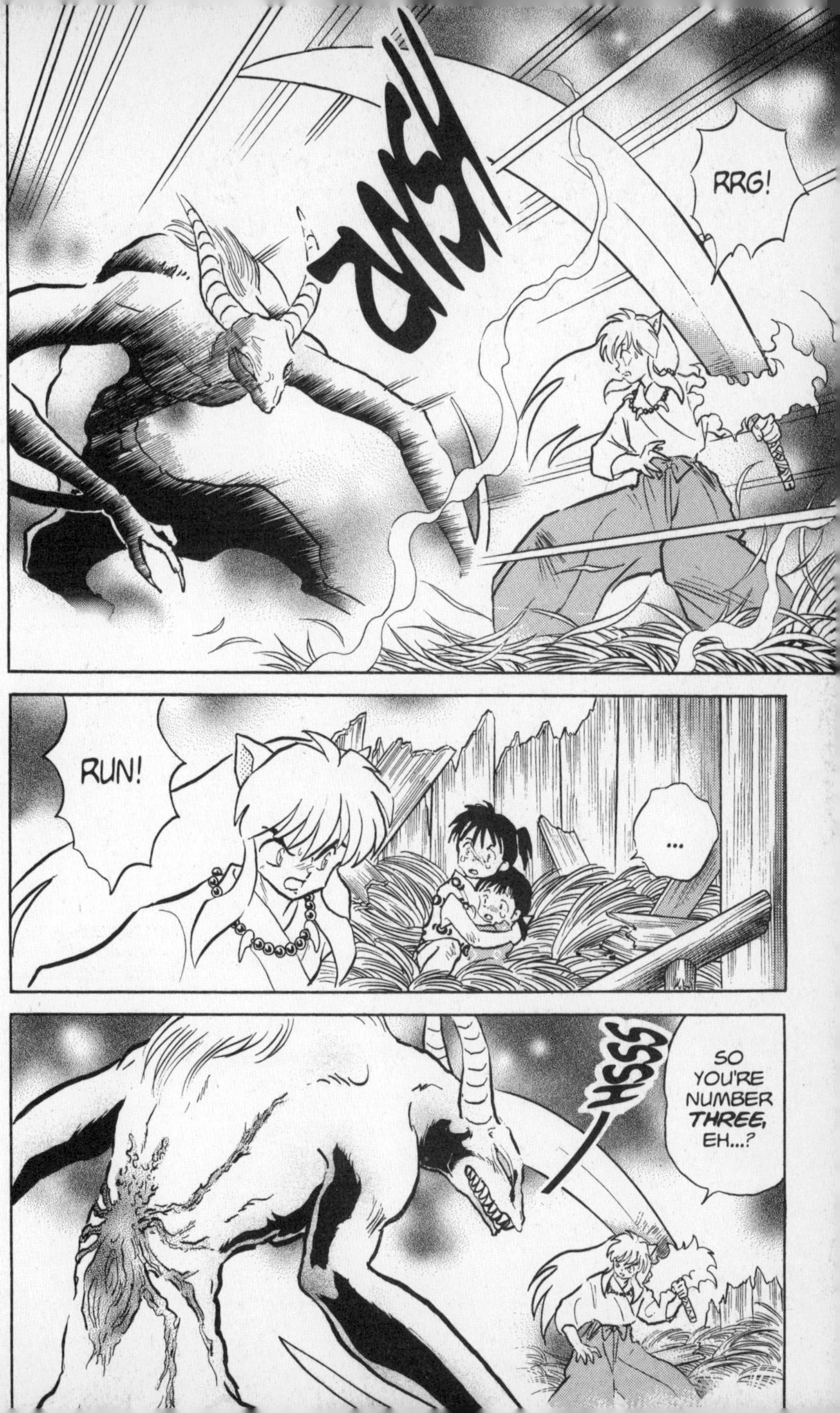
RRG!
RUN!
...
SO YOU'RE NUMBER THREE, EH...?
HSSSS

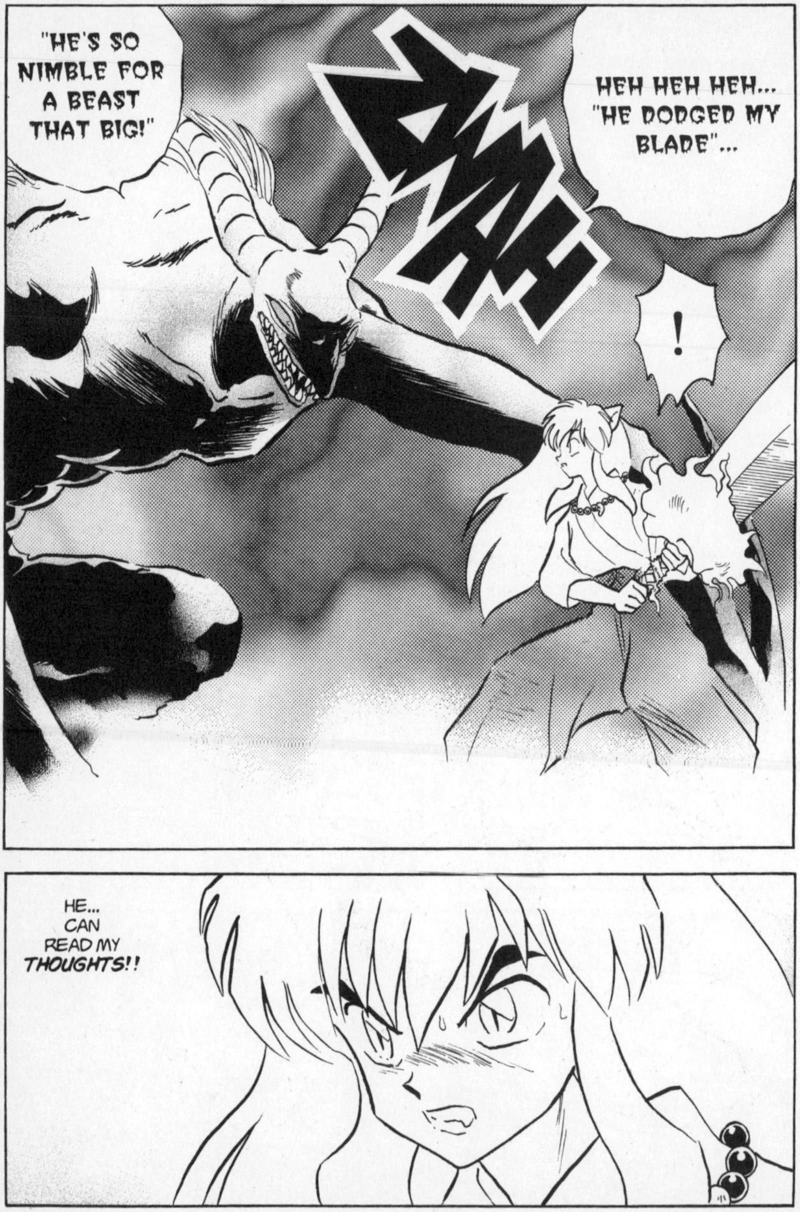
"HE'S SO NIMBLE FOR A BEAST THAT BIG!"
HEH HEH HEH... "HE DODGED MY BLADE"...
!
HE... CAN READ MY ***THOUGHTS!!***

SCROLL SEVEN

THE MIND-READER

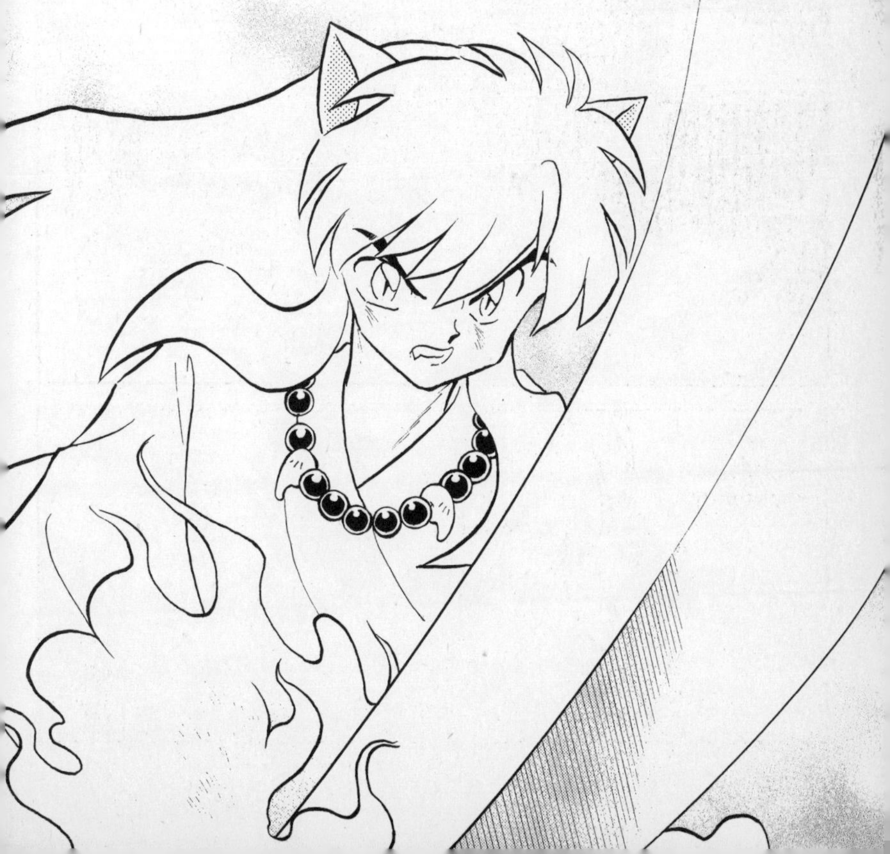

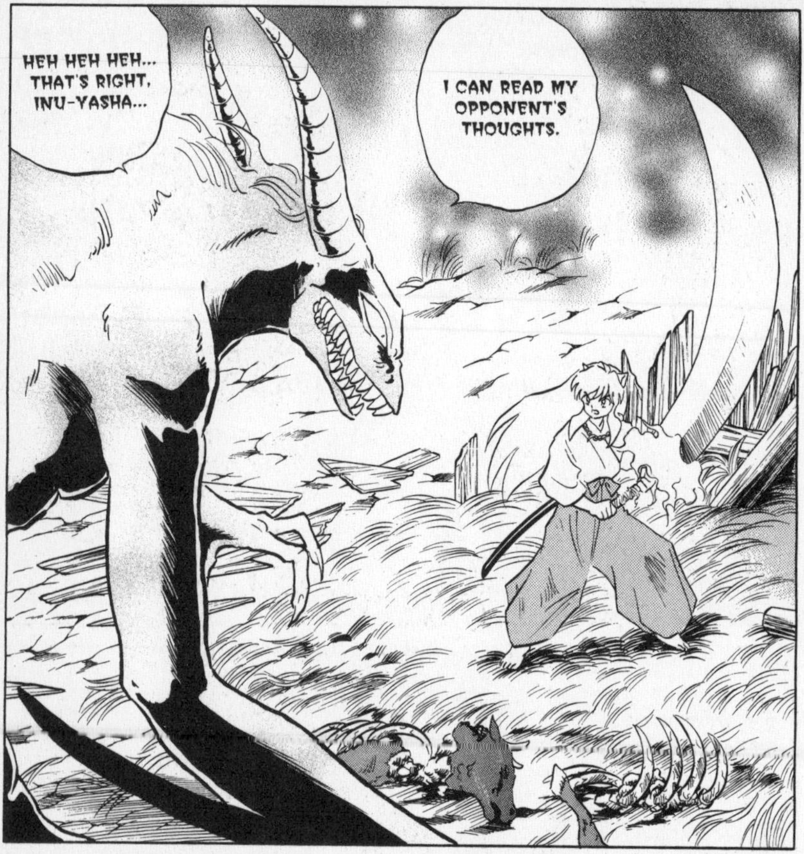
HEH HEH HEH... THAT'S RIGHT, INU-YASHA...
I CAN READ MY OPPONENT'S THOUGHTS.
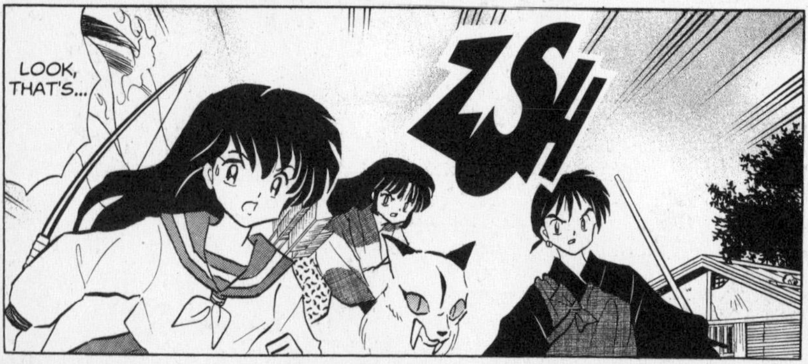
LOOK, THAT'S...
ZSH

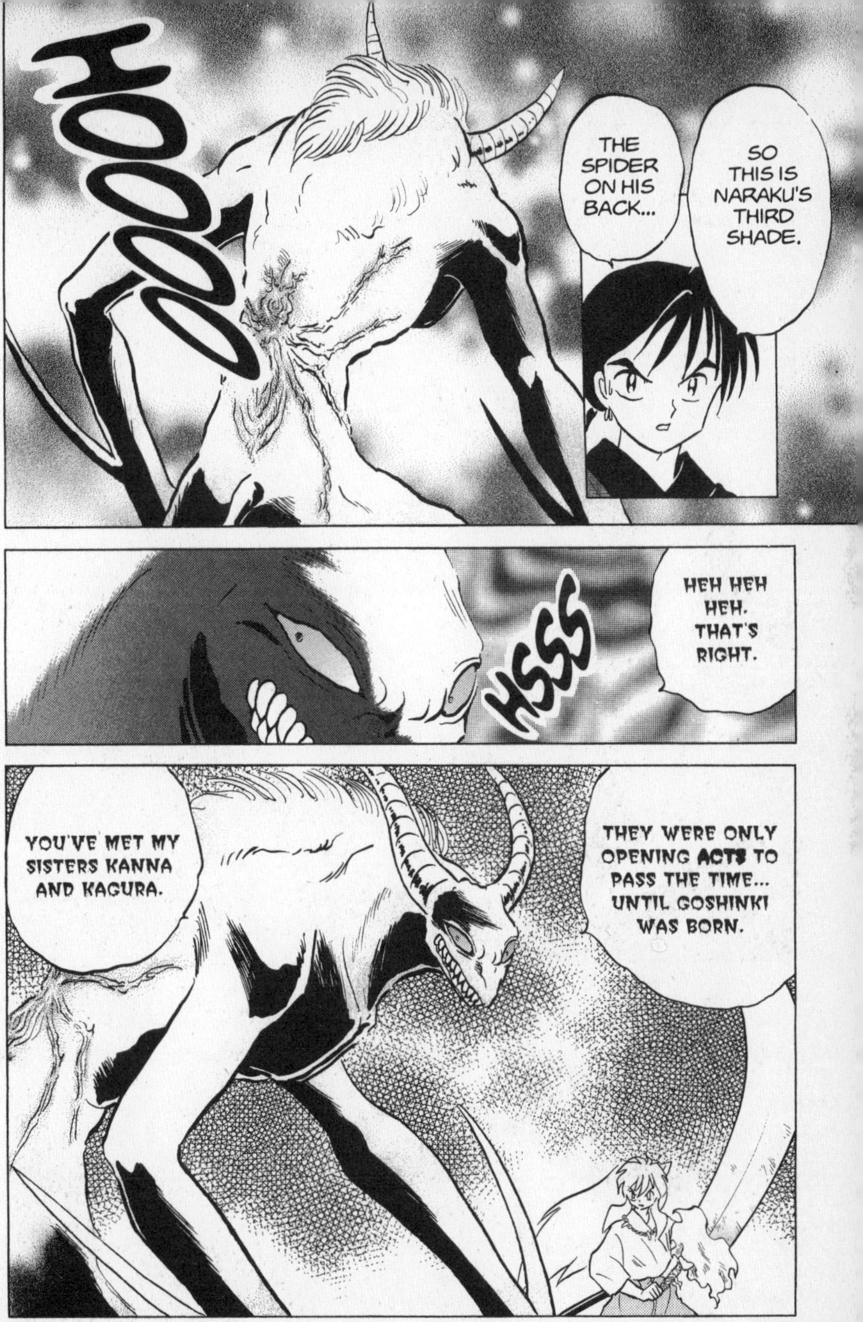
HOOOO
THE SPIDER ON HIS BACK...
SO THIS IS NARAKU'S THIRD SHADE.
HSSS
HEH HEH HEH. THAT'S RIGHT.
YOU'VE MET MY SISTERS KANNA AND KAGURA.
THEY WERE ONLY OPENING **ACTS** TO PASS THE TIME... UNTIL GOSHINKI WAS BORN.

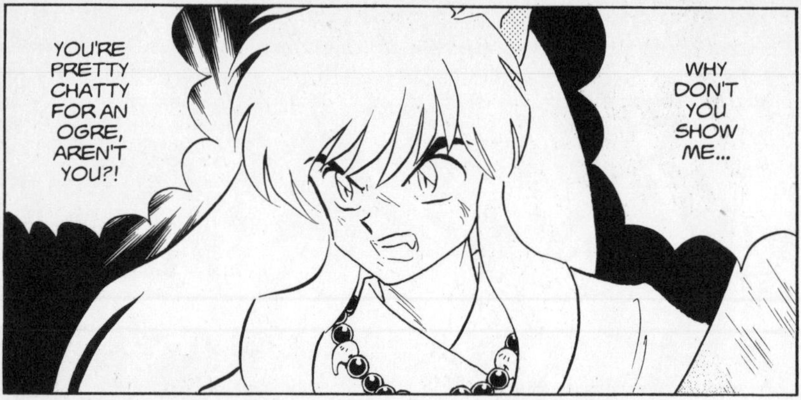
YOU'RE PRETTY CHATTY FOR AN OGRE, AREN'T YOU?!
WHY DON'T YOU SHOW ME...

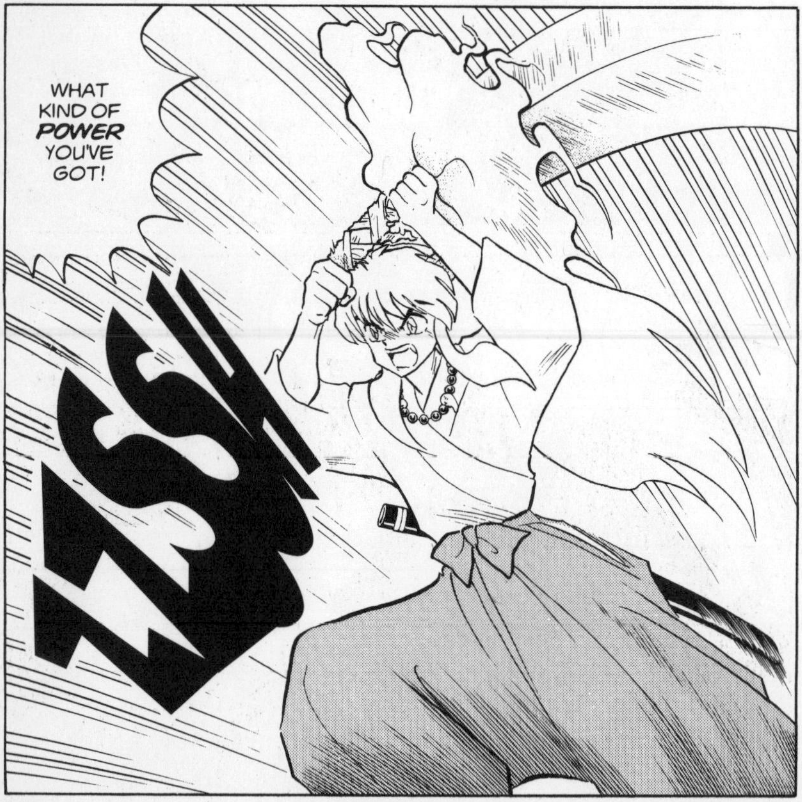
WHAT KIND OF ***POWER*** YOU'VE GOT!
ZSH

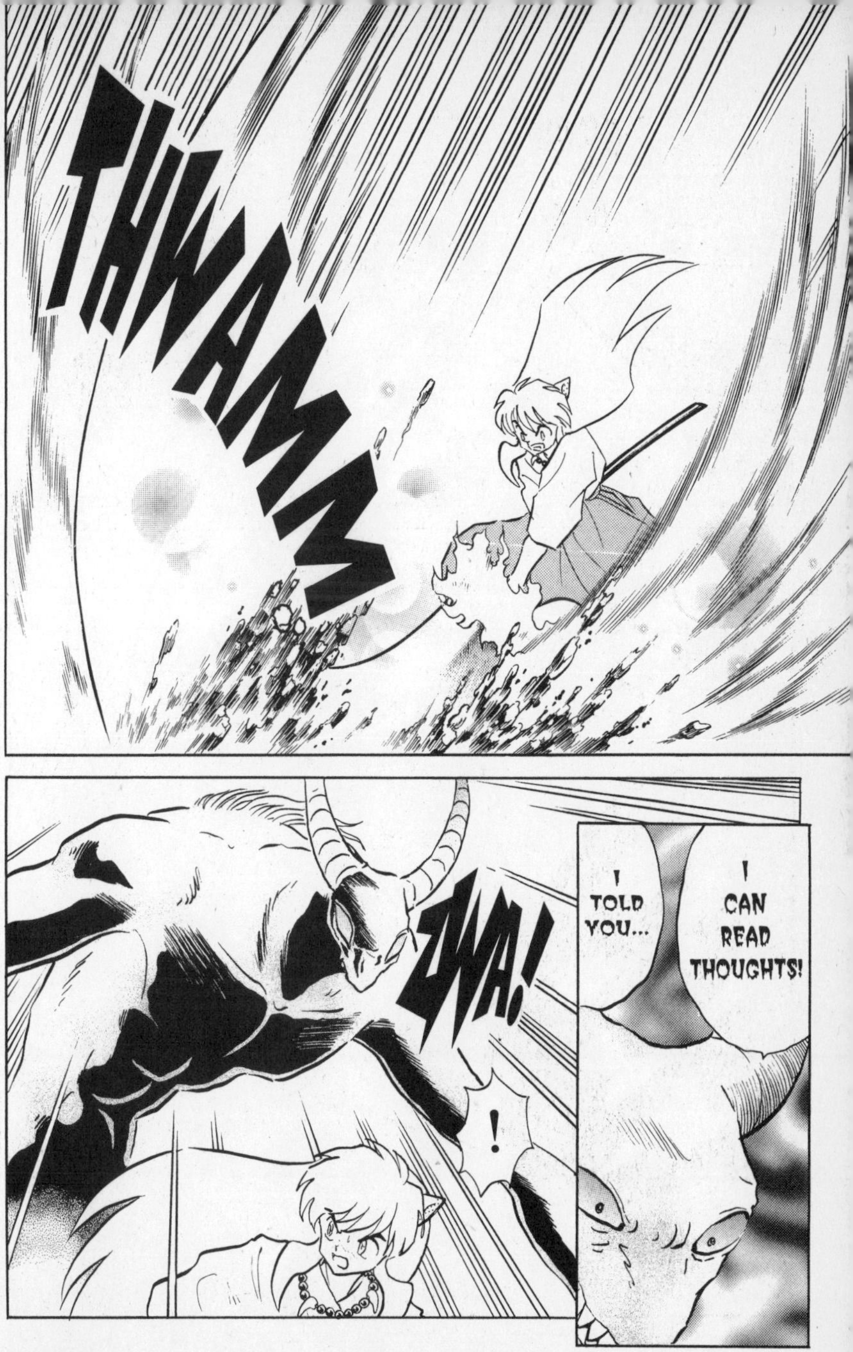
THWAMM
ZWA!
!
I TOLD YOU...
I CAN READ THOUGHTS!

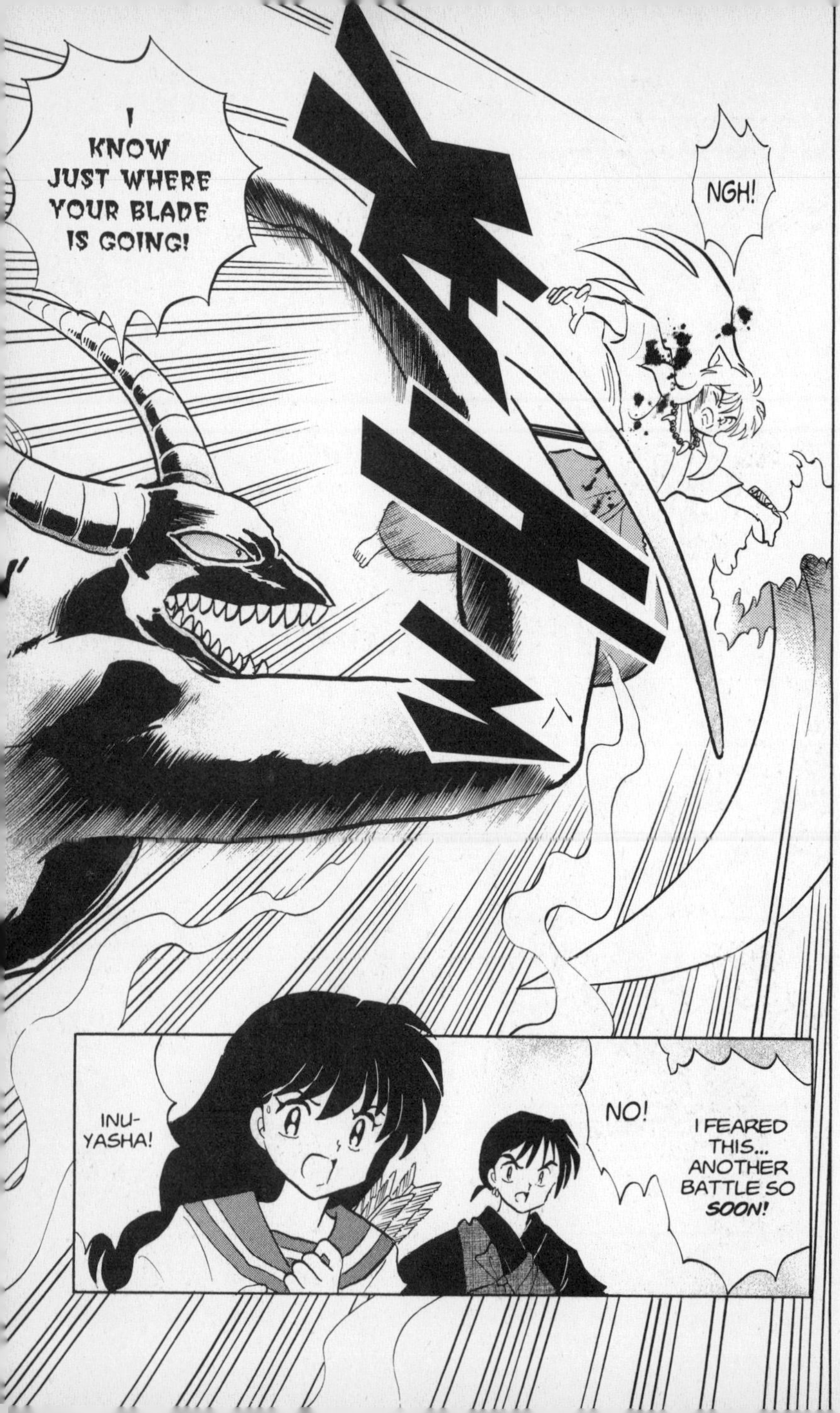
I KNOW JUST WHERE YOUR BLADE IS GOING!
NGH!
INU-YASHA!
NO!
I FEARED THIS... ANOTHER BATTLE SO *SOON!*

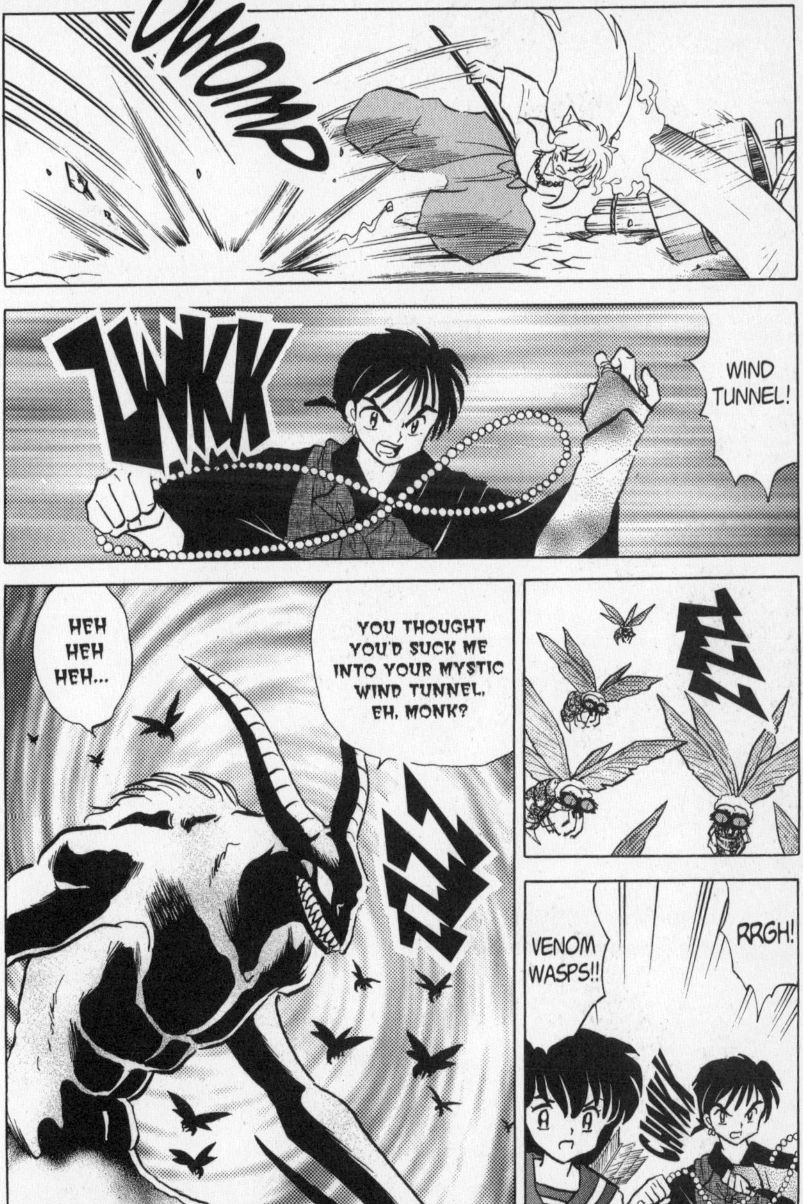
DWOMP
TWKK
WIND TUNNEL!
HEH HEH HEH...
YOU THOUGHT YOU'D SUCK ME INTO YOUR MYSTIC WIND TUNNEL, EH, MONK?
VENOM WASPS!!
RRGH!

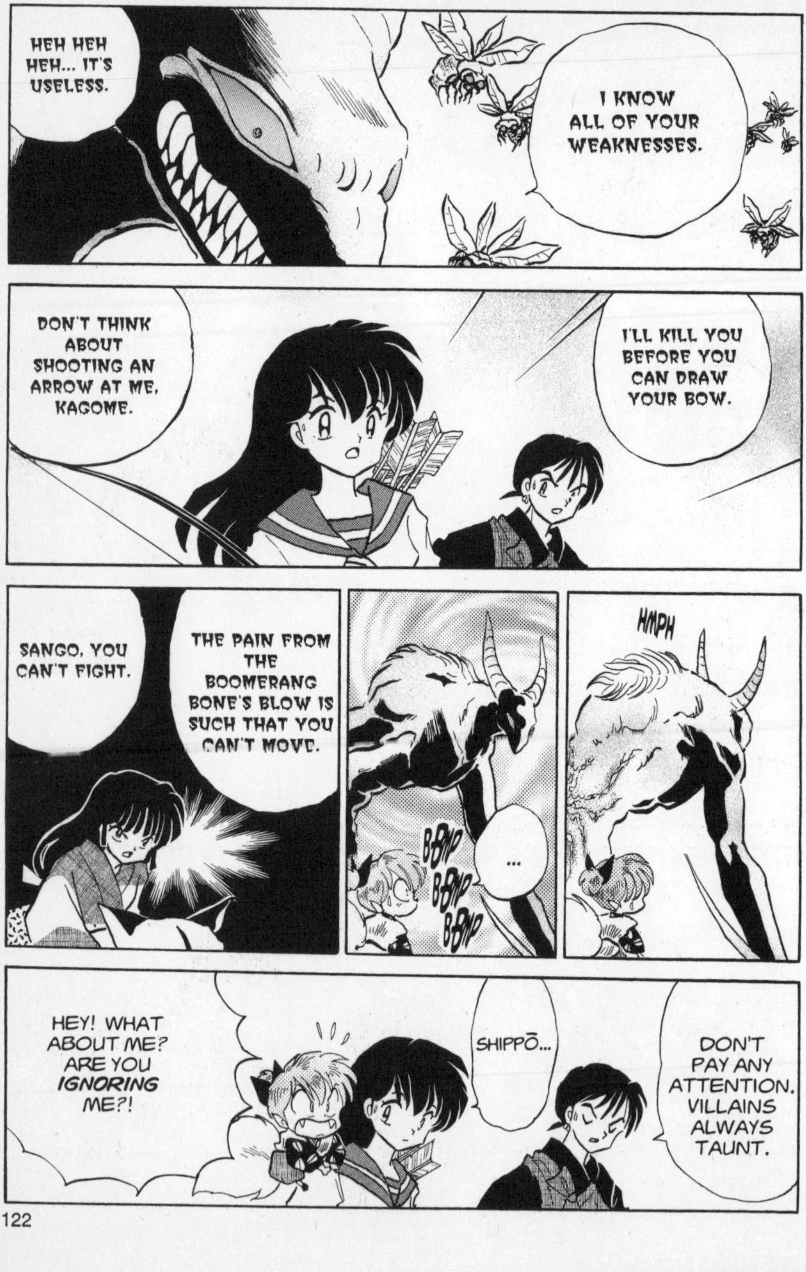
HEH HEH HEH... IT'S USELESS.
I KNOW ALL OF YOUR WEAKNESSES.
DON'T THINK ABOUT SHOOTING AN ARROW AT ME, KAGOME.
I'LL KILL YOU BEFORE YOU CAN DRAW YOUR BOW.
SANGO, YOU CAN'T FIGHT.
THE PAIN FROM THE BOOMERANG BONE'S BLOW IS SUCH THAT YOU CAN'T MOVE.
B-BMP B-BMP B-BMP
...
HMPH
HEY! WHAT ABOUT ME? ARE YOU *IGNORING* ME?!
SHIPPŌ...
DON'T PAY ANY ATTENTION. VILLAINS ALWAYS TAUNT.

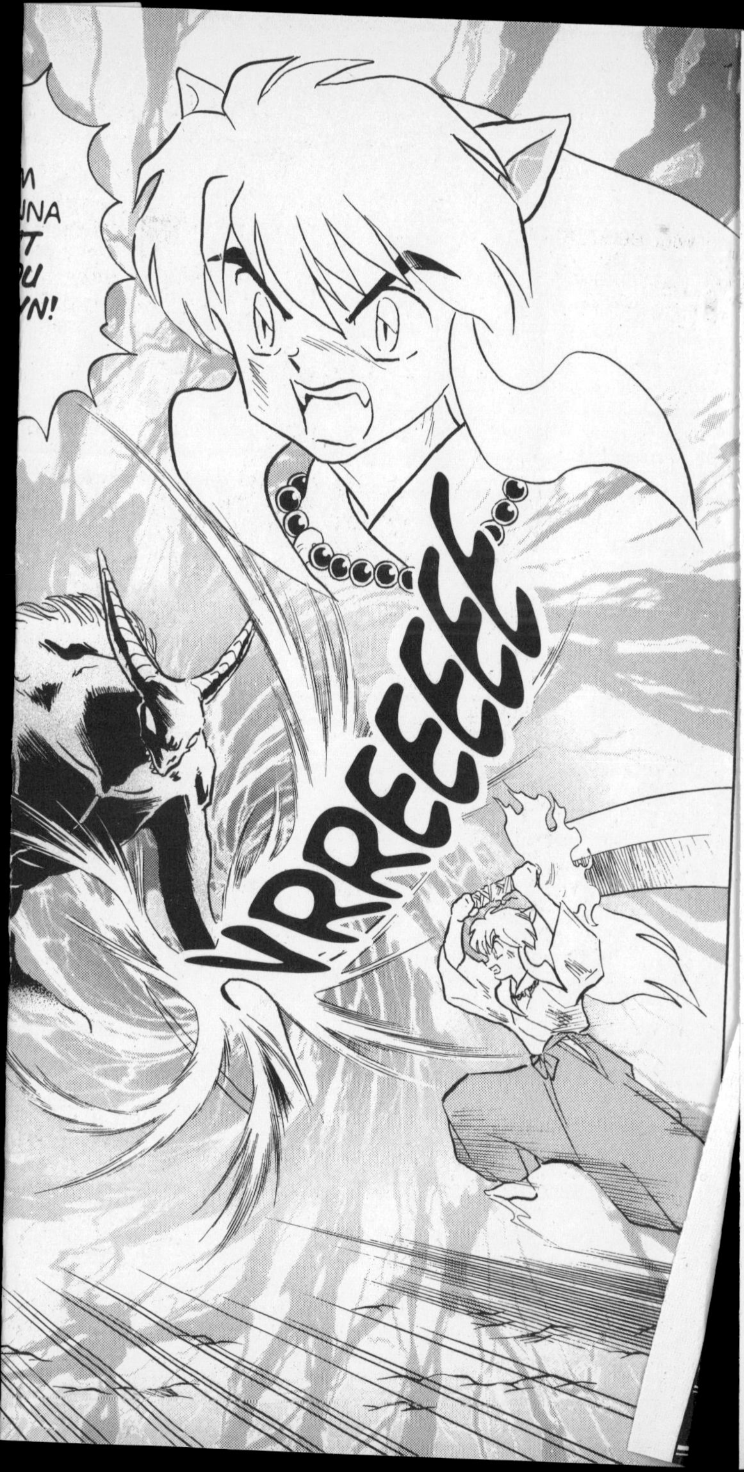
VRREEEEEE

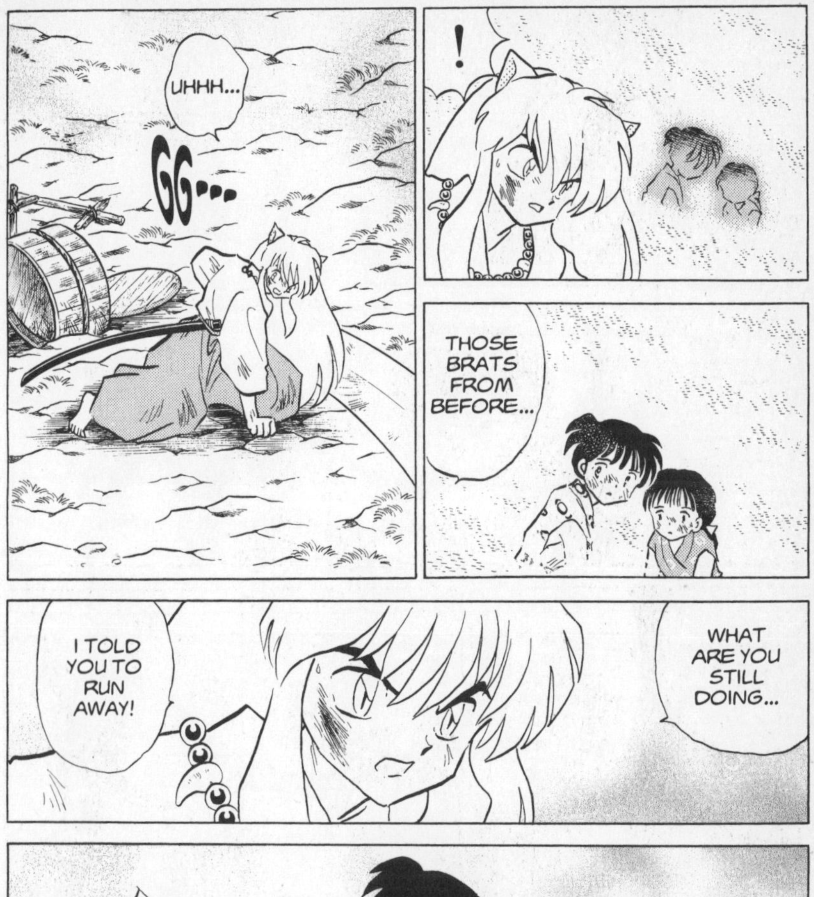
UHHH...
GG...
!
THOSE BRATS FROM BEFORE...
I TOLD YOU TO RUN AWAY!
WHAT ARE YOU STILL DOING...
?!

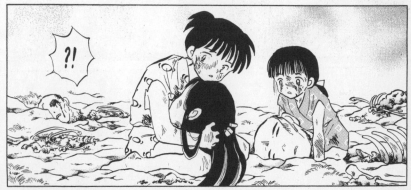

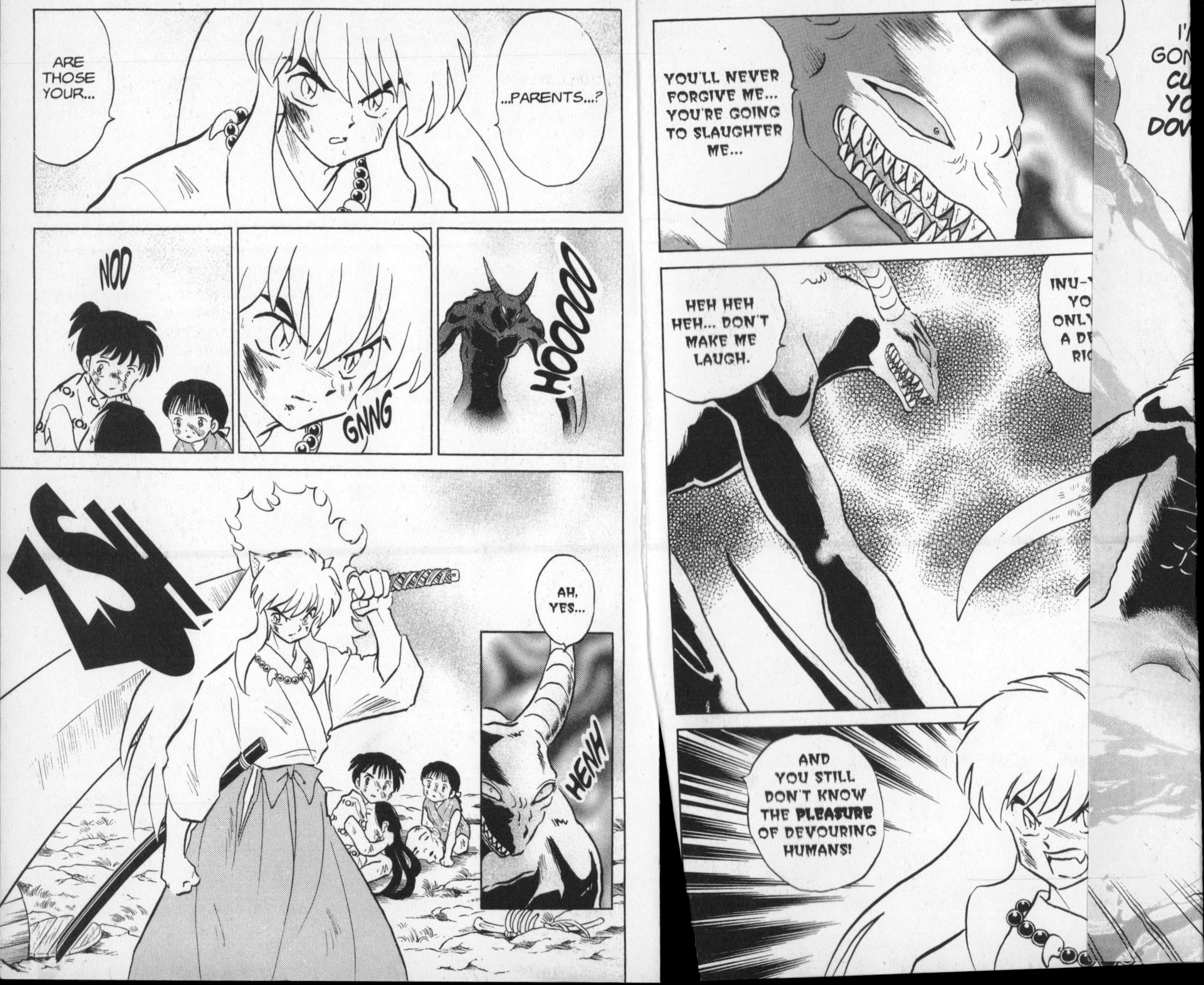
ARE THOSE YOUR...
...PARENTS...?
NOD
GNNG
HOOOOO
TSH
AH, YES...
HENH
YOU'LL NEVER FORGIVE ME... YOU'RE GOING TO SLAUGHTER ME...
HEH HEH HEH... DON'T MAKE ME LAUGH.
AND YOU STILL DON'T KNOW THE **PLEASURE** OF DEVOURING HUMANS!

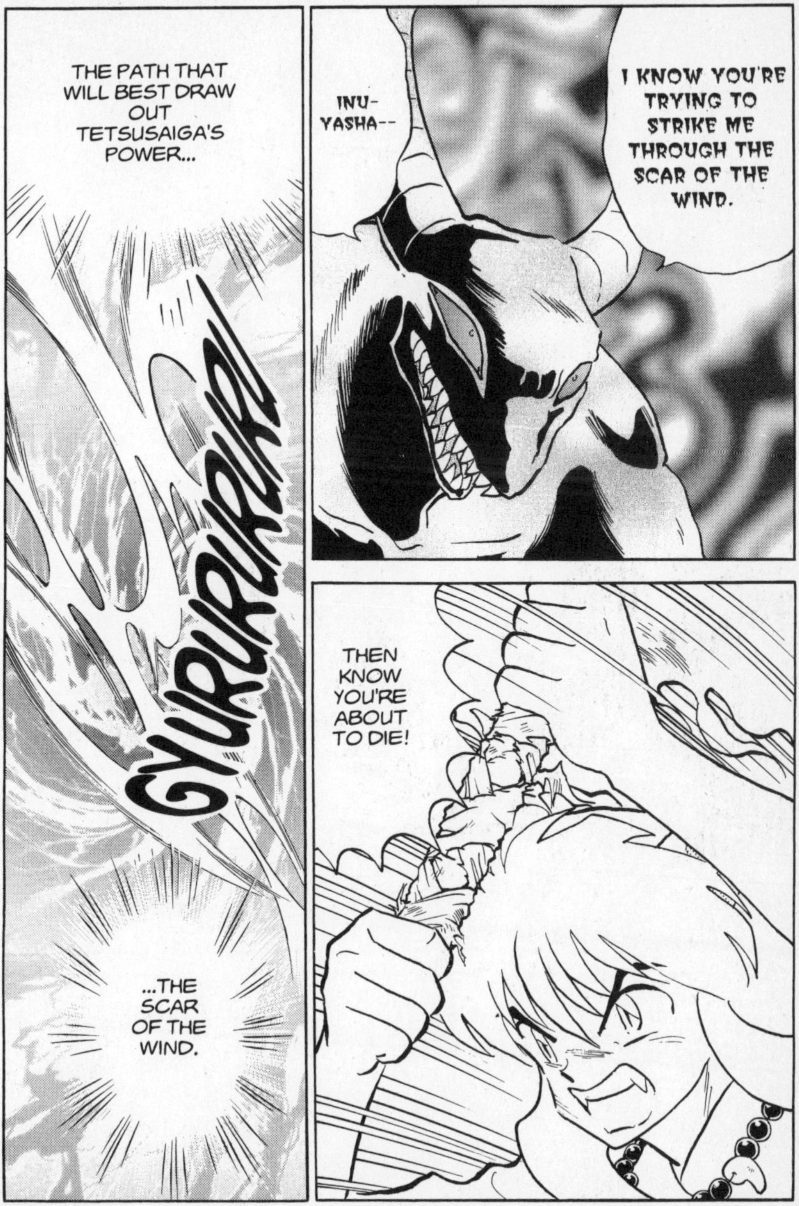
THE PATH THAT WILL BEST DRAW OUT TETSUSAIGA'S POWER...
GYURURURU!
...THE SCAR OF THE WIND.
INU-YASHA--
I KNOW YOU'RE TRYING TO STRIKE ME THROUGH THE SCAR OF THE WIND.
THEN KNOW YOU'RE ABOUT TO DIE!

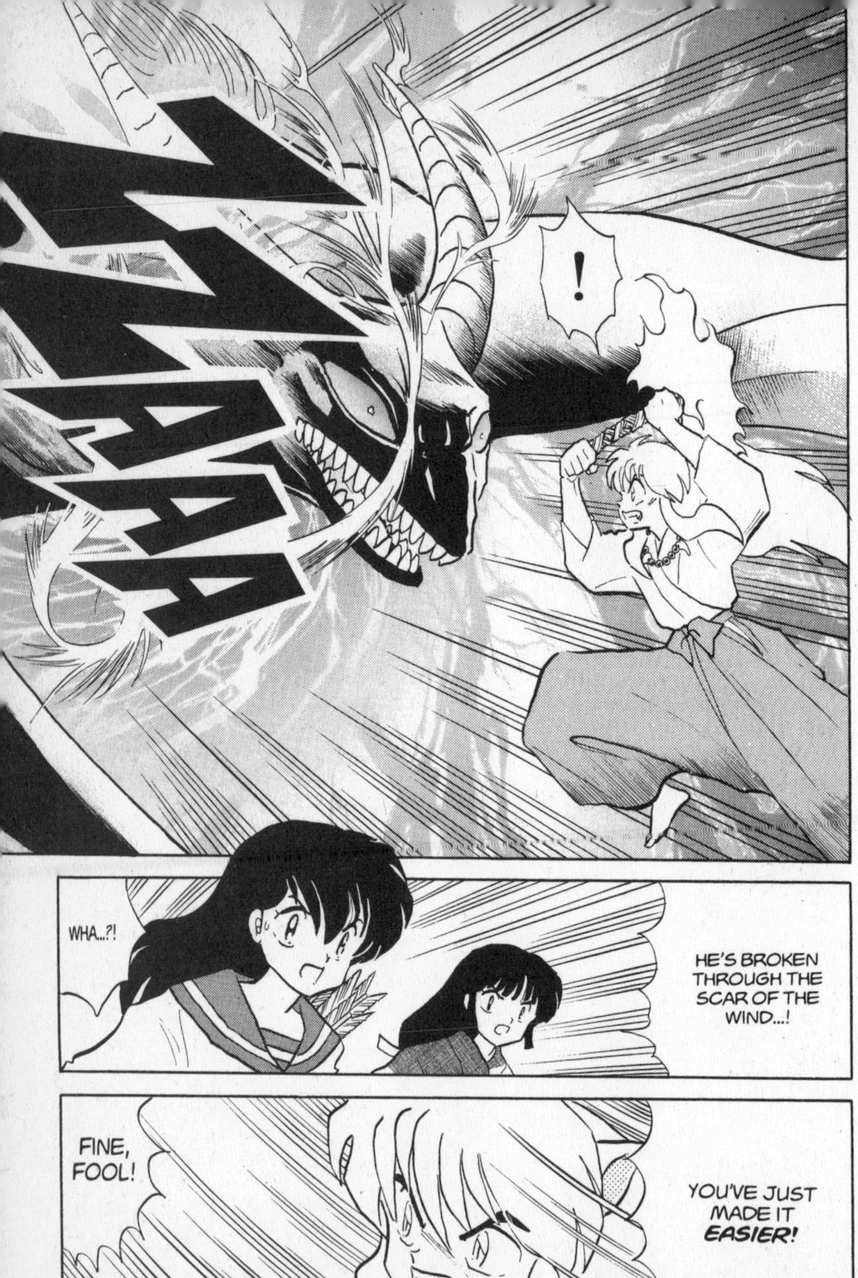
!
WHA...?!
HE'S BROKEN THROUGH THE SCAR OF THE WIND...!
FINE, FOOL!
YOU'VE JUST MADE IT *EASIER!*

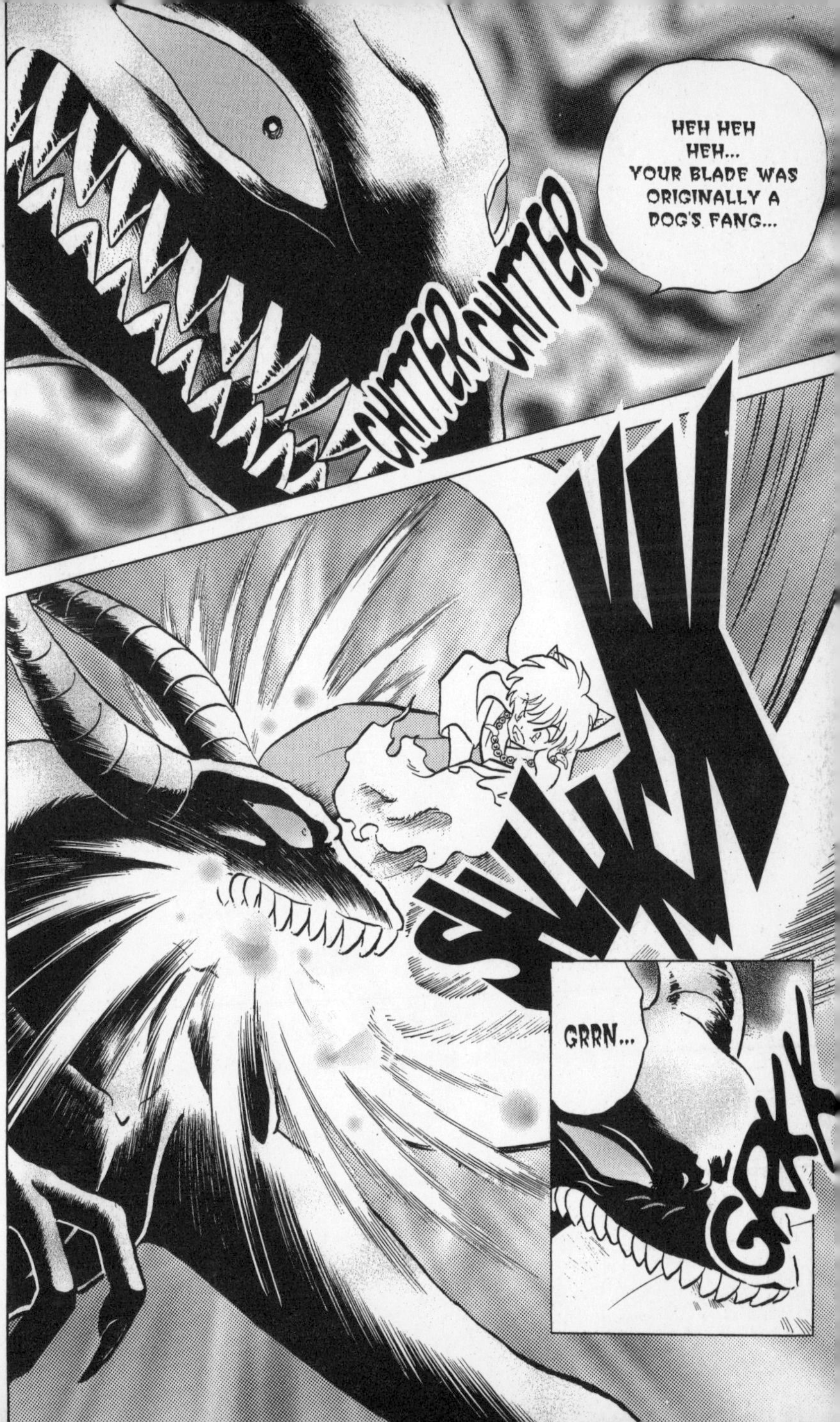
CHITTER CHITTER
HEH HEH HEH... YOUR BLADE WAS ORIGINALLY A DOG'S FANG...
CHINK
GRRN...
GAK

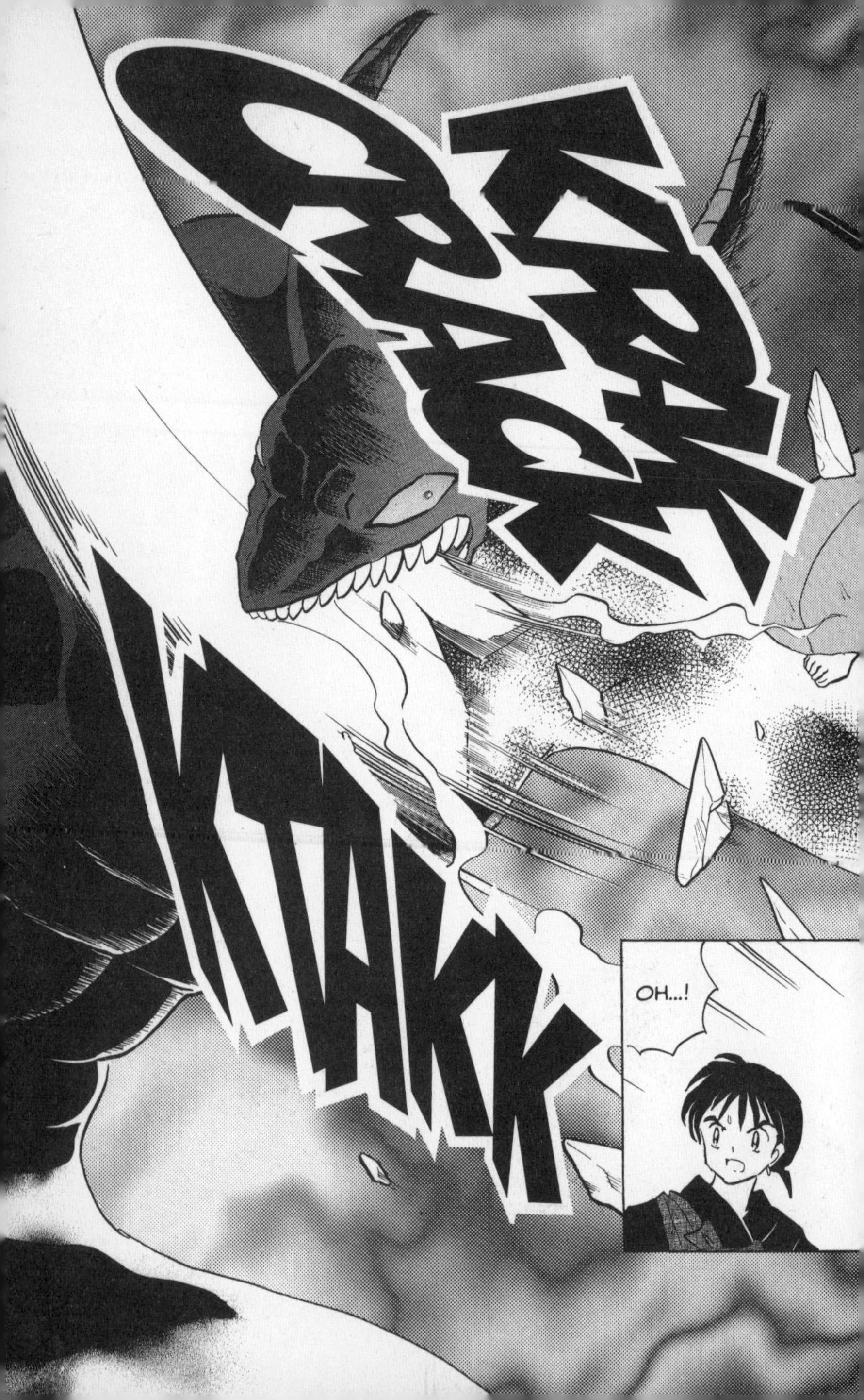
CRAAACK!
KTAKK
OH...!

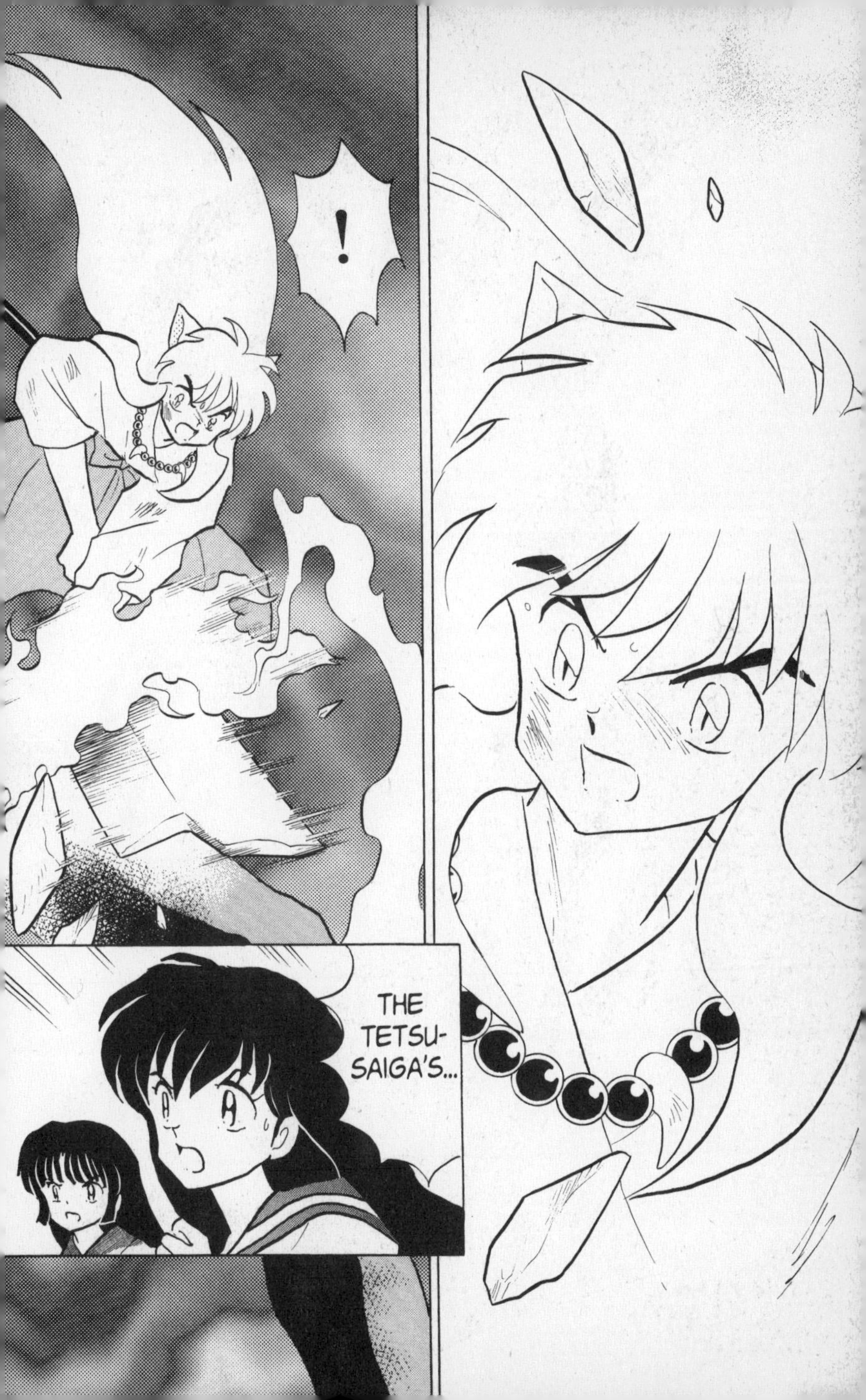
!
THE TETSU-SAIGA'S...

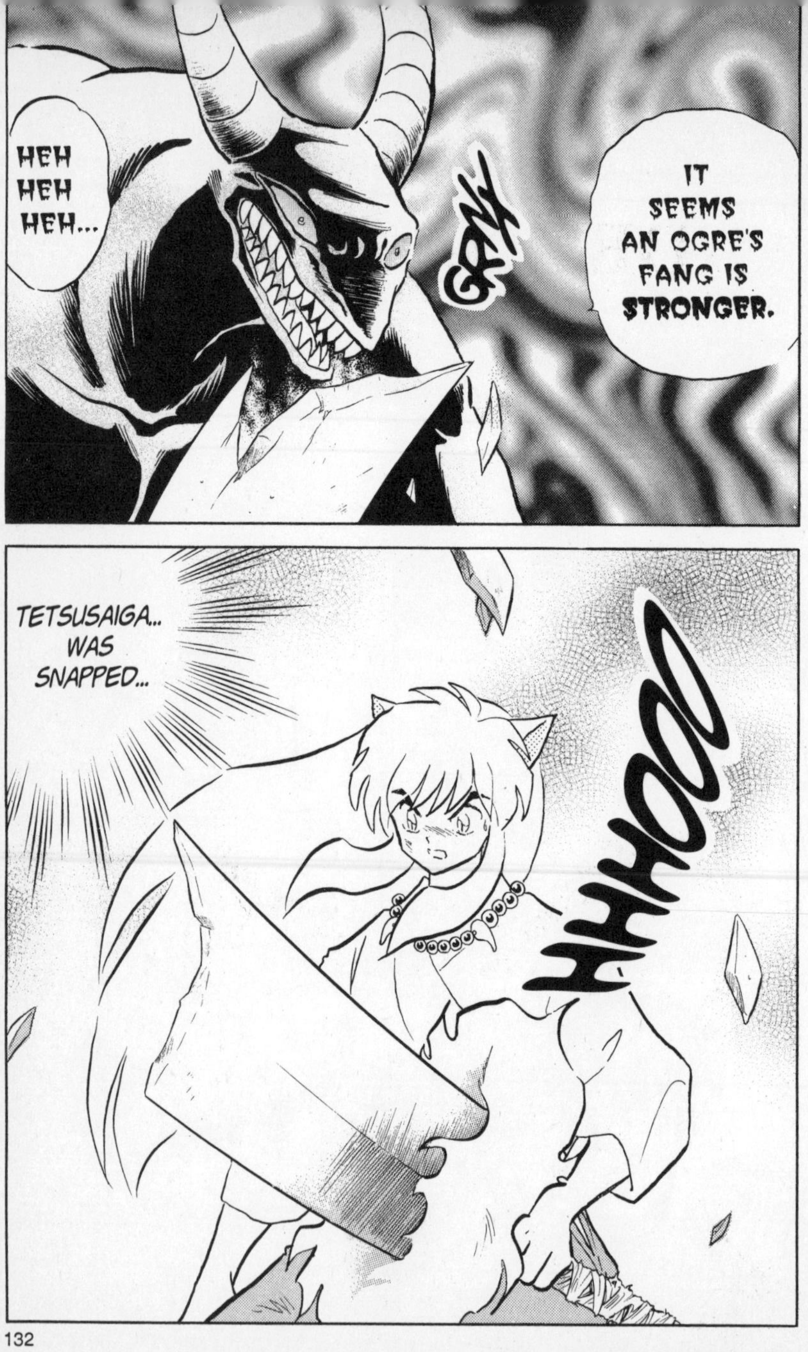
HEH HEH HEH...
GRIN
IT SEEMS AN OGRE'S FANG IS STRONGER.
TETSUSAIGA... WAS SNAPPED...
HHHOOO

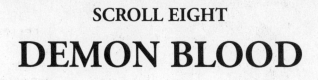

SCROLL EIGHT
DEMON BLOOD

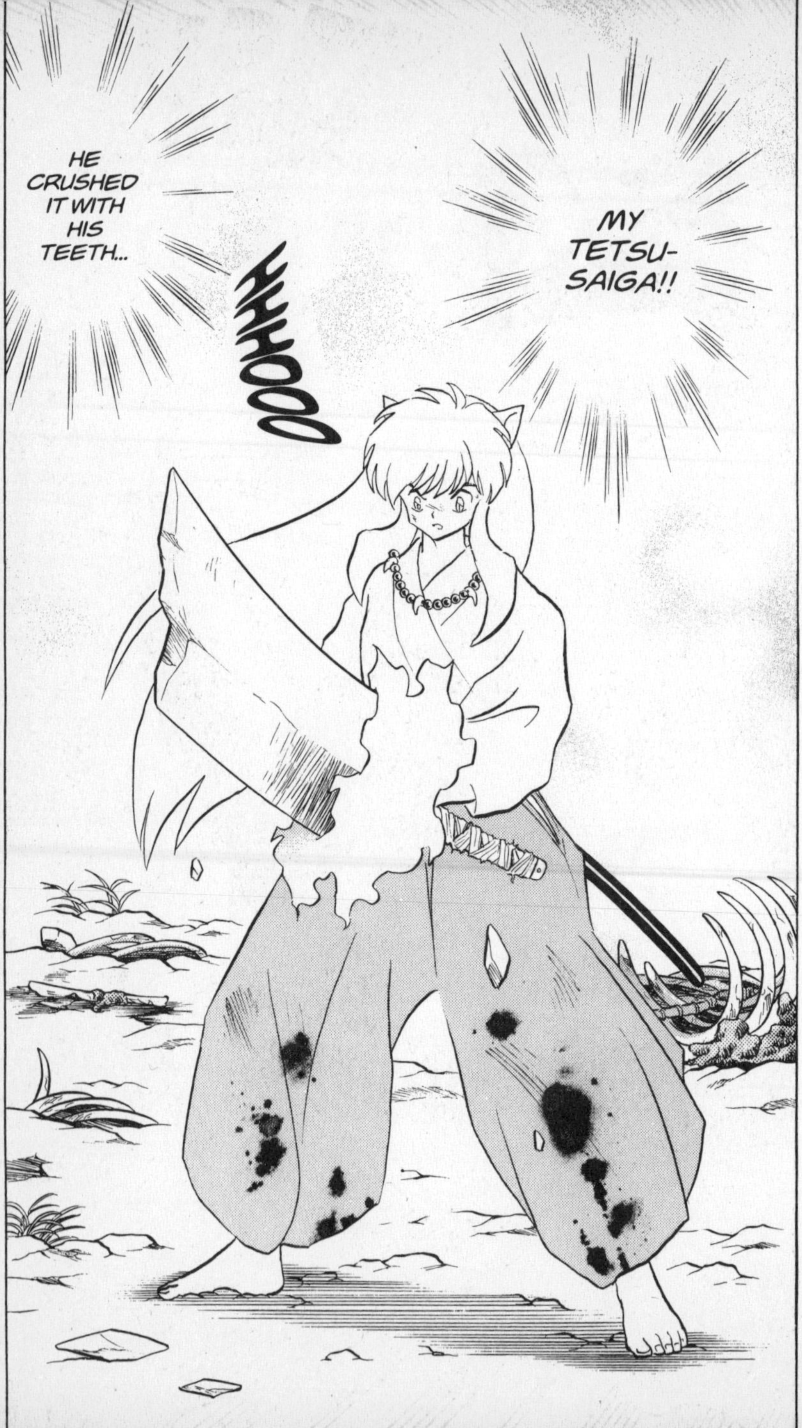
HE CRUSHED IT WITH HIS TEETH...
VOOOOM
MY TETSU-SAIGA!!

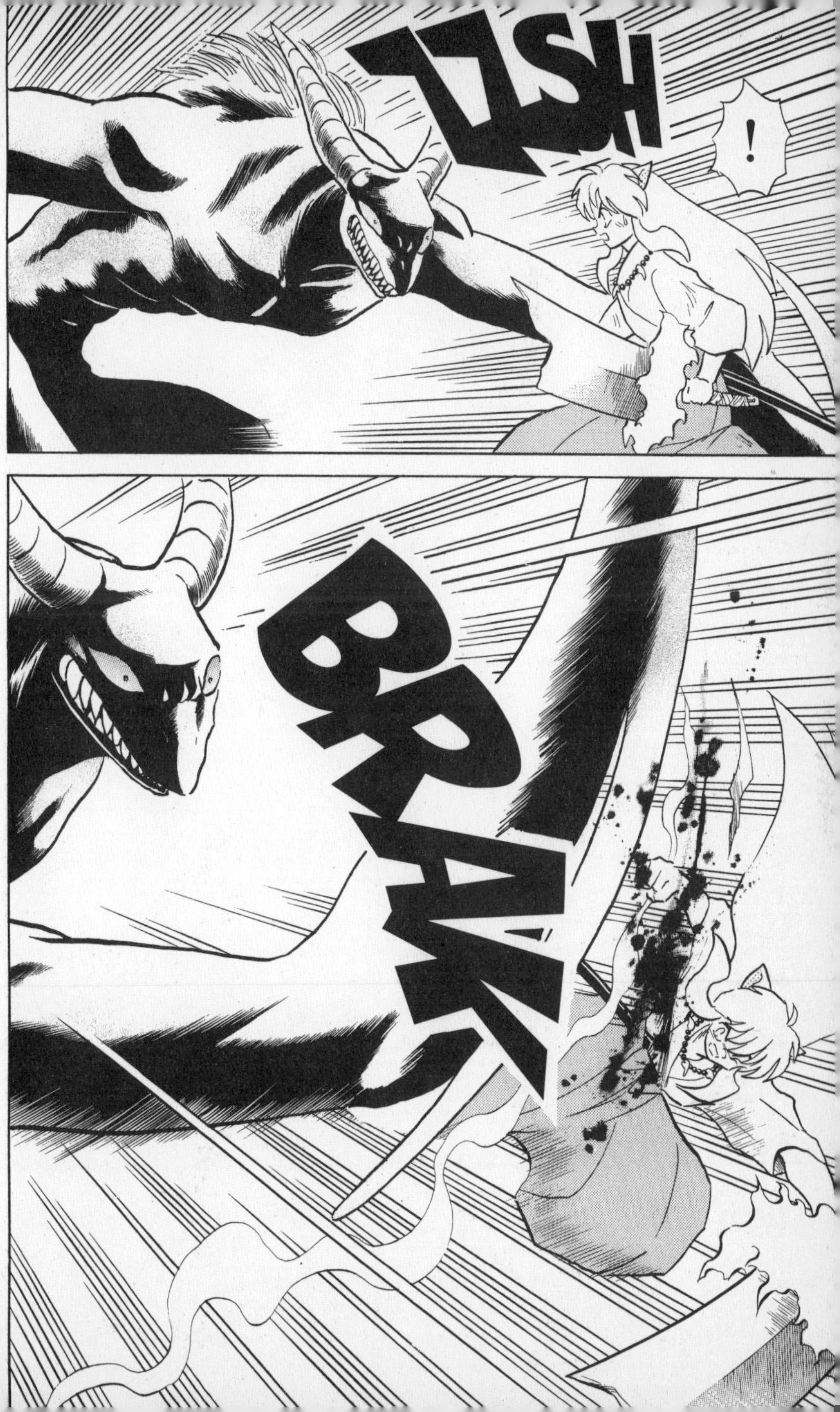

TZSH
!
BRAM

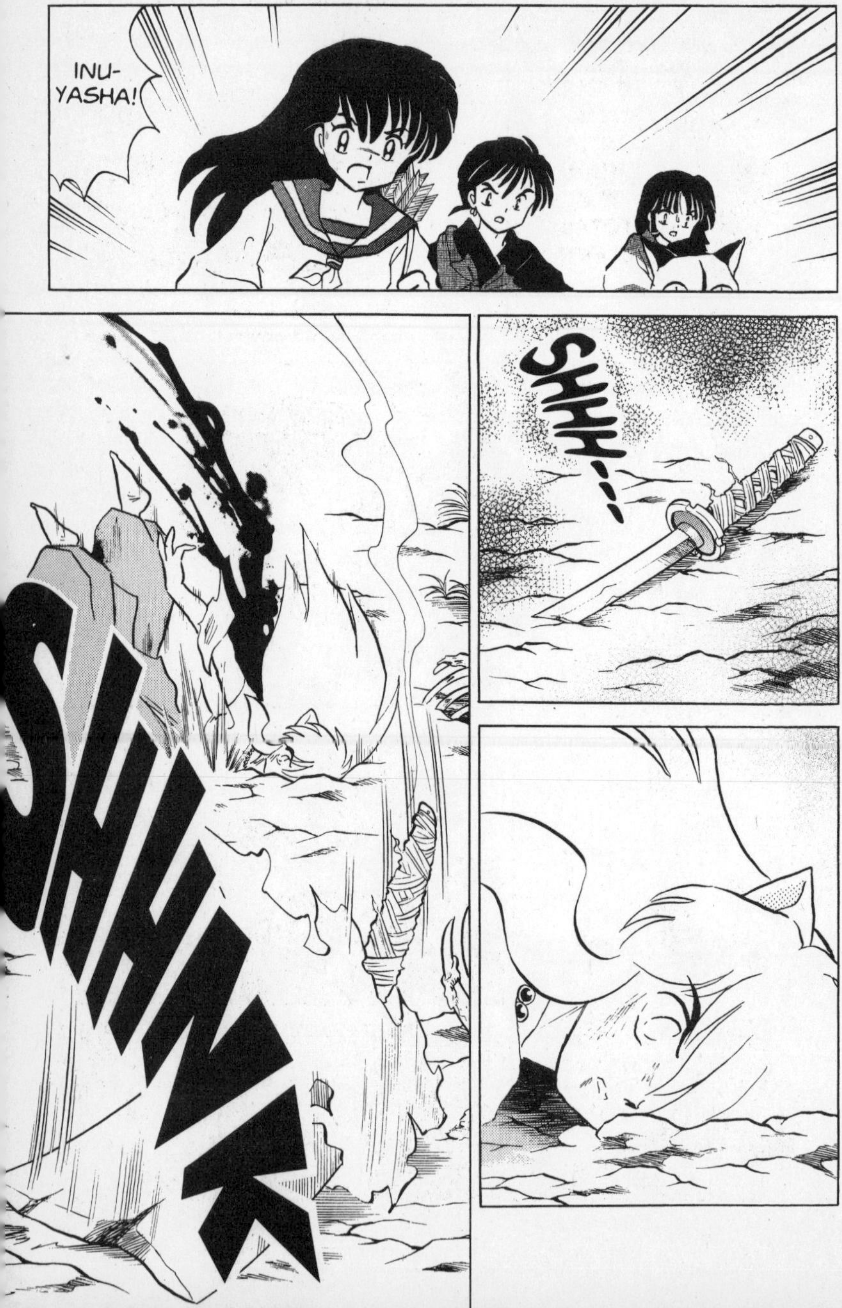
INU-YASHA!
SHANK
SHHH...

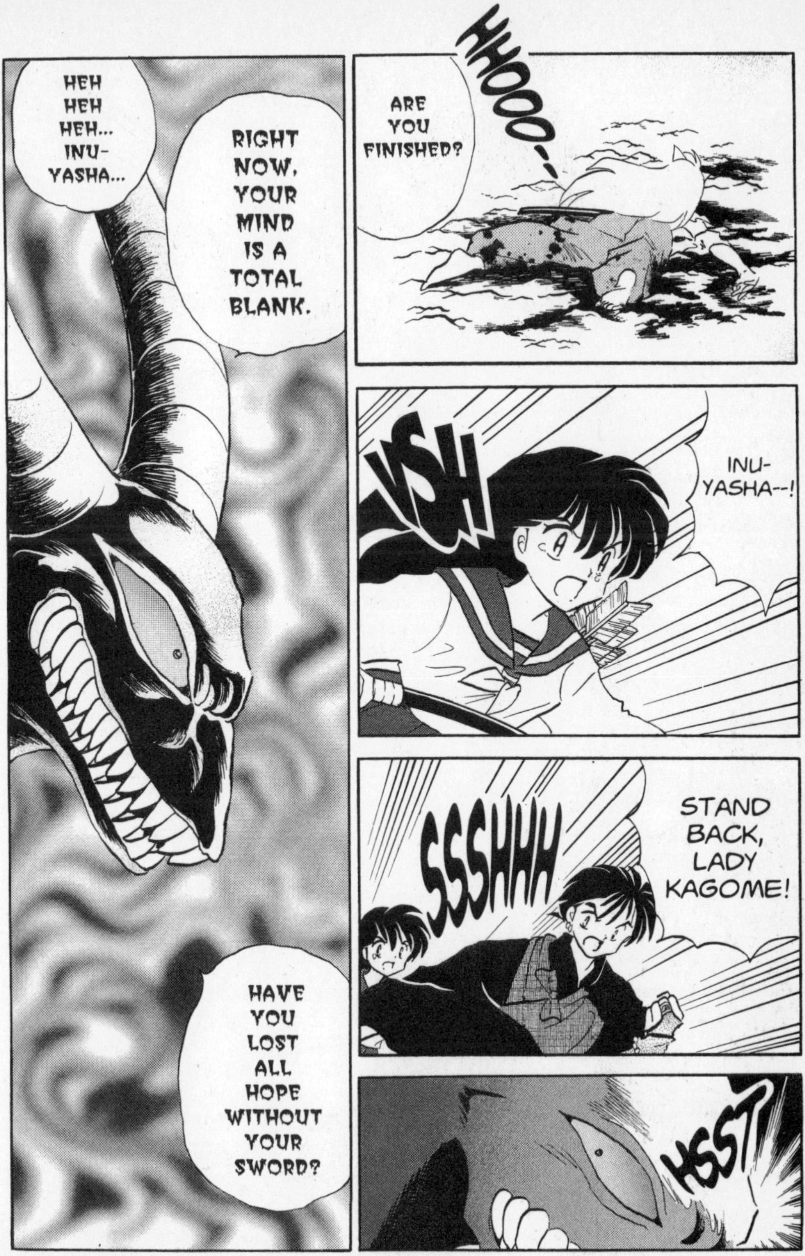
HEH HEH HEH... INU-YASHA...
RIGHT NOW, YOUR MIND IS A TOTAL BLANK.
HAVE YOU LOST ALL HOPE WITHOUT YOUR SWORD?
HHOOO--
ARE YOU FINISHED?
VSH
INU-YASHA--!
SSSHHH
STAND BACK, LADY KAGOME!
HSST

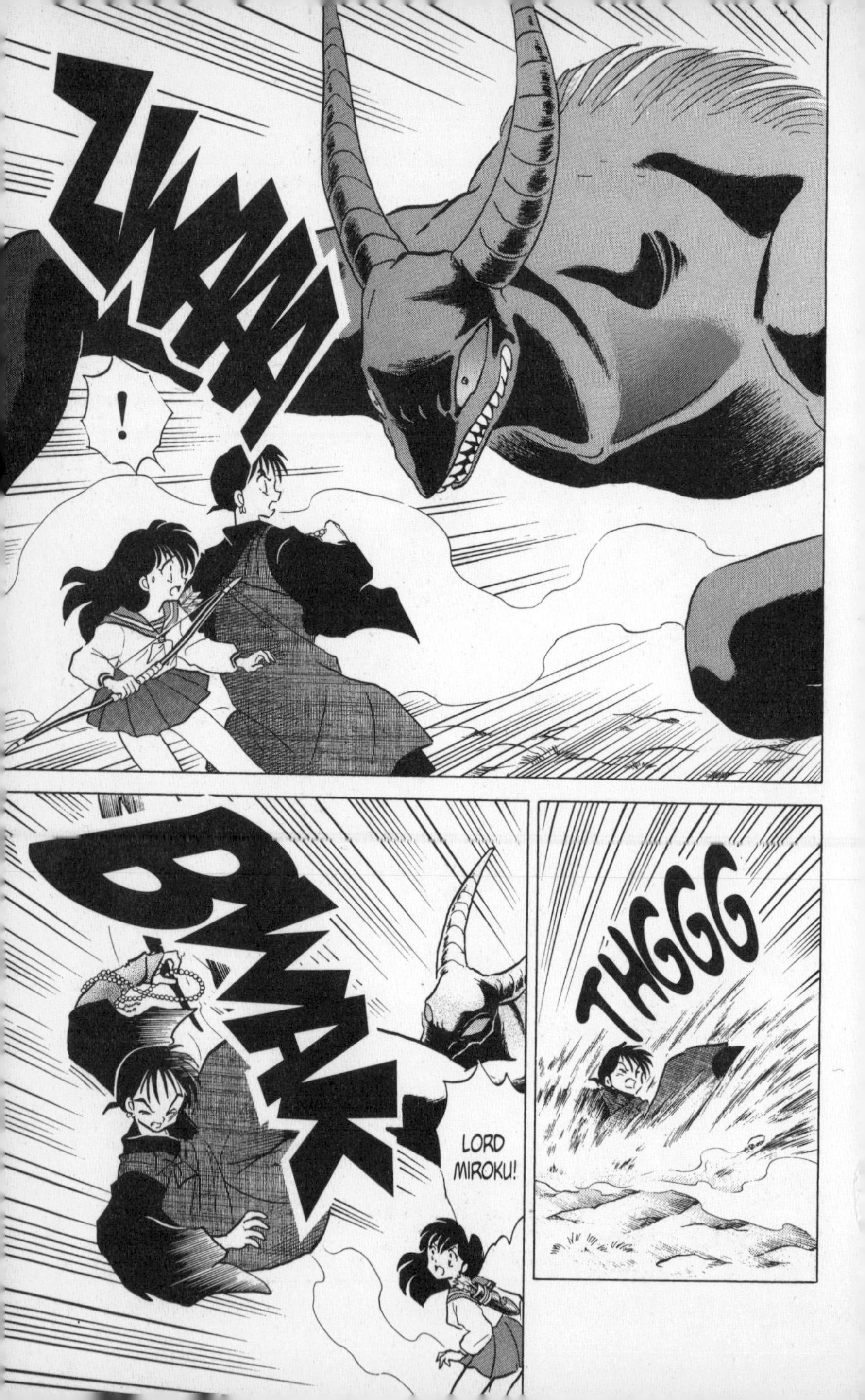
ZWAA
!
BWAK
LORD MIROKU!
THGGG

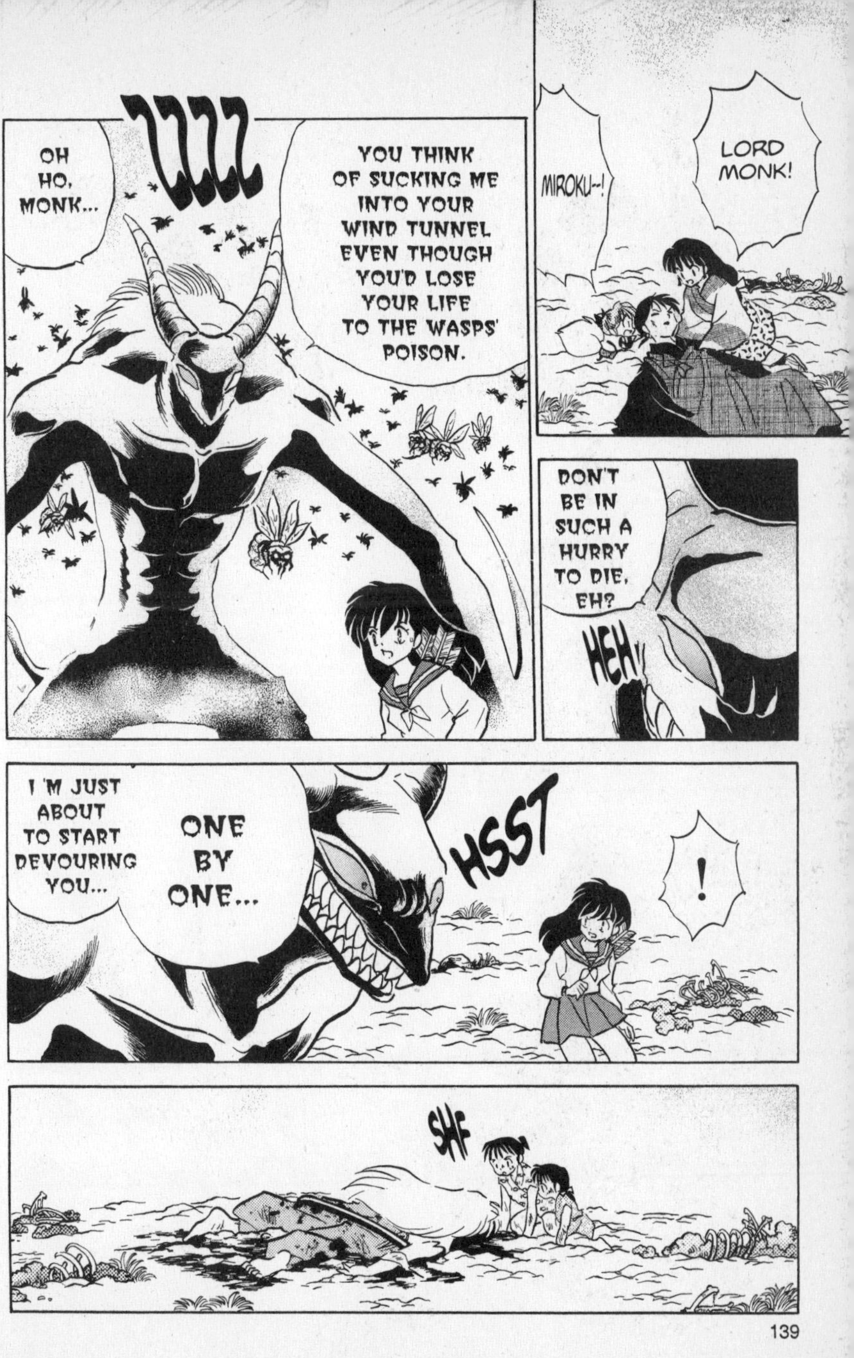
ZZZZ
OH HO, MONK...
YOU THINK OF SUCKING ME INTO YOUR WIND TUNNEL EVEN THOUGH YOU'D LOSE YOUR LIFE TO THE WASPS' POISON.
MIROKU--!
LORD MONK!
DON'T BE IN SUCH A HURRY TO DIE, EH?
HEH
I'M JUST ABOUT TO START DEVOURING YOU...
ONE BY ONE...
HSST
!
SHF

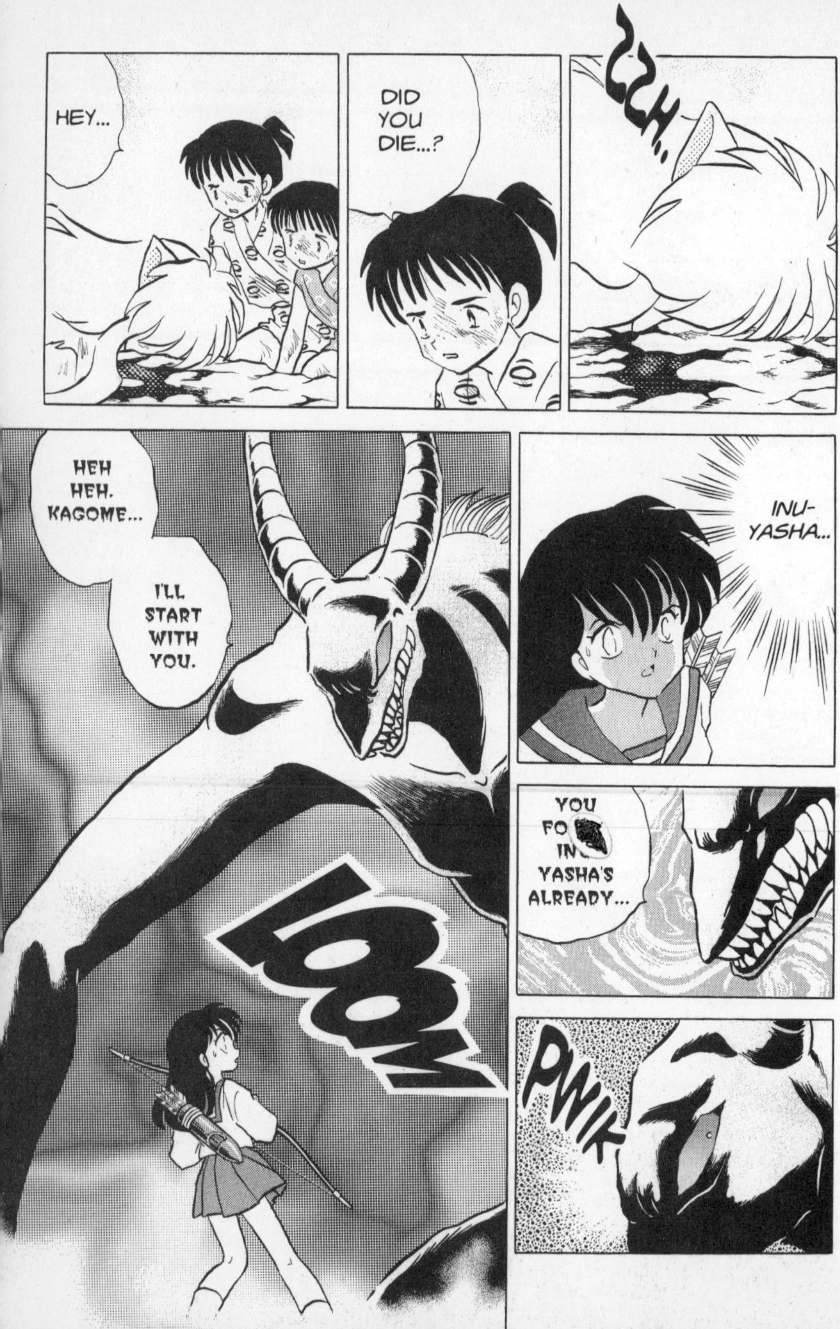
HEY...
DID YOU DIE...?
ZZH...
HEH HEH. KAGOME...
I'LL START WITH YOU.
LOOM
INU-YASHA...
YOU FO
IN
YASHA'S ALREADY...
PWIK

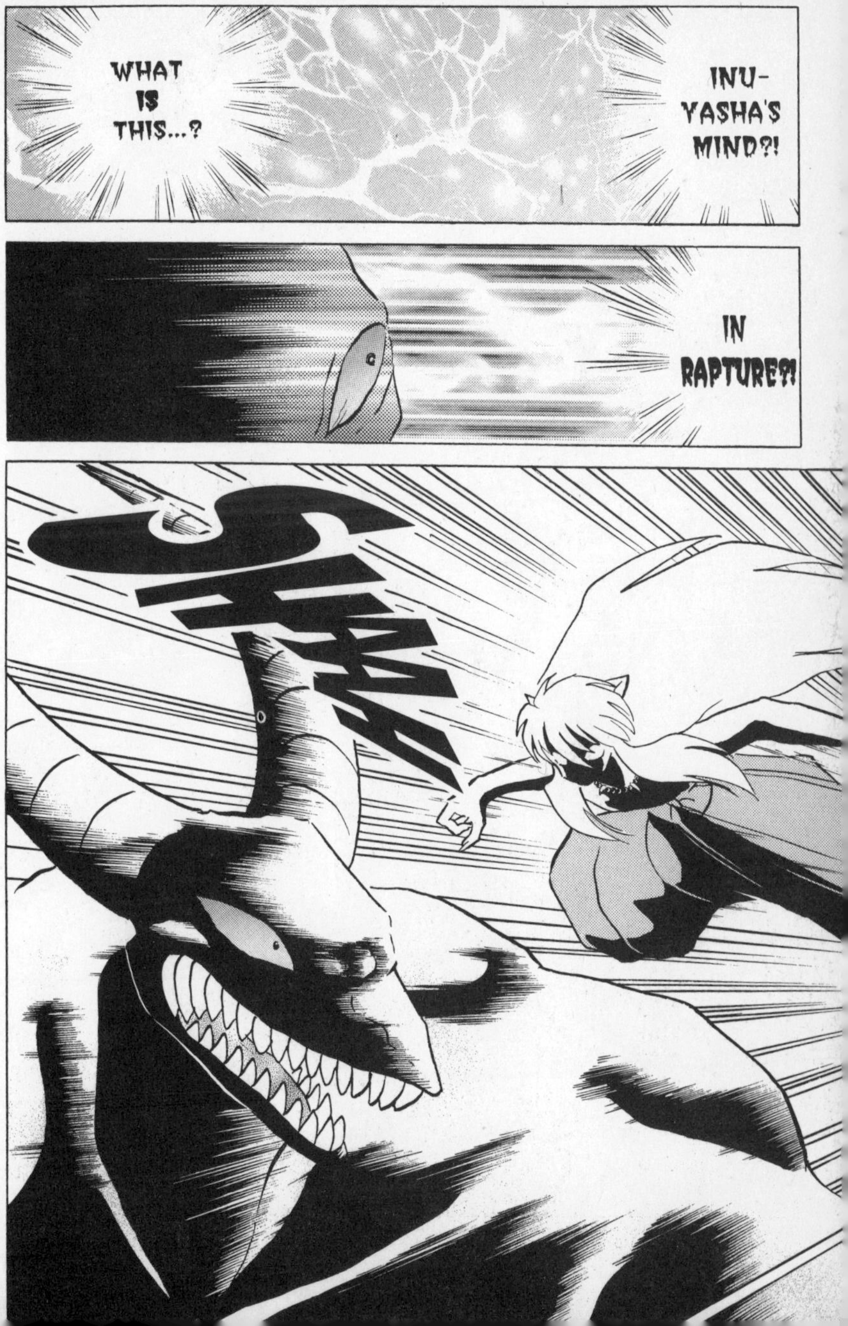
WHAT IS THIS...?
INU-YASHA'S MIND?!
IN RAPTURE?!

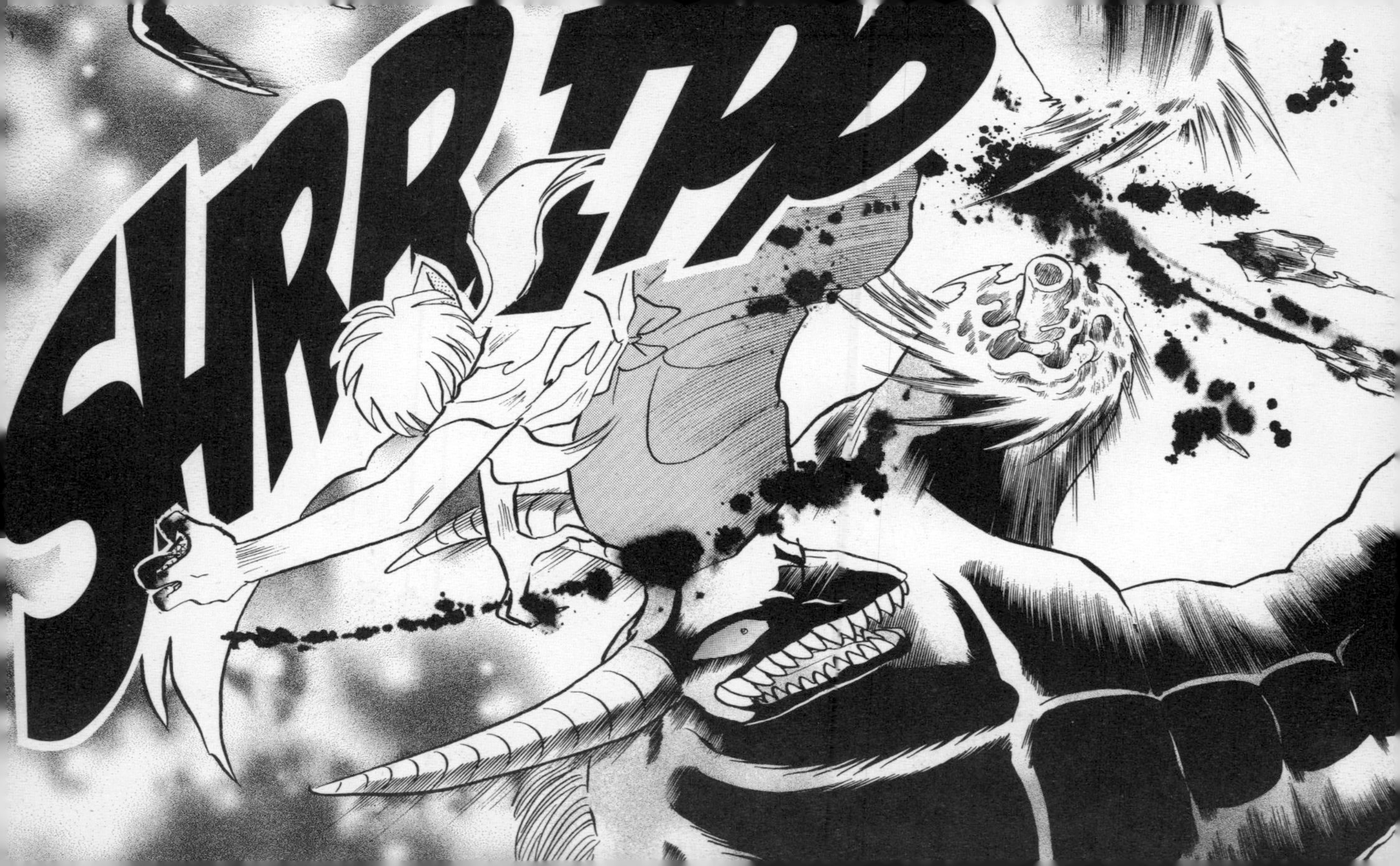
SHRRIPP

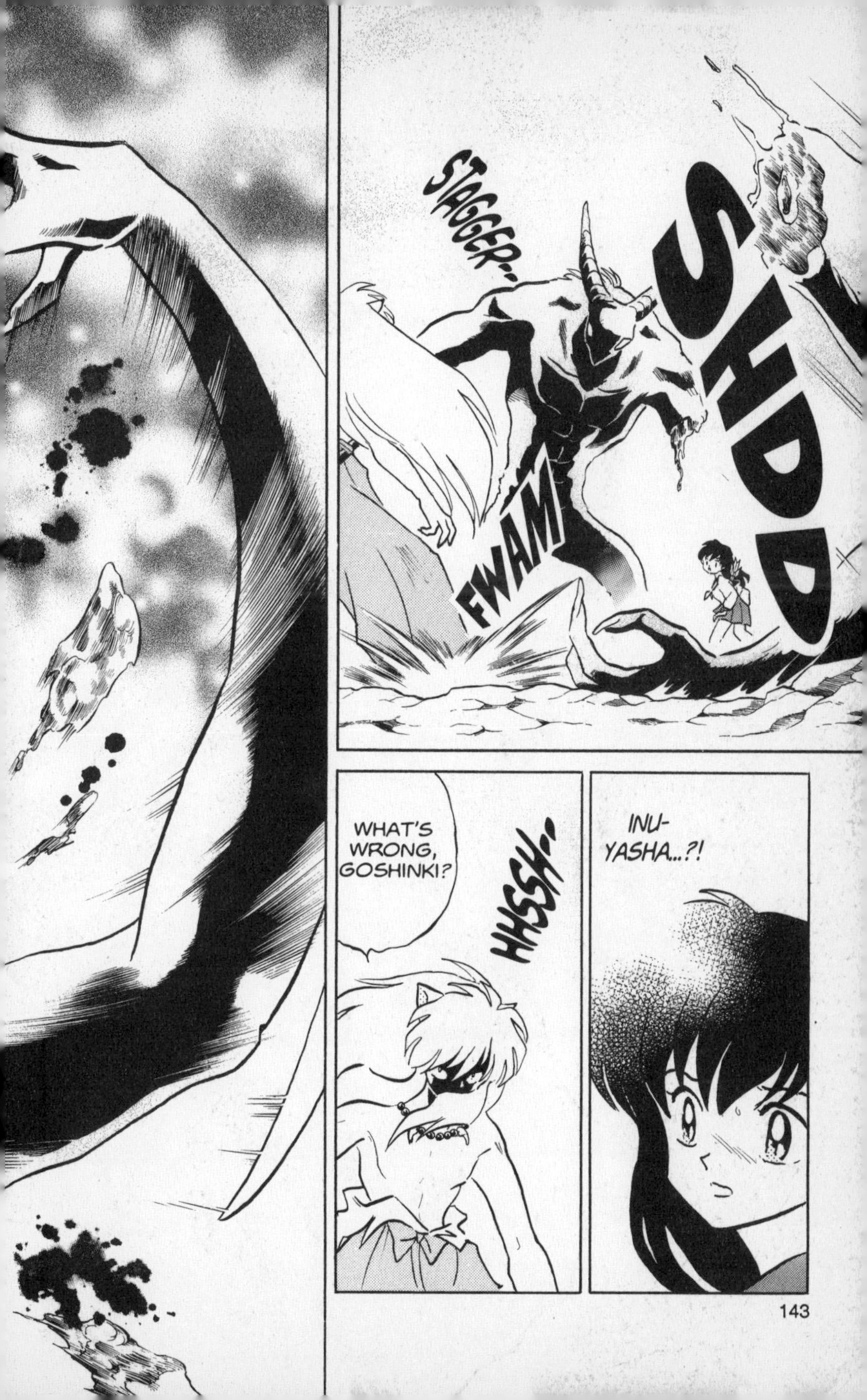
STAGGER..
FWAM
SHDD
WHAT'S WRONG, GOSHINKI?
HHSSH..
INU-YASHA...?!

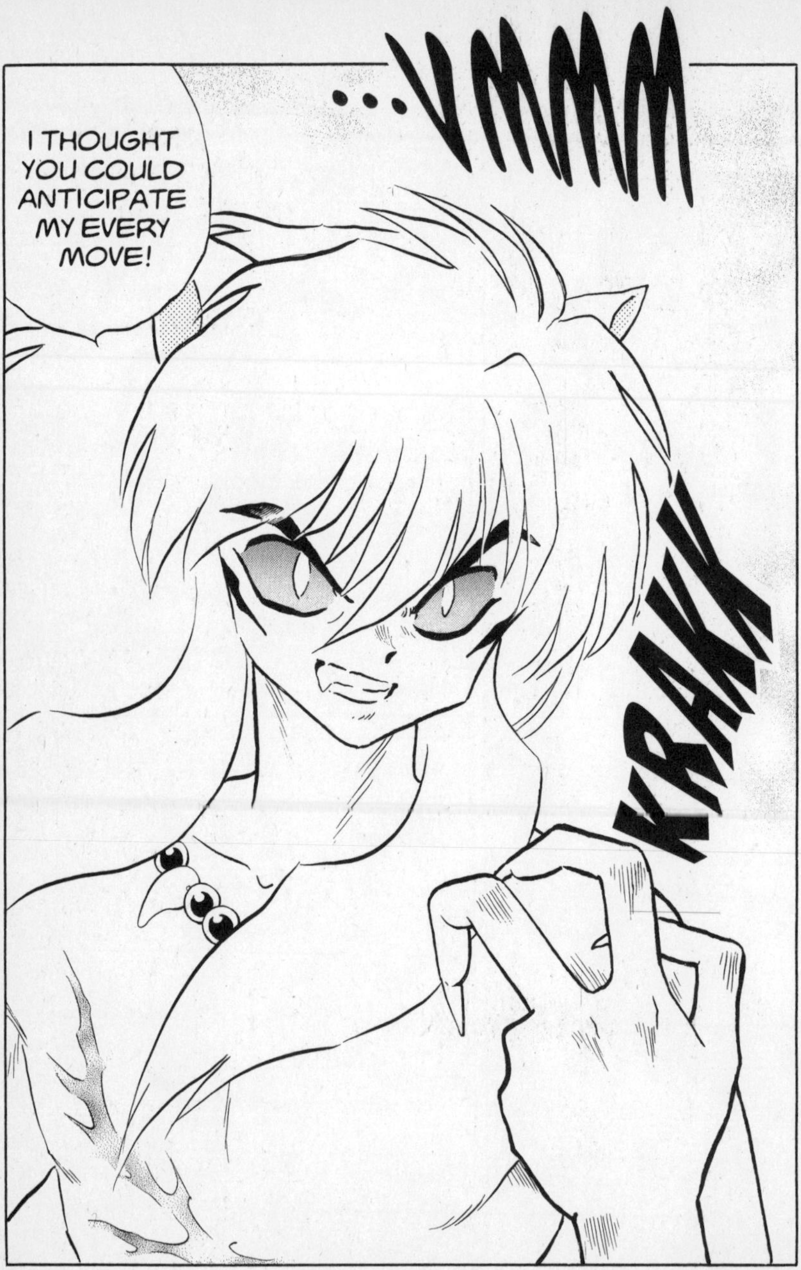
...VMMM
I THOUGHT YOU COULD ANTICIPATE MY EVERY MOVE!
KRAKK

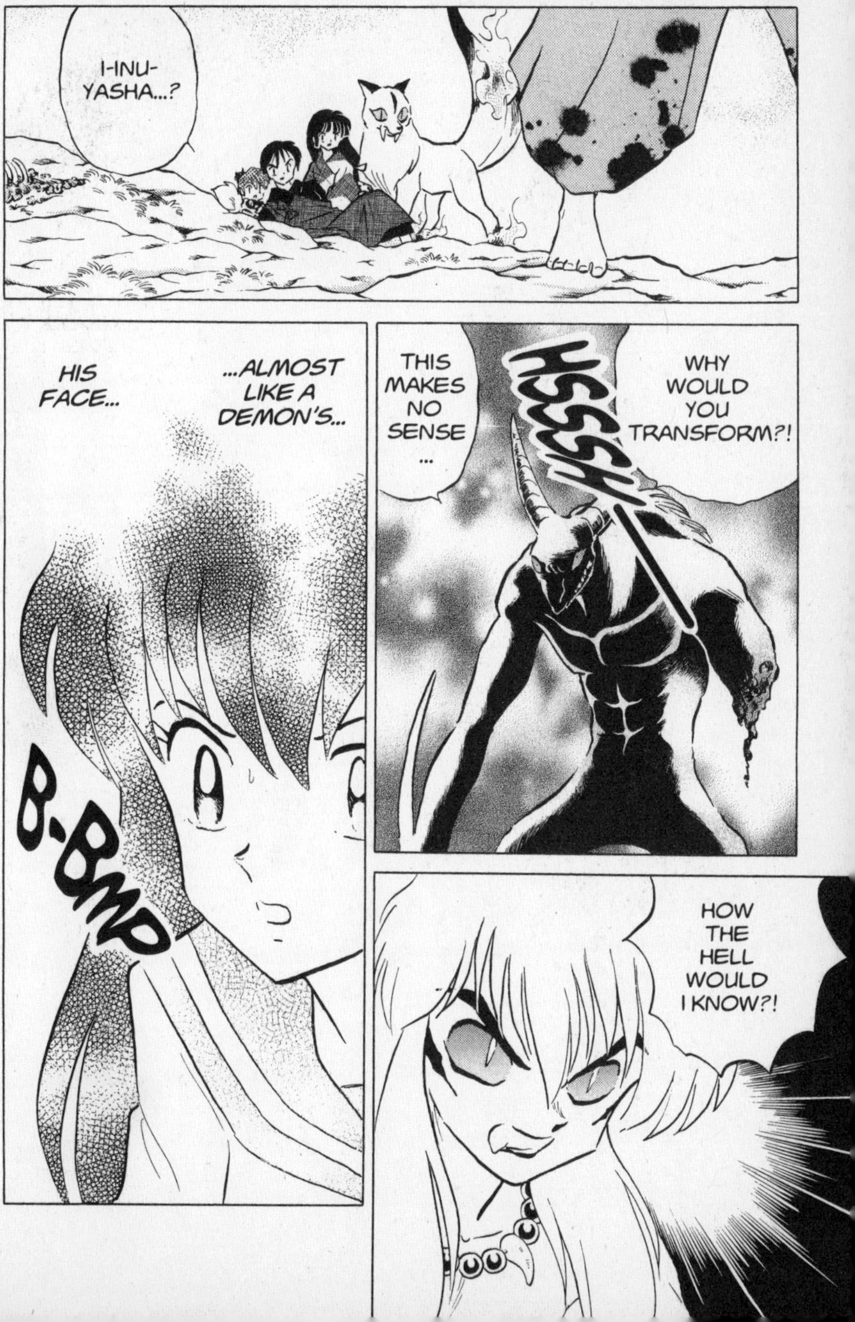
I-INU-YASHA...?
HIS FACE...
...ALMOST LIKE A DEMON'S...
B-BMP
THIS MAKES NO SENSE ...
HSSSH
WHY WOULD YOU TRANSFORM?!
HOW THE HELL WOULD I KNOW?!

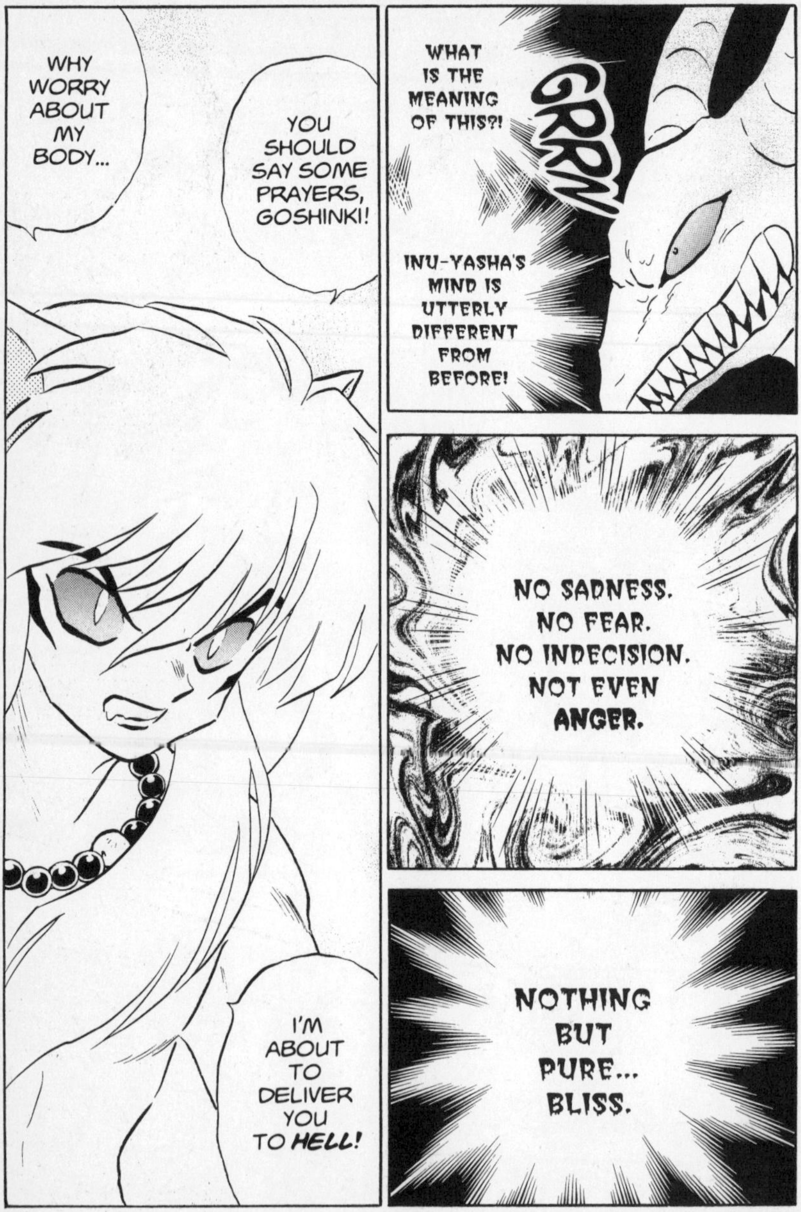
WHY WORRY ABOUT MY BODY...
YOU SHOULD SAY SOME PRAYERS, GOSHINKI!
I'M ABOUT TO DELIVER YOU TO HELL!
WHAT IS THE MEANING OF THIS?!
GRRN
INU-YASHA'S MIND IS UTTERLY DIFFERENT FROM BEFORE!
NO SADNESS. NO FEAR. NO INDECISION. NOT EVEN ANGER.
NOTHING BUT PURE... BLISS.

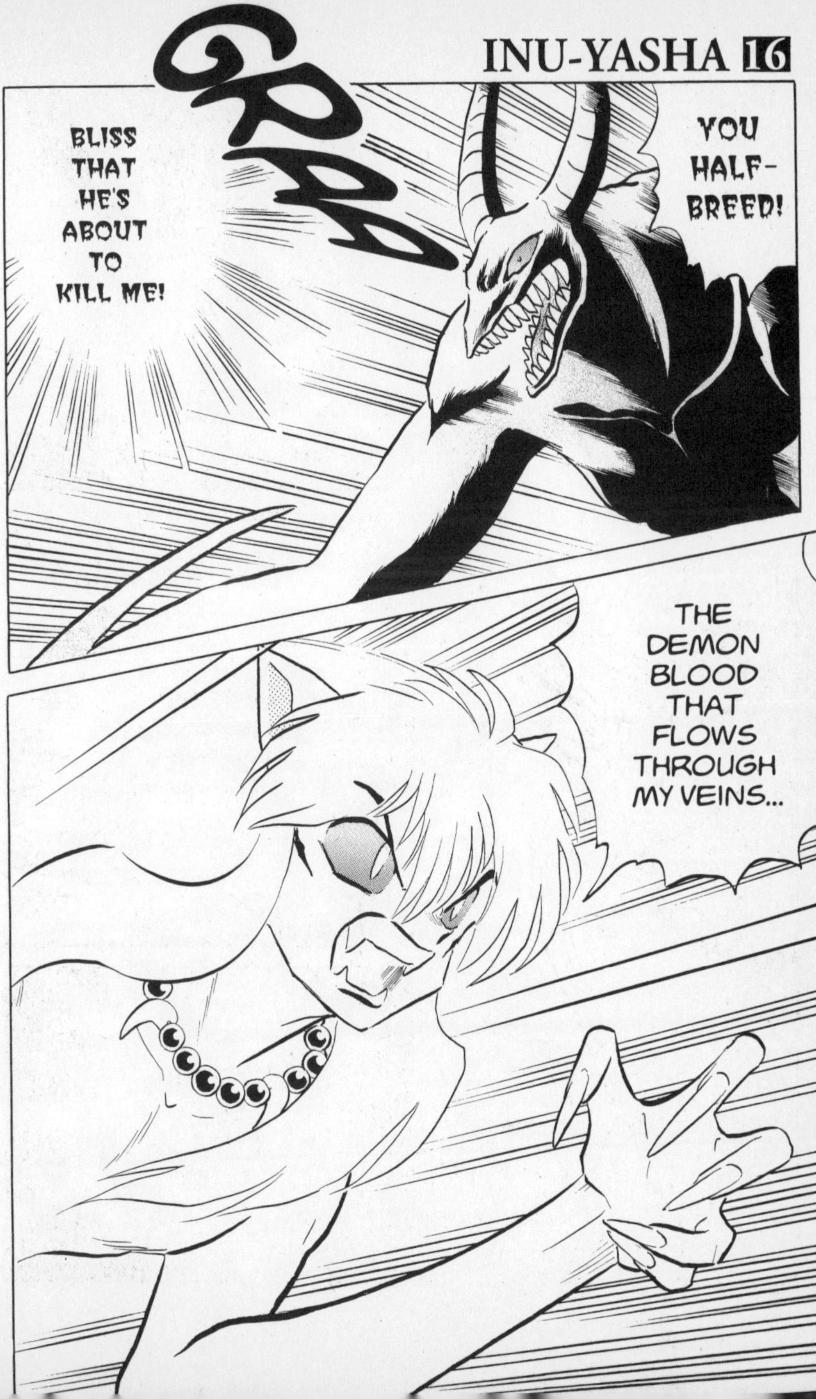
GRRR
BLISS THAT HE'S ABOUT TO KILL ME!
YOU HALF-BREED!
THE DEMON BLOOD THAT FLOWS THROUGH MY VEINS...

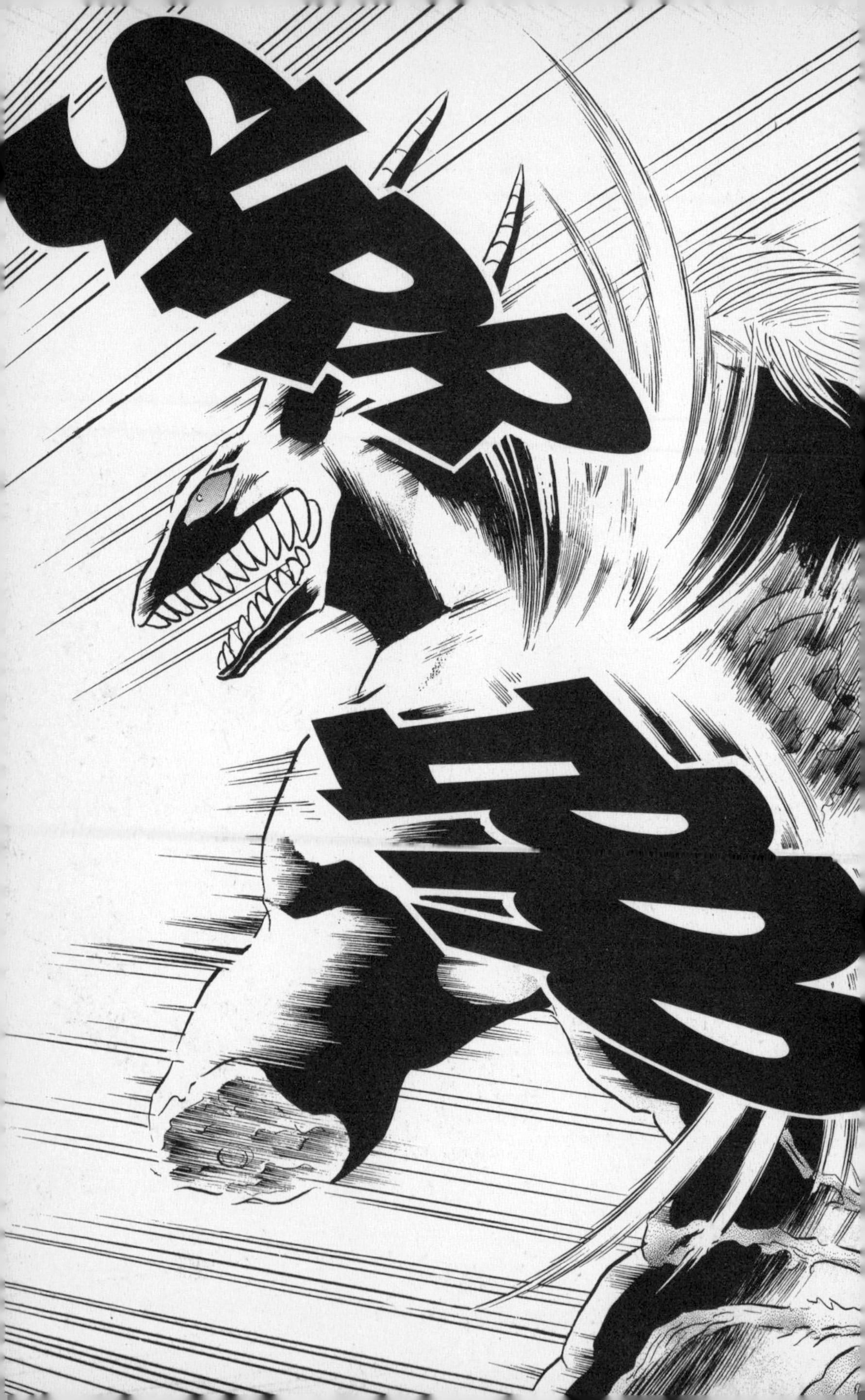

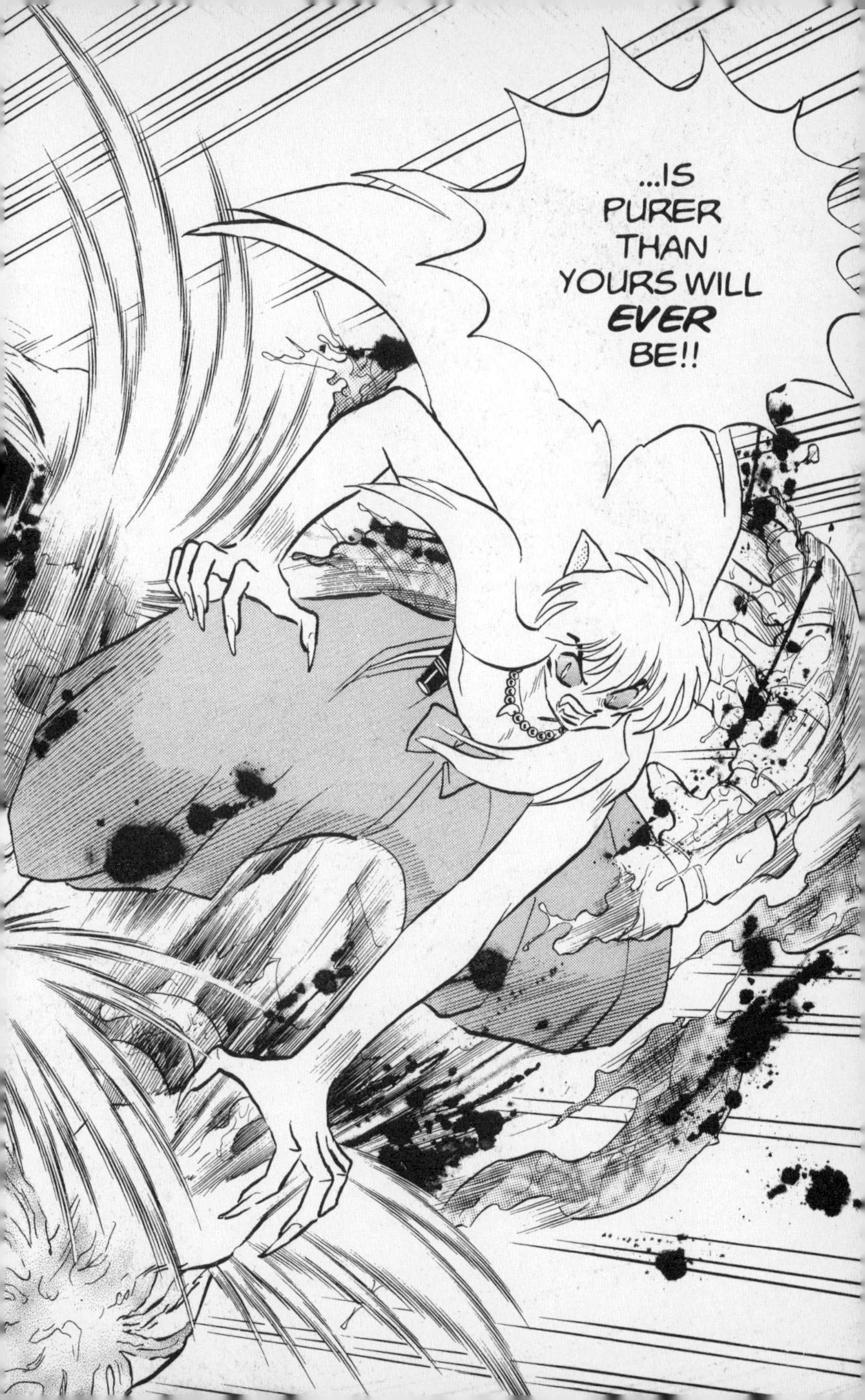
...IS PURER THAN YOURS WILL ***EVER*** BE!!

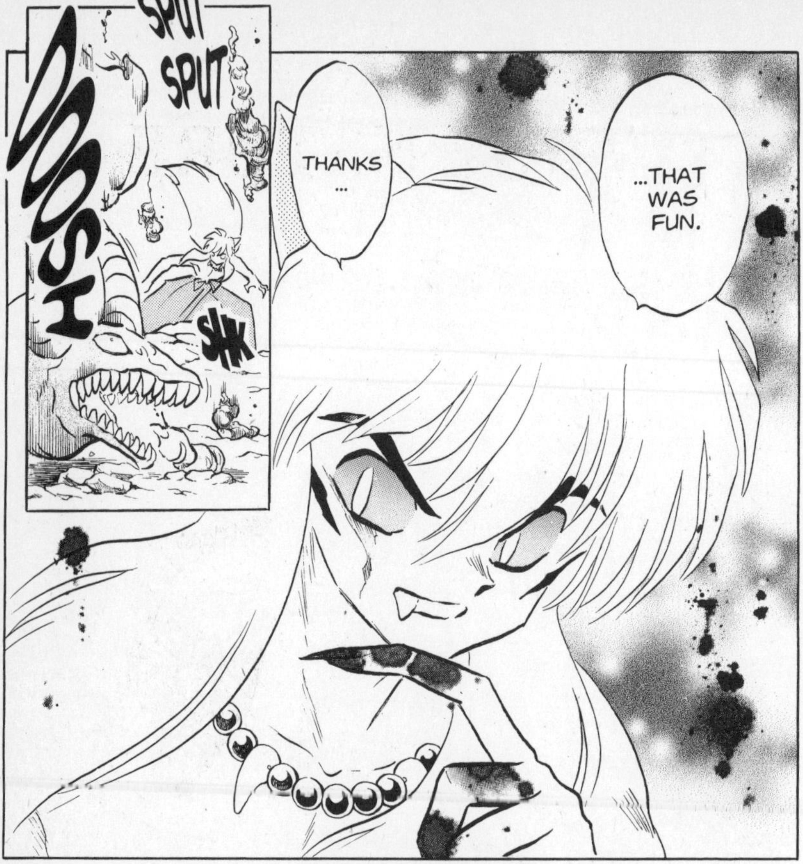
DOOSH
SPUT
SPUT
SHK
THANKS ...
...THAT WAS FUN.
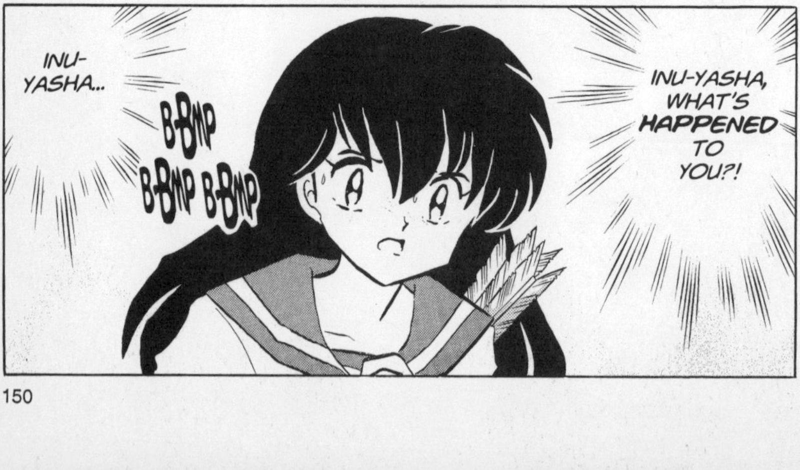
INU-YASHA...
B-BMP
B-BMP B-BMP
INU-YASHA, WHAT'S **HAPPENED** TO YOU?!

SCROLL NINE

TRUE NATURE

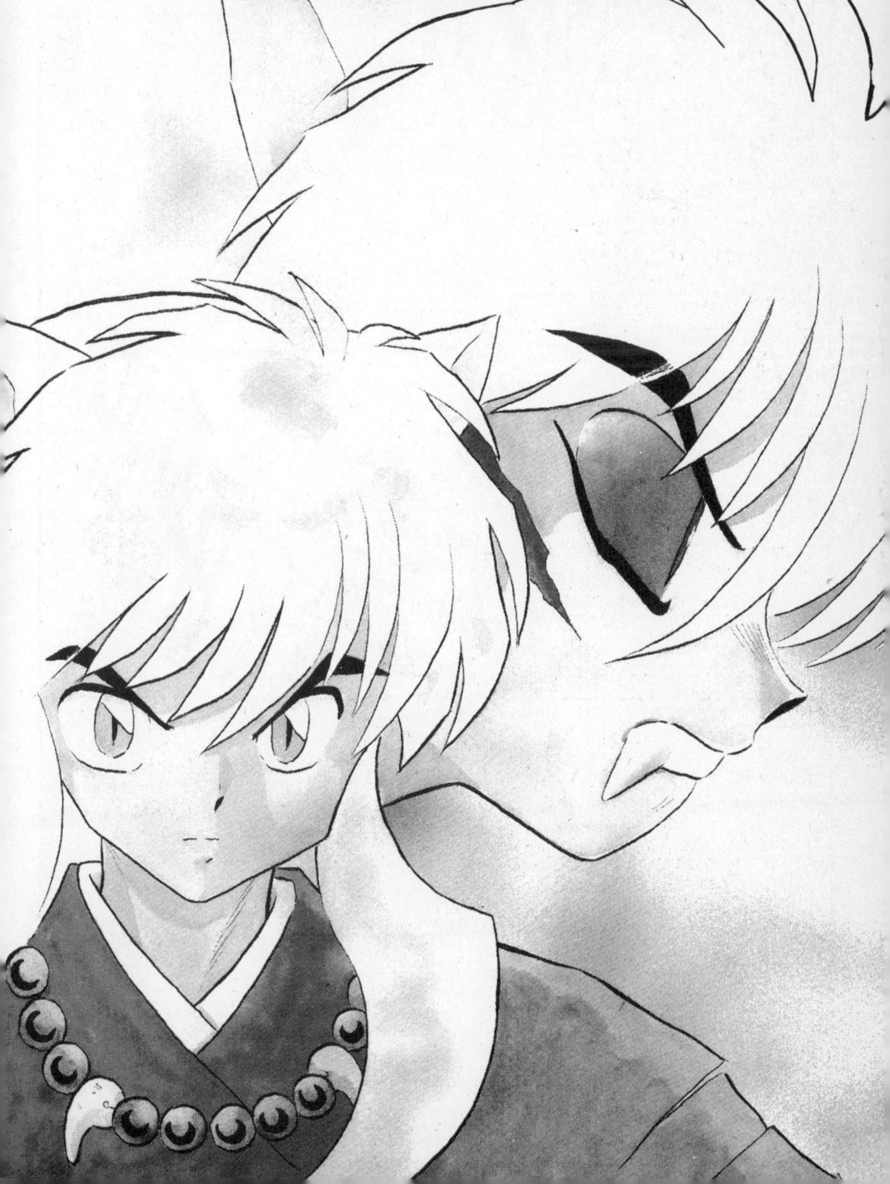

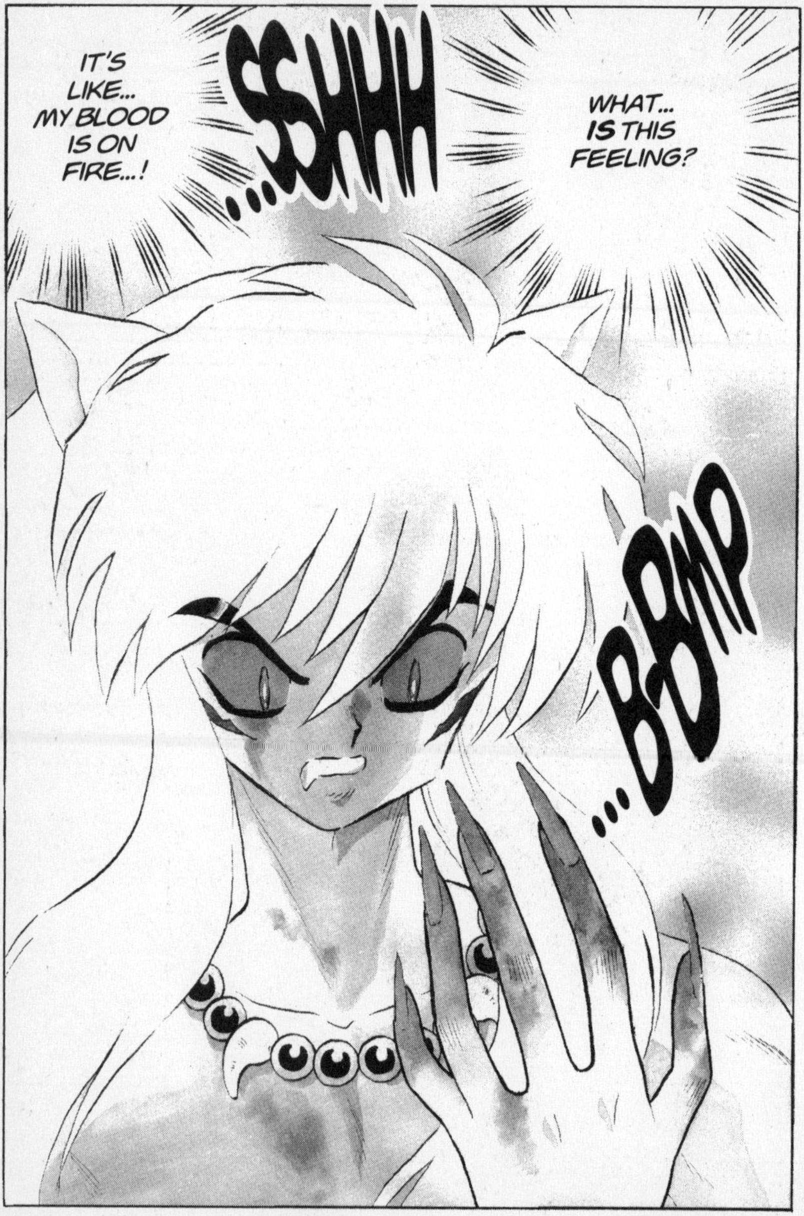
IT'S LIKE... MY BLOOD IS ON FIRE...!
...SSHHH
WHAT... IS THIS FEELING?
...B-BMP

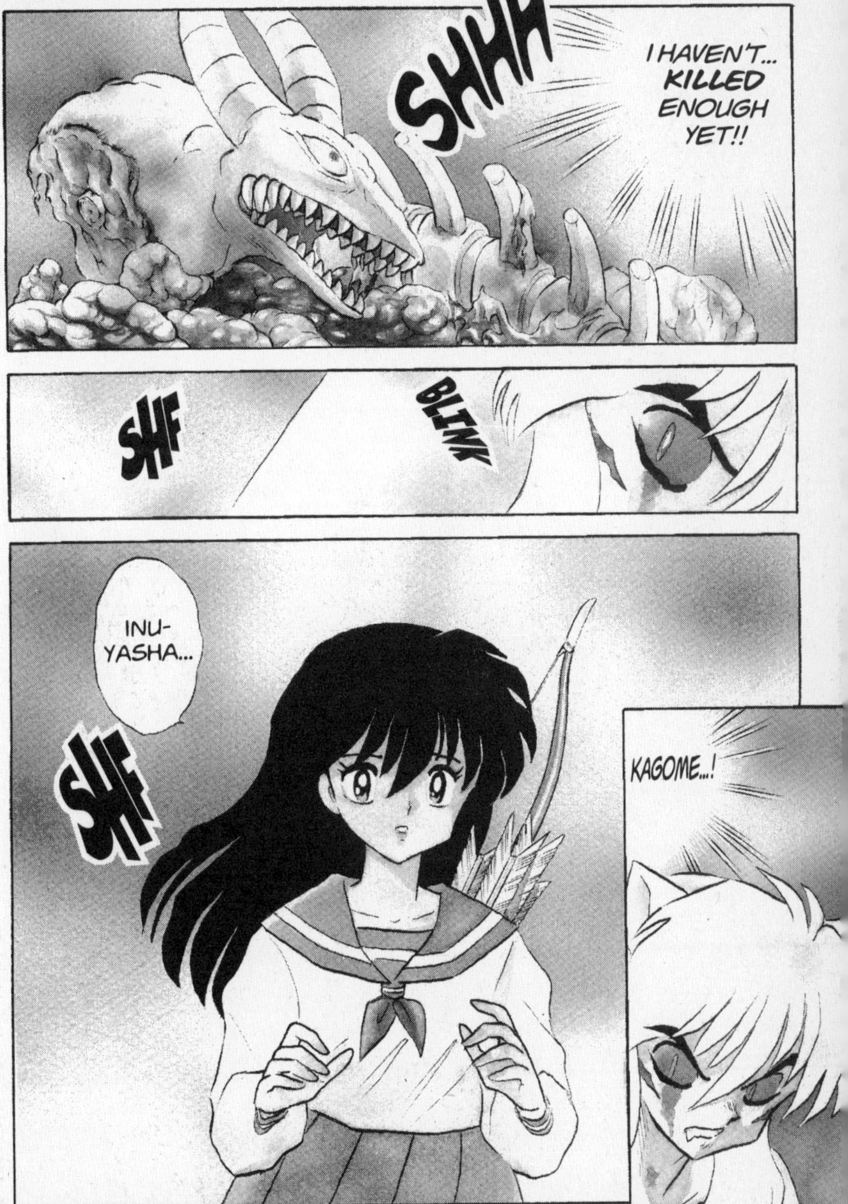
SHHH
I HAVEN'T... KILLED ENOUGH YET!!
SHF
BLINK
INU-YASHA...
SHF
KAGOME...!

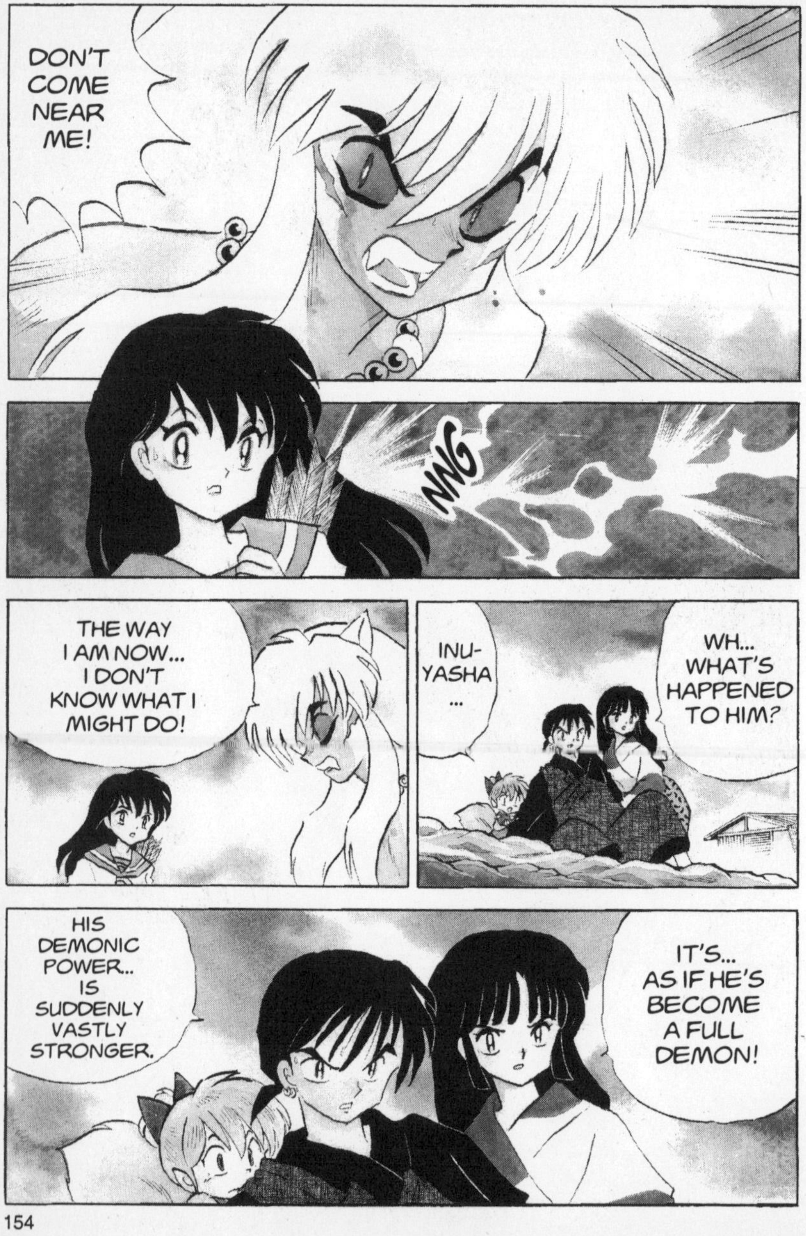
DON'T COME NEAR ME!
NNG
WH... WHAT'S HAPPENED TO HIM?
INU-YASHA ...
THE WAY I AM NOW... I DON'T KNOW WHAT I MIGHT DO!
IT'S... AS IF HE'S BECOME A FULL DEMON!
HIS DEMONIC POWER... IS SUDDENLY VASTLY STRONGER.

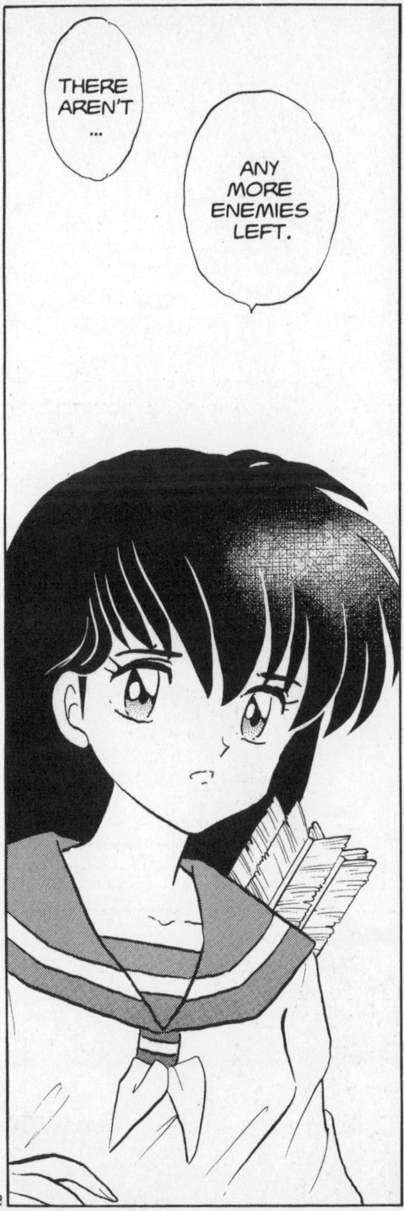
THERE AREN'T ...
ANY MORE ENEMIES LEFT.

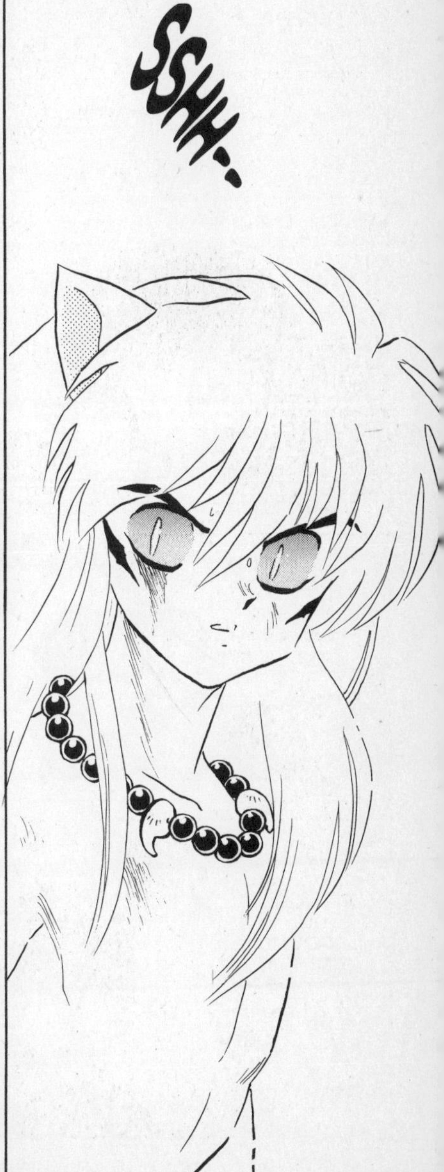
SSHH..

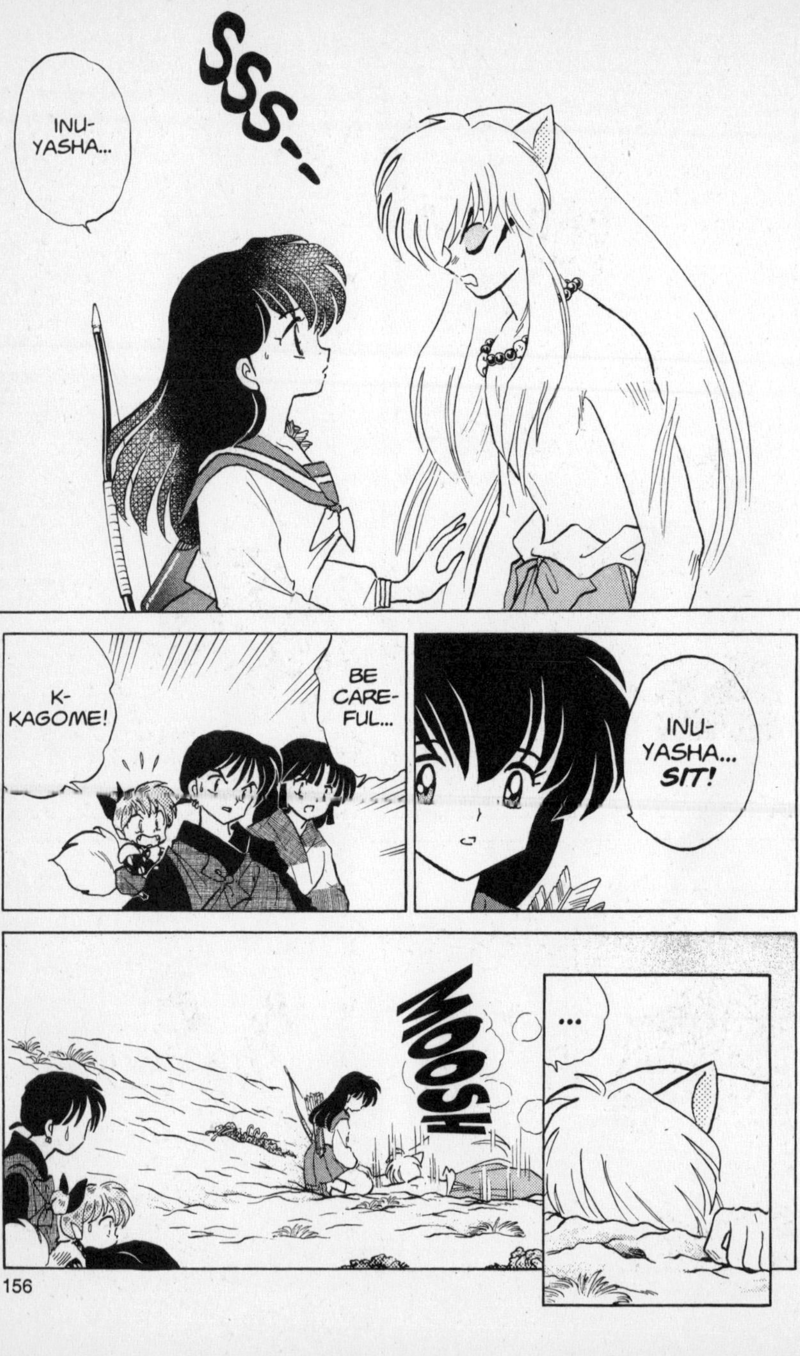
INU-
YASHA...
SSS--
K-
KAGOME!
BE
CARE-
FUL...
INU-
YASHA...
SIT!
WHOOSH
...

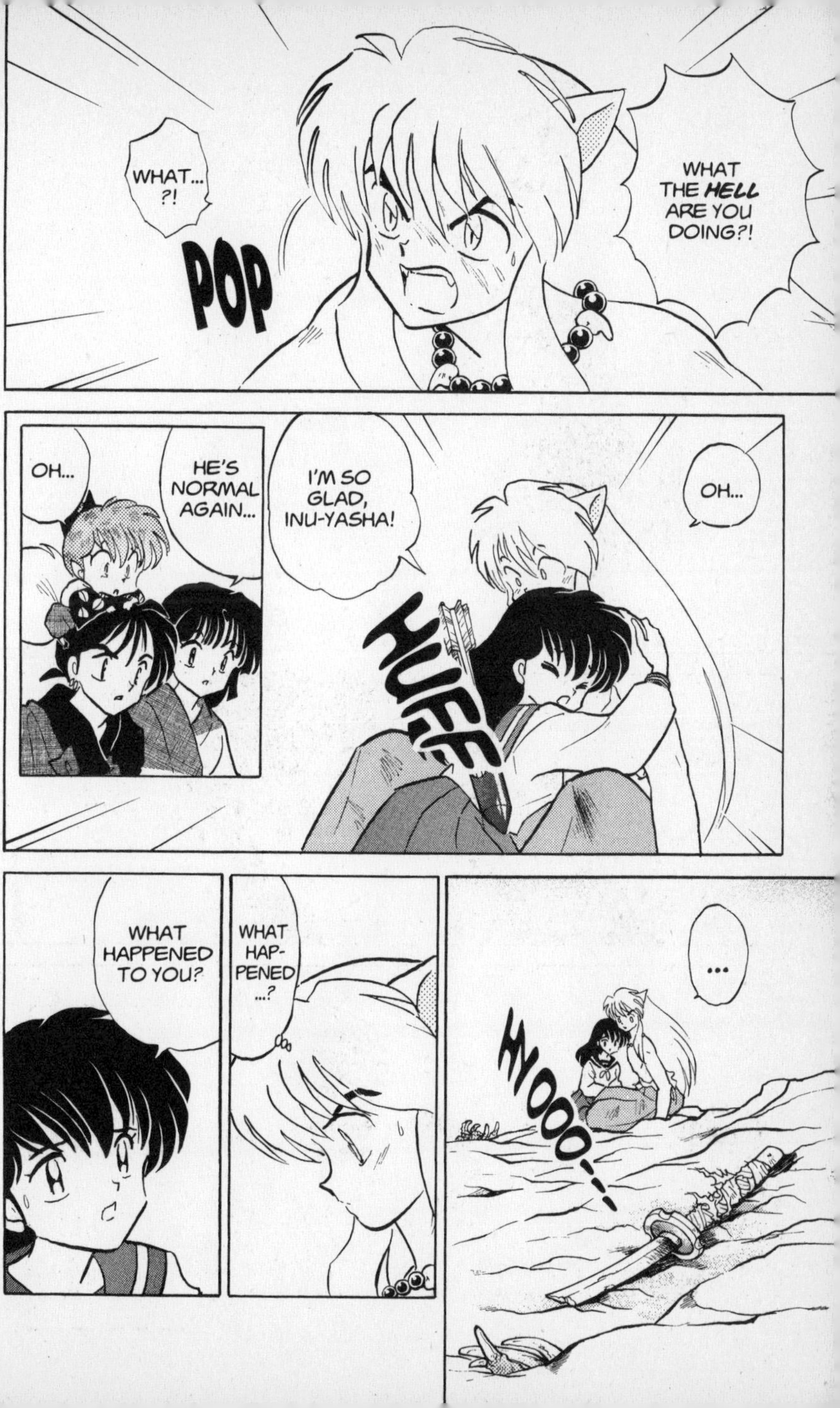
WHAT... ?!
POP
WHAT THE **HELL** ARE YOU DOING?!
OH...
HE'S NORMAL AGAIN...
I'M SO GLAD, INU-YASHA!
HUFF
OH...
WHAT HAPPENED TO YOU?
WHAT HAP-PENED ...?
...
HYOOO...

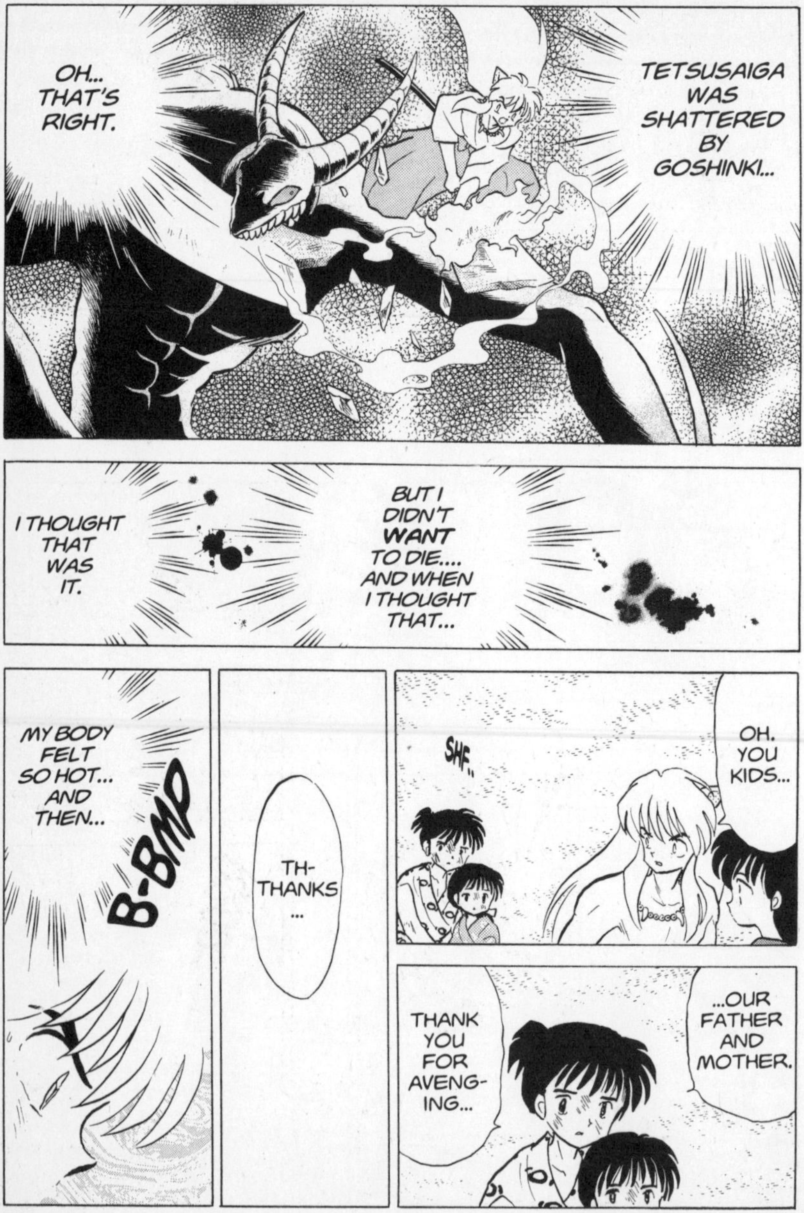

OH... THAT'S RIGHT.
TETSUSAIGA WAS SHATTERED BY GOSHINKI...
I THOUGHT THAT WAS IT.
BUT I DIDN'T WANT TO DIE.... AND WHEN I THOUGHT THAT...
MY BODY FELT SO HOT... AND THEN...
B-BMP
TH-THANKS ...
SHF..
OH. YOU KIDS...
THANK YOU FOR AVENG-ING...
...OUR FATHER AND MOTHER.

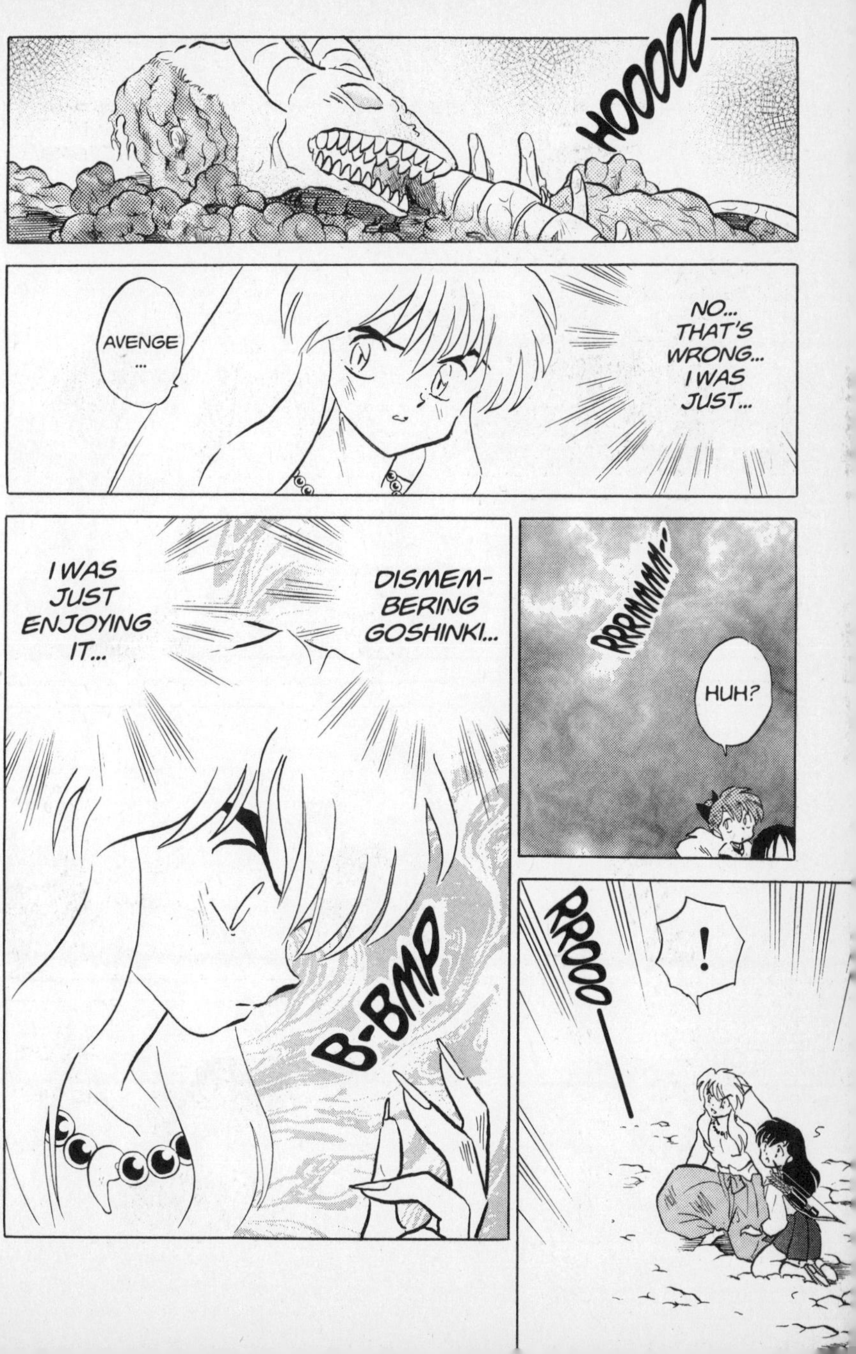
HOOOOO
AVENGE ...
NO... THAT'S WRONG... I WAS JUST...
I WAS JUST ENJOYING IT...
DISMEM-BERING GOSHINKI...
B-BMP
RRRMMMM...
HUH?
RROOOO—
!

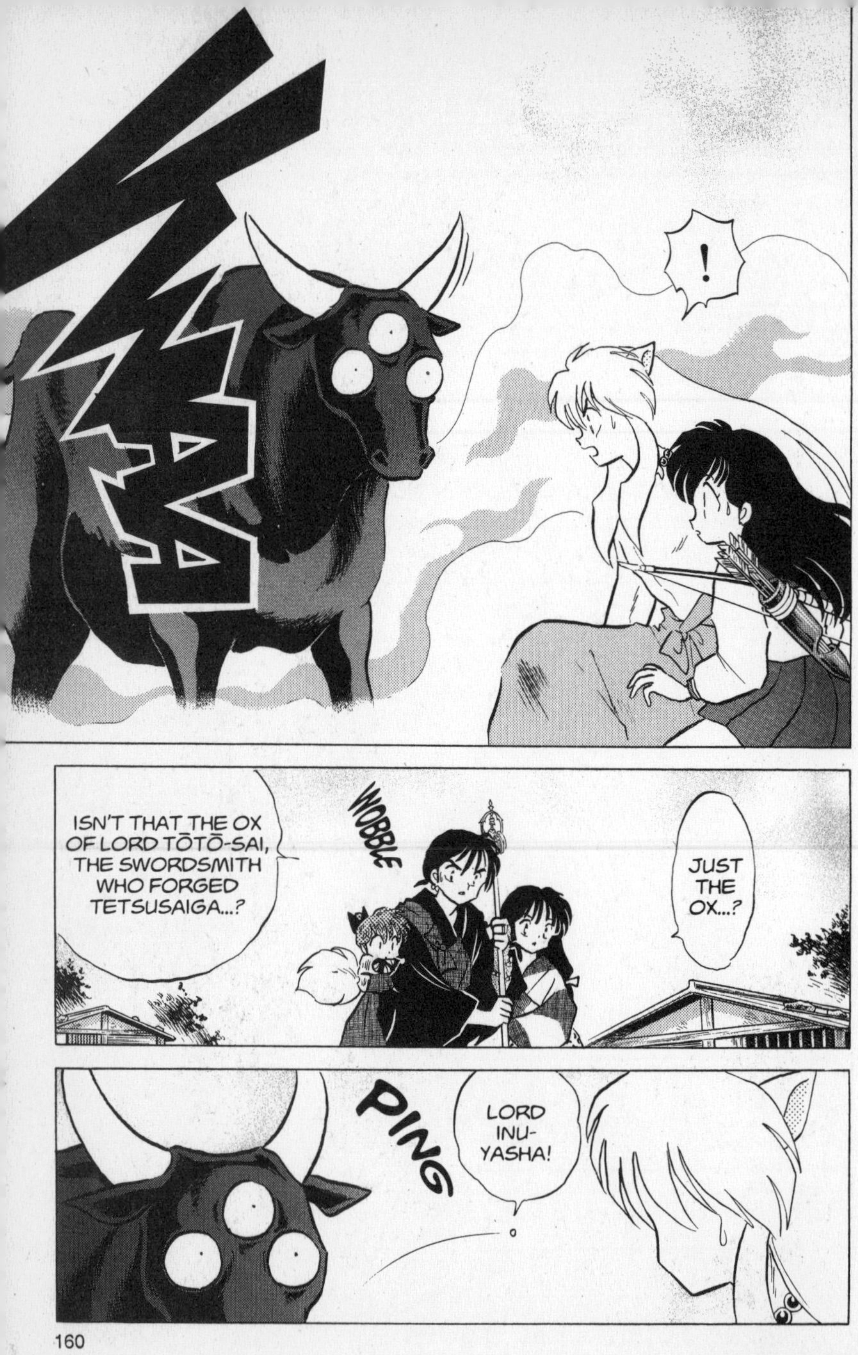
!
ISN'T THAT THE OX OF LORD TŌTŌ-SAI, THE SWORDSMITH WHO FORGED TETSUSAIGA...?
WOBBLE
JUST THE OX...?
PING
LORD INU-YASHA!

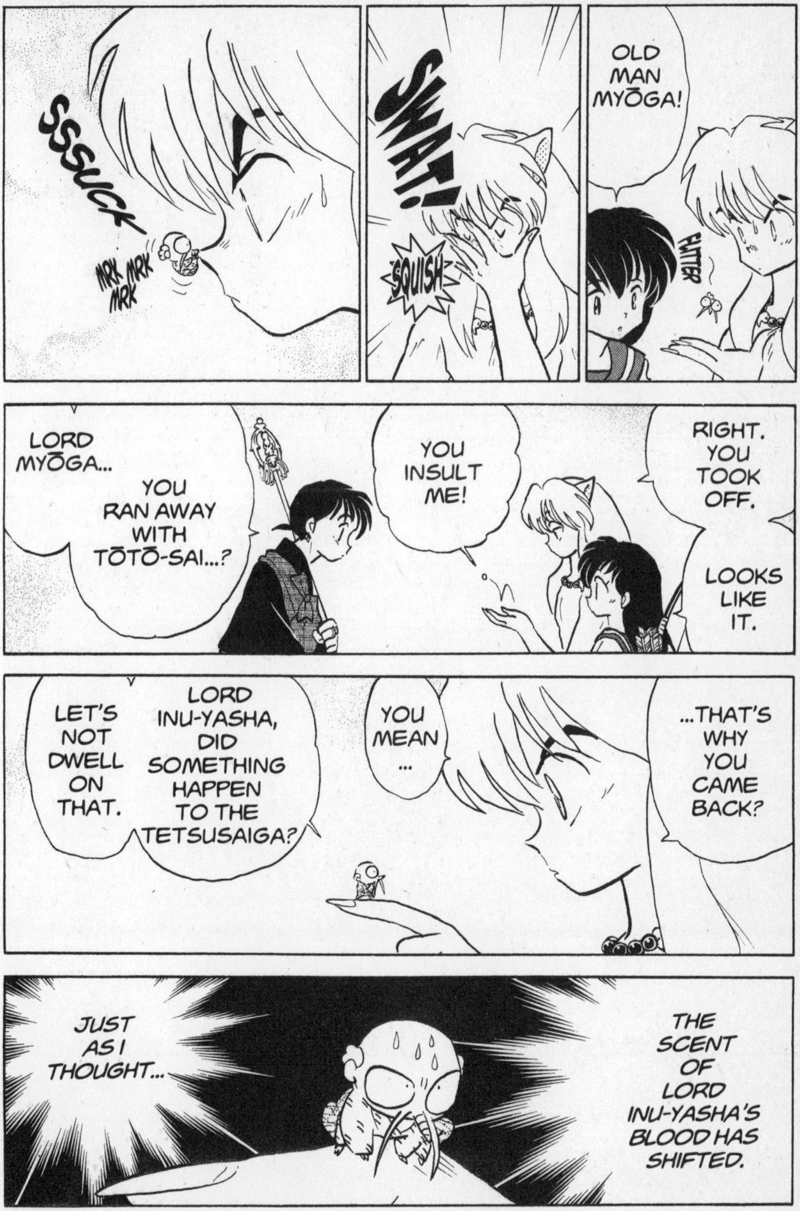
SSSUCK
MRK MRK MRK
SWAT!
SQUISH
OLD MAN MYŌGA!
FLUTTER
LORD MYŌGA...
YOU RAN AWAY WITH TŌTŌ-SAI...?
YOU INSULT ME!
RIGHT. YOU TOOK OFF.
LOOKS LIKE IT.
LET'S NOT DWELL ON THAT.
LORD INU-YASHA, DID SOMETHING HAPPEN TO THE TETSUSAIGA?
YOU MEAN...
...THAT'S WHY YOU CAME BACK?
JUST AS I THOUGHT...
THE SCENT OF LORD INU-YASHA'S BLOOD HAS SHIFTED.

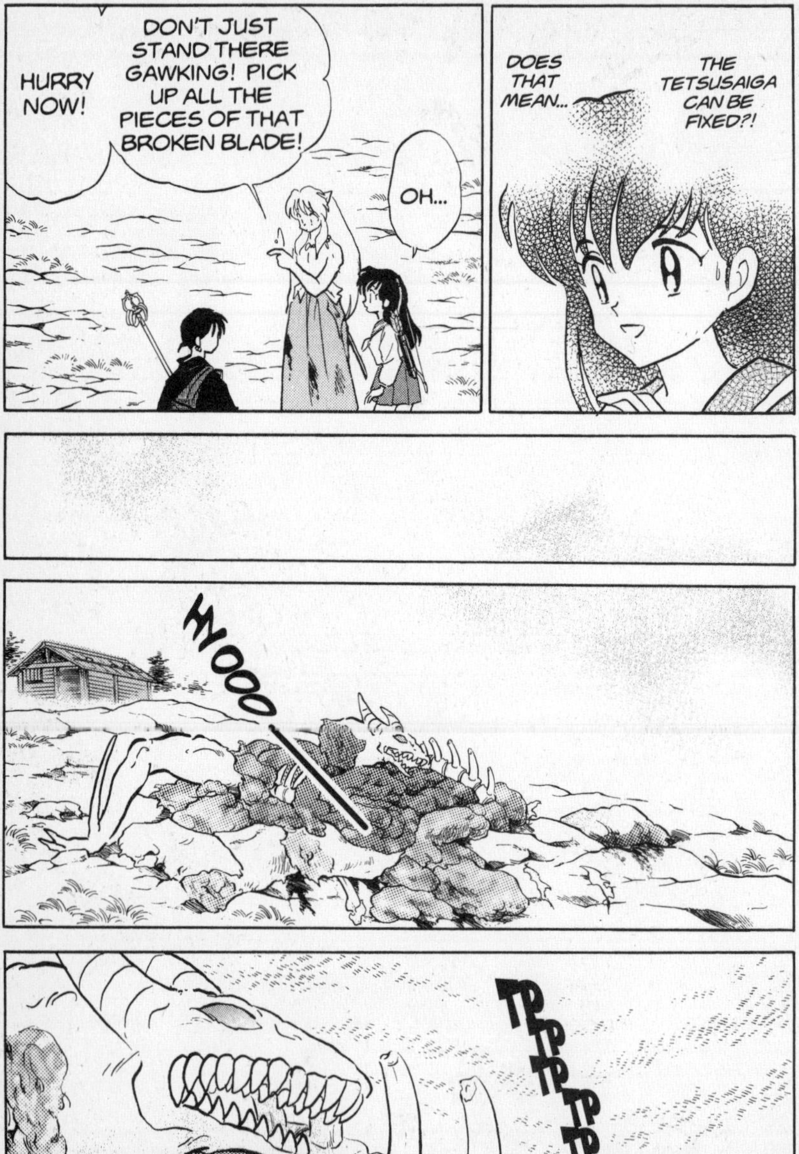
HURRY NOW!
DON'T JUST STAND THERE GAWKING! PICK UP ALL THE PIECES OF THAT BROKEN BLADE!
OH...
DOES THAT MEAN...
THE TETSUSAIGA CAN BE FIXED?!
HYOOO
TP TP TP TP TP

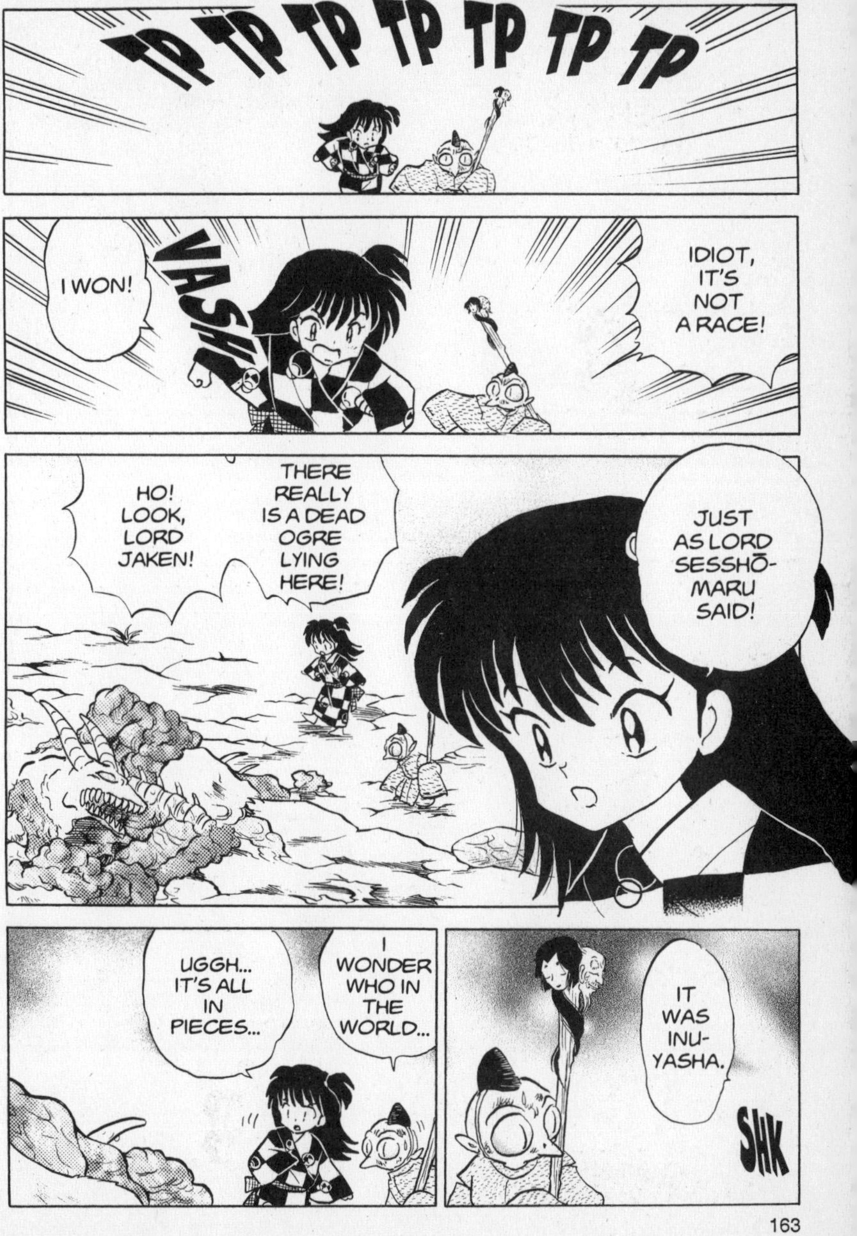
TP TP TP TP TP TP TP
I WON!
VASH!
IDIOT, IT'S NOT A RACE!
HO! LOOK, LORD JAKEN!
THERE REALLY IS A DEAD OGRE LYING HERE!
JUST AS LORD SESSHŌ-MARU SAID!
UGGH... IT'S ALL IN PIECES...
I WONDER WHO IN THE WORLD...
IT WAS INU-YASHA.
SHK

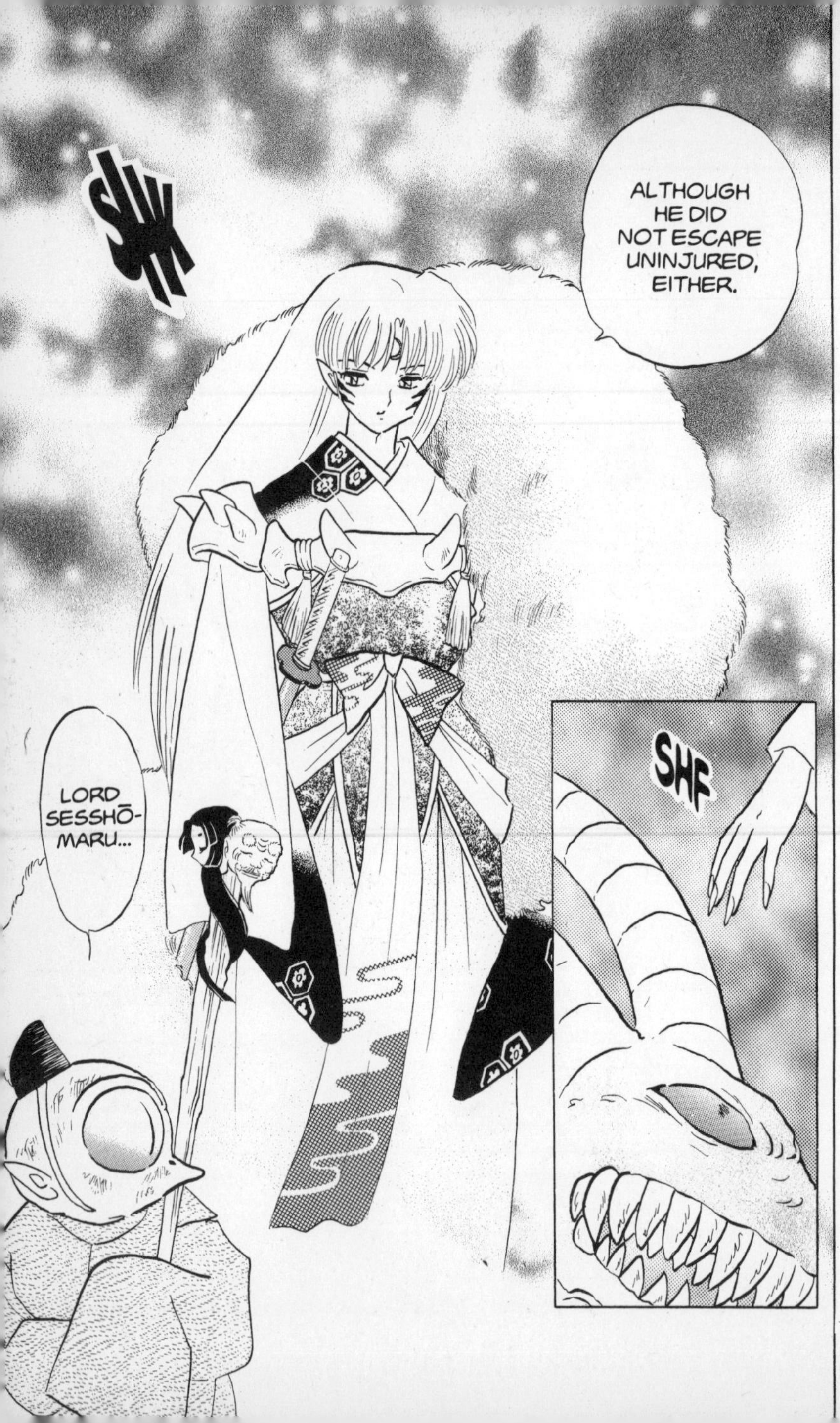
SHK
ALTHOUGH HE DID NOT ESCAPE UNINJURED, EITHER.
LORD SESSHŌ-MARU...
SHF

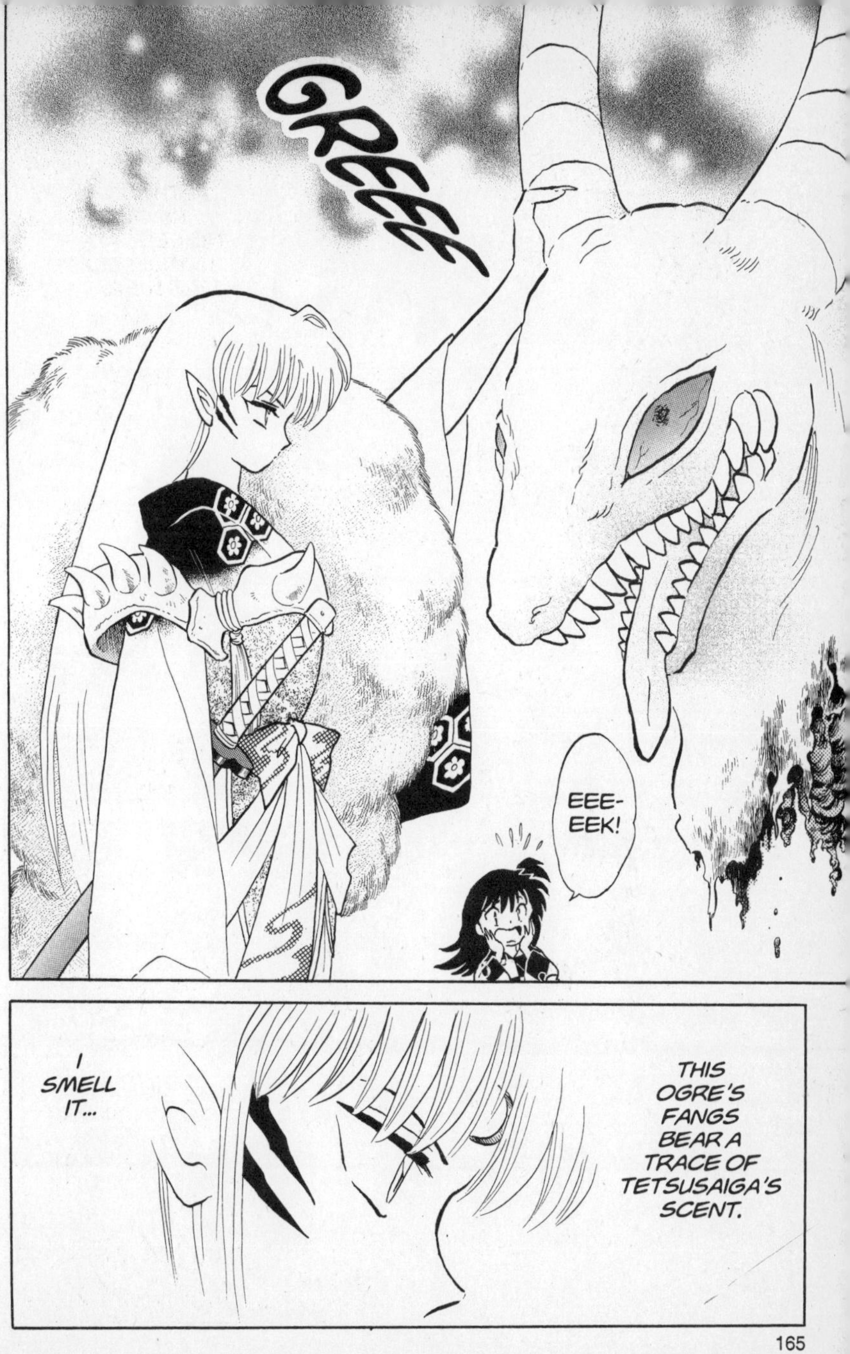
GREEE
EEE-EEK!
I SMELL IT...
THIS OGRE'S FANGS BEAR A TRACE OF TETSUSAIGA'S SCENT.

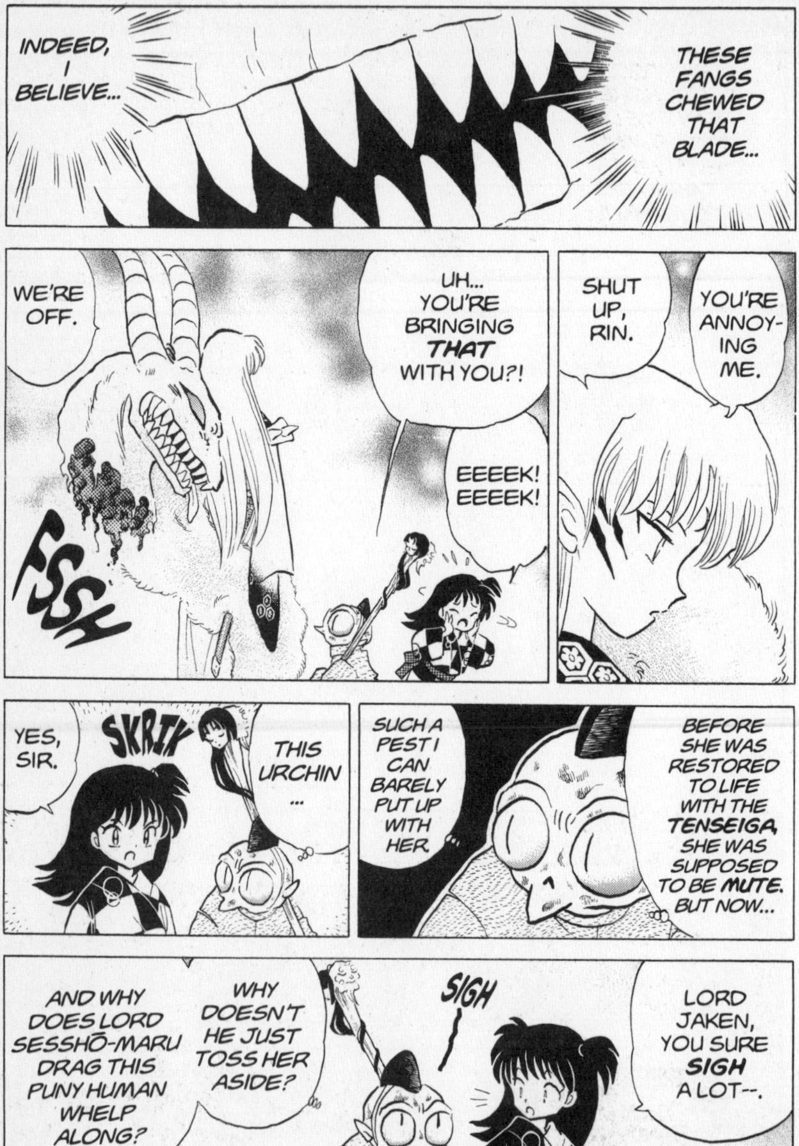
INDEED, I BELIEVE...
THESE FANGS CHEWED THAT BLADE...
WE'RE OFF.
FSSH
UH... YOU'RE BRINGING THAT WITH YOU?!
EEEEK! EEEEK!
SHUT UP, RIN.
YOU'RE ANNOY-ING ME.
YES, SIR.
SKRIK
THIS URCHIN ...
SUCH A PEST I CAN BARELY PUT UP WITH HER.
BEFORE SHE WAS RESTORED TO LIFE WITH THE TENSEIGA, SHE WAS SUPPOSED TO BE MUTE. BUT NOW...
AND WHY DOES LORD SESSHŌ-MARU DRAG THIS PUNY HUMAN WHELP ALONG?
WHY DOESN'T HE JUST TOSS HER ASIDE?
SIGH
LORD JAKEN, YOU SURE SIGH A LOT--.

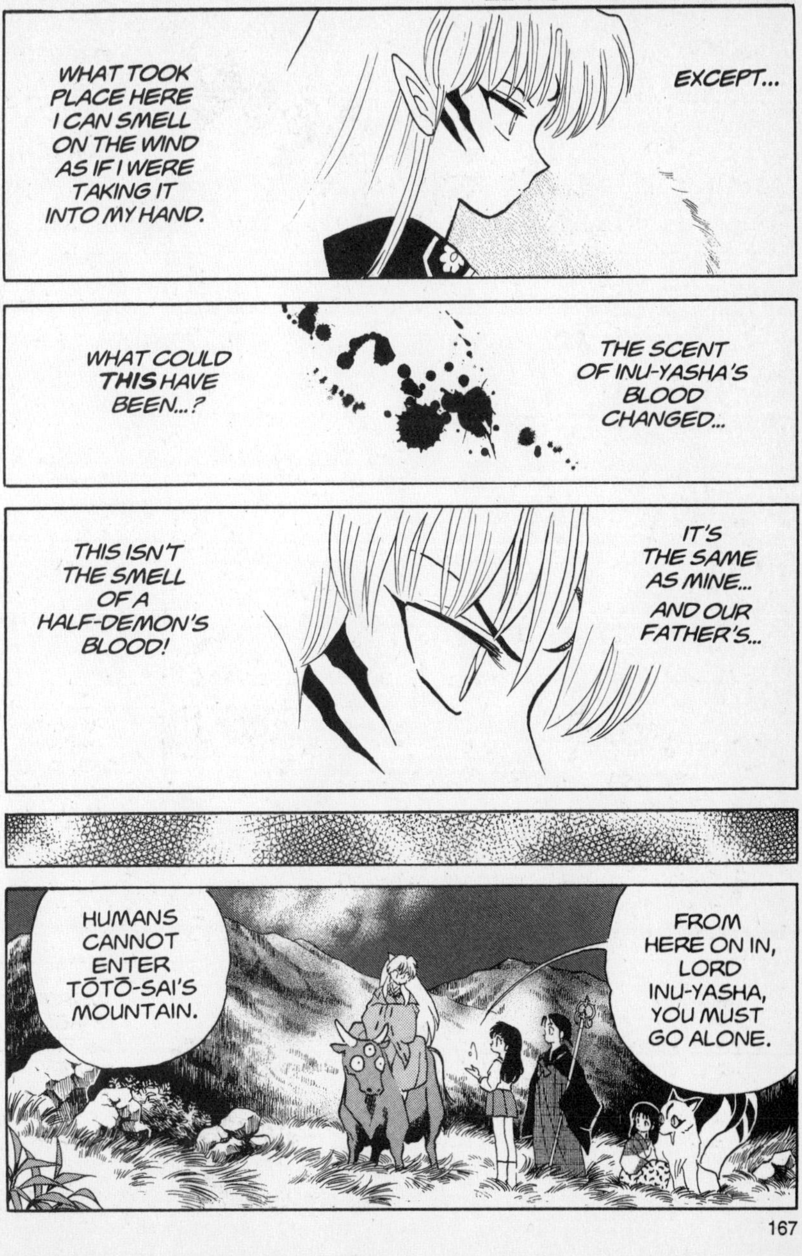
WHAT TOOK PLACE HERE I CAN SMELL ON THE WIND AS IF I WERE TAKING IT INTO MY HAND.
EXCEPT...
WHAT COULD THIS HAVE BEEN...?
THE SCENT OF INU-YASHA'S BLOOD CHANGED...
THIS ISN'T THE SMELL OF A HALF-DEMON'S BLOOD!
IT'S THE SAME AS MINE...
AND OUR FATHER'S...
HUMANS CANNOT ENTER TŌTŌ-SAI'S MOUNTAIN.
FROM HERE ON IN, LORD INU-YASHA, YOU MUST GO ALONE.

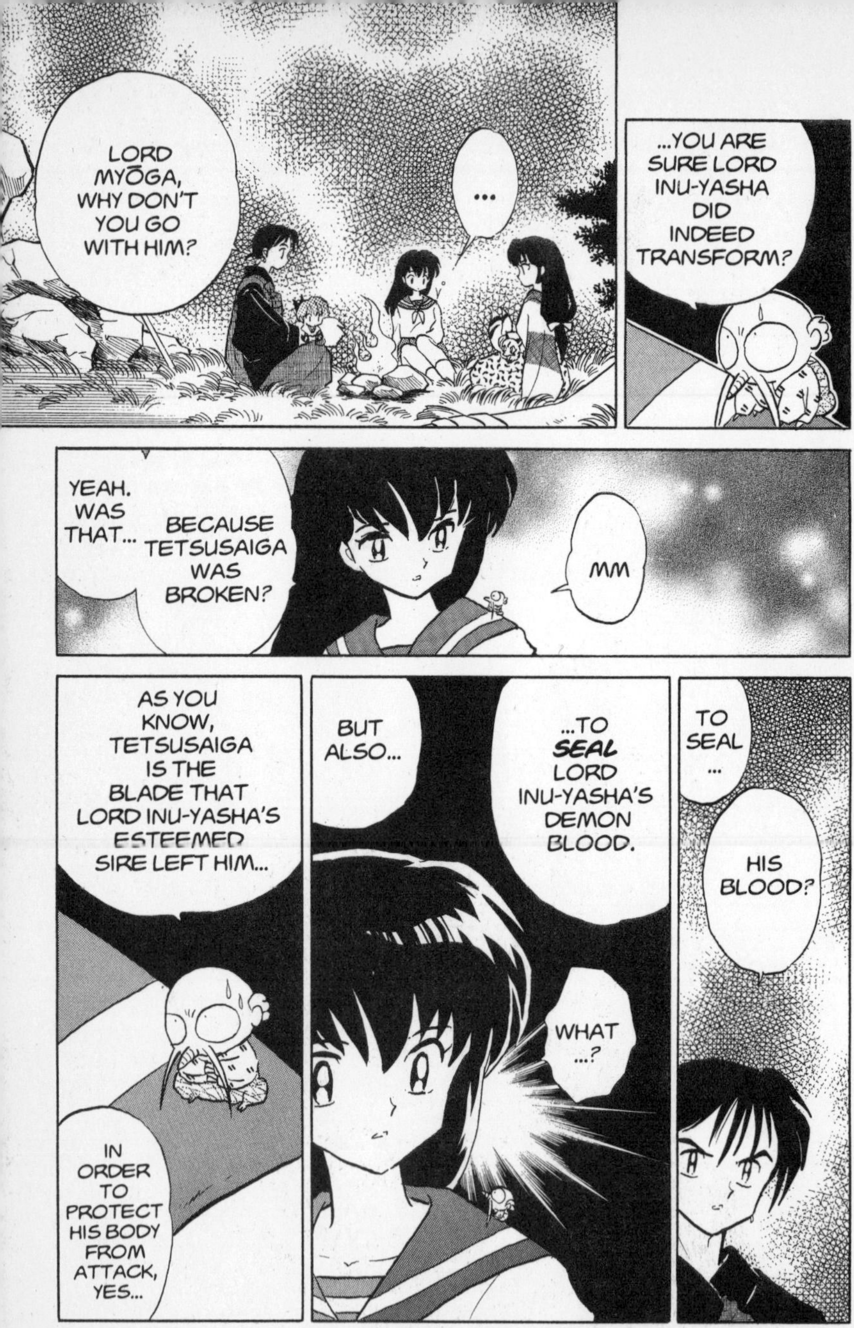

LORD MYŌGA, WHY DON'T YOU GO WITH HIM?
...
...YOU ARE SURE LORD INU-YASHA DID INDEED TRANSFORM?
YEAH.
WAS THAT... BECAUSE TETSUSAIGA WAS BROKEN?
MM
AS YOU KNOW, TETSUSAIGA IS THE BLADE THAT LORD INU-YASHA'S ESTEEMED SIRE LEFT HIM...
IN ORDER TO PROTECT HIS BODY FROM ATTACK, YES...
BUT ALSO...
...TO SEAL LORD INU-YASHA'S DEMON BLOOD.
WHAT ...?
TO SEAL ...
HIS BLOOD?

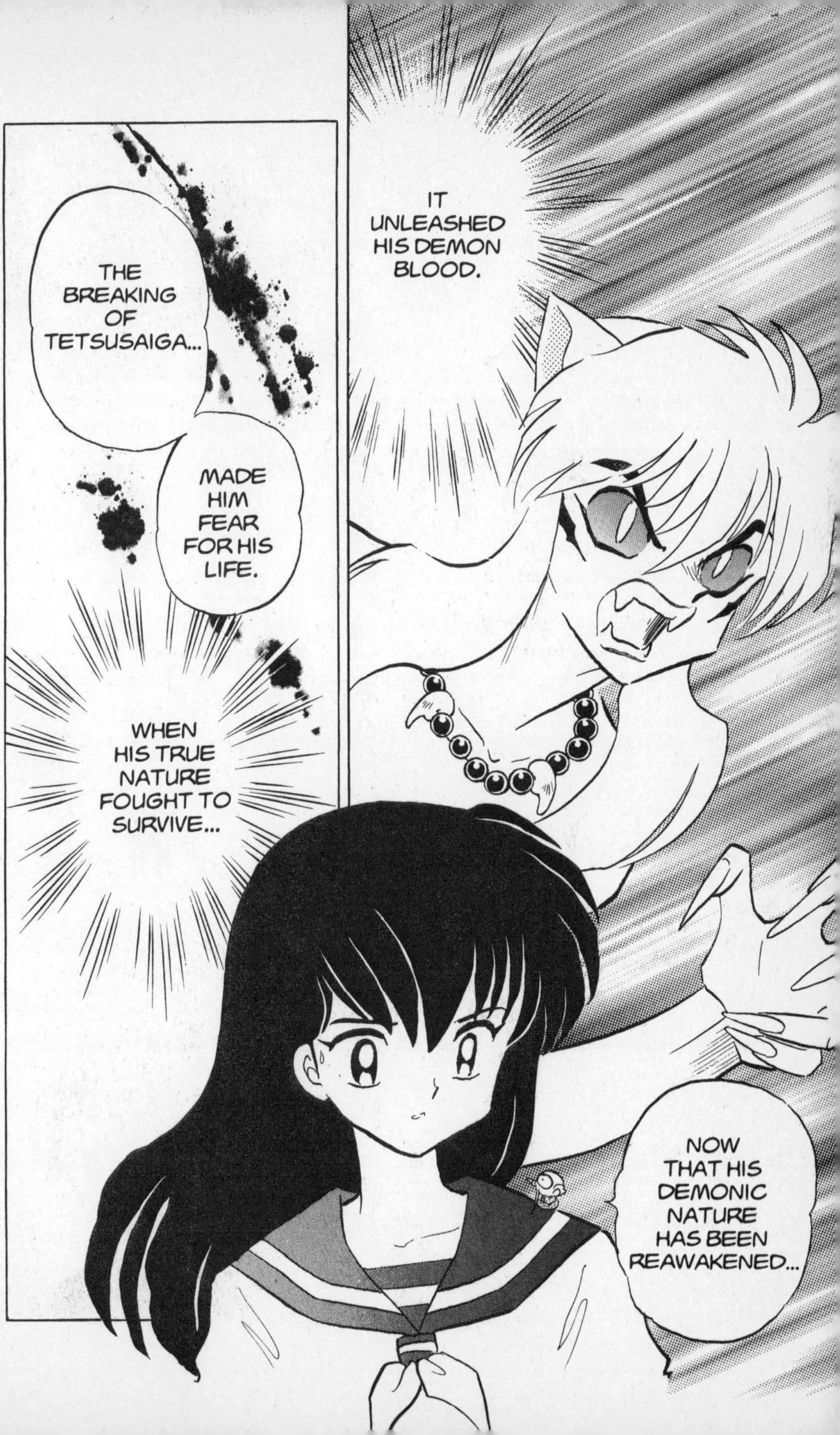
THE BREAKING OF TETSUSAIGA...
MADE HIM FEAR FOR HIS LIFE.
WHEN HIS TRUE NATURE FOUGHT TO SURVIVE...
IT UNLEASHED HIS DEMON BLOOD.
NOW THAT HIS DEMONIC NATURE HAS BEEN REAWAKENED...

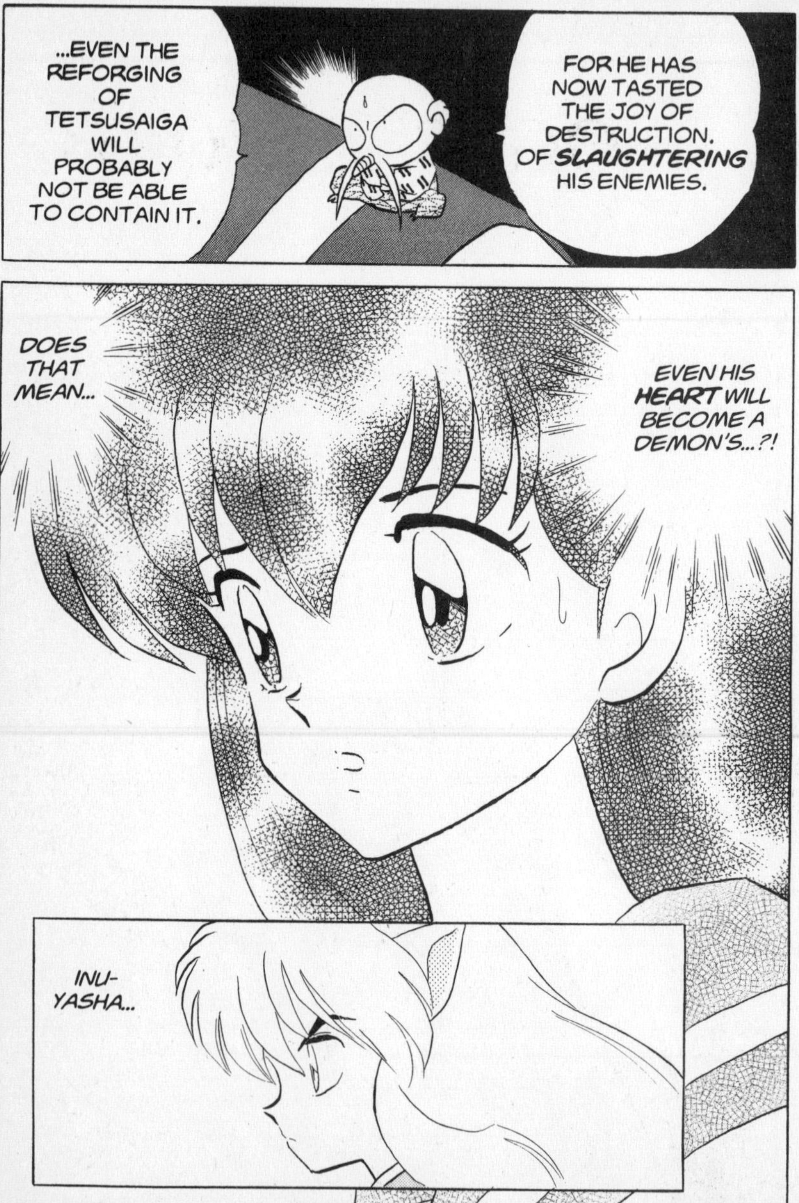
...EVEN THE REFORGING OF TETSUSAIGA WILL PROBABLY NOT BE ABLE TO CONTAIN IT.
FOR HE HAS NOW TASTED THE JOY OF DESTRUCTION. OF **SLAUGHTERING** HIS ENEMIES.
DOES THAT MEAN...
EVEN HIS **HEART** WILL BECOME A DEMON'S...?!
INU-YASHA...

SCROLL TEN

THE OGRE'S SWORD

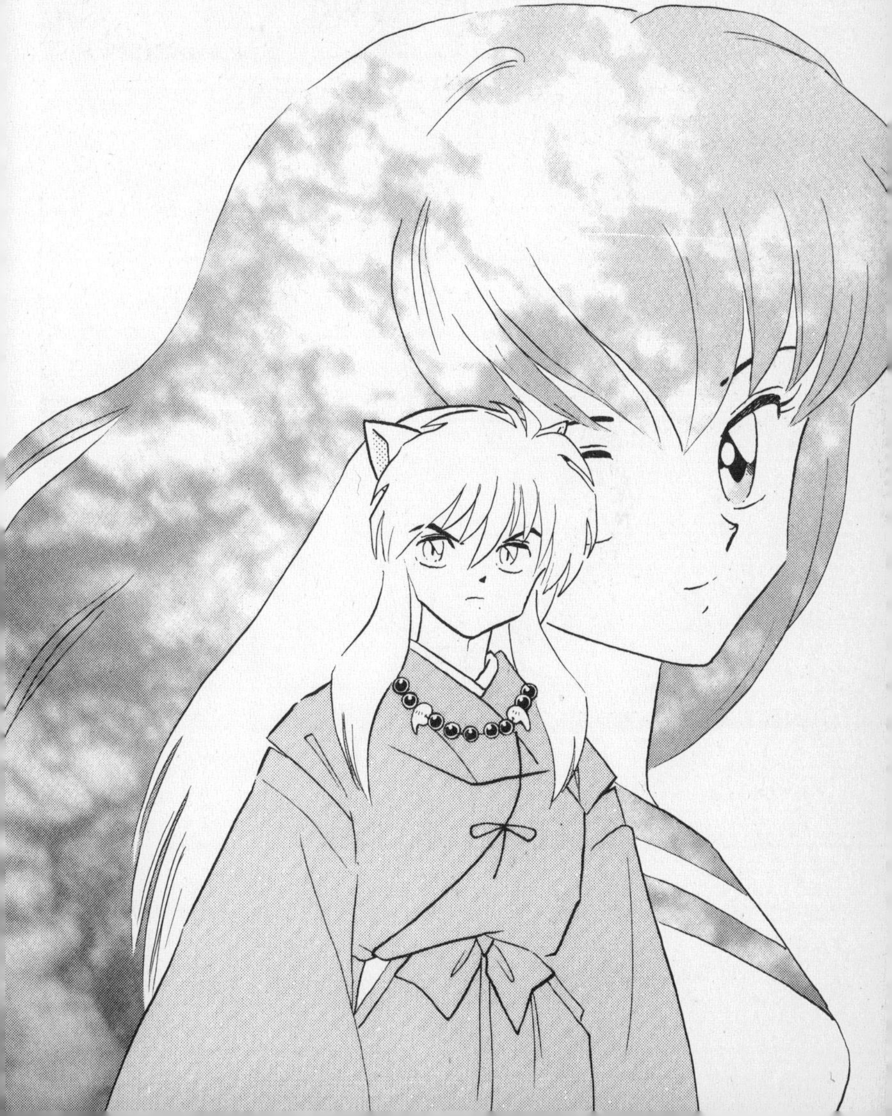

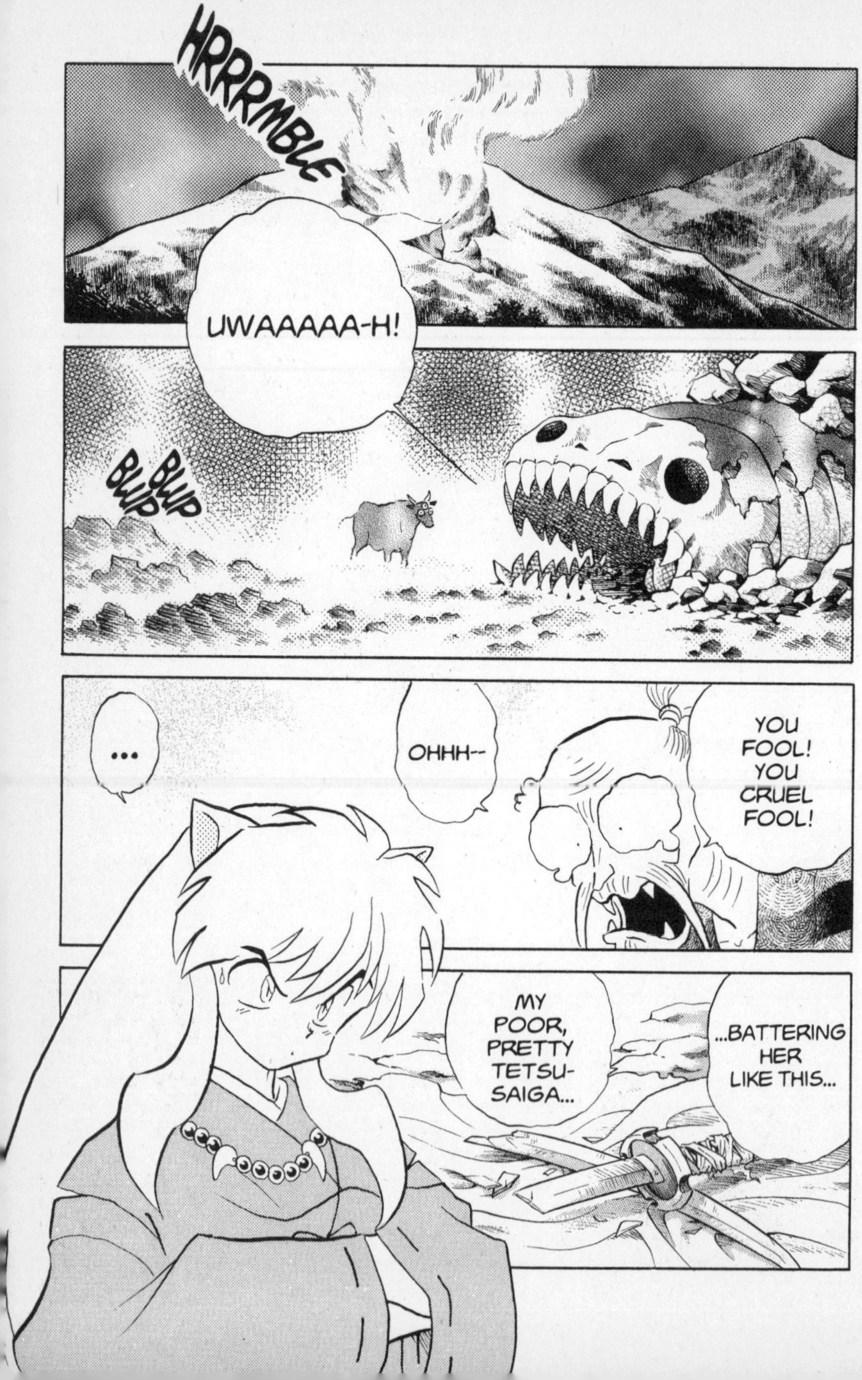
HRRRMBLE
UWAAAAA-H!
BWUP BWUP
...
OHHH--
YOU FOOL! YOU CRUEL FOOL!
MY POOR, PRETTY TETSU-SAIGA...
...BATTERING HER LIKE THIS...

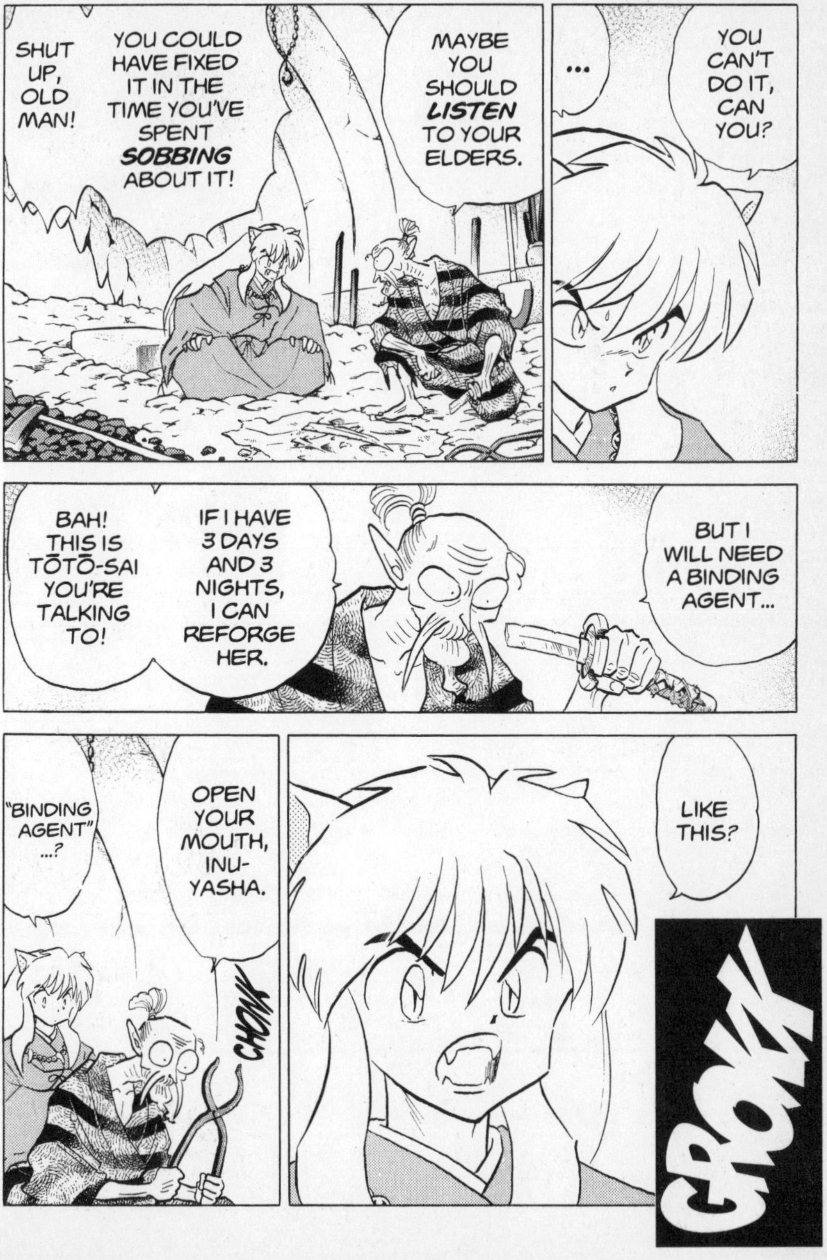
SHUT UP, OLD MAN!
YOU COULD HAVE FIXED IT IN THE TIME YOU'VE SPENT SOBBING ABOUT IT!
MAYBE YOU SHOULD LISTEN TO YOUR ELDERS.
...
YOU CAN'T DO IT, CAN YOU?
BAH! THIS IS TŌTŌ-SAI YOU'RE TALKING TO!
IF I HAVE 3 DAYS AND 3 NIGHTS, I CAN REFORGE HER.
BUT I WILL NEED A BINDING AGENT...
"BINDING AGENT" ...?
OPEN YOUR MOUTH, INU-YASHA.
CHONK
LIKE THIS?
GRONK

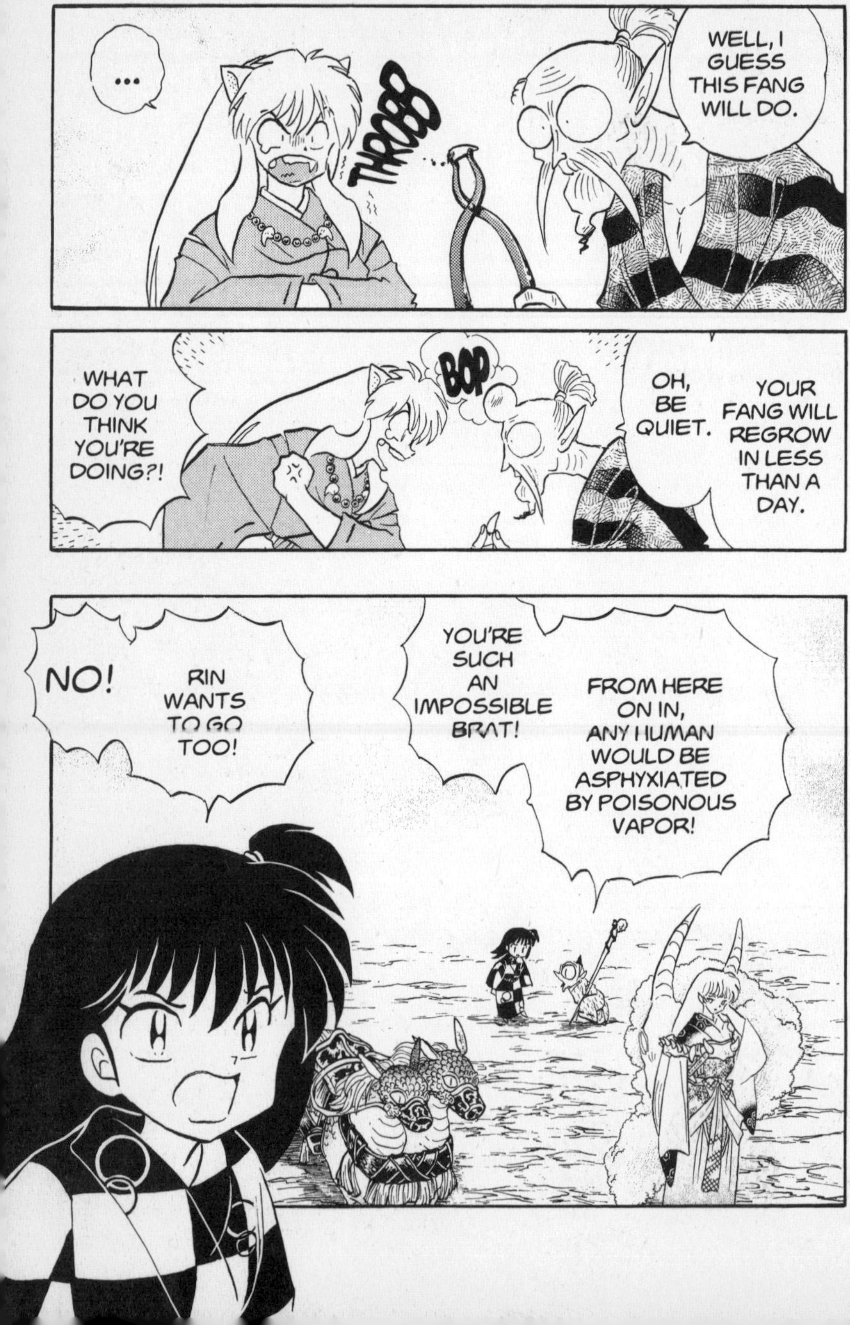
...
THROBB
WELL, I GUESS THIS FANG WILL DO.
WHAT DO YOU THINK YOU'RE DOING?!
BOP
OH, BE QUIET.
YOUR FANG WILL REGROW IN LESS THAN A DAY.
NO!
RIN WANTS TO GO TOO!
YOU'RE SUCH AN IMPOSSIBLE BRAT!
FROM HERE ON IN, ANY HUMAN WOULD BE ASPHYXIATED BY POISONOUS VAPOR!

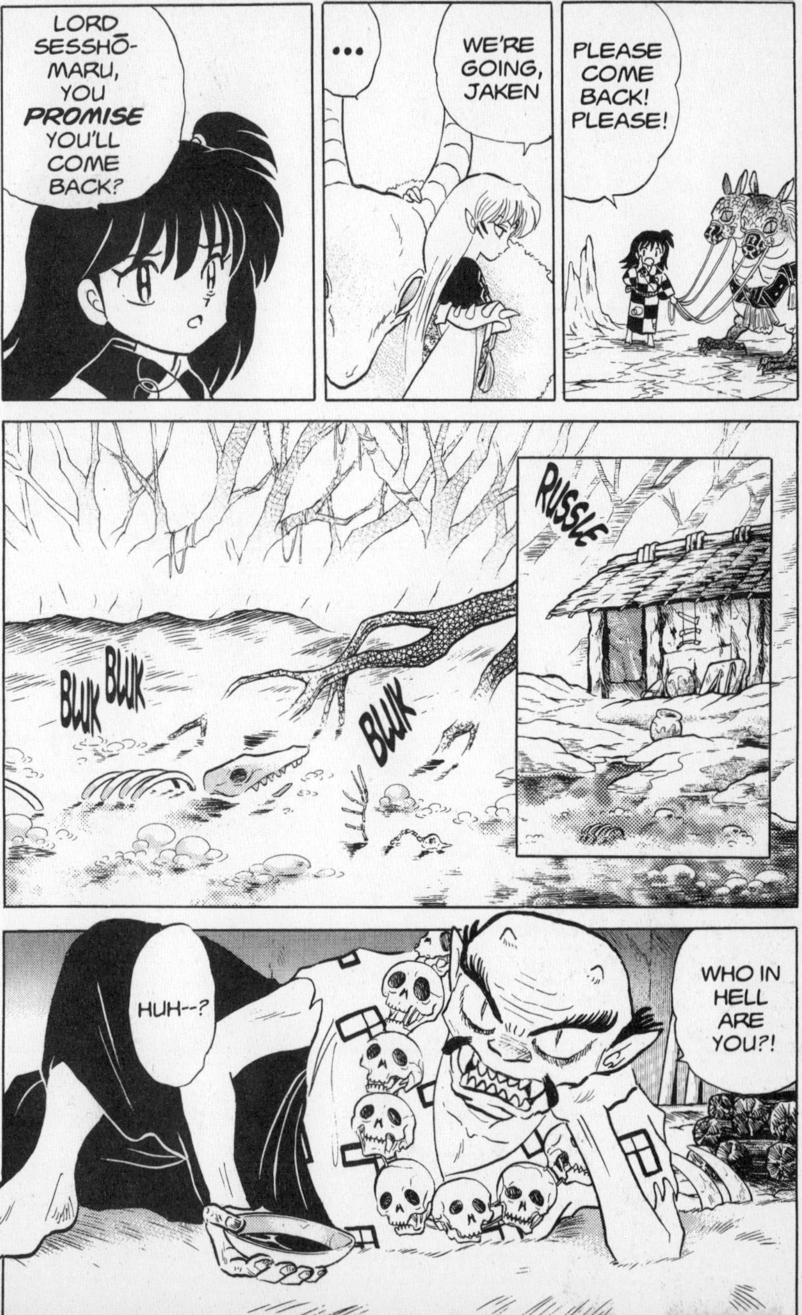
LORD SESSHŌ-MARU, YOU **PROMISE** YOU'LL COME BACK?
...
WE'RE GOING, JAKEN
PLEASE COME BACK! PLEASE!
BLUK
BLUK
BLUK
RUSSLE
HUH--?
WHO IN HELL ARE YOU?!

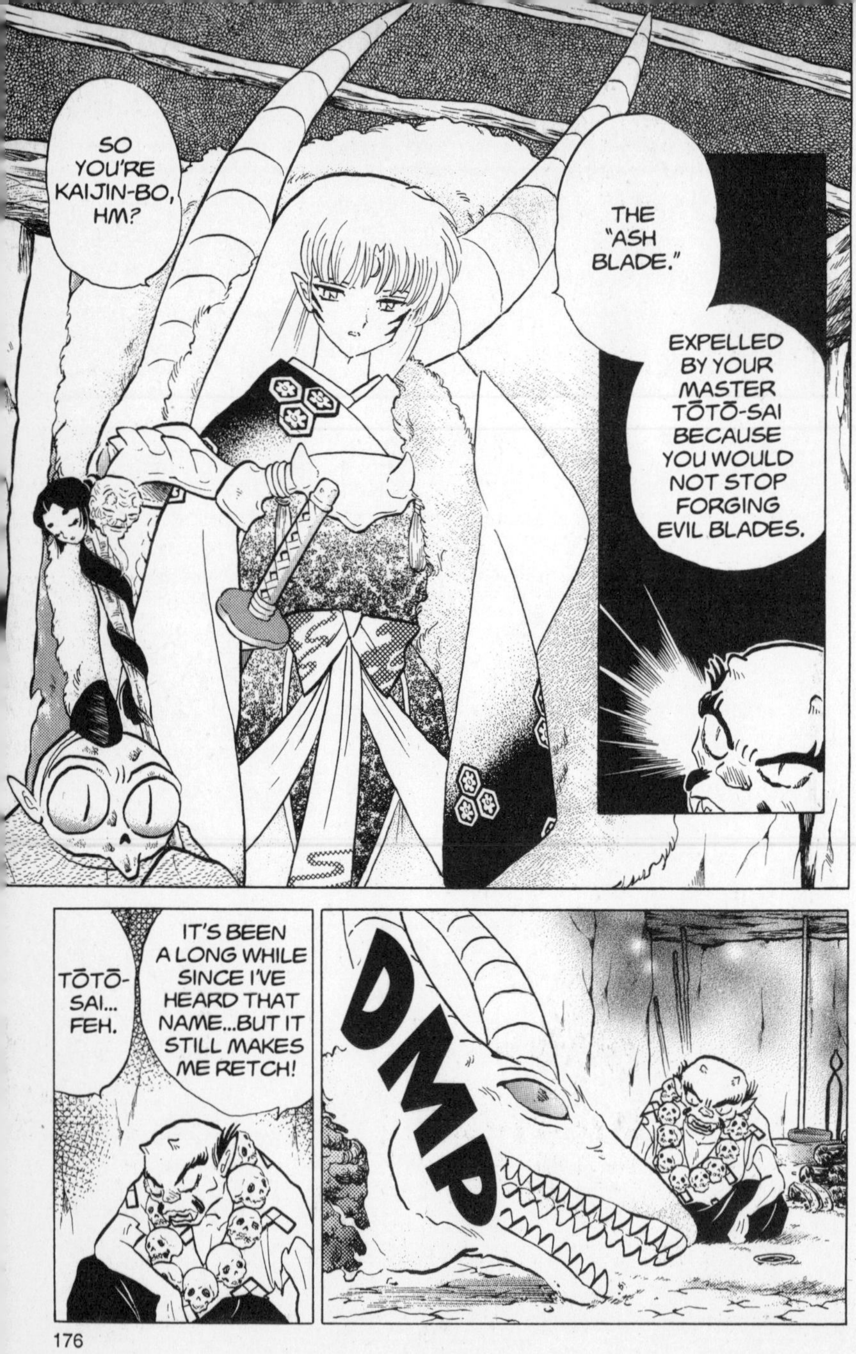
SO YOU'RE KAIJIN-BO, HM?
THE "ASH BLADE."
EXPELLED BY YOUR MASTER TŌTŌ-SAI BECAUSE YOU WOULD NOT STOP FORGING EVIL BLADES.
TŌTŌ-SAI... FEH.
IT'S BEEN A LONG WHILE SINCE I'VE HEARD THAT NAME...BUT IT STILL MAKES ME RETCH!
DMP

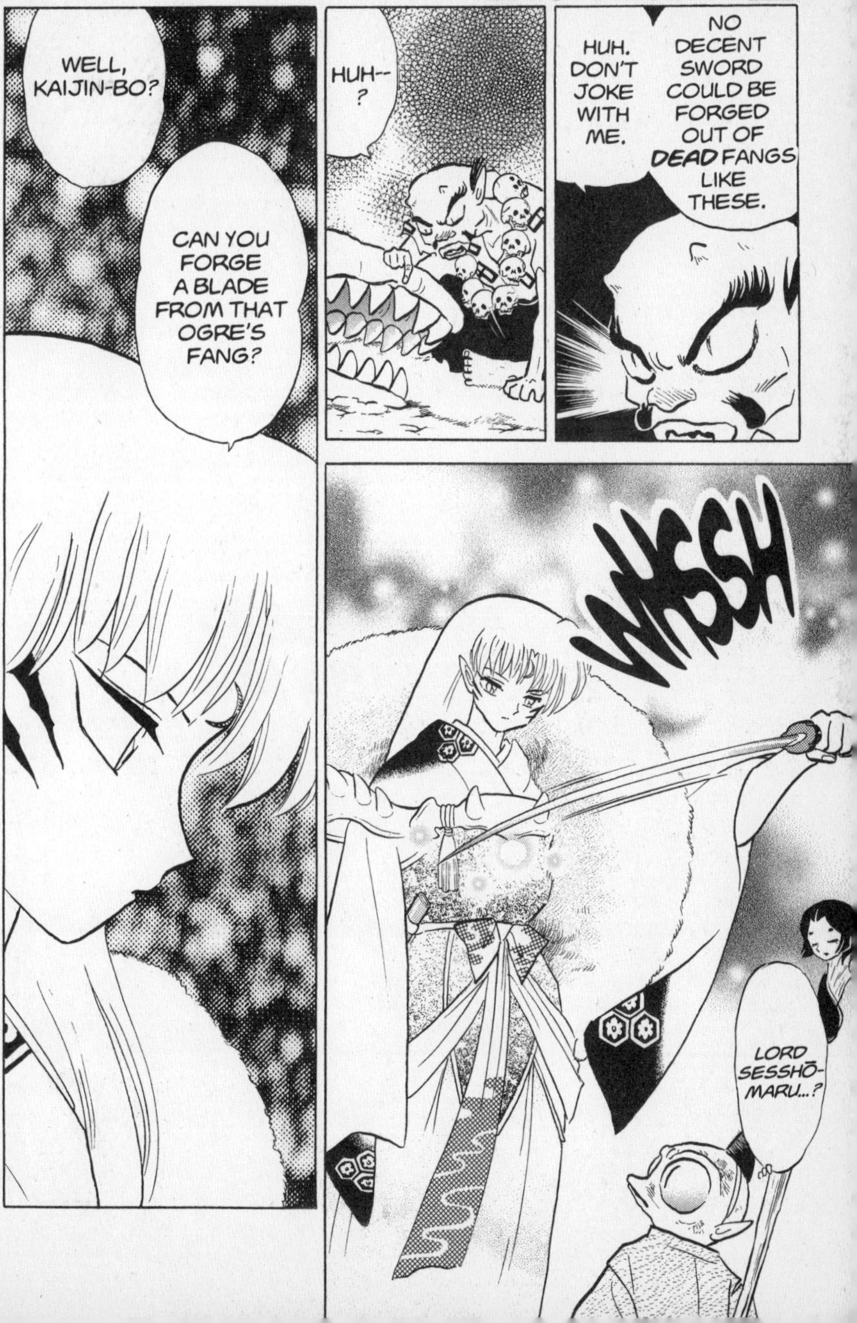
WELL, KAIJIN-BO?
CAN YOU FORGE A BLADE FROM THAT OGRE'S FANG?
HUH-- ?
HUH. DON'T JOKE WITH ME.
NO DECENT SWORD COULD BE FORGED OUT OF DEAD FANGS LIKE THESE.
WSSH
LORD SESSHŌ-MARU...?

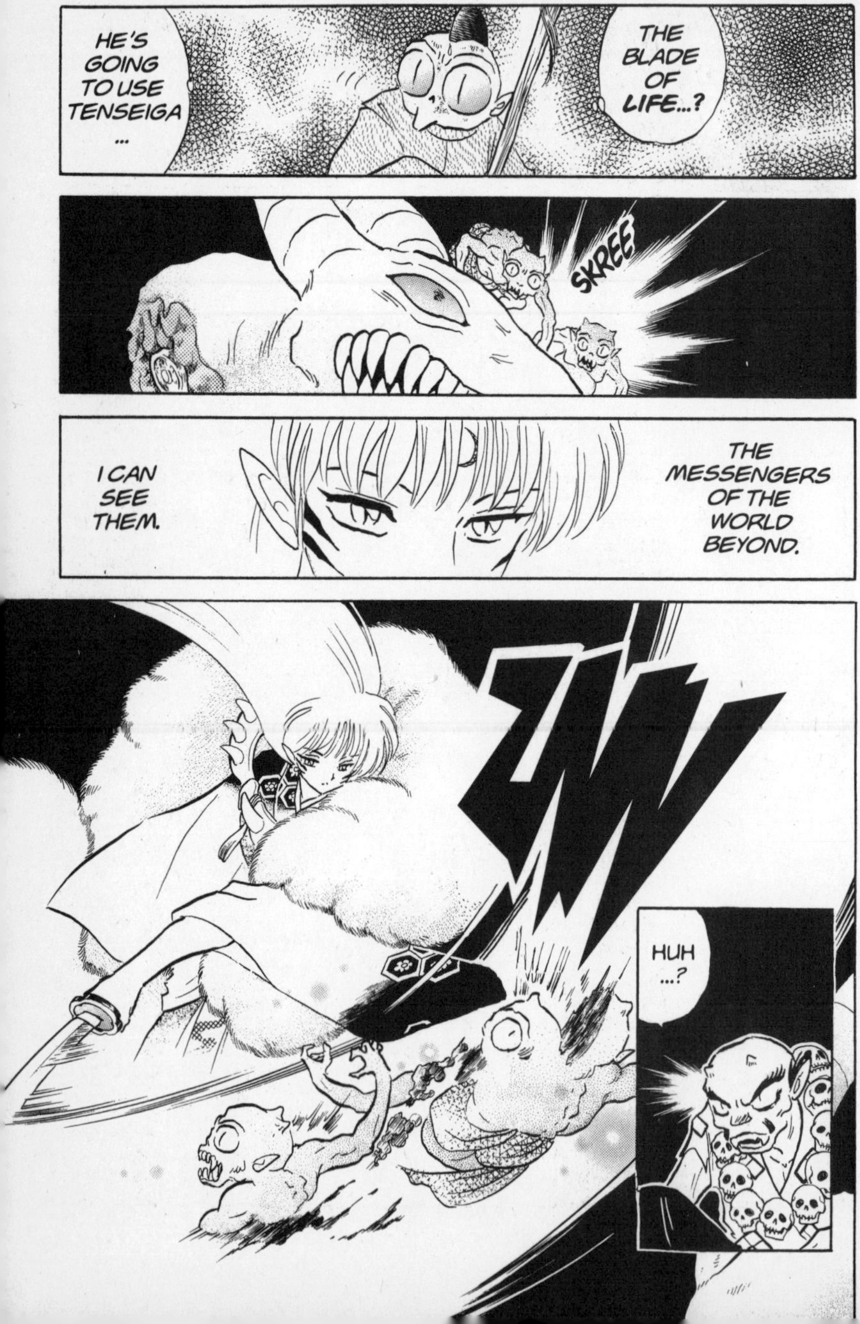
HE'S GOING TO USE TENSEIGA ...
THE BLADE OF LIFE...?
SKREE
I CAN SEE THEM.
THE MESSENGERS OF THE WORLD BEYOND.
HUH ...?

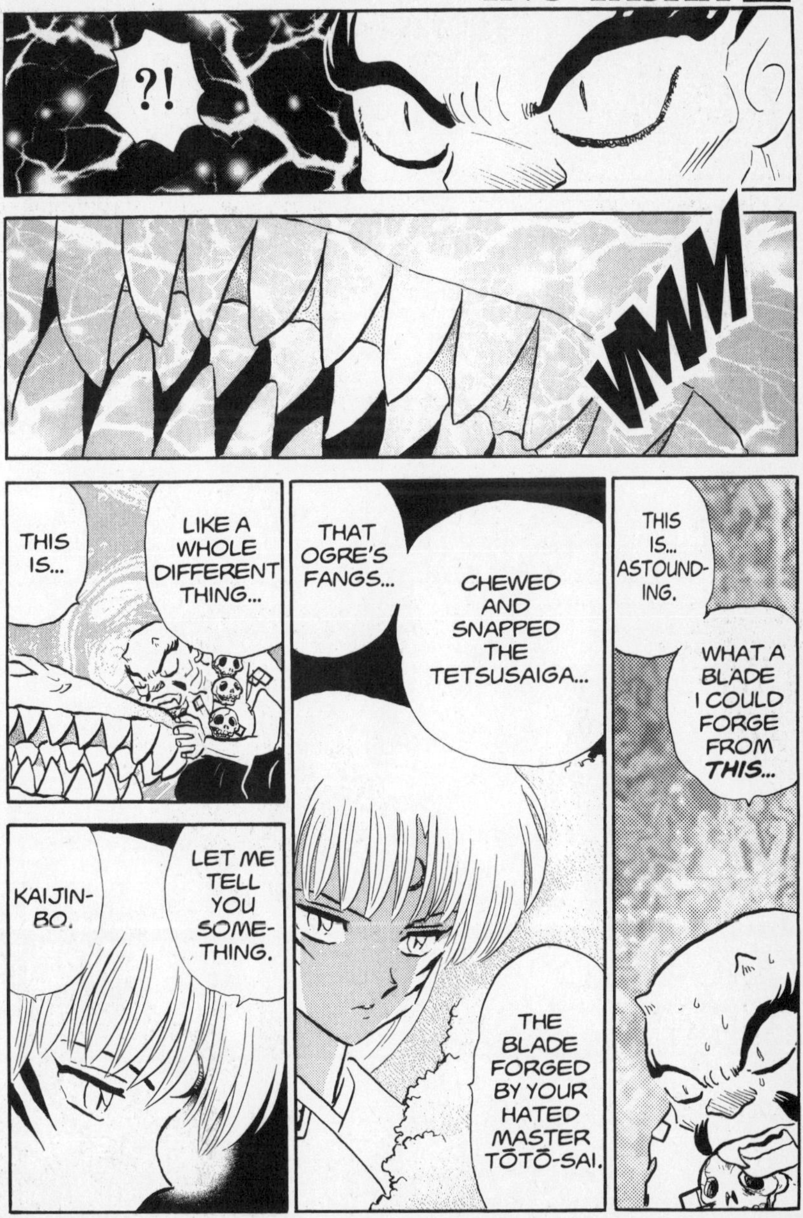
?!
VMMM
THIS IS...
LIKE A WHOLE DIFFERENT THING...
KAIJIN-BO.
LET ME TELL YOU SOME-THING.
THAT OGRE'S FANGS...
CHEWED AND SNAPPED THE TETSUSAIGA...
THE BLADE FORGED BY YOUR HATED MASTER TŌTŌ-SAI.
THIS IS... ASTOUND-ING.
WHAT A BLADE I COULD FORGE FROM ***THIS...***

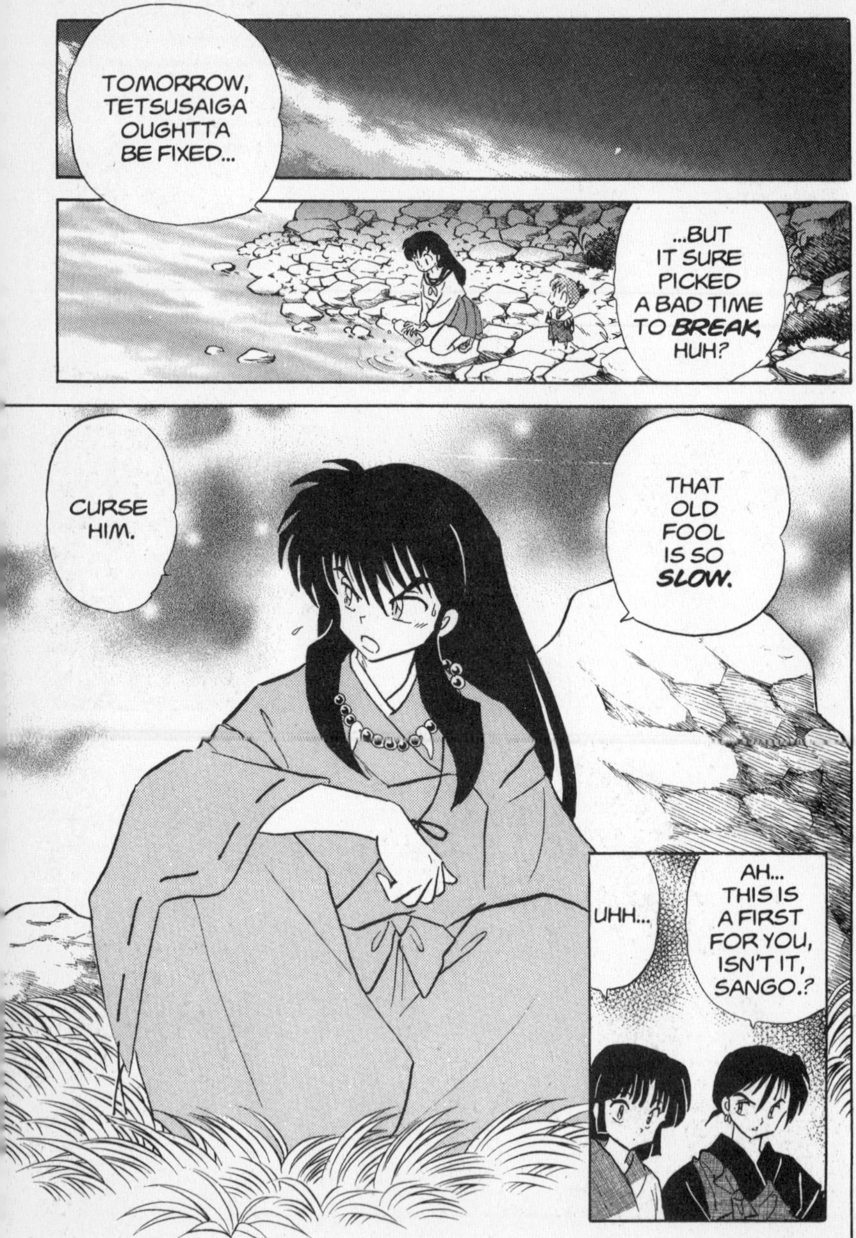
TOMORROW, TETSUSAIGA OUGHTTA BE FIXED...
...BUT IT SURE PICKED A BAD TIME TO **BREAK,** HUH?
CURSE HIM.
THAT OLD FOOL IS SO **SLOW.**
UHH...
AH... THIS IS A FIRST FOR YOU, ISN'T IT, SANGO.?

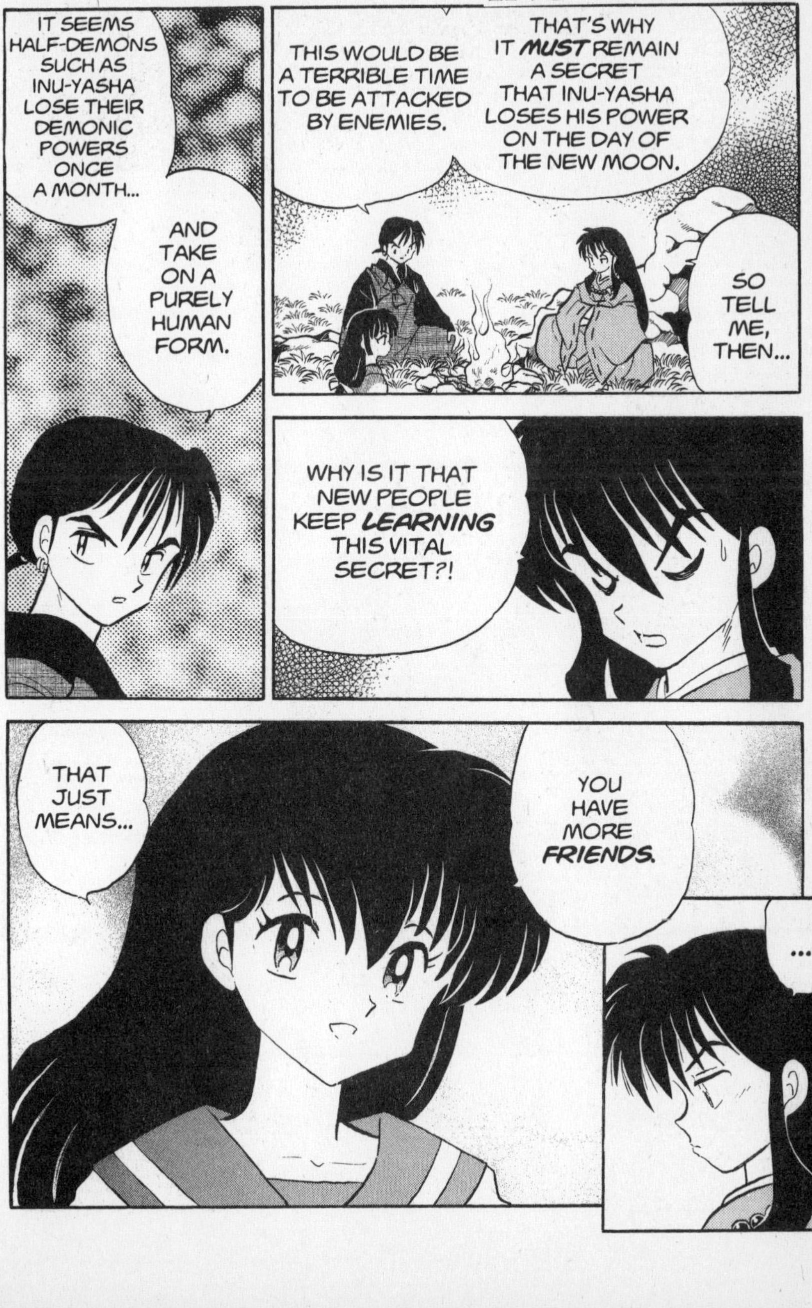
IT SEEMS HALF-DEMONS SUCH AS INU-YASHA LOSE THEIR DEMONIC POWERS ONCE A MONTH...
AND TAKE ON A PURELY HUMAN FORM.
THIS WOULD BE A TERRIBLE TIME TO BE ATTACKED BY ENEMIES.
THAT'S WHY IT *MUST* REMAIN A SECRET THAT INU-YASHA LOSES HIS POWER ON THE DAY OF THE NEW MOON.
SO TELL ME, THEN...
WHY IS IT THAT NEW PEOPLE KEEP *LEARNING* THIS VITAL SECRET?!
THAT JUST MEANS...
YOU HAVE MORE *FRIENDS.*
...

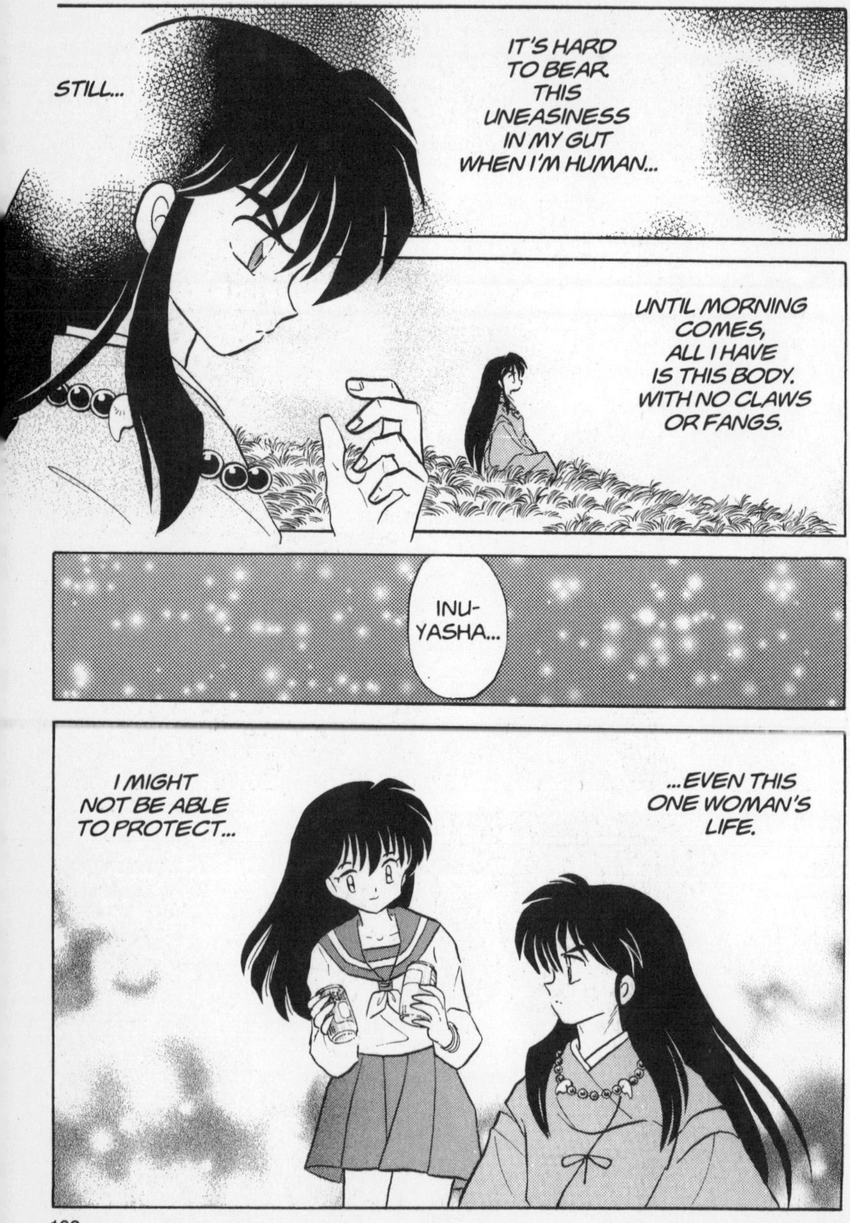
STILL...
IT'S HARD TO BEAR. THIS UNEASINESS IN MY GUT WHEN I'M HUMAN...
UNTIL MORNING COMES, ALL I HAVE IS THIS BODY. WITH NO CLAWS OR FANGS.
INU-YASHA...
I MIGHT NOT BE ABLE TO PROTECT...
...EVEN THIS ONE WOMAN'S LIFE.

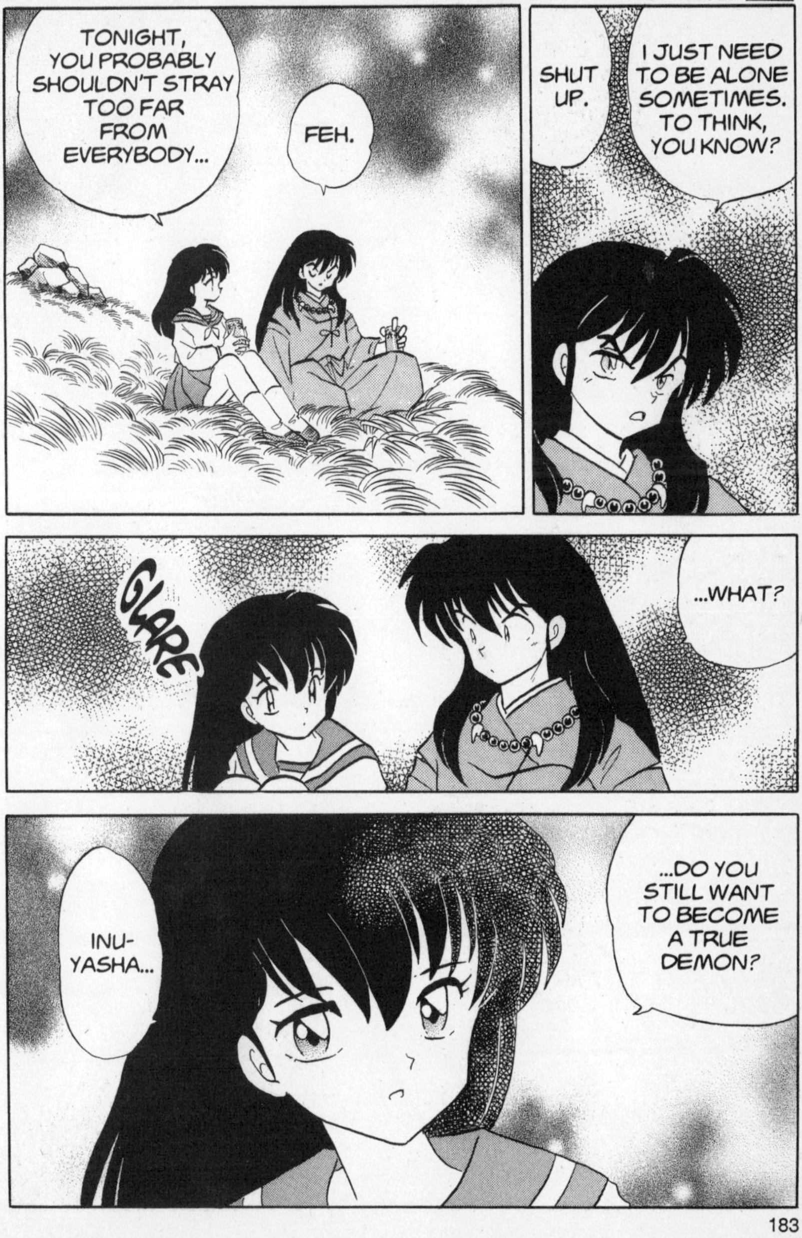
TONIGHT, YOU PROBABLY SHOULDN'T STRAY TOO FAR FROM EVERYBODY...
FEH.
SHUT UP.
I JUST NEED TO BE ALONE SOMETIMES. TO THINK, YOU KNOW?
GLARE
...WHAT?
INU-YASHA...
...DO YOU STILL WANT TO BECOME A TRUE DEMON?

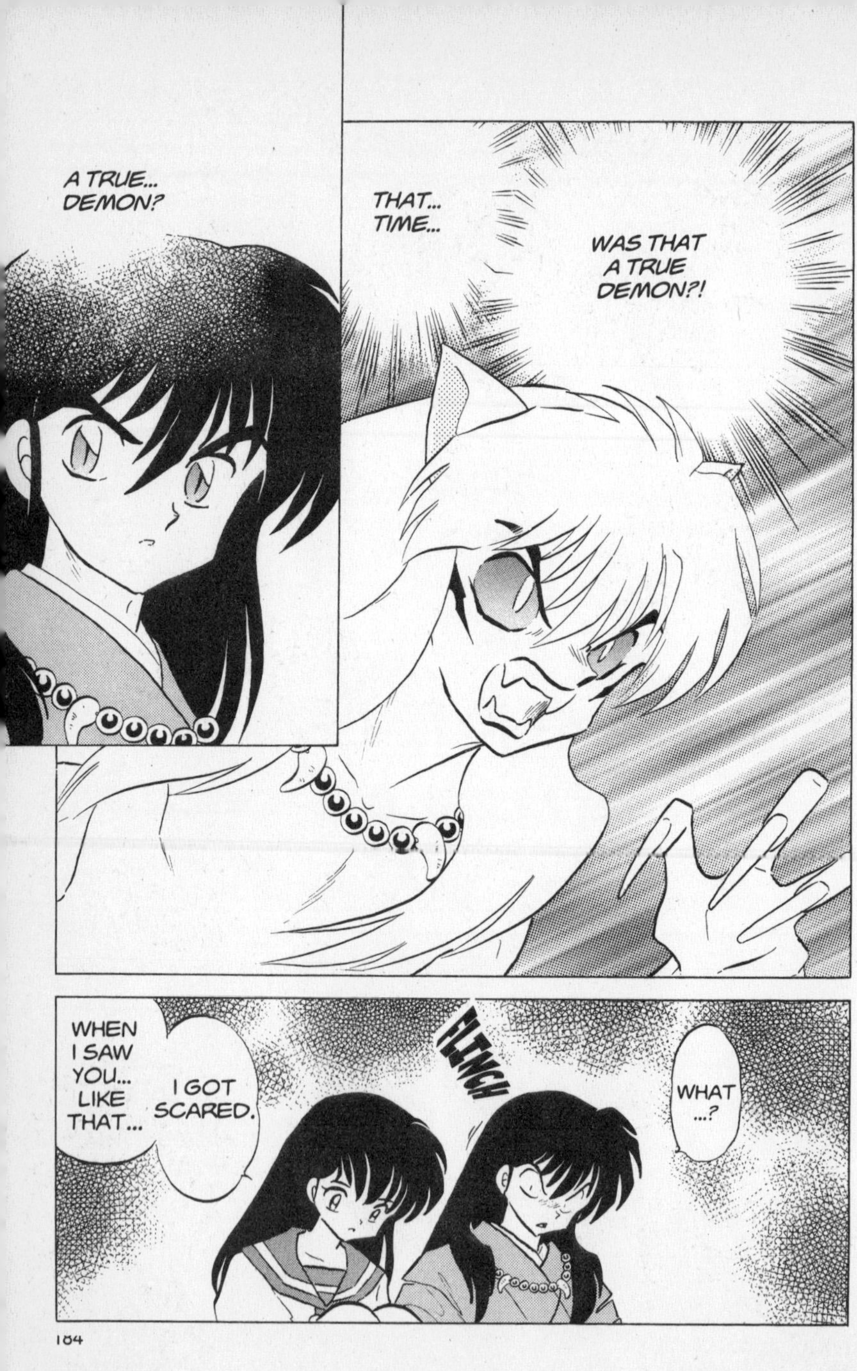
A TRUE... DEMON?
THAT... TIME...
WAS THAT A TRUE DEMON?!
WHEN I SAW YOU... LIKE THAT...
I GOT SCARED.
FLINCH
WHAT ...?

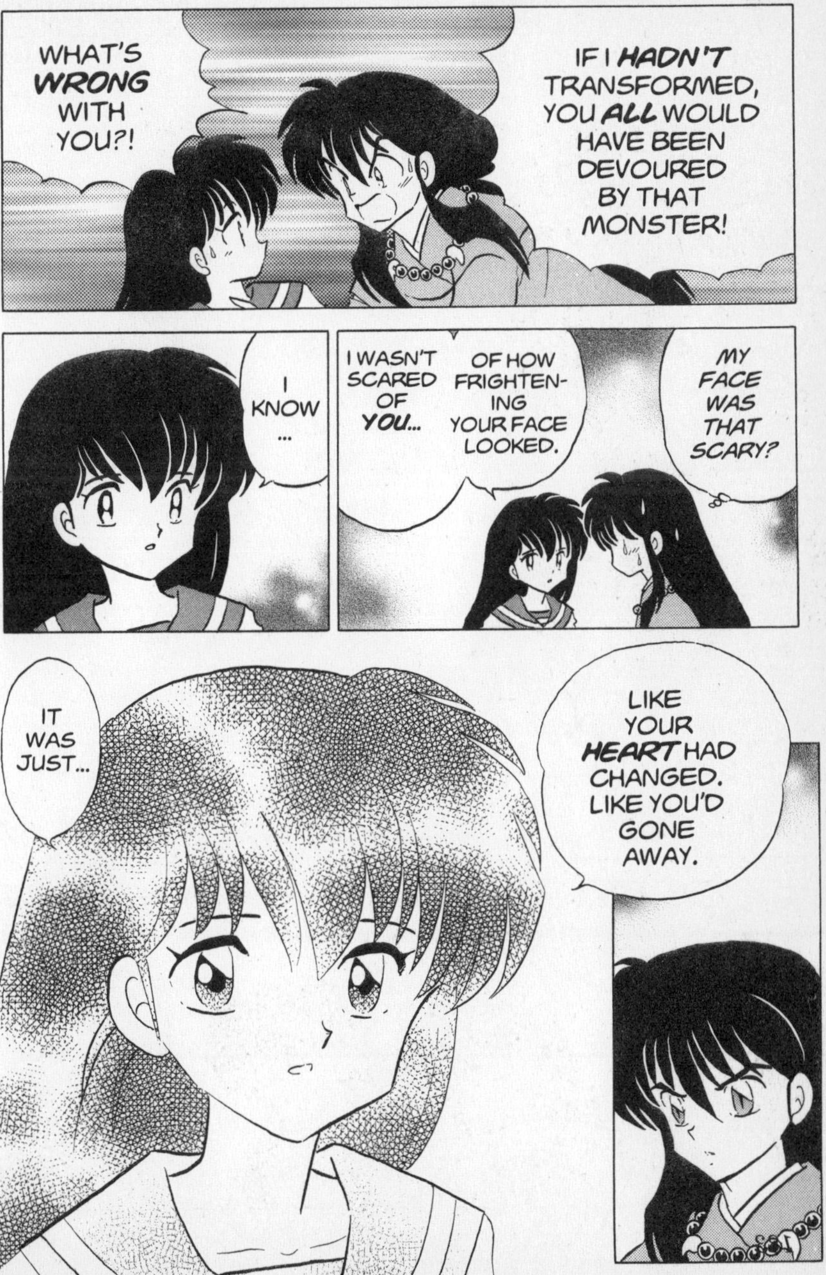
WHAT'S WRONG WITH YOU?!
IF I HADN'T TRANSFORMED, YOU ALL WOULD HAVE BEEN DEVOURED BY THAT MONSTER!
I KNOW ...
I WASN'T SCARED OF YOU...
OF HOW FRIGHTEN-ING YOUR FACE LOOKED.
MY FACE WAS THAT SCARY?
IT WAS JUST...
LIKE YOUR HEART HAD CHANGED. LIKE YOU'D GONE AWAY.

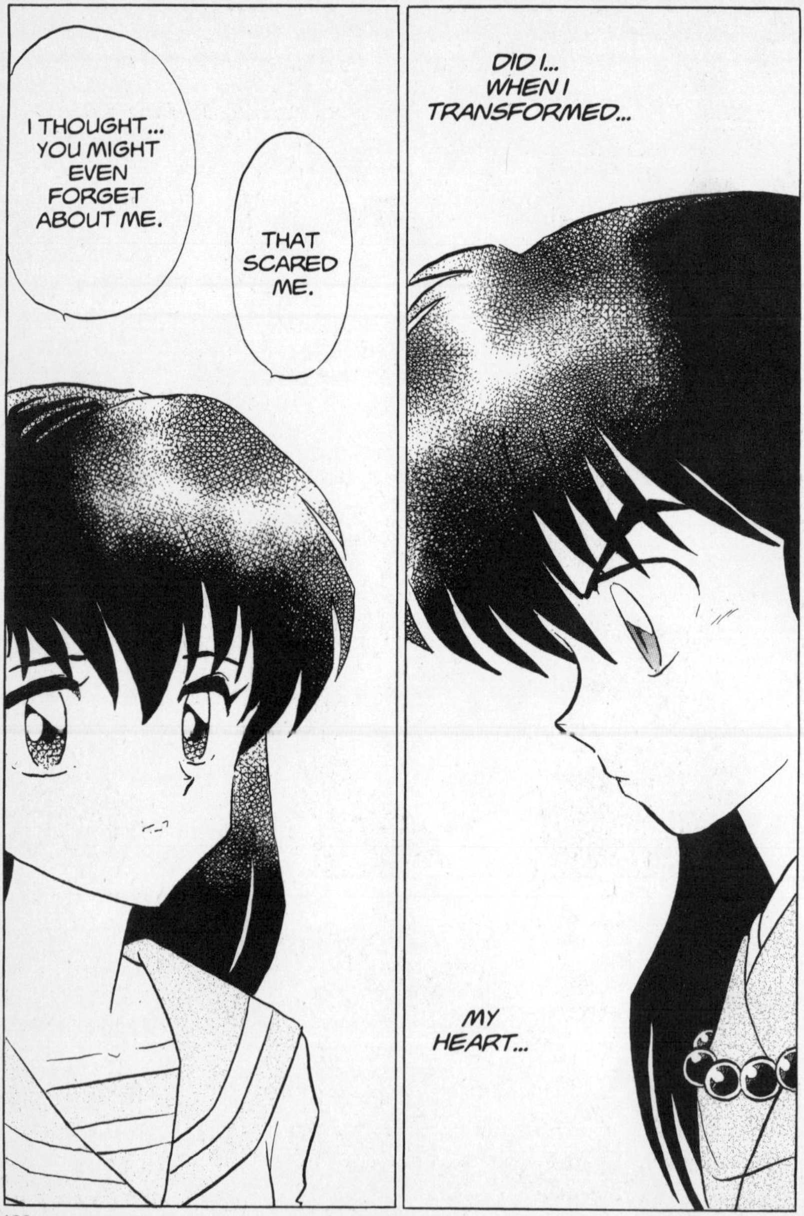
I THOUGHT... YOU MIGHT EVEN FORGET ABOUT ME.
THAT SCARED ME.
DID I... WHEN I TRANSFORMED...
MY HEART...

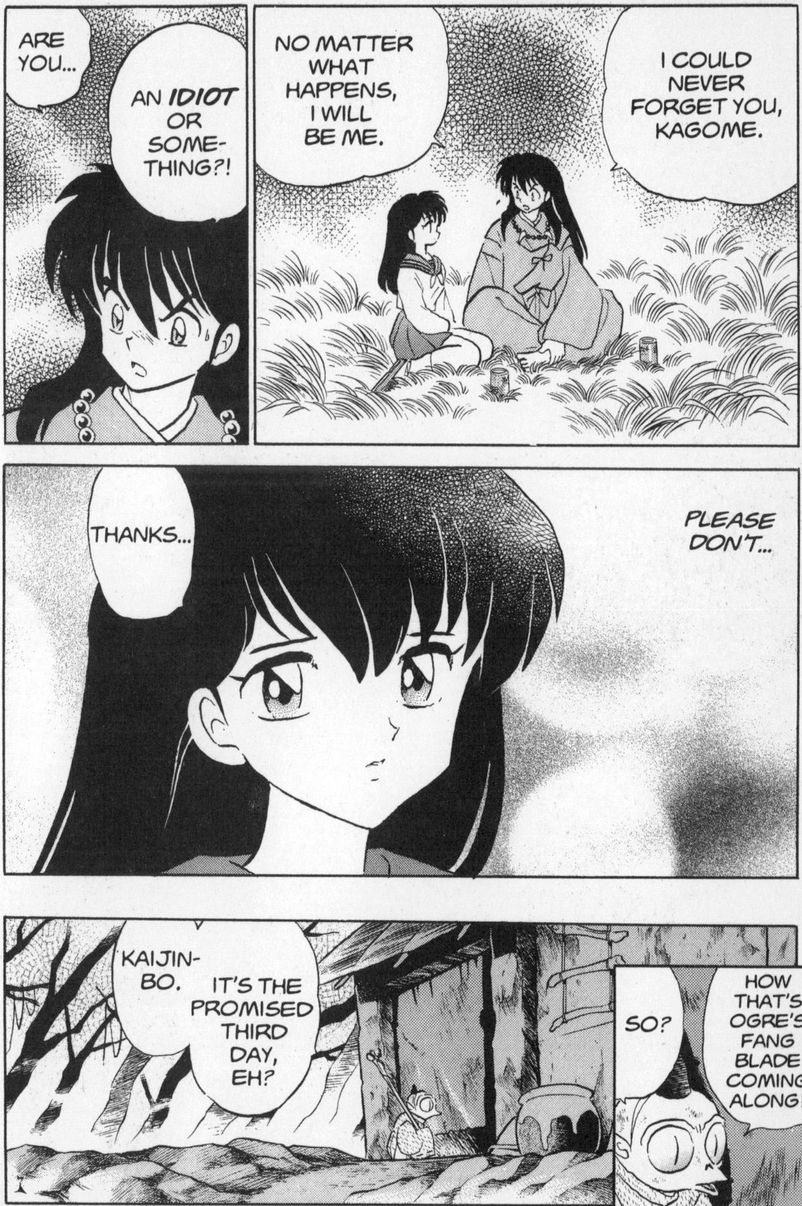
ARE YOU...
AN *IDIOT* OR SOME-THING?!
NO MATTER WHAT HAPPENS, I WILL BE ME.
I COULD NEVER FORGET YOU, KAGOME.
THANKS...
PLEASE DON'T...
KAIJIN-BO.
IT'S THE PROMISED THIRD DAY, EH?
SO?
HOW THAT'S OGRE'S FANG BLADE COMING ALONG?

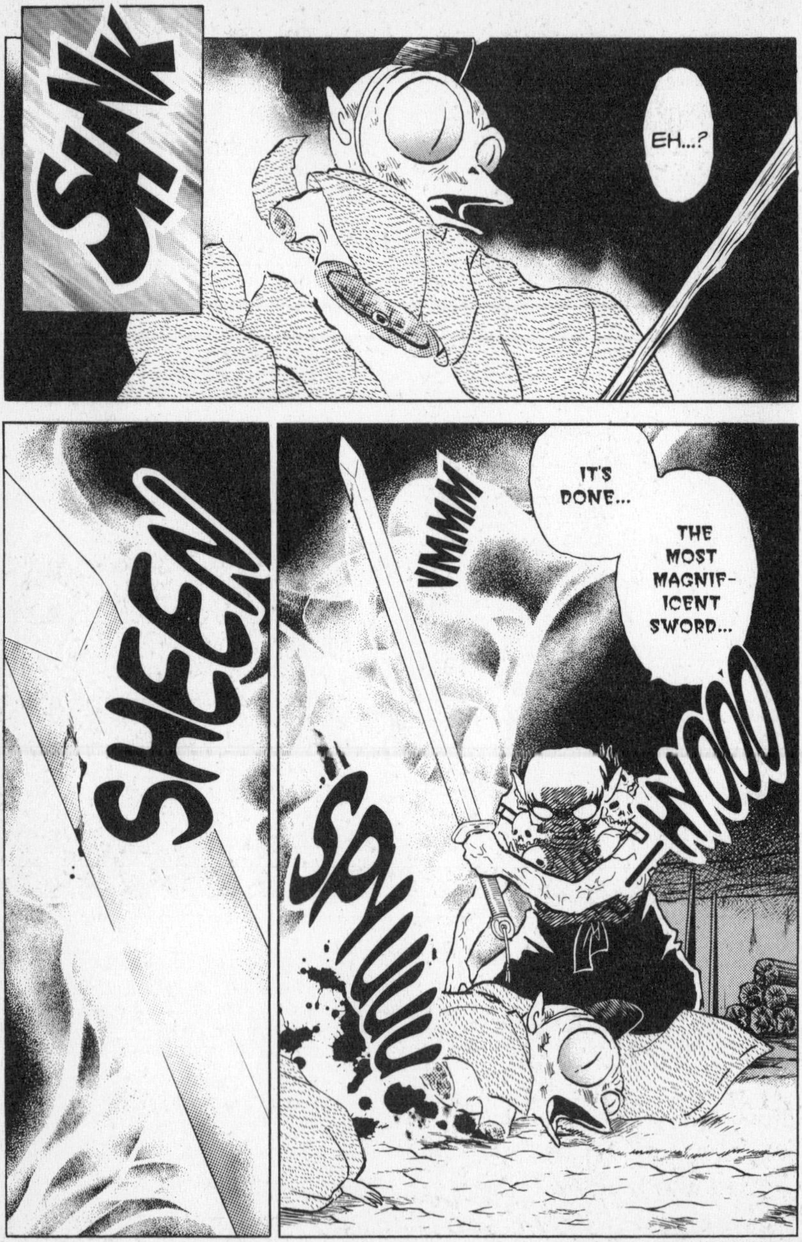
SHINK
EH...?
SHEEN
IT'S DONE...
THE MOST MAGNIF-ICENT SWORD...
VMMM
SPYUUU
WOOO

TO BE CONTINUED

EDITOR'S RECOMMENDATIONS

Story & Art by Saki Hiwatari   Vol. 1

Did you like INUYASHA? Here's what we recommend you try next:

PLEASE SAVE MY EARTH

A sensitive high school student has recurring dreams that she's part of a team of seven alien scientists from the moon. She doesn't believe this could possibly be true until she meets other people who've been having these dreams as well. Fragments of a past life eventually come to light in an intricate, fascinating story of reincarnation, psychic powers, and enternal, tragic love.

© 1986 Saki Hiwatari/HAKUSENSHA, Inc.

story and art by   Yū Watase

ALICE 19TH

Alice was a typical young girl—hopelessly in love and bored, until she follows a magical rabbit that literally jumps in front of her life. In a shôjo twist on *Alice in Wonderland*, this new story by the artist of *Fushigi Yûgi* and *Ceres, Celestial Legend* features two sisters: one who's been pulled into a world of darkness, and another (Alice) who must become a master of the Lotis Words to save her.

© 2001 Yuu Watase/Shogakukan, Inc.

Story & Art by Junji Itoh

GYO

This horror manga by *Uzumaki* artist Junji Ito dredges up a nightmare from the deep—monstrous, mutant fish and sea creatures that invade an Okinawa town. Ito's artwork is gorgeous and unforgettable—if you're looking for something completely different in manga, this is it.

© 2002 Junji Ito/Shogakukan, Inc.

COMPLETE OUR SURVEY AND LET US KNOW WHAT YOU THINK!

☐ Please check here if you DO NOT wish to receive information or future offers from VIZ

Name: _____

Address: _____

City: _____ State: _____ Zip: _____

E-mail: _____

☐ Male ☐ Female Date of Birth (mm/dd/yyyy): ___ / ___ / _____ (Under 13? Parental consent required)

What race/ethnicity do you consider yourself? (please check one)

☐ Asian/Pacific Islander   ☐ Black/African American   ☐ Hispanic/Latino

☐ Native American/Alaskan Native   ☐ White/Caucasian   ☐ Other: _____

What VIZ product did you purchase? (check all that apply and indicate title purchased)

☐ DVD/VHS _____

☐ Graphic Novel _____

☐ Magazines _____

☐ Merchandise _____

Reason for purchase: (check all that apply)

☐ Special offer   ☐ Favorite title   ☐ Gift

☐ Recommendation   ☐ Other _____

Where did you make your purchase? (please check one)

☐ Comic store   ☐ Bookstore   ☐ Mass/Grocery Store

☐ Newsstand   ☐ Video/Video Game Store   ☐ Other: _____

☐ Online (site: _____)

What other VIZ properties have you purchased/own? _____

_____

How many anime and/or manga titles have you purchased in the last year? How many were VIZ titles? (please check one from each column)

ANIME
- ☐ None
- ☐ 1-4
- ☐ 5-10
- ☐ 11+

MANGA
- ☐ None
- ☐ 1-4
- ☐ 5-10
- ☐ 11+

VIZ
- ☐ None
- ☐ 1-4
- ☐ 5-10
- ☐ 11+

I find the pricing of VIZ products to be: (please check one)
- ☐ Cheap
- ☐ Reasonable
- ☐ Expensive

What genre of manga and anime would you like to see from VIZ? (please check two)
- ☐ Adventure
- ☐ Comic Strip
- ☐ Science Fiction
- ☐ Fighting
- ☐ Horror
- ☐ Romance
- ☐ Fantasy
- ☐ Sports

What do you think of VIZ's new look?
- ☐ Love It
- ☐ It's OK
- ☐ Hate It
- ☐ Didn't Notice
- ☐ No Opinion

Which do you prefer? (please check one)
- ☐ Reading right-to-left
- ☐ Reading left-to-right

Which do you prefer? (please check one)
- ☐ Sound effects in English
- ☐ Sound effects in Japanese with English captions
- ☐ Sound effects in Japanese only with a glossary at the back

THANK YOU! Please send the completed form to:

NJW Research
42 Catharine St.
Poughkeepsie, NY 12601

All information provided will be used for internal purposes only. We promise not to sell or otherwise divulge your information.